# Studies in European Economic Law and Regulation

Volume 9

The series shall focus on studies devoted to the analysis of European Economic Law. It shall firstly embrace all features of EU economic law in general (e.g. EU law such as fundamental freedoms and their relationship to fundamental rights, as well as other economic law such as arbitration and WTO law) and more specifically (antitrust law, unfair competition law, financial market law, consumer law). This series shall cover both classical internal analysis (doctrine) as well as external analysis, where European Economic Law and Regulation is the subject of analysis (Law and Economics, Sociological Analysis, Comparative Law and the like).

The series accepts monographs focusing on a specific topic, as well as edited collections of articles covering a specific theme or collections of articles by a single author. All contributions are accepted exclusively after a rigorous double-blind peer-review process.

More information about this series at http://www.springer.com/series/11710

Adriana Almăşan • Peter Whelan
Editors

# The Consistent Application of EU Competition Law

## Substantive and Procedural Challenges

Springer

*Editors*
Adriana Almăşan
Faculty of Law
University of Bucharest
Bucharest, Romania

Peter Whelan
School of Law
University of Leeds
Leeds, West Yorkshire, UK

ISSN 2214-2037 ISSN 2214-2045 (electronic)
Studies in European Economic Law and Regulation
ISBN 978-3-319-47381-9 ISBN 978-3-319-47382-6 (eBook)
DOI 10.1007/978-3-319-47382-6

Library of Congress Control Number: 2016962636



Printed on acid-free paper

This Springer imprint is published by Springer Nature
The registered company is Springer International Publishing AG
The registered company address is: Gewerbestrasse 11, 6330 Cham, Switzerland

# Foreword

It is a great pleasure to introduce and welcome this new book, *The Consistent Application of EU Competition Law: Substantive and Procedural Challenges*, edited by, and with contributions from, Dr Adriana Almăşan and Dr Peter Whelan. The chapters contained in this book examine the important question of how a number of the procedural and substantive challenges created by Regulation 1/2003 have been dealt with in the 10 years following that Regulation's coming into force.

Prior to Regulation 1/2003, the EU antitrust laws (Articles 101 and 102 TFEU) were enforced principally by the European Commission (the 'Commission'). In 2004, however, the Regulation transformed the enforcement landscape by abolishing the notification and exemption system and removing the Commission's exclusive right to decide on the compatibility of an agreement with Article 101(3). These steps have enabled the Commission to focus its resources on, and prioritise, more serious violations of the antitrust laws and paved the way for greater enforcement of the rules at the national level. A more decentralised system has consequently been able to emerge, involving both a network of competition authorities, the European Competition Network (ECN), comprised of the Commission and the national competition authorities (NCAs), and the courts and tribunals of the individual Member States (the national courts). Indeed, both NCAs and national courts are now playing an increasingly important part in the enforcement of Articles 101 and 102.

The changes introduced by Regulation 1/2003 have provided the opportunity for more effective enforcement of the EU antitrust laws across the EU. At the same time, however, they have created a number of significant challenges, for example, how investigations should be coordinated, and cases allocated, between the Commission and NCAs, how cases should be prioritised, how guidance on the compatibility of new business conduct with the antitrust rules can be given, how national and EU law should operate together in this sphere, how parallel proceedings in national courts should be dealt with and how it can be ensured that the various investigators and decision-takers act consistently.

The chapters in this book focus on the issue of consistency and examine the different mechanisms which exist to ensure that discrepancies in procedure and/or in the substantive interpretation of competition law do not undermine an effective, efficient and robust competition law system. With more than 10 years of practice to analyse, they consider whether EU competition policy, the Court of Justice of the European Union, the national courts and a number of the NCAs have successfully combined to achieve consistent application of EU competition law.

This book provides a valuable and timely study of how the competition laws have been enforced since 2004 and how the various actors have sought to meet the challenges posed. It is widely researched and sets out a clear analysis of the complex issues arising. No doubt, it will provide helpful assistance to practitioners, students and researchers working in this area.

King's College London
London, UK
June 2016

Alison Jones

# Preface

Competition law has been a core European competence since the foundation of the European Union. Over the past 60 years, it has proven difficult to achieve the optimal balance of Member States and European Commission involvement in determining the substantive and procedural scope and application of Articles 101 and 102 TFEU. Regulation 1/2003 sought to set out to address the overburdening of the Commission in this area and to carve out a clearer role for the Member States, initiating a move towards a more decentralised and collaborative approach. Over the past 10 years, this has created more space for national actors, both courts and competition authorities, while retaining a central role for the Commission in particularly significant cases and as coordinator through the European Competition Network.

This volume, edited under the expert guidance of Almăşan and Whelan, highlights the substantive and procedural challenges that remain 10 years into this new era of EU competition law. In doing so, this volume addresses several key areas of research with great value for practitioners and academic commentators alike.

The contributions of Chiriţoiu and Rusu in Part I set out the remaining coordinating and centralising features of the system through discussion of the European Competition Network and the role of the Commission. Judge Collins, Nagy and Gherghina build on these coordinating features by discussing the role of the Court of Justice of the European Union and its harmonising influence. Relatedly, Judge Toader and Stuyck's commentary on preliminary rulings in Part IV shows what instruments may be used in order to secure the consistent interpretation of EU competition law. In contrast, in Parts III and V of the volume, Whelan, Thouvenin, Almăşan, Oppermann, Amaro, David, Papp and Kowalik-Bańczyk discuss how jurisdictional challenges and national applications of Articles 101 and 102 TFEU require further attention in order to balance this system of decentralisation and coordination.

The topics confronted by this volume are important and timely in their own right. Their combined treatment by this varied group of scholars in a single volume allows us to identify synergies, clashes and overlaps between practices that would otherwise go undetected. In addition, the inclusion of experiences of Member States that have joined the EU since the adoption of Regulation 1/2003 incorporates perspectives that are vital to the future development of EU competition law.

The expertise combined in this contribution speaks directly to our mission of advancing the critical analysis of European economic law in all its iterations. It therefore gives us great pleasure to welcome this rich volume in the *Studies in European Economic Law and Regulation* series.

Worcester College, University of Oxford
London, UK
Law and Governance Group, Faculty of Law
Wageningen University, Erasmus University
Wageningen and Rotterdam
The Netherlands
July 2016

Josephine van Zeben

Kai Purnhagen

# Introduction

Articles 101 and 102 TFEU contain the EU rules on competition law, and they constitute part of the internal competition law for the European Union Member States, in addition to the specific rules set forth in their domestic legislation. When there is an effect on trade between Member States, a Member State must apply EU competition law when applying national competition law. With anticompetitive agreements in particular, the application of national law cannot be any stricter than the rules contained within Article 101 TFEU. Therefore, a thorough understanding of the EU competition law rules is essential not only for the European Commission and the Court of Justice of the European Union but also for the correct interpretation and application of each Member State's competition law.

As a result of the adoption of Regulation 1/2003, these particular rules are applied in their entirety by the European Commission and the national competition authorities and courts. The decentralisation of enforcement through the involvement of national competition authorities and courts creates potential for an inconsistent application of the EU competition law rules. The spectre of inconsistency is a worry for those who wish to see an effective, efficient and robust competition law system operate within the EU. The creation and maintenance of such a system require, inter alia, certain actions, measures and procedures that aim to render the consistent interpretation of the competition provisions by all of the institutions that have application prerogatives. Indeed, certain instruments, including measures adopted by the European Commission and the jurisprudence of the Court of Justice, not to mention its preliminary rulings, have already been used to smooth the way for the uniform application of competition law. Nonetheless, challenges remain concerning the consistent application of European competition law, despite the existence of all of these instruments. Added to this situation is the fact that the procedural framework concerning the enforcement of competition law may differ across each Member State of the European Union; therefore, the uniform application of competition law across the EU encounters further challenges that stem from the national rules on procedure.

With this particular context in mind, this edited collection examines the main substantive and procedural challenges that relate to the consistent application of EU competition law. Divided into five parts, it comprises 15 detailed chapters.

Part I of the book examines in two chapters how the consistent enforcement of Articles 101 and 102 TFEU operates as a general EU competition policy. The operation of two specific mechanisms is relevant here: Regulation 1/2003, as a whole, and the European Competition Network in particular. Chapter 1, written by Dr Bogdan Chirițoiu from the Faculty of Business Administration, University of Bucharest, examines the process of convergence within the European Competition Network that is characterised by both legislative harmonisation and the enforcement prioritisation at the level of the national competition authorities. Chapter 2 was written by Dr Cătălin Rusu of Radboud University Nijmegen and thoroughly analyses the assessment contained within the 'Commission Communication on Ten Years of Antitrust Enforcement Under Regulation 1/2003', identifying prospective priorities and challenges that are relevant to the consistent application of EU competition law.

Part II of the book comprises three chapters and discusses how the Court of Justice's jurisprudence acts as an instrument of harmonisation. Several recent landmark cases of the Court of Justice on Articles 101 and 102 TFEU are discussed in this context. These cases clearly help to reduce the potential for inconsistent application of EU competition law; they temper the substantive challenges inherent in this context. Moreover, the Court of Justice case law is often cited by the national courts and by the competition authorities; therefore, they also provide scope for impact upon national competition law. The first chapter in this part (Chap. 3, written by Judge Anthony Collins, General Court of the European Union) analyses the Court's extremely important recent review on the concept of restrictions of competition 'by object'. The second chapter (Chap. 4, written by Dr Csongor István Nagy, University of Szeged) presents the landmark cases *Allianz* and *Cartes Bancaires* in comparative assessment with the new De Minimis Notice. The third chapter (Chap. 5, Dr Simona Gherghina, Faculty of Law, University of Bucharest) evaluates the importance of the EU public procurement regulations in the interpretation of the EU competition law provisions.

Part III of the book analyses certain additional, unique jurisdictional challenges to the uniform application of the EU competition law provisions. Three chapters are presented. The first chapter in this part (Chap. 6, Dr Peter Whelan, University of Leeds) examines the extent to which EU competition law (in particular Article 101 and Regulation 1/2003) impacts upon the content and operation of a regime which imposes criminal sanctions for the violation of its cartel law. The next chapter (Chap. 7, Prof. Jean-Marc Thouvenin, Université Paris Ouest Nanterre La Défense) discusses the consistency-related challenges that may result from the private enforcement of competition law under the Brussels 1 Regulation. The final chapter of this part (Chap. 8, Dr Adriana Almășan, University of Bucharest) focuses on the challenges concerning the applicability of Articles 101 and 102 TFEU in national and international arbitration, which are due in large part to the absence in Regulation 1/2003 of a reference to arbitral courts and to the lack of acknowledged access of arbitration to the preliminary reference process. This is clearly an important issue that needs to be resolved in order to ensure the maximum amount of consistency in the application of the EU competition law rules.

Part IV of the book comprises two chapters and focuses on one of the most important instruments that can help to achieve the uniform application of EU competition law in cases handled by the national courts: preliminary rulings. The role that the Court of Justice has in establishing a consistent interpretation of Articles 101 and 102 TFEU by virtue of preliminary references is extremely important and deserves analysis. The first chapter in this part (Chap. 9, written by Prof. Camelia Toader, Court of Justice of the European Union and Faculty of Law, University of Bucharest) provides an overview of preliminary rulings and the role played by the Court of Justice in ensuring consistent application of the TFEU provisions to cartel and abuse of dominant position practices. Chapter 10, written by Emeritus Professor Jules Stuyck, University of Leuven (KU Leuven) and Radboud University Nijmegen, further details technical conditions pertaining to the preliminary referrals of the courts and develops a complex analysis of the special issues that can be engendered by referrals for preliminary rulings.

Finally, Part V of the book provides selective examples of how Articles 101 and 102 TFEU are effectively applied at the national level, thereby providing additional input into how problematic the issue of consistent application of EU competition law is in practice. These examples were chosen so as to include founding Member States of the EU as well as 'younger' Member States. Its five chapters present analyses of the following jurisdictions and their experiences in applying the EU competition law rules: Germany (Chap. 11, Professor Bernd Oppermann and Ahmad Chmeis, both from Leibniz University of Hanover), France (Chap. 12, Dr Rafael Amaro, Université Paris Descartes – Sorbonne Paris Cité (CEDAG)), Romania (Chap. 13, Dr Sorin David, University of Bucharest), Hungary (Chap. 15, Dr Mónika Papp, Eötvös Loránd University, Budapest) and Poland (Chap. 15, Dr Krystyna Kowalik-Bańczyk, Institute of Law Studies, Polish Academy of Sciences).

Taken together, all five parts of the book contribute towards a detailed review of the issue of consistency in the application of Articles 101 and 102 TFEU and of the major substantive and procedural challenges that can be engendered in this context.

Faculty of Law
University of Bucharest
Bucharest, Romania

Adriana Almăşan

School of Law
University of Leeds
Leeds, UK

Peter Whelan

# Contents

# Contributors

**Adriana Almăşan** is an associate professor of law and a former vice dean responsible with international relations at the University of Bucharest, Faculty of Law. She teaches in various areas of competition law and civil law (civil obligations, dynamics of civil obligations, property law, property legal protection and secured transactions and contract negotiation). She is the Director of the European Union Law master programme of the Faculty of Law, University of Bucharest, where she teaches EU competition law. She has introduced in the scholar curricula several new subjects, such as advanced competition law for the master in public acquisitions, concessions and public-private partnership and contract negotiation at the master of business law (for the first time in a faculty of law in Romania). She is member of the panel of arbitrators with the Romanian Court of International Commercial Arbitration by the Chamber of Commerce and Industry of Romania. She is author and co-author of several books and articles on civil law, contract negotiation and competition law. She is a member of the Bucharest Bar, with her main practice involving assistance and representation in competition law (antitrust cases, M&A and state aid cases), contract and business negotiation. Adriana has been Senior European Union Expert on competition law, and she is the co-founder and co-director of the 'Centre for Competition Law Studies', established by the Faculty of Law, University of Bucharest, in cooperation with the Romanian Competition Council. She is the editor of the private law section of the *Judicial Courier*, a law review issued by C. H. Beck România, and sits on the scientific board of Romanian Competition Review, edited by the Romanian Competition Council.

**Rafael Amaro** is an associate professor at the Université Paris Descartes – Sorbonne Paris Cité (CEDAG). He teaches EU and French competition law, contract, tort, civil procedure and human rights law. His research interests focus mainly on the private enforcement of competition law and unfair commercial practices. Prior to his PhD (*Le contentieux privé des pratiques anticoncurrentielles*, Bruylant, 2014), he graduated from Sciences Po Paris (master in economic law, 2007) and Paris Descartes (master in private law, 2008). He was a visiting lecturer at the China University of Political Science and Law in Beijing (2010–2012), at the Sandra Day

O'Connor College of Law at Arizona State University in Phoenix (2014) and at Paris-Sorbonne University – Abu Dhabi in Abu Dhabi (2016). He is also a member of the European network of legal experts Trans Europe Experts (TEE).

**Bogdan M. Chirițoiu** has been a lecturer in economics and European studies at the University of Bucharest since 1999 and is member of the some of the most important Romanian think tanks (the Romanian Society of Political Science, the Network of Institutes and Schools of Public Administration in Central and Eastern Europe (NISPAcee), the Romanian Academic Society and the Aspen Institute of Romania). Dr Chirițoiu has MA degrees in political science (Central European University, Budapest, 1997) and economic studies (London School of Economics and Political Science, 1998). He holds since 2008 a PhD in economics (international economic relations) from the Bucharest Academy of Economic Studies, with a thesis on public health insurance systems in CEE states. Dr Chirițoiu has been the president of the Romanian Competition Council since 2009. From 2005 to 2009, he served as presidential advisor (rank of deputy minister) on economic affairs and public policy and head of the Romanian delegation to the EU Economic Policy Committee.

**Ahmad Chmeis** born in Beirut in 1988, studied law in Hanover and Pune (India). He is a PhD student and legal assistant at the chair for German, European and international civil and commercial law of Prof. Oppermann. Mr. Chmeis is also a scholar of the German Academic Exchange Service and the Friedrich Ebert Foundation. His main research focus is on European antitrust law and antitrust procedural law in particular. He has been teaching European law at the Leibniz University of Hanover since 2014.

**Judge Anthony M. Collins** A legal science graduate of Trinity College, Dublin, Anthony M. Collins practised for over two decades as a barrister-at-law and later as senior counsel at the Bar of Ireland, where he specialised in administrative and EU law. Between 1990 and 1997, he was référendaire at the Court of Justice of the European Communities. He was director of the Irish Centre for European Law from 1997 to 2000 and coeditor of the *Irish Journal of European Law* from 1992 to 2001. Since 16 September 2013, he has been a judge at the General Court of the European Union. He is a bencher of the Honorable Society of King's Inns, an adjunct professor at University College Cork and a member of the board of directors of the Irish Centre for European Law.

**Sorin David** is the managing partner of D&B David si Baias. He has been a member of the Bucharest Bar since 1991. He is an arbitrator of the Court of Arbitration of the Romanian Chamber of Commerce and Industry. Sorin has legal qualifications obtained in Romania (PhD, summa cum laude), the USA (master of laws) and the Netherlands (postgraduate studies). He is also an associate professor of law at the Faculty of Law of the University of Bucharest, teaching commercial law and competition law. He is an expert in corporate law, competition law and M&A. Sorin is the author of more than 20 law journal articles published in Romania and/or abroad.

He is co-author of *Commentaries on Company Law*, one of the leading law books on Romanian company law, that was awarded the Romanian Academy prize. Sorin has been involved in several projects for the alignment of Romanian legislation with EU regulations and international best practice. Sorin specialises in competition, commercial and consumer protection law, among others. He has been involved in many projects in different fields of activity, providing legal advice to clients on various matters and coordinating restructuring projects in respect of Romanian companies or Romanian subsidiaries of international companies.

**Simona Gherghina** is an associate professor with the Faculty of Law of the University of Bucharest, teaching public finance law, banking law and financing of public investments (the latter within the master programme of public procurement, concessions and public-private partnership of the same faculty). She is also the director of that particular master programme. Simona has published several books, articles and contributions to collective volumes on sovereign guarantees, public debt and financing of public investments and successfully participated in national and international research grant competitions, having been awarded a postdoctoral research grant on *Financing Public Investments: Between Budgetary and Legal Limitations and the Public Interest Imperative* (www.publicinvestments.ro) and also acting as a senior researcher in the Romanian-French joint research project *From Fiscal Compact to Constitution: Shaping a Legal Form for the Balanced Budget Rule* (www.fcbb.cdcip.ro). She has recently published with C. H. Beck România a monograph on the financing of public investments and currently sits as deputy editor in chief of the *Romanian Public-Private Partnership Law Review*. Simona has extensive experience as a lawyer in matters related to financing of public investments, public-private partnership projects and concessions.

**Alison Jones** is professor of law at King's College London and a solicitor at Freshfields Bruckhaus Deringer LLP. Prior to joining King's in 1992, Alison read law at Girton College, Cambridge, worked at Slaughter and May and completed a BCL at Christ Church, Oxford. Since joining King's, she has taught competition law (EU, UK and US), trusts, property and EU law. Alison is co-author of *EU Competition Law* (Jones and Sufrin) and a regional editor for the *Restitution Law Review* and writes two of the Centre of European Law's modules for the diploma in EU competition law. She is also director of the LLB law with the European legal studies programme.

**Krystyna Kowalik-Bańczyk** is an associate professor in law at the Institute of Law Studies, Polish Academy of Sciences, where she works at the chair of competition law. She holds a degree in law from the University of Gdańsk, Poland. She accomplished postgraduate studies in EU law at the University of Toulouse, France, as well as an LLM in European law at the College of Europe in Bruges, Belgium. She holds a diploma of the Academy of European Law from the European University Institute in Florence. Krystyna holds a PhD in law from the Institute of Law Studies at the Polish Academy of Sciences. Her PhD on the regulation of electronic commerce in international and European law has been published by Wolters Kluwer Poland. She obtained her professor title on the basis of her book on the rights of defence in EU antitrust proceedings (published by Wolters Kluwer Poland). She teaches European law, public international law and Internet law at the Technical University of Gdańsk. Between the years 2002 and 2010, she lectured at the Centre for Europe of the University of Warsaw, as well as at the European School of Law and Administration in Warsaw. She has led several workshops for judges and public servants on various aspects of the application of EU law in Poland. She has been a visiting scholar at the Max Planck Institute in Münich, Germany, and at the Institute of Comparative Law in Lausanne, Switzerland. She profited from the Natolin Foundation grant at the European University Institute in Florence. Since 2005 she is a coeditor of one of the leading Polish scientific journals on European law: *Europejski Przegląd Sądowy*. She was a visiting professor at the University of Nice Sophia Antipolis; at the University of Luxembourg, teaching EU Internet law; and at the Université Panthéon-Assas Paris 2, teaching some aspects of EU competition law. At present she is a visiting scholar at the Max Planck Institute Luxembourg. On 1 September 2016, she became the Polish judge at the General Court of the European Union in Luxembourg.

**Csongor István Nagy** is research chair at and head of the Federal Markets 'Momentum' Research Group (Hungarian Academy of Sciences) and professor of law at and the head of the Department of Private International Law at the University of Szeged. He is recurrent visiting professor at the Central European University (Budapest/New York), the Sapientia University of Transylvania (Romania) and the Riga Graduate School of Law (Latvia). He is admitted to the Budapest Bar. In 2015–2016, he was Fulbright visiting professor and adjunct professor at Indiana University, Bloomington. Csongor graduated at the Eötvös Loránd University of Sciences (ELTE, Dr. jur.) in Budapest, in 2003, where he also earned a PhD in 2009. During his studies, he was a member of the István Bibó College of Law and Political Sciences and of the Invisible College. He received master (LLM, 2004) and SJD degrees (2010) from the Central European University (CEU) in Budapest/New York. As an exchange student, he pursued graduate studies in Rotterdam, Heidelberg and Ithaca, New York (Cornell University). He earned habilitation at the University of Szeged in 2014 and was promoted to full professor in 2016. He had visiting appointments in the Hague (Asser Institute), Munich (twice, Max Planck Institute), Brno (Masarykova University), CEU Business School (Budapest), Hamburg (Max Planck Institute), Edinburgh (University of Edinburgh), London (British Institute of International and Comparative Law) and Bloomington, Indiana (Indiana University), and was senior fellow at the Centre for International Governance Innovation in Canada. He was Eurojust legal counsel in the European Commission's Representation in Hungary. He has more than 140 publications in English, French, German, Hungarian, Romanian and (in translation) Croatian and Spanish. He is the coeditor of the *Verseny és Szabályozás* (*Competition and Regulation*) yearbook (Hungarian Academy of Sciences, Institute of Economics) and the sole author of ten monographs.

**Bernd Oppermann** born in 1956, is professor at Leibniz University of Hanover, Germany, where he holds a chair for German, European and international private law and commercial law since 1992. He received his first and second state examinations in law at Frankfurt and Wiesbaden in 1981 and 1986; his LLM degree from the University of California (UCLA), School of Law, in 1983; his PhD (Dr. jur.) from J.W. Goethe University of Frankfurt in 1985; and his habilitation from the University of Hamburg for research in private law, civil procedure, business law and legal theory in 1992. He was dean of his faculty in Hanover from 2000 to 2002. Recent publications are found in general private law, in competition law and in comparative law. Professor Oppermann has lectured and is teaching at several European and Asian universities. For his European activities and project coordination (TEMPUS and the ERASMUS MUNDUS schemes 1999–2012), he received the titles Dr. h.c. from the University of Rouen and Prof. h.c. from UMCS at Lublin. For details, see www.jura.uni-hannover.de/oppermann/.

**Mónika Papp** is a law graduate from József Attila University, Szeged (HU). She has a PhD in law from Eötvös Loránd University, Budapest (HU). She is currently senior lecturer at Eötvös Loránd University, Budapest, at the Department of Private International Law and European Economic Law and researcher at the Centre for Social Sciences, Hungarian Academy of Sciences. She passed her bar exam in Hungary in 2000. She is currently part of two research teams. One, financed by the Hungarian Research Council (OTKA) for the period 2013–2016, explores the possibilities of Member States to intervene in the market (the project is titled 'The EU legal framework for the State's active economic engagement') at Pázmány Péter Catholic University, Hungary, School of Law. Her other research team is financed by the Hungarian Academy of Sciences for the period 2013–2018 and deals with the 'Policy Opportunities for Hungary in the European Union-the analysis of the legal framework'. Under this project she is currently preparing legal mapping reports on EU competition law and state aid law. Her key research interests lie primarily in EU internal market law and competition law. She has presented a number of papers at various conferences. Before Hungary's accession to the EU, she has been involved in the training of national administration officials in EU competition law. She is the co-author of various books and articles dealing with European Union law generally and EU competition law specifically. She has recently published the fourth edition of her book (co-authored with Ernő Várnay) on *European Union Law* in Hungarian.

**Cătălin S. Rusu** is an associate professor of European law at the Faculty of Law, Radboud University Nijmegen. He also acts as visiting professor of European competition law at the Faculty of Law, Babes-Bolyai University, Cluj Napoca. He studied law at Babes-Bolyai University, Cluj Napoca; at the International Faculty of Comparative Law, Strasbourg; and at Utrecht University. He obtained his PhD degree in 2009 after publishing his research findings in the field of European merger control. He currently lectures on EU law, European competition law and EU internal market law at both master and bachelor levels. Cătălin's main research interests revolve around the fields of competition law and EU internal market law. More specifically, his research focuses on the dynamic role that EU competition law and policy play in the internal market project, the manner in which competition law regulation adapts to the requirements of modern law making and the distinct approaches to competition law enforcement in different jurisdictions. Cătălin is a member of several professional associations, such as ASCOLA, CLaSF and the Dutch Associations for European Law and Competition Law. He also regularly provides advice on matters of (EU) competition law, as a court-appointed independent specialist.

**Jules Stuyck** has long experience in EU law, both as an attorney and as an academic. He regularly assists private clients as well as the European institutions (Commission and Council), agencies and bodies before the European Courts. In the last 15 years, he has pleaded numerous cases in various fields, including competition, state aid, the customs union, free movement, public procurement, trade mark and trade practices law, media law and environmental law. He represents clients before the European Commission in competition cases, as complainants in internal market, state aid and competition disputes, and before the Belgian Competition Council (in cartel and dominance cases). He is also an experienced litigator in the Belgian courts. Until September 2013, Jules taught substantive European law at the University of Leuven (KU Leuven) and at Radboud University Nijmegen, the Netherlands. He is now emeritus professor from both universities. In recent years, he has been teaching European substantive law at the Université Panthéon-Assas Paris 2, France, and from 2000 to 2015, he has been teaching European competition law at the Central European University in Budapest, Hungary. He is regularly invited as guest professor for EU consumer law at the Université Panthéon-Assas Paris 2. He is the author of more than 400 publications in various fields, including a leading handbook on commercial practices law. He is a member of the editorial board of several Belgian and European legal journals. Jules Stuyck has been with Liedekerke Wolters Waelbroeck Kirkpatrick since 1991 and was a partner from 2002 until 2015. He is now of counsel with this firm.

**Jean-Marc Thouvenin** is professor of international and European law at Université Paris Ouest Nanterre La Défense. He is the director of the CEDIN (Centre de Droit International de Nanterre, ranked 6xA+ by the last French national evaluation (2013)), as well as of master 2 in international and European law and of the College International de Droit. His doctoral thesis was devoted to the EU merger control, and he has published many articles on European competition law. Jean-Marc gives an annual lecture on competition law in Bucharest for students of the College Juridique Franco-Roumain. He is also a practitioner before the International Court of Justice, the European Court of Justice and the national courts within the EU. Before the national courts, his practice is mainly concentrated on competition law disputes.

**Camelia Toader** has degrees in law from the University of Bucharest and a PhD in law from the University of Bucharest (with doctoral studies and research at the Max Planck Institute for Private International Law, Hamburg). She was a lecturer (1992–2005) and has been, since 2005, professor in civil law and European contract law at the University of Bucharest. She is a member of the editorial board of several legal journals, an associate member of the International Academy of Comparative Law (from 2010), an honorary researcher at the Center of European Legal Studies of the Legal Research Institute of the Romanian Academy as well as a member of the consultative committee of the foundation of the Academy of European Law (Trier, from 2012). Formerly judge at the High Court of Cassation and Justice (1999–2007), since 2007, she has been a judge at the Court of Justice of the European Union (CJEU).

**Peter Whelan** is an associate professor in law at the School of Law, University of Leeds, where he is the deputy director of the Centre for Criminal Justice Studies. He has degrees in law from Trinity College, Dublin, and a PhD in law from St John's College, University of Cambridge. A qualified US attorney-at-law and a member of the New York State Bar, Peter is an expert in competition law and criminal law. He sits on the editorial boards of five law journals and has published widely in specialist competition law journals, as well as in generalist law journals (including *Oxford Journal of Legal Studies*, *Cambridge Law Journal* and *Modern Law Review*). He has provided oral evidence on cartel criminalisation to the New Zealand Parliament and recently delivered a commissioned report to the Finnish Ministry of Justice advising it on the desirability of introducing criminal cartel sanctions in Finland. He has provided training in competition law to a variety of judges from different levels of the Romanian judicial system and was a visiting professor at the Institute of International Trade and Law in Moscow, Russia. He has used his research and expertise on cartel criminalisation to advise practising lawyers on criminal investigations affecting their clients. Peter is currently the managing editor of Oxford Competition Law (operated by Oxford University Press) and sits on the Council of the Society of Legal Scholars. He recently published a monograph with Oxford University Press on the criminalisation of European cartel enforcement.

# Part I
# EU Competition Policy and the Harmonized Enforcement of Articles 101 and 102 TFEU

# Chapter 1
# Convergence Within the European Competition Network: Legislative Harmonization and Enforcement Priorities

**Bogdan M. Chiriţoiu**

## 1.1 Introduction

*Motto: "United in diversity"*[1]

On the 1st of May 2004, *Council Regulation (EC) No. 1/2003 from the 16th of December 2002 on the implementation of the rules on competition laid down in Articles 81*[2] *and 82*[3] *of the Treaty*[4] (hereinafter Regulation 1/2003) also called the Modernization Regulation[5] came into force. Regulation 1/2003 was a landmark reform, the most far-reaching review of EU antitrust procedures in more than 40 years. It modernized the procedural rules which govern how the EU antitrust rules are enforced and introduced a decentralized system of direct applicability of the EU competition rules in their entirety, thus replacing the centralized notification and authorization system established by the Council Regulation (EEC) No. 17 from

[1] The European Union's motto.

[2] Article 81(1) (now Article 101(1) TFEU) prohibits agreements which may affect trade between Member States and which have as their object or effect the prevention, restriction or distortion of competition within the common market. Agreements which fall within Article 101(1) are prohibited unless the conditions in Article 101(3) are met.

[3] Article 82 (now Article 102 TFEU) prohibits conduct by one or more undertakings which amounts to an abuse of a dominant position within the common market or in a substantial part of it and which may affect trade between Member States.

[4] By the Treaty of Lisbon, entered into force on the 1st of December 2009, the Treaty establishing the European Community was renamed the Treaty on the Functioning of the European Union and its articles have been renumbered. The Articles 81 and 82 of the Treaty establishing the European Community became Articles 101 and 102 of the Treaty on the Functioning of the European Union (TFEU).

[5] OJ L1, 4.1.03, p1.

B.M. Chiriţoiu (✉)
Faculty of Administration and Business, University of Bucharest, Bucharest, Romania
e-mail: bogdan.chiritoiu@consiliulconcurentei.ro



A. Almăşan, P. Whelan (eds.), *The Consistent Application of EU Competition Law*, Studies in European Economic Law and Regulation 9,
DOI 10.1007/978-3-319-47382-6_1

the 6th of February 1962, the first Regulation implementing Articles 85 and 86 of the Treaty.[6]

Regulation 1/2003 greatly enhanced the role of the National Competition Authorities of the Member States (hereinafter NCAs) and of national courts as enforcers of the EU competition rules.[7] NCAs and national courts not only have the power to apply the EU competition rules in full: they are obliged to do so when applying their national competition laws to agreements or conduct are capable of affecting trade between Member States.

The Regulation also introduced cooperation tools and obligations with the view of ensuring efficient work sharing, effective cooperation in the handling of cases and to fostering coherent application.[8] According to Article 11(1) of Regulation 1/2003, the European Commission and the NCAs enforce in close cooperation the European antitrust rules within the European Competition Network (hereinafter the ECN).[9]

The ECN is a framework for debates on competition related aspects, exchange of experience and information, including confidential information, and also a cooperation mechanism set by the provisions of Regulation 1 (Article 11(4)) according to which NCAs have to inform the Commission of any prohibition or commitment decision relating to the application of Articles 101 and 102 TFEU and any decision withdrawing the benefit of a block exemption regulation not later than 30 days before it is adopted.

Within this network, the exchange of information, including confidential information, can take place, thus helping enforcers to detect and sanction the violations of the rules on competition. The Commission must transmit a copy of the most important documents and, at the request of the competition authorities, furnish any document necessary to an assessment of the case pursued by it.[10]

The new enforcement system enabled the Commission to take more effective action against serious infringements of the rules on competition. It also constitutes a remarkable model of cooperation of NCAs that are more or less independent and that reach a common agreement on economic and legal aspects and enforce the competition provisions of the TFEU.[11]

The 1st of May 2004 also marked a fundamental change in the history of the EU: ten new Member States joined the European Union. The modernization of EU com-

---

[6] OJ P 013, 21.2.1962, p. 204–211.

[7] Cf. 2009 Report on Regulation 1/2003, part 5.

[8] Communication from the Commission to the European Parliament and the Council, *"Ten Years of Antitrust Enforcement under Regulation 1/2003: Achievements and Future Perspectives"* (http://ec.europa.eu/competition/antitrust/legislation/antitrust_enforcement_10_years_en.pdf).

[9] The functioning of the ECN is regulated by the provisions of the *Commission Notice on cooperation within the Network of Competition Authorities* (OJ C 101, 27.04.2004). This Notice is based to a significant extent on a Joint Statement of the Council and the Commission on the functioning of the network of competition authorities.

[10] http://europa.eu/legislation_summaries/competition/firms/l26092_en.htm

[11] Helen Wallace, Mark A. Pollack, Alasdair R. Young, Romanian European Institute, *Elaborarea politicilor in Uniunea Europeană*, 6th edition, p. 127.

petition law enforcement has in fact taken place against the background of enlargement. The enlargement and the modernization of the law enforcement have been closely connected one to another.[12] Regulation 1/2003 formed part of the legal requirements of the candidate countries' accession to the EU.[13]

The discussion on the impact of European competition law on national competition law concentrated on the question as to how far the new Member States managed to align their legislation with that of the EU and how effectively and accurately the new Member States implemented the *acquis communautaire*.[14] This approach was concerned about the ability of these countries to meet the requirements of accession and later membership. This approach was based on controlling compliance with the conditions set by the EU.[15]

The Copenhagen European Council of December 2002 found that 10 candidate countries (Cyprus, Estonia, Hungary, Poland, the Czech Republic, Slovenia, Latvia, Lithuania, Malta and Slovakia) fulfilled the conditions necessary for joining the EU. These countries together with the existing EU Member States enjoyed the application of the provisions of Regulation 1/2003 since its entry into force. Romania through its national competition authority, i.e. the Romanian Competition Council (hereinafter the RCC), applied the mentioned provisions since its accession date, namely from the 1st of January 2007.

The present chapter will provide in its first part (Sect. 1.2) a comprehensive overview of the legislative approximation/harmonization process of the national compe-

---

[12] KJ Cseres, *The Impact of Regulation 1/2003 in the New Member States*, The Competition Law Review, Volume 6 Issue 2 pp 145–182 July 2010.

[13] The legal, economic and political conditions have been first laid down in the so-called Copenhagen criteria of the 1993 Copenhagen European Council and later in more detail in the 1995 White Paper, which was drafted in order to assist the candidate countries in their preparations to meet the requirements of the internal market. The conditions that pre-accession candidates have to fulfil are specified in a Commission report entitled 'Europe and the Challenge of Enlargement'. They were made formal by the Member States at the Copenhagen European Council in June 1993, and then expanded upon by the Commission in a Communication called 'Agenda 2000', dated 16 July 1997. Agenda 2000 is an action program adopted by the Commission on the 15th of July 1997.

[14] The Community *acquis* is the body of common rights and obligations which bind all the Member States together within the European Union. It is constantly evolving and comprises: the content, principles and political objectives of the Treaties; the legislation adopted in application of the treaties and the case law of the Court of Justice; the declarations and resolutions adopted by the Union; measures relating to the common foreign and security policy; measures relating to justice and home affairs; international agreements concluded by the Community and those concluded by the Member States between themselves in the field of the Union's activities.

Applicant countries have to accept the Community *acquis* before they can join the Union. Derogations from the *acquis* are granted only in exceptional circumstances and are limited in scope. To integrate into the European Union, applicant countries will have to transpose the *acquis* into their national legislation and implement it from the moment of their accession.

[15] Ojala, M, *The competition law of Central and Eastern Europe* (Sweet & Maxwell, 1999); D Geradin, D Henry, 'Competition Law in the New Member States – Where Do We Come From? Where Do We Go?', in: D. Geradin, D. Henry (eds.) *Modernisation and enlargement: two major challenges for EC Competition law* (Intersentia, 2005); J. Fingleton, M. Fritsch, H Hansen, (eds.), *Rules of competition and East-west integration* (Boston: Kluwer Academic Publishers, 1997).

tition legislations of the Member States with the provisions of Regulation 1/2003 (with an emphasis on investigative and decision making powers), highlighting the legislative convergence especially from the Romanian perspective. The second part (Sect. 1.3) will address the enforcement activity in the ECN, evaluating the convergence of enforcement priorities between the European Commission and the NCAs from the Member States. Additionally, the chapter will present other fields that may play a significant role in the convergence of the competition policy at European level. The chapter will finally provide concluding remarks and discuss the benefits of legislative and enforcement convergence and the critical features that should be improved.

## 1.2 The Legislative Approximation/Harmonization Process of the National Competition Legislation with the Provisions of Regulation 1/2003

For Romania, its efforts to be part of the European Union started with legislative harmonization in the competition field. The Romanian Competition Council (RCC) made constant endeavours to bring in line the national legislation with the European competition rules.[16] For shaping the national antitrust framework, the European antitrust provisions represented the model and the base to start from. This fact was also justified by the criteria that the Romania had to fulfil as candidate country to the European Union (the Copenhagen criteria), namely the administrative and institutional capacity to effectively implement the *acquis* and the ability to take on the obligations of membership.[17] In terms of legal and institutional convergence of Romania competitive environment with the EU acquis in the field, studies have shown a high degree of compliance of Romanian competition legislation since the period of the accession negotiation on Chapter 6-Competition, with EU accession removing some of the incompatibilities due to compulsory full harmonization of legislation in this area.[18]

The obligations of the Association Agreement between Romania and the European Union regarding the policy in the field of competition were fulfilled through the Law no. 21/1996 and the secondary legislation issued in its application.[19] The Competition Law no. 21/1996[20] is the legal act that regulates competition at national level and the Competition Council is the national authority enforcing it. From 2003 to the present, the Romanian antitrust legislation has passed through

---

[16] B. Chiriţoiu, European Competition Day, Rome, Italy, 2014.

[17] http://ec.europa.eu/enlargement/policy/glossary/terms/accession-criteria_en.htm

[18] Fuerea, A.; Sandu, S.; Scarlat, C.; Hurduzeu, Gh.; Păun, C.; Popescu, R.M. 2004. *Evaluarea gradului de concordanţă a legislaţiei române cu acquis-ul comunitar, la nivelul anului 2002, pe capitole de negociere*, Institutul European din România – Studii de impact (PAIS II), Bucureşti.

[19] Popescu-Cruceru A., *Economic-juridic în economia concurenţială*, Editura Economică, Bucureşti, 2006.

[20] Published in the Official Journal of Romania no. 240/03.04.2015.

several reviews envisaging the transposition of the European antitrust rules stipulated in Regulation 1/2003.

### *1.2.1 Brief Presentation of the Amendments Brought to the Competition Law No. 21/1996 to Align it with the Provisions of Regulation 1/2003*

In the pre-accession phase, among the first important legislative improvements[21] inspired by Regulation 1/2003 was the introduction of new investigative powers, namely the possibility to request information, to carry out inspections and to take declarations. In the subsequent amendments of the national antitrust framework these investigative powers have been improved and reshaped almost identically to those of the European Commission (Articles 18, 19 and 20 of Regulation 1/2003).

The further major legislative amendments[22] of the national antitrust provisions provide for substantial developments into the procedural framework for enforcing the competition rules. Elements of novelty concern the abolition of the notification system, to insure convergence with Regulation 1/2003. Targeting the regime of the national block exemption regulations, the amendments to the Romanian competition law make reference to the conditions and criteria set by the EU regulations, for both national and cross-border agreements. Thus, the categories of agreements, decisions and concerted practices exempted and the conditions and criteria for the classification into categories are those set out in the EU Block Exemption Regulations. This amendment brought in line the Competition Law with the Article 29 of Regulation 1/2003.

With regard to sanctions, the amendments introduced the possibility for the Competition Council to take into account, while fixing the fine for violation of Articles 5 and 6 of the national law (the equivalent of Articles 101 and 102 TFEU) and/or Articles 101 and 102 TFEU, a specific type of cooperation provided during the administrative procedure as a mitigating circumstance justifying a reduction of the total fine (acknowledgment of the deed). Such cooperation covers the case where, after having received the investigation report and after having exercised its right of access to the file or during the hearing, the undertaking expressly admits to having engaged in anticompetitive behaviour. Independently from the sanctions applied in accordance with the provisions of the competition law, the amendments foresee that natural or legal persons have the right to ask for the complete remedy of damages caused to them by anticompetitive practices. This amendment was also

[21] The amendment was introduced by the Emergency Government Ordinance no. 121/2003 published in the Official Journal of Romania no. 875/10.12.2003.

[22] The Competition Law no. 21/1996, republished, was further amended in 2010 by the Emergency Government Ordinance no.75/30.6.2010, approved one year later by the Law no. 149/5.7.2011. The latter act not only approved the EGO no. 75/2010 but also brought new amendments to the Competition Law.

aimed at introducing at national level legal provisions after the model of the *settlement* procedure that the European Commission implements, but it was partially taken over.

Another important improvement brought to the legal framework consists in the assimilation, at national level, of the Article 19 of Regulation 1/2003 i.e. the legal possibility of the Romanian Competition Council to interview any natural or legal person that gives its consent to be interviewed in order to obtain information on the subject of the investigation, thus harmonizing the national competition legislation with Article 19 of Regulation 1/2003.

As mentioned before, the inspections powers introduced in 2003 have been improved by new important amendments that not only fully align this power with that of the European Commission (Article 20 of Regulation 1/2003) but also expressly introduced at national level the concept of 'legal professional privilege' in the competition procedures and the applicable procedure.[23] At Community level, the European Court of Justice recognized the concept of "legal privilege" to guarantee the right of defence of the undertakings under investigation.

The latter amendment pursued the taking over in the national legislation the minimum limits which guarantee this right in the form established at EU level having in mind that the national competition law implemented the system of parallel application by the national authority of both national and EU competition rules. The concept of "legal privilege" is expressly regulated in other Member States' competition legislations as well (Hungary, Netherland). Those amendments reflected the jurisprudence of the European Court of Justice as was that of the *Akzo* case.[24] The amendment pursued the observance of this concept as it was developed by the jurisprudence of the Community courts.

Another legal amendment envisaged the possibility to adopt commitments decisions after the model of Regulation 1/2003 (Article 9). The national procedure that was introduced enables the undertakings under investigation for possible anticompetitive practices to voluntarily assume a number of obligations so as to address certain issues that might constitute violations of the national and Community legislation in the field of competition. The initiative of presenting the commitments belongs exclusively to the undertakings investigated by the Competition Council for the possible violation of the law. The closure of an investigation by a decision accepting commitments is an exceptional situation, limited to those cases whereby through this procedure the competitive environment is restored more rapidly and efficiently than it would have been achieved by imposing fines and/or corrective measures through a decision asserting an infringement of the law. The decision for accepting commitments has a compulsory legal force. If the undertakings fail to comply with the commitments made, the Competition Council will apply penalties, comminatory fines when the implementation of the compulsory obligations is

---

[23] OECD – Romania Peer Review, February **2014**, Questionnaire for Competition Policy.

[24] T-125/03 and T-253/03. *Akzo Nobel Chemicals Ltd and Akcros Chemicals Ltd v Commission of the European Communities.*

delayed or it may reopen the procedure ex-officio or upon request.[25] The improvement of the national legislation framework with the commitments decision power was also meant to reduce the duration of the investigations and the number of the Competition Council's cases pending in courts.

The power to adopt interim measures was also taken over in the national competition law. The respective provisions also clarified the conditions grounding the adoption of interim measures and assimilated the principles established in Article 8 of Regulation 1/2003 making as well a clear distinction between the interim measures for antitrust and merger cases.

Following the amendment of the Competition Law, a comprehensive process of adapting the secondary legislation was performed.[26]

As a preliminary conclusion, it may be argued that, based on the above mentioned amendments of the Romanian competition framework, there is a consistent level of harmonisation of national legislation in the antitrust field with that Community one (at least from the decision making and investigative powers' perspective).

This assessment is also sustained by the OECD and the Wold Bank, which made positive remarks within the peer-review and the functional assessment of the competition authority carried out in the period 2013–2014 concerning the investigative tools used by the Competition Council as well as the alignment to the antitrust Community rules.[27]

They pointed out that: "The Romanian competition regime has greatly benefited the Europeanisation and 'internationalization'. Competition law in Romania is firmly anchored in European enforcement standards: the framework for substantive analysis, secondary regulations, and law enforcement practices are essentially in line with the European enforcement model."[28] And also: "***The RCC has an extensive range of instruments in its toolbox***, from antitrust enforcement and merger review to actions against anticompetitive measures by public authorities such as advocacy, impact assessment opinions, informal working relationships with other authorities, and unfair competition laws. Maintaining an organization centred on industrial sectors will enable the RCC to prioritize among the various tools it has to address problems in the market, and benefit from previous experience when using new tools to address competitive problems in a sector."[29]

---

[25] Romanian Competition Council, 2010 Annual Report.

[26] The secondary legislation contains: the *Guidelines on the conditions, terms and procedure applied in order to accept and evaluate the commitments for anticompetitive practices* (enforced by Order no. 724 of the 28th of December 2010 and published in the Official Journal of Romania no.11/05.01.2011) with further amendments and completions and the *Guidelines on the conditions, terms and procedure followed to adopt interim measures according to article 47 of the Competition Law no. 21/1996*, enforced by Order no. 40 of the 24th of January 2011 and published in the Official Journal of Romania no. 91/04.02.2011.

[27] The debate of the *peer-review* on the competition policy and law in Romania took place in Paris on the 27th of February 2014 in the framework of the OECD Global Forum on Competition.

[28] OECD: Competition Law and Policy in Romania, a peer review (pg. 7).

[29] Ibid, (pg. 55).

### 1.2.2 *Harmonization of the NCAs' Antitrust Legislative Provisions Concerning the Investigative and Decision-Making Powers with Those of Regulation 1/2003*

In the specialized economic and legal literature it is often argued that Regulation 1/2003 is in itself a regulation oriented towards convergence while the ECN represents its driving force.

In 2009 the European Commission published the first ECN Report[30] on the functioning of Regulation 1/2003 emphasizing that "the EC Treaty's antitrust rules have at a greater extent become the *law of the land* for the whole of the EU".[31] It also revealed a number of limited areas which merit further evaluation, such as aspects related to the investigations and procedures and the sanctions applied by NCAs.

Based on the aspects raised in the 2009 ECN Report, the ECN – as the NCAs' forum for discussions and cooperation – carried out an in-depth assessment work through a series of projects in order to improve the level of convergence of national competition legislations on specific issues of interest concerning the investigative and decision-making powers of the NCAs.

Two of these projects have been finalized in two reports, namely the Investigative Powers Report and the Decision-making Powers Report. They were made public in October 2012 and provide an overview of the different systems and procedures for antitrust investigations within the ECN.[32]

Furthermore, the ECN has also endorsed and published a set of Recommendations on key investigative and decision-making powers.[33] These Recommendations were intended to be used as advocacy tools vis-à-vis policymakers and they set out the ECN's position on the powers that authorities in the Network should have in their competition toolbox.[34] The ECN's 7 recommendations showed a strong consensus on the tools needed for enforcement[35]:

- investigative powers, enforcement measures and sanctions in the context of inspections and requests for information;
- the power to collect digital evidence, including by forensic means;
- assistance in inspections conducted under Articles 22(1) of Regulation 1/2003;

[30] Commission staff working paper accompanying the Communication from the Commission to the European Parliament and Council – Report on the functioning of Regulation 1/2003 {COM(2009)206 final}/* SEC/2009/0574 final */(http://ec.europa.eu/competition/antitrust/legislation/regulations.html).

[31] Press release IP/09/683: *Commission adopts report on functioning of key antitrust Regulation* (http://europa.eu/rapid/press-release_IP-09-683_en.htm?locale=en).

[32] ECN, Investigative Powers Report (http://ec.europa.eu/competition/ecn/documents.html).

[33] Communication from the Commission to the European Parliament and the Council *Ten Years of Antitrust Enforcement under Regulation 1/2003: Achievements and Future Perspectives* (http://ec.europa.eu/competition/antitrust/legislation/regulations.html).

[34] ECN Decision Making Report (http://ec.europa.eu/competition/ecn/documents.html).

[35] Alexander Italianer, *Completing Convergence*, speech European Competition Day, Rome 2014.

- the power to set priorities;
- interim measures;
- commitment procedures; and
- the power to impose structural remedies.

The table below presents in a synthetic manner an overview on the level of harmonization of NCAs legislation with the EU antitrust rules related to investigation and decision-making powers (Table 1.1).

The table contains information concerning the national competition laws of all Member States and Norway highlighting as far as the transposition of EU rules on investigation and decision-making powers is concerned:

(A) a very positive situation regarding the adoption of decisions finding and terminating an infringement, the power to request information and the general power to conduct inspections: all NCAs are endowed with these powers;
(B) a positive situation for the following powers: to order interim measures, to adopt commitments decisions, to conduct sector enquiries, to take statements, to seal business premises, books and records and to inspect non-business premises where the vast majority of the NCAs possesses this powers;
(C) a less positive situation in relation to the power to set priorities and the power to impose structural remedies, as fewer NCAs dispose of these powers.

The net outcome, based on the voluntary convergence sustained by the Member States and the ECN soft laws, is appreciated as satisfactory and reflects a degree of transposition above average with important variations and levels of harmonization from one Member State to another. As for Romania, it is worth mentioning that the national competition authority may use a complete set of the investigative and decision-making powers under assessment.[36]

By way of example, the recent amendments brought to the Romanian Competition Law provide for the prioritization of cases in terms of the potential impact upon effective competition, consumers general interest or strategic importance of the relevant economic sector. This is in line with *the ECN Recommendation on the Power to set Priorities*. The RCC is also empowered to take commitments decisions, to pursue inspections in both business and private premises and to impose structural and behavioural remedies. These investigative and decision powers may be exercised more or less by all NCAs, their complexity depending on the specificities of each national legal system. To overcome the limits imposed by the national particularities, in a number of Member States (e.g. Greece, Ireland, Portugal and Austria) similar investigative and decision powers have been introduced following the

[36] B. Chirițoiu, President of the Romanian Competition Council, European Competition Day, Rome, Italy, 2014: "For Romania, the efforts to integrate in the European Union started with legislative harmonization in the competition field. The Romanian Competition Council (RCC) made constant endeavours to bring in line the national legislation with the European competition rules."

**Table 1.1** Convergence of national competition laws with regulation 1/2003

| EC | NCAs | | |
|---|---|---|---|
| | Fully convergent | Partially convergent | Not convergent |
| **Abolition of notification system for agreements and introduction of a legal exception system (Art. 1)** | All NCAs (**RO**: art. 5 of the Competition Law) except for: | | DK, IT, LV |
| **Parallel application of community and national antitrust rules** *(***Art. 3.2)** | All NCAs (**RO**: art. 3 (2) of the Competition Law) except for: | | IT |
| **Power to adopt decisions finding and terminating an infringement (Art. 7):** if the Commission finds there to be an infringement of Article 101 or 102 TFEU, it may adopt a decision requiring the undertakings and associations of undertakings concerned to bring the infringement to an end or finding that the infringement has been brought to an end. | All NCAs (**RO**: art. 44 a) of the Competition Law) | | |
| **Power to set priorities** | CY, CZ, DK, EL, FI, LT, MT, NL, PT, RO, UK (**RO**: art. 33(2) of the Competition Law) | | AT, BE, BG, DE, EE, ES, FR, HR, HU, IE, IT, LU, LV, PL, SE, SL, SK |
| **Power to impose structural remedies (Art. 7)** | All NCAs (**RO**: art. 44 e) of the Competition Law) except for: | FR, HU, IT, LU | DK, EE, FI, LT, PL, SK, SV |
| **Power to order interim measures (Art. 8):** in cases of justified urgency, the Commission, acting on its own initiative, may, on the basis of a *prima facie* finding of infringement, order interim measures. | All NCAs (RO: art. 44 b) of the Competition Council) except for: | | NL |
| **Power to adopt commitments decisions (Art. 9):** where the Commission intends to adopt a decision requiring that an infringement be brought to an end and where the undertakings concerned offer commitments to meet its concerns, it may make those conditions binding for a specified period. It may reopen the proceedings if the facts of the case change, the undertakings act contrary to their commitments or the decision is based on incomplete, incorrect or misleading information. | All NCAs (**RO**: art. 44 c) of the Competition Law) except for: | LV | |

(continued)

**Table 1.1** (continued)

| | NCAs | | |
|---|---|---|---|
| EC | Fully convergent | Partially convergent | Not convergent |
| **Power to conduct sector inquiries**: where the trend of trade between EU countries, the rigidity of prices, or other circumstances, suggest that competition may be being restricted or distorted within the common market, the Commission is able to conduct an inquiry into a particular sector of the economy or into a particular type of agreement across various sectors. | All NCAs (**RO**: art. 25 g) of the Competition Law) except for: | | NL |
| **Power to request information:** the Commission may, by simple request or by decision, ask undertakings and associations of undertakings to provide any information it needs to carry out the duties assigned to it by this regulation; any natural or legal person who might have useful information is required to supply any information asked of them; the Commission may also ask governments and national competition authorities for any information it requires to carry out its duties. | All NCAs (**RO**: art. 34 of the Competition Law) | | |
| **Power to take statements:** the Commission may interview any natural or legal person who consents to be interviewed. | All NCAs (**RO**: arts. 35 and 36 of the Competition Law) | ES, PL | DK, HR |
| **Power to conduct inspections:** the Commission may conduct any necessary inspections of undertakings and associations of undertakings, and the latter are required to submit to such inspections | All NCAs (**RO**: art. 36 of the Competition Law) | | |
| **Power to seal business premises, books and records (Art. 20)** | All NCAs (**RO**: art. 36 e) of the Competition Law) except for: | UK | CZ, EE, FR, IT |
| **Power to inspect non-business premises (Art. 21)** | All NCAs (**RO**: art. 37 of the Competition Law) except for: | | BG, DK, IT |

Source: Updated results of the questionnaire on the reform of Member States' national competition laws after EC Regulation No. 1/2003 (2013) and of the Reports on Investigative and Decision-making Powers (ECN Working Group on Cooperation Issues, *Results of the questionnaire on the reform of Member States (MS) national competition laws after EC Regulation No. 1/2003*, 22 May 2013 (http://ec.europa.eu/competition/ecn/convergence_table_en.pdf))

Programme Countries[37] and the European Semester.[38] These represent other ways in which enhanced procedural convergence has been sought and attained in the area of commitment decisions and investigative powers.[39]

While the progress made in the convergence of the substantive side of the national competition laws with the EU antitrust provisions is satisfactory, it is appreciated that more efforts are required to improve the procedural side of the convergence.

Above all, it has to be underlined that in the majority of the Member States the competition rules are applied according to an administrative procedure while in a few Member States (Denmark, Estonia, Germany, Ireland, Portugal, Slovenia, and United Kingdom) the rules are applied according to a two-tracked procedure, namely criminal procedure and administrative procedure as well.

To better illustrate this situation of diversity of national procedures for the application of the same substantial antitrust rule, the following exemplifications of comparison for certain procedural areas has been drafted below (Graphs 1.1 and 1.2). If all NCAs may conduct inspections, the powers they may use during the inspections vary significantly across Member States. Graph 1.1 emphasizes the differences that exist between national jurisdictions in relation to the ability of NCAs to seize the original documents (19 NCAs are endowed with these powers, 9 NCAs may not do that, while only one NCA may seize the original documents under certain fulfilled conditions). The same may be said about the addressee of a request for information: Graph 1.2. Whereas in several jurisdictions (AT, BE, CZ, DK, EU, FI, FR, MT, PL, RO) requests for information (RFIs) may be addressed only to undertakings and/or associations of undertakings, in the majority of jurisdictions (BG, CY, DE, EE, EL, ES, HU, IE, IT, LT, LV, LU, NL, PT, SV, SI, SK, UK) requests may also be addressed to natural persons (mostly representatives of the undertaking concerned).[40]

---

[37] Programme Country is an EU financial support program granted through an Economic Adjustment Programme when the country is passing through serious financial situation. The aim is to support the government's efforts to restore fiscal sustainability and to implement structural reforms in order to improve the competitiveness of the economy, thereby laying the foundations for sustainable economic growth. (http://ec.europa.eu/economy_finance/assistance_eu_ms).

[38] EU Member States have committed to achieving the Europe 2020 objectives, translating them into national targets and policies conducive to economic growth. The European Semester is a cycle of economic and fiscal policy coordination within the EU. It focuses on the period of 6 months from the beginning of the year, hence its name, "semester". During the European Semester, Member States shall align their budgetary policies and economic objectives and rules agreed at EU level. The European Semester means, essentially, that the EU and Euro area coordinate ex-ante their economic and fiscal policies in line with the Stability and Growth Pact and Europe 2020. This coordination concerns the drafting of national stability programs or the convergence programs, of Member States' national budgets and of the national reform programs. Every year, the European Commission analyzes in detail the programs of Member States on economic and structural reforms and provides recommendations for the next 12–18 months.

[39] B. Chiriţoiu, President of the Romanian Competition Council, European Competition Day, Rome, 2014.

[40] Investigative Powers Report, 31st of October 2012, ECN Cooperation Issues and Due Process Working Group (http://ec.europa.eu/competition/ecn/documents.html).

**Graph 1.1** Ability to seize original documents

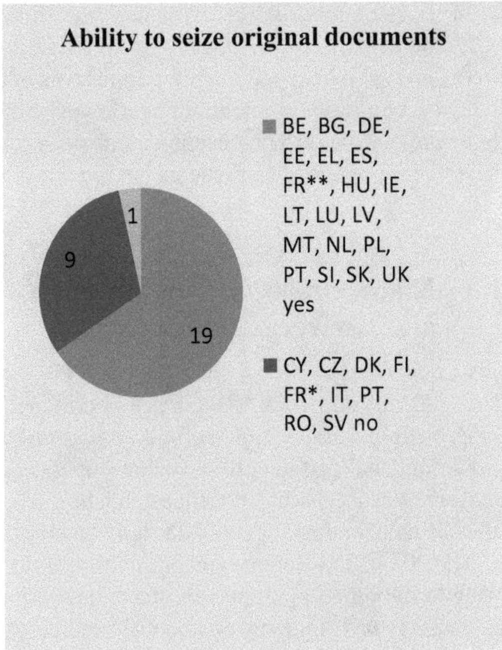


**Graph 1.2** Addressee of a RFI (Source: ECN Investigative Powers Report, 2012)

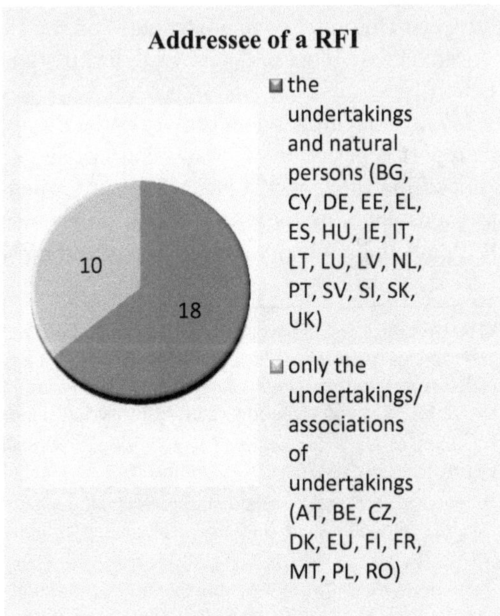

In its 2014 reporting documents,[41] the European Commission concluded that: "Currently many basic elements of investigative and decision making powers and procedure, which are the main working tools of competition authorities, are present in the vast majority of jurisdictions. However, the divergences subsist for some fundamental questions. This results in a disperse picture where NCAs have strong and convergent powers in some fields but are not-convergent in others."

## 1.3 Enforcement Activity of the ECN: Priorities and Convergence

The competition policy has a major importance for creating the right environment for growth and innovation. It is the basis for keeping markets undistorted and for providing legal certainty to businesses operating on the market. Having clear competition rules is a necessity[42] for establishing a level playing field.[43] The competition rules bring economic benefits through the enforcement activity.

The 2014 EC's Report on the last 10 years of enforcement of Regulation 1/2003 bring to light the impressive enforcement work that the European Commission and the NCAs have undertaken together in the respective period, i.e. May 2004 – December 2014. There were altogether more than 700 enforcement decisions of different type of antitrust practices and related to specific territorial areas of the European Union. A comparison between the European Commission and NCAs as concerns the number of decisions issued by type of infringement is provided below (Graph 1.3).[44]

In terms of enforcement activity of the European Commission and NCAs, during the reported period the Commission has adopted 122 decisions enforcing the EU competition rules, whilst NCAs have informed the Commission of 665 envisaged decisions applying these provisions.[45] This means an impressive work and one of the pillars upon which the well-recognized ECN's success is grounded.

[41] The Commission staff-working document: *Enhancing competition enforcement by the Member States' competition authorities: institutional and procedural issues* accompanying the EC's Report on *Ten year of antitrust enforcement under Regulation 1/2003: achievements and further perspectives* (http://ec.europa.eu/competition/antitrust/legislation/regulations.html).

[42] A. Italianer, *EU Priorities and Competition Enforcement*, Institute for European and International Affairs, the 25th of March 2011, Dublin.

[43] Economic and legal environment in which all competitors, irrespective of their size or financial strength, follow the same rules and get equal opportunity to compete.

[44] C. Esteva Mosso, *International Convergence in Competition Policy and Enforcement: A View from the EU* (http://www.bruegel.org/fileadmin/bruegel_files/Events/Event_materials/2014/January/140218_Comp/Esteva_Mosso.pdf).

[45] The Commission staff working document: *Enhancing competition enforcement by the Member States' competition authorities: institutional and procedural issues* accompanying the EC's Report on *Ten year of antitrust enforcement under Regulation 1/2003: achievements and further perspectives* (http://ec.europa.eu/competition/antitrust/legislation/regulations.html).

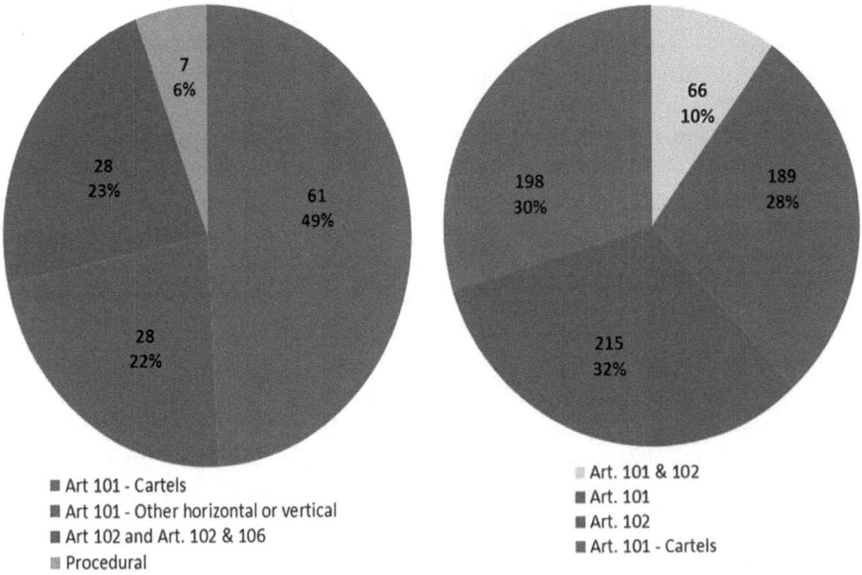


**Graph 1.3** Decisions by European Commission and NCAs by type of infringement (Source: Communication from the Commission to the European Parliament and the Council, "Ten Years of Antitrust Enforcement under Regulation 1/2003: Achievements and Future Perspectives")

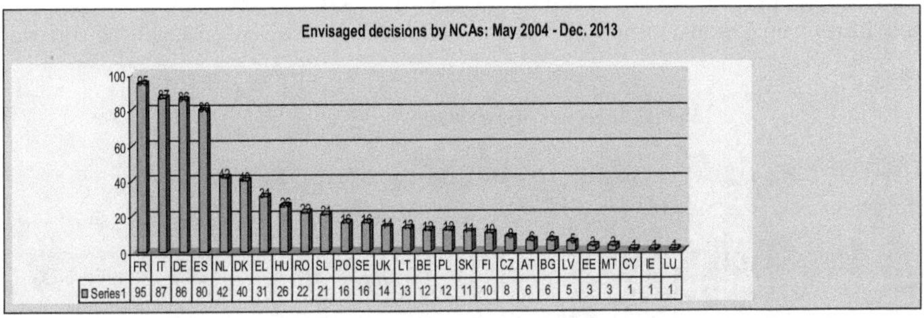


**Graph 1.4** Envisaged decisions by NCAs: May 2004–Dec. 2013 (Source: C. Esteva Mosso, "Ten Years of Regulation 1/2003: Taking Stock", International Forum on EU Competition Law, 04.04.2014)

The graph below points out the envisaged decisions of each NCA from the Member States submitted for consultation with the European Commission within Article 11(4) of Regulation 1/2003. For Romania, the specific cases have been submitted since January 2007 when it officially became a European Union's Member State (Graph 1.4).

The level of convergence in the application of Articles 101 and 102 of TFEU was qualified as satisfactory, being facilitated by the formal consultation mechanisms established by Article 11(4) of Regulation 1/2003 and by the informal dialogue within ECN.[46]

Having in view that the European Commission's aim is to assist the coherent application of competition rules across the EU, the NCAs' objective is to cooperate fully with each other and to exchange opinions and information with the aim of effectively and efficiently applying the competition rules in their respective jurisdictions. Under Article 11(4) of the Regulation, an NCA must inform the Commission no later than 30 days before the adoption of a decision requiring that an infringement would be brought to an end, accepting commitments or withdrawing the benefit of a block exemption Regulation. This information may also be made available to the other members of the ECN.[47] This formal consultation provides the best mechanism of checking the quality of the legal and economic reasoning of NCAs cases involving the application of Articles 101 and 102 of TFEU and gives a greater comfort not only in terms of the robustness of the evidence and the standard of proof but also higher chances in front of the national courts.[48] The coherent, effective and efficient application of EU antitrust rules across Europe was also sustained by the activity of the working groups and sectoral sub-groups set within ECN. All these instruments contributed to assuring the convergence on substance when the NCAs have enforced the competition rules at EU level set in Regulation 1/2003.

A very interesting finding of the Report emphasizes, based on the number of decisions issued by the European Commission by type of procedure (Graph 1.5), the European Commission's approach in relation to the enforcement priorities,

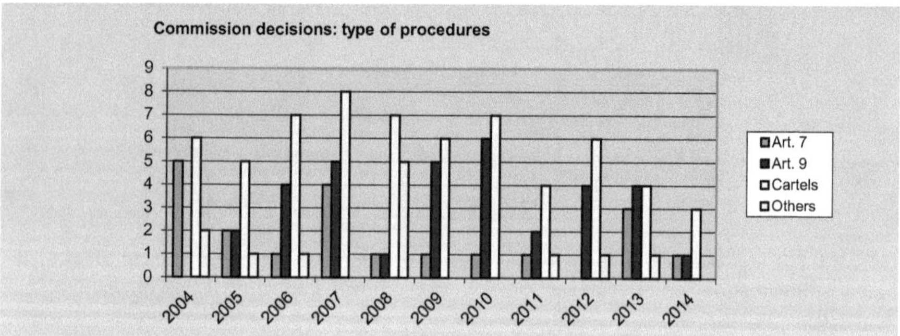


**Graph 1.5** Commission decisions: type of procedures (Source: C. Esteva Mosso, "Ten Years of Regulation 1/2003: Taking Stock", International Forum on EU Competition Law, 04.04.2014)

[46] C. Esteva Mosso, *Ten Years of Regulation 1/2003:Taking Stock*, Studienvereinigung Kartellrecht, International Forum on EU Competition Law, 04.04.2014.

[47] "*The European Competition Network: What It Is and Where It's Going*", The Antitrust Source, July 2005.

[48] B. Chirițoiu, President of the Romanian Competition Council, European Competition Day, Rome, Italy 2014.

meaning that the focus of these priorities was obviously the hard-core cartels. A slightly difference seems to appear on this aspect between the European Commission and the Member States, because the same may not be argued about the enforcement activity of the NCAs of which enforcement appears to concentrate on non-secret infringements.

The enforcement activity of the European Commission and of Member States in the application of Articles 101 and 102 of TFEU complements each other. The unbalanced statistical data on cartel cases between the Commission and the NCAs may be also found in the building blocks of Regulation 1/2003 (applied in conjunction with the Guidelines on the effect on trade and the Commission Notice on ECN cooperation). It is well known that complex cases, covering at least three Member States are cases of Community interest that are obviously dealt exclusively by the Commission while the NCAs' actions are usually limited to the national territory.

On the other hand, each NCA's enforcement activity depends on the national situation of the economy meaning that the enforcement priorities are influenced by the national economic specificities. All NCAs handle cartels if they found them, all NCAs assess vertical agreements if they affect competition on their national markets, but the enforcement priorities at national level is closely linked to national economic particularities. Even if the general picture shows that the NCAs' enforcement activity appears to be oriented towards non-secret infringements, this idea may not be generalized at least for two reasons. First of all, there are NCAs of which enforcement activity may contradict this statement. For Romania, the statistics of cases in the recent years confirm that the enforcement of the Romanian Competition Council is changing its direction from vertical anticompetitive agreements to horizontal agreements seriously affecting competition.[49] The creation of a dedicated Cartel Unit within Romanian Competition Council in 2012 also reveals the key interest in fighting against cartels (Graph 1.6).

---

[49] OECD: Competition Law and Policy in Romania, a Peer Review (p. 7, p. 84). (http://www.consiliulconcurentei.ro/uploads/docs/items/id9183/peer-review-romania-2014-en.pdf).

"The enforcement process is transparent overall, with a strong separation of investigative and decision making functions within the authority. The RCC has moved toward a more pro-active enforcement approach and considerably reduced the number of investigations based on complaints. Less time is spent on vertical cases, ***and more resources are used for cartels and abuse of dominance investigations***. The RCC is highly respected in Romania for its professionalism and expertise."

"Cartels are unambiguously prohibited, the RCC has effective investigative powers, the leniency programme is consistent with European and international standards, fines can reach 10 % of a defendant's annual revenues, and the law provides for individual criminal sanctions for bid rigging and other cartels. The RCC focuses on the fight against cartels. It has created a Directorate for Public Procurement and has a dedicated cartel unit to ensure that the necessary resources and expertise are available. The Procurement Directorate focuses not only on the prosecution of bid rigging, but also works with procurement authorities to improve procurement procedures. Among other initiatives, the RCC has successfully lobbied for the introduction of a certificate of independent bid determination, which can increase both deterrence and enforcement opportunities."

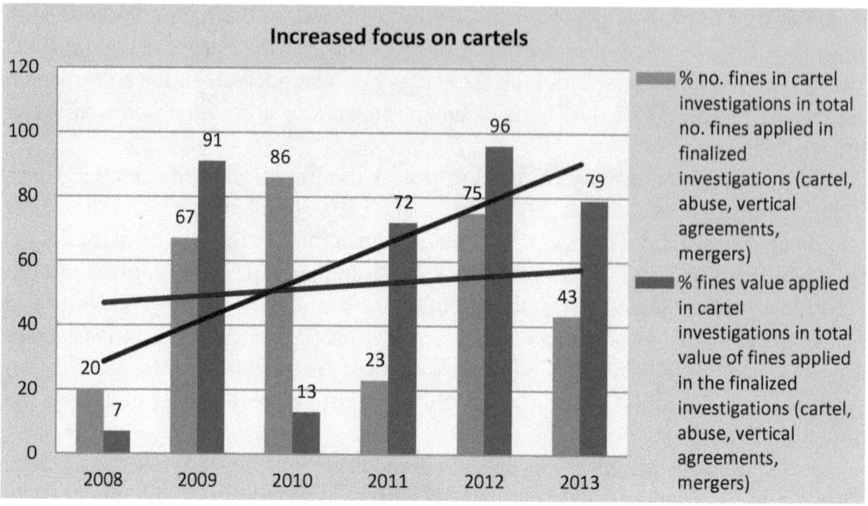


**Graph 1.6** Increased focus on cartels (Source: Romanian Competition Council's Annual Reports 2008–2013)

The easily observable linear trend lines in this graph show a tendency to focus on the most important cartel cases. It may be noticed as well that, while the trend of the number of fines for cartel cases is steadily increasing, the percentage of fines shows an accelerating trend that supports this conclusion.[50]

Secondly, cartels as the most harmful anticompetitive practices are undoubtedly the main target for all NCAs. But in the same time cartels are hard to be disclosed in the absence of effective leniency enforcement and adequate forensic IT tools. To develop these tools, investment is needed in human resources and specific equipment. The effectiveness of leniency policies is also interrelated with putting into place a deterrent sanctioning policy. In Romania's case it's still room for further improvement. Romania has a leniency program in place since 2009 and yet it had only one leniency case where the company qualified for a fine reduction, although intensive advocacy actions were carried out over the last years. Nevertheless, the spectacular results are still delaying.

Cartels are without any doubt the most harmful infringements of competition and the European Commission's approach in this respect should be a trend for all NCAs. Nevertheless, the enforcement activity especially that related to cartels not only depends on the economic environment in a Member State but it implies as well other complex and sensitive issues such as the sanctioning policy and the leniency program an NCA has in place.

[50] B. Chiriţoiu, President of the Romanian Competition Council, *Latest Developments in Competition Law and Policy in Romania*, OECD Peer review of competition law and policy in Romania, Global Competition Forum, 27 February 2014.

## 1.4 Conclusions

Since the entry into force of Regulation 1/2003, the convergence of competition rules has remained high on the agenda of the ECN. Whether done voluntarily or based on different actions at national level (European Semester, Programme Country) or based on the ECN's Recommendations, a satisfactory level of harmonization on substance as concerns the investigative and decision making powers at NCAs level has been achieved. Despite the progress made, the same may not be stated about procedural convergence, as the reality shows that the same substantive rules are applied according to different national procedures within the ECN. As part of the ECN, Romania invested all efforts required both pre- and post- accession to align the competition legislation with the *acquis communautaire*, equipping the competition authority with a set of investigative and decision making instruments similar to that of the European Commission. Although a full alignment is not characterizing either the Romanian competition legislation, still its level of harmonization with the EU antitrust rules is high.

A solid degree of convergence insures a smooth application of competition rules along the internal market. Similar procedural and substantive rules are meant to simplify cooperation across the various jurisdictions of the European Union and to bring more efficiency for both enforcers and businesses. Apart from the investigative and decision making powers, the sanctioning and leniency policy at ECN level are other areas that are even more problematic for convergence. That is why this topic still remains a "must" for the ECN.

Having in view the close relation between the legislation and enforcement, a satisfactory level was also achieved in applying the EU antitrust rules. The number of over 700 decisions taken within the ECN in the last 10 years of enforcement of Regulation 1/2003 speaks for itself. If one assesses the enforcement record from the type of infringement perspective, it may be affirmed that the European Commission was cartel-oriented while the NCAs tackled especially non-secret infringements. This different enforcement result does not represent a different competition policy approach. The fight against cartels as the most harmful antitrust practice is also a priority for all NCAs, but the enforcement record by NCAs inevitably depends on the state and particularities of the national economy. By taking Romania as example, one may again support the claim that cartels are *the most sought after* anticompetitive practices. The trend of the last years' enforcement, the leniency program in place since 2009, the creation of a dedicated Cartel Unit within the competition authority and the intensive advocacy in the field are solid enough to point out that the enforcement trend of the European Commission is also followed by other NCAs.

Apart from that, as the Vice President of the European Commission who is responsible for competition policy stated when presenting the 2014 EC Annual Report, "all competition policy instruments help Europe's companies and economies to become more efficient, increase productivity and foster innovation:

- antitrust and cartel enforcement creates the conditions for lower input prices and better quality services for EU industry and consumers by ensuring that new entrants are not kept away from the market and by preventing collusive arrangements between companies;

- merger control keeps markets open and efficient; and
- State aid policy helps to steer public resources towards growth-enhancing objectives."

Taking that statement as a starting point, it may be further argued that a convergent approach at ECN level of all competition policy's instruments (including mergers, state aid and advocacy) will better complement the antitrust enforcement actions and unify the strategies to promote pro-competitive reforms that foster growth and consumer welfare.

Finally, although at this moment one may speak about more or less convergent areas of EU antitrust rules and enforcement records, the general view highlights a constant progress attained since May 2004 until present in these areas. This progress is grounded on the NCAs' commitment based on Regulation 1/2003 and was highly supported by the ECN's "can do" attitude and the way it has been embraced by all Member States and the willingness shown by all to attempt to accommodate each other.[51]

[51] "*The European Competition Network: What It Is and Where It's Going*", The Antitrust Source, July 2005.

# Chapter 2
# The Commission Communication on Ten Years of Antitrust Enforcement Under Regulation 1/2003 – Prospective Priorities and Challenges

**Cătălin S. Rusu**

## 2.1 Introduction

In July 2014, the Commission issued a Communication,[1] accompanied by two Staff Working Documents,[2] marking 10 years of EU competition law enforcement under Regulation 1/2003.[3] These documents have a dual purpose: to provide a facts-based review of the public enforcement of the competition law rules, performed by the Commission and the National Competition Authorities (hereinafter NCAs), during the past decade; and to examine some institutional and procedural aspects relating to the enforcement by the NCAs, with a view to its further enhancement.[4] The 2014 COM's scope and main propositions were also briefly previewed by the Commission's 2013 Report on Competition Policy.[5]

The Commission, in issuing this Communication, offers a good opportunity to evaluate the achievements of probably the most prominent component of the 2004 Modernization Package. This occasion provides the appropriate ambit to also look

[1] Communication from the Commission – Ten Years of Antitrust Enforcement under Regulation 1/2003: Achievements and Future Perspectives, COM(2014) 453, 09.07.2014 (hereinafter 'the 2014 COM').

[2] Commission Staff Working Document SWD (2014) 230 – Ten Years of Antitrust Enforcement under Regulation 1/2003, SWD(2014) 230/2, 09.07.2014 and Commission Staff Working Document SWD (2014) 231 – Enhancing competition enforcement by the Member States' competition authorities: institutional and procedural issues, SWD(2014) 231/2, 09.07.2014.

[3] Council Regulation 1/2003 on the implementation of the rules on competition laid down in Articles 81 and 82 of the Treaty, OJ L 1, 04.01.2003.

[4] 2014 COM, [2].

[5] COM(2014) 249 final, 6.5.2014, available at: http://ec.europa.eu/competition/publications/annual_report/2013/part1_en.pdf, accessed on 7 May 2015.

C.S. Rusu (✉)
Radboud University Nijmegen, Nijmegen, Netherlands
e-mail: c.rusu@jur.ru.nl



A. Almăşan, P. Whelan (eds.), *The Consistent Application of EU Competition Law*, Studies in European Economic Law and Regulation 9,
DOI 10.1007/978-3-319-47382-6_2

forward and dwell upon the prospective lines of development when it comes to enforcing the EU competition law rules. These two facets of the enforcement evaluation exercise highlight a number of challenges, past on the one hand, and present and eventually prospective, on the other hand. With regard to the former, one may notice that some challenges have successfully been tackled, while others were left more or less untouched; with regard to the latter, they seem to reflect not only the actual development of the law (be it hard-law or soft-law), of the enforcement priorities, and of the means of practical enforcement, but also the constant shaping exercise that the Court of Justice of the EU (hereinafter CJEU) has been engaging in, with a view to accommodating the wide variety of interests at stake.

In this respect, the 2014 COM invites one not only to look back and appreciate the benefits of the decentralized enforcement system, but also to engage in a forward-looking exercise, in an attempt to decipher the challenges that still lie ahead and the priorities of enforcement that seem bound to arise given the latest developments in the field. This contribution aims to do just that, by attempting to answer one apparently straightforward question: after a decade of challenging expansion of the enforcement activities, which is the correct way ahead?

In order to accomplish this endeavour, this contribution, in Sect. 2.2, will first briefly recall the added value of the enforcement system introduced by Regulation 1/2003. Then, Sect. 2.3 will look into some of the puzzles that surround the issue of enforcement of the EU competition law rules, in an attempt to assert whether the existing achievements are indeed owed to the system introduced by Regulation 1/2003. In Sect. 2.4, the existing degree of substantive and procedural convergence is discussed, while also contextualizing some of the main concerns highlighted by the 2014 COM. Section 2.5 will then set the scene for previewing the answer to the main research question of this contribution: after looking back to 10 years of enforcement which is the correct way to look ahead? Lastly, Sect. 2.6 will provide the conclusions of this contribution.

## 2.2 Achievements

It is by now generally accepted that Regulation 1/2003 brought about radical changes in the manner in which Articles 101 and 102 TFEU are enforced.[6] These changes were triggered by the need to freshen up the old enforcement system based on Regulation 17/62.[7] Completely renouncing the notification system for practices that may infringe the competition law rules and decentralizing the enforcement activities have yielded important consequences not only for the Commission but also for the NCAs.

---

[6] See also W. Wils, 'Ten Years of Regulation 1/2003 – A Retrospective', 4 *Journal of Competition Law and Practice* 4, 2013.

[7] First Regulation 17/62 Implementing Articles 85 and 86 of the Treaty, OJ 013, 21.02.1962.

Of course, it is important to acknowledge the achievements of Regulation 1/2003, which is essentially viewed by the Commission as having positively contributed to stronger enforcement of the EU competition rules.[8] Without attempting to exhaustively list here all the noteworthy aspects of the reform's consequences, one should mention at least the following:

1. Regulation 1/2003 has given the Commission greater scope to set its priorities and devote resources to investigating problematic cases and conducting inquires in key sectors of the economy, at the end of the day for the overall benefit of consumers.[9]
2. The Commission was equipped with a renewed set of enforcement powers.[10]
3. Regulation 1/2003 aimed at enhancing the enforcement of the EU competition rules by NCAs and national courts, entities that are obliged to apply the EU competition rules when applying national competition law to agreements or conducts are capable of affecting trade between Member States.
4. The Regulation also introduced cooperation tools to ensure work sharing and cooperation in the handling of cases and to foster the coherent application of the law.[11]

For now, one may draw a general observation to the effect that the last 10 years have witnessed a proliferation of competition law enforcement. The achievements listed above have been based on the reliance on multiple enforcers, which have guaranteed a wider application of the EU competition law rules. What is more, the larger number of enforcers has not lead to major gaps in the manner in which these rules are applied.[12] This is primarily because over the last 10 years a somewhat satisfying level of enforcement convergence has been reached in the EU, based on the following four building blocks[13]:

1. The joint enforcement of EU substantive rules, namely Articles 101 and 102 TFEU. This has rendered the NCAs and the domestic courts as solid enforcement pillars.
2. Information exchanges between NCAs and the Commission, which nowadays seem to be essential tools of cooperation, although as discussed below, are not always problem-free.

---

[8] 2014 COM, [3].

[9] *Ibid,* [4].

[10] *Ibid,* [5].

[11] *Ibid,* [7].

[12] See also J. Almunia, 'Weaving Europe's Single Competition Enforcement Area', Speech/14/678 delivered at the *European Competition Day*, Rome, 10 October 2014, available at: http://europa.eu/rapid/press-release_SPEECH-14-678_en.htm, accessed on 12 May 2015.

[13] See also A. Italianer, 'Completing Convergence', Speech delivered at the *European Competition Day*, Rome, 10 October 2014, available at: http://ec.europa.eu/competition/speeches/text/sp2014_05_en.pdf, accessed on 12 May 2015.

3. The European Competition Network (ECN). This building block pertains to the division of labour between the NCAs, in the context of the system of reallocation of cases within the ECN. This system has been rarely used, which may very well mean that the current setup of work sharing within the ECN works well. However, once again, this proved to be not always problem-free, especially in light of some recent General Court rulings, which will be dealt with briefly below.
4. Lastly, the notification of envisaged NCA decisions to the Commission, by virtue of Article 11 of Regulation 1/2003, which may result in the Commission exercising its power to take over a case, if there is a serious risk of the NCAs applying the EU competition law rules contrary to established case-law and practice. This power has been granted to the Commission, yet it has never been used, although the Commission has not been shy in exercising its prerogative to provide comments to the NCAs.

Observing these building blocks constitutes an important step in achieving what can be labelled as a common competition culture in Europe. Based on a system of parallel enforcement of the EU competition law rules, this approach is likely to add value when it comes to the mutual reinforcement of the work done by both the Commission and the NCAs. At the end of the day, this approach may be beneficial as far as the impact on the markets is concerned. If these are in general terms the achievements of Regulation 1/2003 and the building blocks on which they are based on, one has to dig deeper and inquire whether these achievements are indeed verifiable and whether the building blocks are as solid as presented above.

## 2.3 Solved and Unsolved Puzzles

The 2014 COM takes stock of these developments and their impact in the EU Internal Market. This exercise is done while taking account of several perspectives relating to the enforcement activities: the types of infringements tackled,[14] the sectors investigated,[15] the procedures used,[16] and the manner in which the cooperation with the national courts has unfolded.[17] In this context the performance of the Commission and of the NCAs is taken into account. Certain interesting findings stem from the 2014 COM's provisions, regarding the focus of enforcement of these authorities.

First, a large number of decisions were taken by the NCAs. In the words of the 2014 COM, we are witnessing a considerably larger number of decisions taken by the NCAs than the Commission could have ever adopted on its own, should decentralization have never taken place. Indeed, as mentioned above, we are witnessing a

[14] 2014 COM, [11]–[14].
[15] *Ibid*, [15]–[18].
[16] *Ibid*, [19]–[21].
[17] *Ibid*, [22].

proliferation of competition law enforcement in the EU and in this respect the 2014 COM puts forward an estimate of 122 Commission decisions and 665 NCAs decision adopted under Regulation 1/2003, over a period of almost 10 years.[18] Still, do the numbers tell the real story? This discussion has to be viewed from the perspective of both the Commission and the NCAs. Regarding the former, Wils shows that although there are variations in the number of decisions adopted from year to year, if one looks at the averages, the figures are rather stable: 7.5 prohibition decisions and 2 exemption decisions with conditions per year under Regulation 17/62 and 7 prohibition decisions and 3 commitment decisions per year under Regulation 1/2003.[19] One may easily observe here that the projections of the 1999 White Paper on the modernization of the rules implementing Articles 85 and 86 of the Treaty,[20] namely an increase in the number of prohibition decisions after the abolition of the notification system, do not necessarily stand, as far as the Commission is concerned. If this is so, this proliferation of competition law enforcement must pertain to the NCAs. The opinions are divided here. Whereas some[21] see that the NCAs seem to have a larger decision output than the Commission, other authors[22] are more sceptical and claim that the value of Regulation 1/2003 remains unclear: it should be regarded more as of incremental value, rather than a revolution, since NCAs have been coordinating even before Regulation 1/2003 came into force, and the possibility to apply Articles 101 and 102 TFEU has not changed much in the work of NCAs (including here no considerable increase in enforcement activities), since in substance the domestic rules on cartels and the dominant position abuse were roughly similar.

Second, with regard to the type of infringements tackled by the Commission and the NCAs, the 2014 COM[23] notes that a large proportion of the resources were allotted to tackling cartels and other horizontal practices. What is interesting to notice is that the numbers show a higher propensity of the NCAs to investigate vertical practices, than of the Commission. This may very well be a matter of coincidence, but at the same time, one has to appreciate the manner in which the Vertical Restraints Block Exemption Regulation and its predecessor[24] have gotten the job done at EU

[18] *Ibid*, [8].

[19] See Wils, *supra* n. 6.

[20] OJ C 132/1, 28.04.1999.

[21] See for example Almunia, *supra* n. 12.

[22] See for example the keynote speech of G. Monti, 'A Plea for 'Extraterritorial' Antitrust Enforcement by National Competition Authorities', *Fourth ACELG Annual Conference, Amsterdam,* 14 November 2014, summarized by O. Brook, 'Ten Years of Decentralized EU Competition Law Enforcement – Success or Failure?', available at http://acelg.blogactiv.eu/2014/12/10/ten-years-of-decentralized-eu-competition-law-enforcement-success-or-failure-2/, accessed on 12 May 2015.

[23] [11]–[12].

[24] Regulation 330/2010 on the application of Article 101(3) of the TFEU to categories of vertical agreements and concerted practices, OJ L 102/1, 23.04.2010 and Regulation 2790/1999 on the application of Article 81(3) of the Treaty to categories of vertical agreements and concerted practices, OJ L 336, 29.12.1999.

level. As far as Article 102 TFEU enforcement is concerned, a clear focus of the Commission may be detected when it comes to exclusionary abuses, by virtue of the 2009 Enforcement Priorities Communication,[25] whereas NCAs, while being also preoccupied with this type of abuses, they seem to be more prone to investigate exploitative abuses than the Commission is.[26] This discussion has to be framed in the context of the first achievement listed in the previous section of this contribution, namely that Regulation 1/2003 has given the Commission greater scope to set its priorities and devote resources to investigating problematic cases. Still, certain nuances must be inserted in this discussion. Prioritization in competition matters stems from the provisions of Article 105 TFEU and the case-law of the Courts[27]: essentially, the Commission defines and implements the orientation of the EU competition policy, while ensuring the application of the principles laid down in Articles 101 and 102 TFEU.[28] If this is so, one may ask the question whether it is Regulation 1/2003 indeed that gave more room for prioritization, or whether the ability for the Commission to prioritize its actions was always there. Furthermore, has prioritization actually taken place more evidently since 2004? With regard to the former question, it is easily noticeable that room for prioritization was present before 2004, since a number of Block Exemption Regulations[29] were in force even before the enactment of Regulation 1/2003. Further testimony to the Commission's ability to prioritize stems from the *Automec* ruling,[30] which provides that the Commission must weigh up the significance of the alleged infringement regarding the functioning of the Internal Market, against the probability of establishing the existence of the infringement, and the extent of the necessary investigative measures. If at the end of the day there is no EU interest in pursuing the case, the Commission may refuse taking on an investigation, without needing to go as far as adopting a final decision on the existence or non-existence of an infringement. This is a specific ground for the Commission to do so, which is built both on Recital 18 of Regulation 1/2003 and on Article 105 TFEU.[31] Regarding the second question, namely whether prioritization has actually taken place more evidently since 2004, one could argue that by empowering the domestic authorities to apply the EU competition law rules, some resources must have been freed up in the Commission's structures, and there-

[25] Guidance on the Commission's enforcement priorities in applying Article 82 of the EC Treaty to abusive exclusionary conduct by dominant undertakings, OJ C 45, 24.02.2009.

[26] 2014 COM, [14].

[27] See for example case C-344/98 *Masterfoods*, ECLI:EU:C:2000:689 and case T-24/90 *Automec v. Commission*, ECLI:EU:T:1992:97.

[28] See also C.S. Rusu, 'Workload Division after the *Si.mobil* and *easyJet* Rulings of the General Court', *CLaSF Competition Law Review*, Volume 12, Issue 1, forthcoming 2015.

[29] For example, see Regulation 2659/2000 on the application of Article 81(3) of the Treaty to categories of research and development agreements, OJ L304, 05.12.2000, Regulation 2658/2000 on the application of Article 81(3) of the Treaty to categories of specialisation agreements, OJ L304, 05.12.2000, Regulation 2790/1999 on the application of Article 81(3) of the Treaty to categories of vertical agreements and concerted practices, *supra* n. 24.

[30] T-24/90 *Automec v. Commission*, [23].

[31] Rusu, *supra* n. 28.

fore prioritization should be more evident. Indeed, the Commission seems to have taken upon itself a more overseeing task, embodied in its coordination and monitorisation role, when it comes to the enforcement performed by the domestic authorities. This may be one facet of how prioritization has been conceived after 2004. At the same time, it may very well be the case that available resources may have been redirected to other policy areas (such as merger control and state aid, where the Commission fulfils more resource intensive functions); also, prioritization may be conceived in the context of the Commission seeking to engage its focus on the more problematic and complex cases, which obviously require a more pressing need for resources.[32] In any case, the stagnating number of prohibition decisions adopted by the Commission after 2004 may also be explained by an increased level of the competitive analysis' quality, resulting in a low number of successfully challenged Commission prohibition decisions. In essence, this may be perceived as entailing a certain degree of (internal) prioritization, which should be appreciated.

Third, as far as the sectors investigated during the past decade are concerned, both the Commission's and the NCAs' efforts were directed at a broad range of sectors: basic and manufacturing industries, recently liberalized sectors (telecom, media, transport, energy), which are characterized by a high degree of market concentration and/or market power. After 10 years of enforcement under Regulation 1/2003, no significant differences may be identified, from the perspective of the sectors investigated, between the Commission's and the NCAs' approaches. Thus, the 2014 COM does not bring any big surprises to the table: it is business as usual for the competition law enforcers.

Fourth, regarding the type of procedure used, the 2014 COM reveals that prohibition decisions and commitments are key tools for both the Commission and the NCAs. The Communication's text seems to give a shy preference to commitments, due to the advantages that stem from such proceedings: efficient use of resources, speed, reaching a resolution of the problem on a more cooperative basis.[33] In the same vein, more than once has former Commissioner Almunia highlighted the importance of commitments and settlements.[34] Furthermore, the 2014 COM seems to provide a clearer indication of the limited circumstances in which a prohibition decision is appropriate: when fines for past behaviour should be imposed, when cessation of behaviour is the only remedy available, or when there is a need for clear legal precedent.[35] This method seems reasonable. But will this approach be carried out in the future too? It seems that Commissioner Vestager feels less strongly about

---

[32] See to this effect Wils, *supra* n. 6 and W. Wils, 'Discretion and Prioritisation in Public Antitrust Enforcement, in Particular EU Antitrust Enforcement', 34 *World Competition* 3, 2011.

[33] 2014 COM, [21].

[34] See for example J. Almunia, 'Some Highlights from EU Competition Enforcement', Speech/14/608 delivered at the *IBA 18th Annual Competition Conference*, Florence, 19 September 2014, available at: http://europa.eu/rapid/press-release_SPEECH-14-608_en.htm, and J. Almunia, 'Looking Back at Five Years of Competition Enforcement in the EU', Speech/14/588 delivered at the Global Antitrust Enforcement Symposium, Washington, 10 September 2014, available at: http://europa.eu/rapid/press-release_SPEECH-14-588_en.htm, accessed on 14 May 2015.

[35] 2014 COM, [21].

commitments and settlement decisions. In her first appearance as Commissioner-Designate in front of the European Parliament, a somewhat stronger stance relating to competition law infringements seemed to be evident.[36] Commissioner Vestager stated: '[…] the commitment procedure is a very useful tool to speed up our decisions and a more efficient use of resources; […] But let me remind you that the priority is always how best to address the competition concerns in a specific case. I will not negotiate or compromise by accepting commitments that do not fully address the Commission's competition concerns.' In this respect, it should not come as a surprise that, after years of attempts by former Commissioner Almunia to find common ground with Google, regarding the alleged abuse of a dominant position, 6 months after taking office, Commissioner Vestager departed from the commitments path and opted for a statement of objections. In this particular case, the Commission's preliminary view is that in its general Internet search results, Google artificially favours its own comparison shopping service and that this constitutes an abuse.[37]

The 2014 COM thus presents us with a glowing picture of how the enforcement of the EU competition law rules has boomed over the past decade. Yet, the analysis above shows that tentative progress existed even if one excludes the changes brought about Regulation 1/2003 from the discussion. If this is so, one needs to consider where the true value of Regulation 1/2003 rests and whether any glitches occurred as far as the proliferation of competition law enforcement is concerned.

## 2.4 Convergence?

Despite the more or less controversial findings as revealed in the previous section of this contribution, while returning to the first building block mentioned above, namely the joint enforcement of EU substantive rules (Articles 101 and 102 TFEU), rendering the domestic authorities as solid enforcement pillars, one must appreciate that after 10 years of enforcement, a substantial level of convergence has been achieved as far as the substance of the law is concerned.[38] While although before Regulation 1/2003 came into force the same substantive rules were used in some of the Member States, nowadays, by virtue of the said Regulation, the Commission and all the NCAs and domestic courts apply the same substantive rules to cartels and abuses of dominant positions which impact trade between Member States.

[36] See 'Answers to the European Parliament: Questionnaire to the Commissioner-Designate Margrethe Vestager', available at http://ec.europa.eu/commission/sites/cwt/files/commissioner_ep_hearings/vestager-reply_en.pdf, accessed on 16 May 2015.

[37] See M. Vestager, 'Statement on Antitrust Decisions Concerning Google', STATEMENT/15/4785, Brussels, 15 April 2015, available at: http://europa.eu/rapid/press-release_STATEMENT-15-4785_en.htm?locale=en, accessed on 15 May 2015.

[38] See also 2014 COM, [24].

Articles 101 and 102 TFEU have become the law of the land throughout the EU,[39] thus ensuring the creation of a level playing field, and affording a higher degree of legal certainty for the market players active in the EU Internal Market. Alexander Italianer exemplifies how substantive convergence works in practice, by pointing to several sectors where this has become evident (food, payments, manufacturing, etc).[40] Since these sectors are highly prone to cartelization they are amongst the most examined by both the Commission and the NCAs. Italianer emphasizes that in the enforcement performed, it is important that the same rules are applied (Article 101 TFEU), while maintaining close cooperation with all the authorities involved. When it comes to Article 102 TFEU enforcement, one of the most evident examples relates to the postal services sector, where the NCAs and the Commission have been known to cooperate closely. Lastly, substantive convergence is also highly visible in the liberal professions sectors, which are traditionally regulated within domestic ambits. Consequently, it is the NCAs who perform most of the investigations, however, again using the same antitrust legal provisions, and while benefiting from the direction and guiding principles as established by the Commission.[41]

Notwithstanding the evident substantive convergence achieved in the field of enforcing the EU competition law rules, the 2014 COM emphasizes that divergences still subsist.[42] One issue often raised is that the convergence achieved in substance is not sufficiently supported by convergence when it comes to procedures. Indeed, Regulation 1/2003 has not gone that far, and as things stand, the procedures for applying the EU competition law rules by NCAs are governed by domestic laws, subject to the general principles of EU law, in particular the principles of effectiveness and equivalence.[43] Regulation 1/2003 may be viewed as providing only the bare basis for procedural convergence, as far as the (basic) powers conferred by Article 5 of the Regulation onto the NCAs are concerned. This is so especially after the CJEU's ruling in *Tele2Polska*,[44] which considerably undercut the Article 5-based powers of the NCAs. According to this ruling, in light of the need of uniform application of the EU competition law rules, Article 5 of Regulation 1/2003 is to be interpreted as restrictively defining the decisions which the domestic authorities may take: i.e. domestic authorities may not adopt negative decisions regarding infringements of these EU law rules.

---

[39] *Ibid*, [23].

[40] Italianer, *supra* n. 13.

[41] See for example the 'Report on Competition in Professional Services' – Commission Communication COM(2004) 83 final, 09.02.2004, 'Professional Services – scope for more reform' Follow-up to the Report on Competition in Professional Services – Commission Communication COM(2005) 405 final, 05.09.2005, 'Progress by Member States in reviewing and eliminating restrictions to Competition in the area of Professional Services' – Commission Staff Working Document SEC(2005) 1064, 05.09.2005.

[42] 2014 COM, [24].

[43] *Ibid*, [30]. See case C-453/99 *Courage Ltd v. Crehan*, ECLI:EU:C:2001:46.

[44] Case C-375/09 *Tele2Polska*, ECLI:EU:C:2011:270.

From this point on, voluntary procedural alignment towards the provisions of Regulation 1/2003 and towards certain soft law mechanisms, such as the Commission's leniency programme, took place to a certain extent.[45] Further, the work of the ECN has added some value as far as the desired procedural convergence is concerned, and in this respect the 2014 COM points to the ECN Recommendations on key enforcement powers, which may be used by the NCAs as advocacy tools vis-à-vis policymakers.[46] This seems too little to suffice though, especially since such a lack of procedural convergence results from divergences on three additional fronts, comprehensively dealt with in the 2014 COM: the institutional positioning of the NCAs, their staffing and funding policies, and the powers allotted to them in relation to day-to-day enforcement activities.[47]

First, the institutional positioning of the NCAs is lightly 'controlled' by Regulation 1/2003: Article 35's only criteria to keep in mind is that NCAs should be designated in such a way that the provisions of the Regulation are effectively complied with. From this point on, there is no EU law provision meant to govern the institutional setup of NCAs, as opposed to the fields of telecoms or energy, for example, where EU law outlines detailed requirements for the independence of national supervisory authorities. However, this has not stopped the Commission and the EU judiciary to occasionally touch upon this matter during proceedings in front of the General Court.[48] Although the position of some NCAs has recently evolved in the direction of more autonomy and effectiveness, their independence may often be regarded as being at risk, due to lack of sufficient autonomy from the respective governments in matters such as overlapping competences, dismissals of heads of NCAs, management and other decision makers etc.[49]

Second, there are no specific EU rules requiring adequate human and financial resources, other than the general obligation to ensure the effective implementation of EU law. The result of this is that NCAs may be understaffed and underfinanced, and as a consequence, they may not be able to do their job properly. The 2014 COM points again to the work of the ECN in this respect, which highlighted via its Resolution of the Heads of NCAs[50] the need for appropriate infrastructure and expert resources. In the same vein, in the words of Alexander Italianer, 'NCAs should have control over the people they appoint. NCAs should be able to recruit their own staff, based on their own specific needs, and should draft clear guidelines to prevent conflicts of interests. [...] Last but certainly not least, NCAs should have control over their own budgets. This first of all means that NCAs need sufficient and

---

[45] See also K. Cseres, 'The Impact of Regulation 1/2003 in the New Member States', 6 *Competition Law Review* 2, 2010.

[46] 2014 COM, [31].

[47] *Ibid,* [26] *et seq.*

[48] See for example case T-201/11 *Si.mobil v. Commission*, ECLI:EU:T:2014:1096.

[49] 2014 COM, [26] and the following.

[50] See http://ec.europa.eu/competition/ecn/ncas.pdf, accessed on 27 May 2015.

stable resources to be able to pay for their own personnel, accommodation, investigations, etc.'[51]

Third, other than the provisions of Article 5 of Regulation 1/2003, there are no provisions in EU law on the enforcement powers that NCAs should have. This results in some NCAs lacking fundamental enforcement powers such as the powers to set their enforcement priorities, the power to adopt remedies, ensuring compliance with commitment decisions, the power to inspect premises, imposing effective and deterrent fines, establishing parent–daughter companies liability, etc.[52]

All in all, while the substantive convergence of the competition law rules in the EU is rather visible, this is not supported by the same degree of procedural convergence. On top of this, certain technical challenges are still present when it comes to the day-to-day work performed by the NCAs. These preliminary conclusions allow us to place attention on the main research question of this contribution.

## 2.5 Which Way Forward?

With regard to the above, if convergence has only been partially completed, the natural question that follows is 'what next?' The obvious straightforward answer would be that more efforts should be directed to addressing the problems of procedural convergence. Further, the 2014 COM seems to ring the alarm, by pointing to the priority areas where further progress is needed, in order to ensure that the right balance is achieved between the NCAs' ability to prevent and sanction anti-competitiveness and the respect of due process (i.e. enforcement priorities and the policies designed are clear and predictable). First of all, account should be taken of guaranteeing the independence of the NCAs and making sure they have sufficient resources. Second, the 2014 COM emphasizes that ensuring that all NCAs have a complete set of effective investigative and decision-making powers at their disposal is essential to the correct development of the enforcement activities. Third, guaranteeing that all NCAs have powers to impose effective and deterrent fines and ensuring that well designed leniency programs are available in all Member States are both key to the same ends.[53]

In other words, if the NCAs are not independent, if they do not have the staff, finances or enforcement powers to fulfil their tasks, or cannot impose adequate fines, then this affects their credibility, their impartiality, and their capacity to properly enforce the competition law rules.[54] This last assertion pertains a great deal to consistency in the procedures used and, to take the argument one step further, this

---

[51] A. Italianer, 'The Independence of National Competition Authorities', Speech delivered at the *Best Practice in Investigations Competition Conference*, Vienna, 12 December 2014, available at: http://ec.europa.eu/competition/speeches/text/sp2014_08_en.pdf, accessed on 15 May 2015.

[52] See 2014 COM, [32], [35]–[38] and also Italianer, *supra* n. 13.

[53] See 2014 COM, [46].

[54] See Italianer, *supra* n. 13.

also pertains to the convergence of procedural mechanisms, discussed above, or the current lack thereof. If this is so, the achievements of the convergence on substance risk being jeopardized. Therefore, in order to prevent such an outcome, the convergence of procedures seems highly desirable. How can this occur in the future?

The question of whether there is room for more consistency in the procedural ambit can be answered both in the negative and in the affirmative. First, such consistency should initially stem from the Commission, as a trend-setter. But this may not necessarily be the case at all times. For example, the 2014 COM (and also former Commissioner Almunia in his latest speeches)[55] praise the added value of settlement procedures and commitments in the context of an idea of more efficient and cost-effective competition law enforcement. However, as we have seen above, Commissioner Vestager seems less likely to negotiate and compromise. This stance may already be an indicative sign that the new Commission is already busy in developing its own ideas about how to achieve the goals of procedural consistency. This may take some time, but for now, one may agree that the first 10 years of antitrust enforcement under Regulation 1/2003 offer a good breeding ground in this respect.

One option of fostering procedural convergence is, according to the statements of Alexander Italianer,[56] to build on the success story of the ECN. Is this sufficient though, having in mind that we are actually talking about soft-law? Some may say yes, if we look at the example of leniency (soft-law, with a rather high, even if not perfect altogether, level of convergence reached through the works of the ECN). Similarly, soft convergence of enforcement powers may be reached. The ECN's latest recommendations seem to point to the right direction – a strong consensus on the tools needed for enforcement: power to set priorities, investigative powers, powers to gather digital evidence, the ability of staff from other NCAs to assist with inspections, the power to adopt interim measures and impose structural remedies, etc. Former Commissioner Almunia has also pointed to these elements, while emphasizing the importance of soft convergence reached through the ECN.[57] He further referred to certain country specific recommendations which deal with, among other issues, competition policy too (Ireland, Cyprus and Portugal). Then, along the lines of the 2014 COM, he continued by acknowledging the lack of a clear legal basis to make sure that all NCAs can enforce EU antitrust rules with the same degree of effectiveness. This seems reasonable, bearing in mind that some issues pertaining to this matter currently rest (more or less) uncomfortably outside EU law. Yet, former Commissioner Almunia previewed that the debate will develop in the coming years, and thus placed the ball in Commissioner Vestager's court, to decide how to promote the most appropriate reforms: soft-law and continuing on the path of soft convergence (probably primarily via the ECN) or hard-law (following the example of the long desired Directive concerning private damages). The merits of this choice are interesting to investigate, and although they go a bit beyond the scope of this contribution, I will return to the matter of public v. private enforcement below. Still,

[55] See *supra* n. 34 and 35.

[56] Italianer, *supra* n. 13.

[57] Almunia, *supra* n. 12.

at this particular point an indication of the future directions on the soft-law v. hard-law matter may be previewed.

Commissioner Vestager delved into this discussion during European Parliament hearings,[58] while seemingly previewing a break in the development of hard-law future convergence. When answering the question related to involving the Parliament in the design of the Commission's fining policy, Commissioner Vestager acknowledged that 'fines are a key element of deterrence, and I will always be happy to explain the criteria set out in the Fining Guidelines, and have an open dialogue with the Parliament on the underlying principles. The current fining guidelines ensure transparency and predictability, while at the same time allowing some discretion to take the specificities of each individual case into account. The European Courts have upheld the Commission's approach on this matter in many occasions; few provisions have had such intense scrutiny by the Courts. Should there be a need for any legislative step, the content of this initiative will determine the legal basis.' Consequently, it seems that soft-law is still the way to go forward in this respect, at least for now.

Still, this does not mean that the soft-law path will be a 'one-size-fits-all' solution. In the paragraphs that follow, I will try to pinpoint some of the remaining challenges that the 2014 COM has not necessarily dwelled upon. By no means are the following discussions to be looked at as an exhaustive set of issues still in need of some sort of resolution. More likely, the elements approached below are various facets that deal with the issue of enforcement of the EU competition law rules, either in a direct or in an incidental manner, and that may provide a better-tailored shape to the 'what next' question that lingers from this contribution's research endeavour. In this respect, I will return to some of the elements discussed above and further qualify them in light of the more or less recent developments of the respective law.

First, not too far above I have mentioned that the Commission, and for that matter I do not see a reason why the CJEU would not follow suit, should act as a trendsetters. Consistency when it comes to enforcement activities may be indeed conceived as originating from the centre. In this regard, the issue of parent–daughter companies' liability has the potential of being a good start, given that the 2014 COM has emphasized that some NCAs lack the power of establishing such liability.[59] To this end, one may look at the recent Commission decision fining Slovak Telekom and its parent, Deutsche Telekom, for abusive conduct (refusal to supply and margin squeeze) in the Slovak broadband market.[60] Such an approach should be adopted and implemented by all NCAs too, especially since even more recently, further guidance on the concept of an economic unit comprising the parent company and its subsidiary has been given by Advocate General Kokott, in the *Fresh Del*

[58] *Supra* n. 36.

[59] 2014 COM, [37].

[60] See http://europa.eu/rapid/press-release_IP-14-1140_en.htm, accessed on 17 May 2015.

*Monte* case.[61] Actually, on several occasions former Commissioner Almunia called for further convergence in this area, with regard to the fining principles within the EU (a lack of which may be currently observed). This is important as it was regularly highlighted that the effectiveness of penalties is a condition for the consistent application of EU competition rules.[62]

Second, if the NCAs are encouraged to emulate the Commission's approaches in the domestic arena, it seems reasonable that more deference to the work done in the domestic realms should be duly accepted. This very much pertains to the work of the ECN, to the close cooperation between the authorities involved when it comes to work sharing, and to the trust that they should place on their counterparties' efforts and results. Let me clarify these assertions by referring to two of the recent General Court rulings, namely *Si.mobil* and *easyJet*.[63] These rulings seem to have reframed the manner in which workload division is conceived within the ECN, by providing the Commission with a *carte blanche*, or in other words, a lower threshold to meet, when it comes to refusing to act on a complaint which was submitted to it, if the same case (i.e. the same alleged infringements, on the same markets, within the same timeframe) is being dealt with, or has been dealt with by a NCA. In such a setting, the Commission must not engage in a full-blown *Automec* cumbersome process of balancing the EU significance of the alleged infringement against the probability of, and resources necessary for, establishing the infringement. It can simply defer to the analysis performed in the domestic jurisdiction, even if the respective NCA has dismissed the case based on priority grounds. While this approach seems to further empower the domestic authorities and sends the signal that more trust has to be placed in the work of the NCAs when they apply the EU competition law rules, this comes at a price for the complainants. This is because now more than ever, they must exercise the utmost diligence when filling their complaints with one or another authority, since after *Si.mobil* and *easyJet* case reallocation seems more difficult to uphold.[64]

Either way, if this is the message that is put forward by the EU judiciary, one would expect increased transparency to accompany this reliance on the NCAs' enforcement actions. Yet, things do not necessarily seem to progress in this respect. Not too long after *Si.mobil* and *easyJet*, the same General Court held in the *UAHE* case[65] that the documents exchanged between the Commission and an NCA, in proceedings concerning an infringement of the competition rules are not, in principle, accessible to the public. This is because disclosure of those documents could in fact undermine the protection of the commercial interests of the undertakings concerned, as well as the protection of the purpose of the investigations. This seems

[61] Opinion of AG Kokott, Joined cases C-293/13 and 294/13 *Fresh Del Monte Produce v. Commission*, ECLI:EU:C:2014:2439.

[62] *Supra* n. 12 and 34.

[63] Case T-201/11 *Si.mobil v. Commission*, *supra* n. 48 and case T-355/13 *EasyJet Airline v. Commission*, ECLI:EU:T:2015:36.

[64] For a more detailed analysis of these two rulings see Rusu, *supra* n. 28.

[65] Case T-623/13 *Unión de Almacenistas de Hierros de España v. Commission*, ECLI:EU:T:2015:268.

reasonable bearing in mind the rationale of the Public Access to Documents Regulation.[66] Still, the General Court has accepted the Commission not granting access to documents, while basing its decision not on specific and individual examination of the application for access, but on a general presumption that disclosure would be detrimental to the interests mentioned above. What is more, the presumption seems to apply even if the investigation procedure is already closed. The Court concludes that this approach serves the effectiveness of the ECN mechanism for the exchange of information.

Indeed, the ECN comes out on top if viewed through the lens of these recent developments. It may very well be the case that, as already pointed out above, fortifying the ECN and its functioning constitutes a reasonable breeding ground for furthering the coherent enforcement of the EU competition law rules. Still, the price to pay should not be unreasonable to those dealing with the competition authorities (complainants, undertakings under investigation, third parties requesting access to documents, etc). Further fine-tuning regarding all interests at stake may be something to take into account in the future.

Speaking of all interests at stake, the discussion must inevitably shift to some of the latest developments in the field, pertaining not only to some of the key elements of public enforcement, but also their relationship with the instruments of private enforcement which seem to have been gaining ground during the past few years. The discussion to follow relates not only to the Commission's central role when it comes to acting as an enforcer, but also to its trend-setter position. Furthermore, what follows impacts also on the place that NCAs and the domestic courts have in the context of enforcing the EU competition law rules. Lastly, this discussion may be related to one of the remarks made in the introduction of this contribution, namely the constant shaping exercise that the CJEU has been engaging in, with a view to accommodating the wide variety of interests at stake. With regard to this last statement, it may be interesting to see how the stance of the EU judiciary is to be integrated in the future enforcement activities. One can ask whether the Commission is apt to complete this task.

Some signs are there that the Commission is indeed up to the task. For example, not too long after the CJEU's ruling in the *Expedia* case,[67] the Commission reacted. One may recall that in *Expedia* the Court ruled that an agreement that may affect trade between Member States and that has an anti-competitive object constitutes, by its nature and independently of any concrete effect that it may have, an appreciable restriction on competition. The Commission incorporated this rationale in a new *De minimis* Notice.[68] Yet, the Commission's reaction may not be characterized as swift and as accommodating at all times. The relationship between public and private

[66] Regulation 1049/2001 of the European Parliament and of the Council regarding public access to European Parliament, Council and Commission documents, OJ 2001 L 145.

[67] Case C-226/22 *Expedia Inc. v. Autorité de la Concurrence and Others*, ECLI:EU:C:2012:795.

[68] Communication from the Commission – Notice on agreements of minor importance which do not appreciably restrict competition under Article 101(1) of the Treaty on the Functioning of the European Union (*De Minimis* Notice), OJ C 291, 30.08.2014.

enforcement of the EU competition law rules stands out in this respect. However, the 2014 COM does not touch upon this very actual and interesting debate.

In 2011 and 2013 the CJEU handed down two interesting judgments in the *Pfleiderer* and *Donau Chemie* cases.[69] These rulings touch upon the relationship between the leniency programmes, as essential tools of public enforcement, on the one hand and the access to documents of parties aiming to obtain compensation for loss sustained as a result of an infringement of the EU competition law rules, on the other hand. The Court pointed out that such parties in need of redress may not be precluded from being granted access to documents relating to a leniency procedure involving the perpetrator of an infringement and, furthermore, such access cannot be made subject solely to the consent of all the parties to those proceedings, without leaving any possibility for the national courts of weighing up the interests involved. Thus, the CJEU send the message that private actions for damages are favoured over the value of leniency programmes, despite the potential chilling effect this approach may have on leniency applications.[70] What is more, in the 2014 *Kone* ruling,[71] the CJEU continued on a similar path by embracing the 'umbrella effects' doctrine and consequently changing the recipe of the 'prisoner's dilemma' concept. Now, cartelists when deciding whether to blow the whistle and apply for leniency have to factor in not only the (reduced or completely erased) fine and the damages owed to their customers in future private damages law suits, but also the potential private damages repercussions stemming from the non-cartelists raising the prices under the protection of the cartel's umbrella anti-competitive results. Again, support for private enforcement seems to rest high on the Court's agenda.

From the outset, these three rulings seem to have placed the Commission in an unpleasant position: while needing to observe the Court's rationale and also to integrate it in the further enforcement-related regulatory regime, the Commission faced the difficult task of not jeopardizing the importance of its leniency tools, when finally establishing a coherent regime of private enforcement. The latter seems more and more essential in the context of enforcing the competition law rules, especially since, not too long ago, the Commission itself benefited from the stance of any person being able to claim damages for loss suffered due to a contract or conduct liable to restrict or distort competition.[72] The long awaited 2014 Private Damages Actions Directive[73] opts for an ingenious approach to the leniency (and for that matter public enforcement in general) versus private enforcement matter. First, the Directive protects leniency statements and settlement submissions by preventing their disclosure

[69] Case C-360/09 *Pfleiderer AG v. Bundeskartellamt*, ECLI:EU:C:2011:389 and case C-536/11 *Bundeswettbewerbsbehörde v. Donau Chemie AG and Others*, ECLI:EU:C:2013:366.

[70] See also C.S. Rusu, J.M. Veenbrink, 'Case Comment – C-557/12 Kone', 10 *Competition Law Review* 1, 2014.

[71] Case C-557/12 *Kone AG and Others v. ÖBB-Infrastruktur AG*, ECLI:EU:C:2014:1317.

[72] See case C-199/11 *Europese Gemeenschap v. Otis NV and Others*, ECLI:EU:C:2012:684.

[73] Directive 2014/104/EU on certain rules governing actions for damages under national law for infringements of the competition law provisions of the Member States and of the European Union, OJ L349/1, 05.12.2014.

for the purpose of civil damages actions; thus, the legal position of cooperating companies is not worsened and the incentives to cooperate with competition authorities are maintained. Second, the Directive safeguards the attractiveness of leniency programs by providing that the undertaking receiving full immunity from fines is primarily liable only towards its own customers. In other words, the infringer's joint and several liability towards cartel victims is limited and it may be revived only in limited circumstances. One may observe here a tougher stance taken by the Commission when it comes to integrating the Court's rationale in the enforcement activities. While the value of private damages actions for the purpose of the overall idea of enforcing the EU competition law rules is hard to be doubted, time will tell whether the Commission's approach when it comes to the already mentioned relationship with the EU judiciary's stance is prone to pay off.

Lastly, in order to paint a more complete picture of the discussions surrounding the enforcement of the EU competition law rules, I believe that the matter has to be also framed in the broader context of the EU Internal Market. After all, a coherently functioning system of competition should also serve the further development of the Internal Market. In this respect, a few words on the latest enforcement activities that the Commission is engaging in seem appropriate. I am referring here to the antitrust inquiry into the e-commerce sector in the EU, launched in early May 2015.[74] This sector inquiry fits nicely with and complements the actions that are taken in the context of the EU's Digital Single Market Strategy.[75] Also, as a more general observation, launching this inquiry restates the value that such enforcement tools have in the context of the Commission's activities, and shows the new Commission's propensity to work on multiple fronts when it comes to EU competition policy. Commissioner Vestager emphasized that the purpose of this endeavour is to identify the nature, prevalence and effects of the potential barriers erected by companies to cross-border online trade in goods and services where e-commerce is most widespread, with the end goal of using the knowledge gained for the purpose of better enforcement of competition law in the e-commerce sector. Once again, Commissioner Vestager affirmed her tough stance and unwillingness to compromise: 'If [the barriers] are anti-competitive we will not hesitate [to open case investigations and] to take enforcement action under EU antitrust rules.' Either way, the Commission expects to publish a final report after concluding this sector inquiry by early 2017.

The paragraphs above highlight some of the latest challenges that the enforcement of the EU competition law rules phenomenon is currently facing. Furthermore, they point out the rough directions that the said enforcement activities seem to be aimed at for the coming period. While acknowledging the dynamic stance the Commission is embarked on, the discussions above show that challenges still exist, some of them being of a rather fundamental nature, especially when referring to the relationship between the public and private enforcement mechanisms.

[74] See http://europa.eu/rapid/press-release_IP-15-4921_en.htm, accessed on 27 May 2015.

[75] See http://europa.eu/rapid/press-release_IP-15-4919_en.htm, accessed on 27 May 2015.

## 2.6 Concluding Remarks

The contribution at hand aims to place the largely debated proliferation of competition law enforcement in the past decade in the correct context. In this respect, it tries to evaluate whether the success of the past 10 years of competition law enforcement in the EU may indeed be associated with the developments brought about by Regulation 1/2003. While the achievements of this piece of the 2004 Modernization Package cannot be denied, there are certain indications that solid competition law enforcement took place even in the absence of the complex system of decentralization and ECN-driven cooperation between NCAs. Still, one of the greater merits of Regulation 1/2003 is the stimulation of convergence. If convergence in substance is more or less achieved when it comes to the competition law rules, the procedural convergence seems to lag behind. This is what the 2014 COM draws the attention to, by pointing to the areas on which the focus should be directed. This contribution briefly assesses the validity of the mechanisms intended to further foster consistent competition law enforcement throughout the EU.

But the further developments in this respect go, in my opinion, beyond the elements discussed in the 2014 COM. To this end, certain prospective challenges relating to the future enforcement priorities of the Commission are delved into, with a view to elucidate whether the Commission's enforcement policy choices are indeed coherently established. The role of soft-law, the integration of the EU judiciary's views in the enforcement regime and in the authorities' enforcement activities, the relationship between the public and private enforcement tools, the Commission–NCAs workload division and cooperation, are some of the issues that will, in my opinion, require due attention in the (near) future.

The conclusion that this contribution can draw may be as straightforward as its main research question: it is not unexpected that more work needs to be done when it comes to the enforcement of the EU competition law rules. However, the challenge now remains how to further foster the enforcement activity not only at domestic level (which the 2014 COM rightfully tackles), but also in the broader context. This context may be painted in various colours, as the challenges listed above show. All in all, interesting times lie ahead for the new Commission, but also for the other interested parties out there: consumers, market players, NCAs, judges, practitioners, and academics.

# Part II
# Court of Justice Jurisprudence as an Instrument of Harmonization

# Chapter 3
# Of Cattle, Crashes & Cards – Recent Case-Law of the Court of Justice on Restrictions by Object

**Anthony M. Collins**

## 3.1 COWS – Case C-209/07 *Competition Authority v. Beef Industry Development Society Ltd & Barry Brothers (Carrigmore) Meats Ltd*

### *3.1.1 Outline of Facts*

The bulk of beef cattle in Ireland are reared on grass, so they are slaughtered once the pasture is exhausted. To meet this peak in demand beef processors were required to have the capacity to slaughter and de-bone large numbers of animals between September and November.

In 1992, the Common Agricultural Policy introduced a de-seasonalisation premium. This gave farmers an incentive to deliver cattle to processors throughout the year, thereby eradicating peaks in demand. This ought to have led to less efficient processors leaving the market: however, another branch of the Common Agricultural Policy simultaneously provided grants of between 50 and 75 % towards the cost of building processing plants. This led to an overcapacity of approximately 30 % in the Irish beef processing market.

In 1998, the Government of Ireland and representatives of the beef industry commissioned a study. It concluded it was necessary to reduce the number of processors from 20 to between 4 and 6. The report also recommended that the undertakings that were to remain in the sector ('the stayers') should compensate those forced to withdraw ('the goers'). A task force set up by the Minister for Agriculture and Food came to a similar conclusion in the following year.

A.M. Collins (✉)
President of Chamber, General Court of European Union, Luxembourg, Luxembourg
e-mail: anthony.collins@curia.europa.eu



A. Almăşan, P. Whelan (eds.), *The Consistent Application of EU Competition Law*, Studies in European Economic Law and Regulation 9,
DOI 10.1007/978-3-319-47382-6_3

In 2002, the 10 principal beef processors established BIDS. BIDS prepared a draft rationalisation plan which provided, *inter alia*, for a reduction in processing capacity of about 25 %. To this end, BIDS prepared a standard form of contract to be entered into by stayers and goers. Stayers agreed to compensate the goers. BIDS was to compensate the goers. The stayers were to repay BIDS by means of a levy of EUR 2 per head of cattle up to their traditional cattle kill volume and EUR 11 per head above that volume. The goers undertook to decommission their plant, not to use the land on which the plant had been located for beef processing for 5 years and not to compete with the stayers on the beef processing market for 2 years.

BIDS notified the Irish Competition Authority of these arrangements. In June 2003 it held that these arrangements were contrary to Article 81 (1) EC (now Article 101(1) TFEU). Since the Competition Authority did not have the power to take coercive measures, it applied to the High Court of Ireland for orders to prevent the implementation of the arrangements.

The High Court dismissed that application in July 2006. It held that the BIDS arrangements were not prohibited by Article 81(1) EC: however, had they been, they would not have been exempted by Article 81(3) EC (now Article 101(3) TFEU).

The Competition Authority appealed that decision to the Supreme Court of Ireland, which decided to refer a question to the Court of Justice. In essence, it asked whether the aforementioned arrangements were to be regarded as anti-competitive by reason of their object, or whether it was necessary for the Competition Authority to show that they had an anti-competitive effect.

### 3.1.2 Court of Justice Judgment[1]

In its response, the Court of Justice distinguished between "*infringements by object*" and "*infringements by effect*" since certain forms of collusion between undertakings can, by their very nature, be considered injurious to the proper functioning of normal competition. Such forms of collusion can be condemned as anti-competitive without the necessity to show that they in fact distort competition.

Had a similar finding to this effect been available earlier it might have been of considerable practical importance in the management of the BIDS litigation. Notwithstanding the Competition Authority's view that the BIDS arrangements constituted an infringement by object, it took slightly over 3 years for the High Court to reach the contrary conclusion. Whilst some of this delay can be attributed to the mechanism for the enforcement of competition law in Ireland, it demonstrates the considerable resources that often must be deployed in order to show that a measure has an anti-competitive effect, as distinct from an anti-competitive object.

The Court of Justice also observed that the existence of an anti-competitive "object" falls to be determined by reference to "*the precise purpose of the agreement, in the economic context in which it is to be applied.*"

[1] EU:C:2008:643; [2008] ECR I-8637.

The first leg of this test is satisfied by paying "*close regard*" to the text of the arrangements and the objectives they seek to attain. The test is to be applied objectively and without reference to the parties' subjective intentions. That the arrangements were made for what might be regarded as legitimate objectives, such as to remedy the effects of a crisis, is thus irrelevant in determining whether they constitute an infringement "*by object*". The pursuit of such objectives is considered at the stage when Article 81(3) EC falls to be applied.

At paragraphs 31–39 of its judgment, the Court of Justice examined the precise purpose of the BIDS arrangements in the economic context in which they were applied. From the information provided by the Supreme Court it found that:

- the BIDS arrangements were intended to improve the overall profitability of undertakings supplying more than 90 % of the beef and veal processing services on the Irish market by enabling them to approach their minimum efficient scale; and
- this was to be done by reducing significantly the number of undertakings supplying processing services, thereby eliminating almost 75 % of excess production capacity.

On that basis the Court of Justice held that the BIDS arrangements clearly conflicted with the concept inherent in Article 81(1) EC according to which each economic operator must determine independently the policy it intends to adopt on the common market and which prohibits any form of coordination that deliberately substitutes practical cooperation between undertakings for the risks of competition. Without the BIDS agreements the undertakings which had entered into them would have had no means of improving their profitability other than by intensifying their commercial rivalry or resorting to concentrations. The Court of Justice also found that the mechanisms to attain these objectives included restrictions with an anti-competitive object (the €11 levy discouraged stayers from increasing output, whilst the restrictions on the use of plant were an obstacle to new operators entering the market).

On one reading of the judgment it was possible to submit that these paragraphs could be read as a response to the argument that BIDS had unsuccessfully advanced to the effect that the concept of infringement by object should be interpreted narrowly which viewpoint the Court of Justice did not share.

When the matter came back before the Supreme Court it took the view that since the trial judge had examined the arrangements under Article 81(3) EC in circumstances where, by his own reasoning, he had not been obliged to do so, he ought to be given an opportunity to conduct a more detailed analysis. Upon the remittal of the matter to the High Court, and prior to the case being re-heard for this purpose, the European Commission submitted written observations pursuant to Article 15(3) of Council Regulation (EC) No 1/2003. Whilst a majority of the Supreme Court seemed to imply that the High Court ought to conduct its Article 81(3) EC analysis by reference to the evidence of market conditions that had been adduced some 4 years earlier, the issue then arose as to whether the High Court, which the relevant Irish legislation had designated as a competition authority for the purposes of

Regulation 1/2003, could lawfully exercise its powers under Article 81(3) EC by reference to prior market conditions or those existing at the time it was called upon to carry out its analysis. Before that issue could be adjudicated upon BIDS withdrew its defence and the matter was settled.

After BIDS the law appeared to be reasonably clear. But Ireland was not the only Member State where competition authorities sought to rely upon the concept of restriction by object. And it was not long before the Court of Justice was asked to consider the application of the concept against a more complex factual background.

## 3.2 CRASHES – Case C-32/11 *Allianz Hungaría Biztosító*

### *3.2.1 Outline of Facts*

To make a living as a motor dealer in Hungary one must, it seems, do more than buy and sell cars. Many dealers repair damaged vehicles. They also sell motor insurance to their customers.

Acting on behalf of many motor dealers, their national association ("GÉMOSZ") negotiated annual framework agreements with insurance companies to fix the hourly charges for the repair of damaged cars. These framework agreements facilitated individual insurers and individual dealers entering into agreements whereby the latter repaired damaged cars insured by the former. Under these individual agreements insurers gave incentives to dealers to sell insurance to their customers. These incentives consisted of insurers increasing the amount they would pay for the repair of damaged cars by reference to the number and percentage of insurance contracts that the motor dealer/repairer sold on the insurer's behalf.

Applying provisions of domestic law effectively identical to Article 101(1) TFEU, the Hungarian Competition Authority held that the following had, as their object, the restriction of competition in the car insurance contracts market and the car repair services market:

- three GÉMOSZ decisions that recommended the prices charged by dealers to insurers for the repair of cars;
- framework agreements concluded between the insurers and GÉMOSZ and individual agreements between the insurers and certain dealers that made the hourly repair charge dependent on the number of insurance policies signed; and
- various agreements between insurers and dealers acting as insurance brokers which specified that the latter had to obtain a minimum amount car insurance policies over a given period of time and which fixed the remuneration for these contracts according to the number of policies taken out with the insurer.

The Hungarian Competition Authority proceeded to fine those undertakings. They challenged that decision in proceedings that ultimately led to the Magyar

Köztársaság Legfelsőbb Bíróság[2] referring a single question to the Court of Justice for preliminary ruling. The Court of Justice summarized that question as asking whether agreements whereby motor insurers make bilateral arrangements with either motor dealers or their representatives to fix an hourly charge for the repair of the vehicles they insure and whereby the level of that charge is determined by reference to the volume of insurance contracts sold by the motor dealer as an intermediary, are restrictions of competition by object for the purposes of Article 101(1) TFEU.

### 3.2.2 Court of Justice Judgment[3]

At paragraphs 33–34 of its judgment the Court of Justice reiterated its established case-law[4] whereby the application of Article 101(1) TFEU requires consideration of the precise object of the agreement in the economic context in which it is applied. Once the anti-competitive object of the agreement is established it is unnecessary to examine its effects on competition. Where, however, the analysis of the content of the agreement does not disclose the presence of a sufficient degree of harm to competition, the effects of the agreement must then be considered in order to determine if factors are present that show that competition has in fact been prevented, restricted or distorted to an appreciable extent.

The Court of Justice then described the distinction between 'infringements by object' and 'infringements by effect' as arising from the fact that certain forms of collusion between undertakings can, by their very nature, be regarded as injurious to the proper functioning of normal competition.[5]

In order to determine whether an agreement involves a restriction of competition 'by object', the Court of Justice would have regard to the content of its provisions, its objectives and the economic and legal context of which it forms a part.[6] In order to determine that context account had to be taken of the nature of the goods or services affected and the real conditions of the functioning and structure of the market or markets in question. The parties' intentions might also be relevant as to context, although the Court of Justice did not indicate whether those intentions were to be ascertained by reference to an objective or a subjective standard.

---

[2] Supreme Court of the Republic of Hungary.

[3] EU:C:2013:160.

[4] Case 56/65 *LTM* EU:C:1966:38; [1966] ECR 337.

[5] Paragraph 35 of the judgment, citing Case C-209/07 *BIDS*, paragraph 17; Case C-8/08 *T-Mobile Netherlands* EU:C:2009:343; [2009] ECR I-4529, paragraph 29 and Case C-226/11 *Expedia* EU:C:2012:795, paragraph 36.

[6] Citing Joined Cases C-501/06 P, C-513/06 P, C-515/06 P & C-519/06 P *GlaxoSmithKline Services v Commission* EU:C:2009:610; [2009] ECR I-9291, paragraph 58; Joined Cases C-403/08 and C-429/08 *Football Association Premier League* EU:C:2011:631; [2011] ECR I-9083, paragraph 136; and Case C-439/09 *Pierre Fabre Dermo-Cosmétique* EU:C:2011:649; [2011] ECR I-9419, paragraph 35.

At paragraphs 40–42 of the judgment, the Court of Justice observed that the agreements under consideration linked the level of remuneration insurers paid for the car repair service to the amounts the dealers earned by way of commission on the sale of insurance. This link between two very different services arose because, in their dealings with the insurers, the dealers acted in a dual capacity. The existence of a link between two activities that are, in principle, independent did not automatically result in a finding that the agreements had as their object the restriction of competition: however in the Court of Justice's view it could constitute an important factor when determining whether those agreements were, of their very nature, injurious to the proper functioning of normal competition. Account had also to be taken of the fact that the agreements were likely to affect two markets and that their object had to be determined in respect of both of them.

The fact that the agreements regulated vertical relationships did not exclude the possibility that they might constitute restrictions of competition by object. While vertical agreements are often less damaging to competition as compared with the effect of horizontal agreements, in some cases they can have a particularly significant potential to restrict competition.

As for the agreements in the *car insurance market*, the Court of Justice observed that the insurance companies entered into them with the aim of maintaining or increasing their respective market shares. In assessing the economic and legal context of those agreements account could be taken of the fact that, under Hungarian law, insurance intermediaries act on behalf of policyholders, not insurers, and that they therefore must be independent of the latter. In determining whether competition on that market would be eliminated or seriously weakened by the agreements under consideration, the Supreme Court of Hungary was also required to take into consideration the structure of the market, the existence of alternative distribution channels and their respective importance, and the market power of the companies concerned.

As for the object of the agreements at issue in the market for *car repair services*, account had to be taken of the fact that the agreements appeared to have been concluded on the basis of 'recommended prices' established in the three decisions of GÉMOSZ to which reference has already been made. Recommendations that established fixed or minimum prices would fall foul of the prohibition of restrictions by object.

The Court of Justice concluded that Article 101(1) TFEU was to be interpreted to mean that agreements whereby car insurance companies make bilateral arrangements, either with car dealers acting as car repairers, or with an association representing those dealers, concerning the hourly charge to be paid by the insurance company for repairs to vehicles insured by it, stipulating that that charge depends, *inter alia*, on the number and percentage of insurance contracts that the dealer has sold as intermediary for that company, may constitute a restriction of competition by object, where, following a concrete and individual examination of the text and aim of those agreements and of the economic and legal context of which they form a part, it is apparent that they are, by their very nature, injurious to the proper functioning of normal competition on one of the two markets concerned.

Notwithstanding the statements in its judgment to the effect that it had followed the same approach as it had taken in *BIDS*, the Court of Justice's application of these provisions in *Allianz* fell short of being a model of clarity. At times the analysis as to whether the agreements were restrictions by object seemed to veer into an examination of the measures' effects. Whilst acknowledging that the line is a fine one, paragraphs 45 and 46 of the Court's judgment discussed the application of the rule in the hypothesis of a horizontal agreement or a concerted practice between the insurance companies designed to partition the market, the relevance of which does not appear to be immediately obvious in the context of an analysis as to the existence of a restriction by object. Again the legal position of insurance intermediaries as a matter of Hungarian law, whilst clearly relevant to an "effects" analysis, seemed somewhat out of place in the context of an "objects" analysis.

The uncertainty as to the distinction to be made between an "objects" and an "effects" analysis set the stage for the Court of Justice's later pronouncement on the subject, delivered on 11 September 2014.

## 3.3 CARDS – Case C-67/13 P *Groupement des cartes bancaires (CB) v. European Commission*

### *3.3.1 Outline of Facts*

*Groupement des cartes bancaires* was a direct action to annul a Commission decision declaring certain measures adopted by the Groupement des cartes bancaires ("CB") as having an anti-competitive object.[7]

In 1984 the main French banks created CB to enable bank cards issued by members to be used (a) to make payments to all traders affiliated to the CB system through any member bank and (b) to withdraw cash from automatic teller machines (ATMs) operated by member banks.

Over time certain member banks expanded their activities as issuers of CB cards ("issuers"), whilst others invested more in affiliating traders with the CB system and operating ATMs ("acquirers"). The perception became established that certain issuers of CB cards were "free-riding" on investments made by acquirers and/or that the CB system was capable of being so exploited by new entrants to the market.

Ostensibly, in order to introduce a better balance between the interests of issuers and acquirers, in 2002 CB informed the Commission that it intended to make the changes to the CB system:

- A levy ("MERFA"),[8] calculated by reference to the ratio between a member's activities as an acquirer and as an issuer. It applied where the ratio of acquisition

[7] C (2007) 5060 final of 17 October 2007 relating to a proceeding under Article [81 EC] (COMP/D1/38606—Groupement des cartes bancaires 'CB').

[8] *Mécanisme de régulation de la fonction acquéreur.*

activities to issuing activities was less than 0.5. Sums collected by the MERFA were distributed between those members that did not pay the levy by reference to their activities as acquirers.

- A fee per active CB card issued in the 3 years after a new member had joined the CB system, together with a supplementary fee for members that tripled the number of CB cards they issued between the end of their third and sixth years of membership.
- A further fee per CB card issued by members that had been inactive prior to the entry into force of the new measures and had more than tripled the level of issuing activity in the following 3 years.

Finding that these measures were contrary to Article 81(1) EC and could not be justified under Article 81(3), the Commission held that they had an anti-competitive object that was "*...evident from the actual formulas envisaged for those measures...*" First, the measures were inappropriate for encouraging acquisition activities as they either imposed additional charges or limited members' issuing activities. Second, the imposition of supplementary membership and dormant member fees was inconsistent with the additional acquisition activity that MERFA was intended to stimulate. Third, the principal members of CB had indicated that the real purpose of the measures was (i) to impede competition from new entrants; (ii) to safeguard their revenue and (iii) to limit price reductions for the issue of bank cards.

By a judgment of 29 November 2012, the General Court dismissed the applicant's action to annul the Commission Decision.[9] The applicant appealed to the Court of Justice.

### 3.3.2 *Opinion of Advocate General Wahl*[10]

Advocate General Wahl identified the distinction between restrictions "by object" and "by effect" as being of a procedural character, going to the standard of proof required to show the anti-competitive impact of the conduct at issue. A finding that conduct constituted a restriction by object had two important consequences. First, once it is established that an agreement is a restriction by object, the ensuing prohibition has a very broad scope and applies irrespective of the agreement's effects. Second, enforcement authorities can rely on an analytical framework without the need to prove the anti-competitive effects of an agreement or practice.

The advantage in terms of predictability and in easing the burden of proof that follows from by identifying agreements that are restrictive by object would be undermined if the identification of such conduct required a thorough examination of the consequences for competition of that behaviour.

[9] Case T-491/07 *CB v. Commission* EU:T:2012:633.

[10] EU:C:2014:1958.

It followed that an uncontrolled extension of the conduct covered by restrictions by object would undermine the principles governing the evidence required to demonstrate anti-competitive conduct. The classification of an agreement as restrictive by object must be circumscribed and apply only to agreements that are inherently harmful, *i.e.* agreements that seem highly likely to have a negative impact on competition without the need to evaluate their actual or potential effects.

Wahl AG was thus of the opinion that the assessment of the existence of a restriction by object requires a detailed, individual examination of the conduct in question, which examination must be clearly distinguished from that of the actual or potential effects of that conduct. Determining whether a conduct has a restrictive object cannot be divorced from considering the economic and legal context in which it occurs. Wahl AG gave the example of horizontal price agreements, which although in general highly harmful to competition may not be so where the undertakings involved hold a tiny share of the relevant market.

Wahl AG took issue with both the General Court's finding that the "*concept of infringement by object should not be given a strict interpretation*" and its conclusion that *BIDS* supported such an approach. Upon examining the Court of Justice's judgment in *BIDS*, he found that it had decided that the arrangements at issue were restrictions by object on the basis of a close analysis of their terms. At paragraph 78 of his Opinion he described the test in the following terms:

> *...whether the Commission had sufficiently established, following a concrete and individual examination of the content, the aim and the economic and legal context of which they formed a part, that the measures at issue achieved a degree of harm such that their negative effects on competition could be presumed.*

He applied this approach to the agreements at issue by reference to their content, objective and context.

Examining the content of the measures, Wahl AG was of the view that the fact that members of CB might be prompted, by reason of the introduction of these measures, either to limit their issuing activities or to bear costs not borne by other members, cannot be regarded as restrictive by object. Whilst it could not be ruled out that, as a result of these measures, certain CB members would be encouraged either to limit their issuing activities or to increase their acquiring activities – the latter option being one that could prove difficult to implement in practice and lead to their exclusion from the CB system – that question fell to be answered in the context of an examination of the potentially anti-competitive effects of those measures.

Wahl AG also examined the relevance of comments made by the principal members of CB when assessing the presence of a restriction by object. Even if these comments represented the intention of CB (which had not been established), they were insufficient to establish the existence of an anti-competitive agreement and, *a fortiori*, of an agreement entailing a restriction of competition by object. The intention as expressed by the parties to an agreement cannot replace a detailed examination of the actual content of their conduct. Just as the parties to an agreement cannot rely on the absence of an intention to breach the prohibition laid down in Article

81(1) EC, the existence of such an intention is of itself insufficient to show that measures have an anti-competitive object.

The objective of the measures is thus to be assessed objectively, without reference to the legitimacy or otherwise of the objectives sought to be pursued thereby. The new measures were adopted in order to stimulate acquiring activity in respect of CB cards within a payment system with two sides, linked by a number of network effects. They were thus intended to obtain a financial contribution from issuers, the card issuing activities of which benefit directly from membership of the CB and which were derived from the acquirers' investments in the system. The new measures, notably the MERFA, comprised a mechanism to extract a financial contribution from those CB members not active in the field of acquisition. The imposition of a financial contribution on members of a network that benefit, without any consideration, from the contributions made by other members in order to develop that network does not of itself have an anti-competitive object.

Given his findings, Wahl AG concluded that it was unnecessary to consider the context in which the measures had been taken since that could not of itself demonstrate the existence of an anti-competitive object. However, he observed that such an examination cannot be conducted in the abstract. In order to examine the context of the measures with a view to identifying a restriction of competition by object consideration had to be given to the interaction between the issuing and the acquiring faces of the CB system, an exercise quite distinct from that of defining the relevant market.

### 3.3.3 *Judgment of the Court of Justice*[11]

The Court of Justice restated the position that certain forms of collusive behaviour can be considered so likely to have negative effects that it is unnecessary to prove an effect on the market in order to apply Article 81(1) EC. To determine whether such behaviour discloses such a sufficient degree of harm to competition, regard must be had to its content, the objectives it pursues and the economic and legal context of which it forms a part.

In the instant case, the Court of Justice held that the General Court erred in its definition of the legal criteria to assess the existence of a restriction of competition by object in two particulars. First, the General Court failed to have had regard to the essential criterion as to whether the coordination at issue of itself discloses a sufficient degree of harm to competition. Second, the General Court erred in finding that the concept of restriction of competition by object must not be interpreted restrictively.

The Court of Justice then examined whether these errors of law vitiated the General Court's characterisation of the measures at issue. The General Court had held that those measures had the object of discouraging new competitors from

[11] EU:C:2014:2204.

entering the market for the issue of payment cards in France. It ascertained that anti-competitive object from an examination of the calculation formulas for those measures. The General Court had also held that since the only market that had been taken into account was the downstream market for the issue of payment cards, it was not required to take account of the balance between the issuing and acquisition activities of the CB. It was irrelevant that the measures pursued a legitimate objective of combatting free-riding on the CB, particularly as the stated objectives of members of CB had indicated otherwise.

The Court of Justice held that the General Court had failed to explain how the text of the measures disclosed the presence of a restriction of competition by object. Whilst the General Court gave reasons as to why, since the measures required the member banks either to pay a fee or to limit their issuing activities, they had the object of impeding new entrants into the market for the issue of payment cards in France, it did not explain how that restriction of competition of itself disclosed such a degree of harm as to constitute a restriction by object.

Moreover, once the General Court had acknowledged that the formulas for the measures in question sought to establish a certain ratio between the issuing and acquisition activities of CB members, it was at most entitled to infer that the measures aimed at imposing a financial contribution on the members of CB that had benefitted from the efforts of others to develop its acquisition activities. That object could not, of its very nature, be regarded as harmful to the proper functioning of normal competition.

The General Court also erred in holding that the balance between issuing and acquisition activities within the CB could not be maintained on the ground that the relevant market was not that of payment systems in use in France but was rather the downstream market for the issue of payment cards in that Member State. That finding conflated the definition of the relevant market with that of the context to be taken into account in order to ascertain whether the content of an agreement by an association of undertakings is a restriction of competition by object. As per the Court's well established case-law, it is necessary to take into consideration all relevant aspects of the economic or legal context in which that coordination takes place, which cannot be limited to those aspects that relate to the relevant market. This observation is particularly pertinent when that aspect consists of taking into account interactions between the relevant market and a different related market or, as here, where there are interactions between both sides of a two-sided system.

Even if it cannot be ruled out that the measures at issue in fact hindered competition from new entrants, that finding went to an assessment of effects of those measures on competition, not their object. Thus the General Court's assessment of the potential effects of these measures demonstrated that they could not, by their very nature, be considered harmful to the proper functioning of normal competition.

The Court of Justice also held that the General Court had been wrong to draw an analogy between the measures at issue and those examined in *BIDS*. By providing for a reduction of the order of 25 % in processing capacity, the BIDS arrangements were clearly intended to enable several undertakings to implement a common policy which had the object of encouraging some of them to withdraw from the market, thereby reducing overcapacity. The object of the BIDS arrangements was to change appreciably the structure of the market by means of a mechanism devised to encourage the withdrawal of competitors in order to increase the degree of concentration in the sector concerned. There was no similar evidence here. Although the General Court had found that the measures at issue encouraged CB members not to issue more than a certain volume of payment cards, the objective pursued thereby was not to reduce possible overcapacity on the market for the issue of payment cards in France but instead to achieve a given ratio between the issuing and acquisition activities of the members of the CB in order to develop further the CB's activities.

## 3.4 Conclusion

The comparatively straightforward factual background in *BIDS* allowed the Court of Justice to put some shape on the concept of restriction by object. However, it is one thing to state principles and quite another to apply them to a given set of facts. The very complicated facts out of which the reference in *Allianz Hungaría Biztosító* was made were apt to give rise to difficulties. The Opinion of Advocate General Wahl and the judgment of the Court of Justice in *CB* go a long way to restating the relevant principles governing the concept of restriction by object, namely by limiting it to conduct that can be presumed to have a negative impact on competition as ascertained by reference to the nature of the conduct itself and not its possible effects.

# Chapter 4
# The Concept of Anti-competitive Object Under EU Competition Law: Comparative Perspectives and European Realities

**Csongor István Nagy**

## 4.1 Introduction

A couple of years ago, the Court of Justice of the European Union (CJEU) opened a new chapter in the history of anti-competitive object in EU competition law. The ruling in *Allianz*, which broke off with a century-long wisdom of antitrust/competition law, provoked a major uproar.[1] However, the CJEU, instead of overruling this holding, endorsed it in *Cartes bancaires* and it seems that the new (elusive) concept of anti-competitive object is ossifying in EU law: the Commission's De Minimis Notice[2] enshrines this doctrine (of course, the Commission had no choice but to bow to the CJEU's jurisprudence).

Much has been written on the above (unfortunate) developments, which have met little support in the scholarship. The present chapter aims at contributing to this discourse with a specific facet. The usual experience of EU competition law is that 'federal antitrust law' affects the development of national competition laws (profoundly) but examples of reverse influence are rare; this is the truer as regards new Member States that joined the European Union in the last three waives of

[1] See e.g. Harrison Dan. 2013. The Allianz Hungária case. The ECJ's judgment could have ugly consequences. Competition Law Insight 12(6): 10; Harrison, Dan. 2013. The Court of Justice's Judgment in Allianz Hungária is Wrong and Needs Correcting. CPI Antitrust Chronicle May 2013(1); Nagy, Csongor István. 2013. The Distinction between Anti-competitive Object and Effect after Allianz: The End of Coherence in Competition Analysis? World Competition 36(4): 541–564; Nagy, Csongor István. 2015. The new concept of anti-competitive object: a loose cannon in EU competition law. European Competition Law Review 36(4): 154–159.

[2] Notice on agreements of minor importance which do not appreciably restrict competition under Article 101(1) of the Treaty on the Functioning of the European Union [2014] OJ C 291/1.

C.I. Nagy (✉)
University of Szeged & HAS Federal Markets Research Group,
Szeged, Hungary
e-mail: nagycs@juris.u-szeged.hu



A. Almăşan, P. Whelan (eds.), *The Consistent Application of EU Competition Law*, Studies in European Economic Law and Regulation 9,
DOI 10.1007/978-3-319-47382-6_4

enlargement[3]: eleven out of thirteen new Member States[4] were transition economies with little experience in competition law,[5] and they built up their own antitrust systems under the determinant influence of EU competition law. However, *Allianz* is an exception to this tendency; this is one of the rare cases where the tide turned: the Hungarian procedure was carried out under the (at that time peculiar) Hungarian concept of anti-competitive object (in fact, solely Hungarian competition law was applied in this matter) and, as a result of the CJEU's preliminary ruling, this notion re-shaped the EU doctrine of anti-competitive object.

The old (pre-*Allianz*) theory of anti-competitive object was based on category-building; it embedded an exhaustive (but revisable) list of restraints, which were considered to be anti-competitive by nature. Putting it otherwise, not particular agreements but categories of agreements were regarded as anti-competitive by object. The concept of anti-competitive object was used to create specific categories and not the general definition but the specific categories were applied to flesh-and-blood agreements. Furthermore, the analysis was summary and rather formalistic (to ensure that the rule is clear-cut and its operation foreseeable): no market-analysis had to be carried out; context was taken into consideration but only to understand the contractual provision; and, roughly speaking, the examination remained within the four angles of the contract. This was a relatively simple exercise: the relevant question was whether the agreement at stake came under one of the black-listed categories.

The new (elusive) theory did away with the principle of category-building and adopted a case-by-case approach, where the general definition of anti-competitive object has to be applied to individual arrangements. Furthermore, it calls for a perfunctory market-analysis. Although, presumably, traditional categories of anti-competitive object remained intact and can still be used as a rule of thumb, if an arrangement does not come under one of these categories, it has to be tested on the basis of the general test. As a consequence, outside of the enclave that remained of the old theory, the merits of anti-competitive object (foreseeability and clarity) are lost.

This chapter demonstrates how the elusive concept of anti-competitive object found its way to EU competition law and re-shaped this fundamental notion. Furthermore, it argues that the *Allianz* doctrine is an unfortunate development, not only is it in disaccord with the century-long wisdom of antitrust law but also puts the consistent application of EU competition law in danger.

Taking the above object into account, in the following, the Hungarian decisional and judicial practice on anti-competitive object will be presented, followed by the analysis of *Allianz* and *Cartes bancaires*. Afterwards, the new (elusive) concept of anti-competitive object is put in a comparative context. The chapter ends with the

---

[3] In 2004, 2007 and 2013.

[4] With the exception of Cyprus and Malta.

[5] See Varady, Tibor. 1999. The emergence of competition law in (former) socialist countries. American Journal of Comparative Law 47: 229.

author's conclusions, which address specifically the new concept's impact on the consistent application of EU competition law in the Member States.

## 4.2 The Prelude of the *Allianz* Doctrine: Hungarian Competition Law's Conception of Anti-competitive Object

Section 11 of the Hungarian Competition Act (HCA),[6] in line with Article 101 TFEU, distinguishes between agreements anti-competitive by object and agreements anti-competitive by effect; object type agreements are restrictive of competition by nature and, hence, do not necessitate the investigation of the context and the arrangement's repercussions; such agreements violate the general prohibition on restrictive agreements *per se*. The HCA's explanatory memorandum makes it clear that agreements anti-competitive by object are subject to automatic condemnation (at least as to Section 11 HCA, since theoretically they may still benefit from an individual exemption under Section 17 HCA), stating that in case the anti-competitive purpose/object is established, it needs not to be inquired whether the arrangement is in fact susceptible of attaining the desired end.[7]

The concept of anti-competitive object gained a pivotal role in the Hungarian Competition Office's (HCO) investigation practice, since this enables the authority to condemn an agreement without a full-blown market analysis, which is required in case of agreements that are not anti-competitive by object but are to be judged on the basis of an effects-analysis. Object type agreements can be condemned on the basis of what was agreed to (i.e. the text of the agreement); that is, it is to be proven what the parties agreed to but the agreement's market context (definition of the relevant market, the parties' market position, the structure of the market, entry barriers etc.) and its actual and potential consequences need not be discovered. Of course, the legal and economic context may still be relevant concerning the interpretation and assessment of the stipulations. However, the examination of the context does not extend to the investigation of the actual and potential effects the agreement may entail. On the other hand, in case of agreements to be judged by their effects, a market analysis is needed. Although the effects may be actual or potential, direct or indirect, the agreement's market context is to be explored, otherwise it could not be established whether it may entail the prevention, restriction or distortion of competition or not.

The competition authority's interest in grasping anti-competitive object widely appears to be understandable, as this approach relieves the authority of much of its

---

[6] Hungarian Competition Act (in Hungarian: '*A tisztességtelen piaci magatartás és versenykorlátozás tilalmáról szóló 1996. évi LVII. törvény (Tpvt.)*').

[7] Explanatory memorandum, remarks on Sections 11–20 HCA.

burdens and widens its playing field. And Hungarian courts did not halt the HCO's endeavours to make a tool of convenience of anti-competitive object.

For the most part, Hungarian competition law adopted the principles and notions used by EU antitrust law in connection to anti-competitive object. In Case *Vj-74/2003 Magyar Gabonafeldolgozók, Takarmánygyártók és -Kereskedők Szövetsége*, the HCO held that when applying Section 11 HCA the actual effects need not be demonstrated, it suffices if the arrangement's intention or suitability is proved. This implies that one need not examine the conduct's actual effect, if it aims at restricting, preventing or distorting competition.[8] When inquiring whether the agreement is anti-competitive by object, the agreement's characteristics (objective purpose) are relevant and not the parties' subjective intentions.[9] In Case *Vj-180/2004 Magyar Ügyvédi Kamara*, in the context of a decision of an association of undertakings (the Hungarian Bar), the HCO described the difference between anti-competitive object and effect. A conduct that involves the potential of restricting competition has an anti-competitive object. The decision's purpose can be deduced from its text, the objective endeavours of the decision-makers, the legal and economic environment and from the parties' behaviour; it does not depend on the parties' subjective intentions. The decision's method of implementation may also reveal the anti-competitive object. If the anti-competitive object cannot be established, it is to be examined whether the conduct has anti-competitive effects. The latter involves both the actual and potential anti-competitive effects. A decision has anti-competitive effects, if on the basis of the impact on actual or potential competition it can be reasonably expected that in the relevant market it will have a negative effect on prices, output, and innovation, the supply of the products and services, and quality. The negative effects need to be perceivable.[10]

In most cases, it can be relatively easily ascertained on the basis of the agreement's content and characteristics whether the agreement has an anti-competitive object or has to be subjected to an effects-analysis. The anti-competitiveness embedded in the agreement determines whether it is regarded as anti-competitive by object or whether its effects are to be examined. Although, as a matter of principle, there are certain contents that make the agreement anti-competitive by object, in Hungarian competition law the borderline between object and effect type agreements is, unfortunately, blurred. Although the characterization of the agreement does not depend on the parties' subjective intentions, it depends on the context. Hence, although, as a rule of thumb, it is possible to draw a list of agreements that are anti-competitive by object, the HCO follows a case-by-case approach.

The HCO's approach can be boiled down to three principles. First, as noted above, restrictions listed in EU competition law as hardcore, as a rule of thumb, are also automatically condemned under Section 11 HCA. Second, the HCO considers the restraints included in the illustrative list of Section 11 HCA to be 'presumably

[8] Para 73.

[9] *See* Case *Vj-180/2004 Magyar Ügyvédi Kamara*, para 22; Nagy, Csongor István, 2006. Kartelljogi Kézikönyv. A közösségi és a magyar kartelljog kézikönyve. Budapest: HVG-Orac. 349–350.

[10] Para 22.

illegal'; this is a notion peculiar to Hungarian competition law, which has no counter-part in EU antitrust law. Third, the circle of agreements anti-competitive by object is not definite; the HCO can examine on a case-by-case basis whether the agreement is anti-competitive by nature and, as such, qualifies as anti-competitive by object.

As to horizontal agreements, the HCO considers, among others, horizontal price-fixing[11] and market-sharing[12] to be anti-competitive by object. In Case *Vj-28/2003 Baucont and others*,[13] the HCO characterized 'mirror contracts' between undertakings participating in the same tender as anti-competitive by object: here, the enterprises mutually agreed that whoever wins, the winner will hire the unsuccessful bidders as sub-contractors.[14]

As to vertical agreements, Hungarian competition law, in line with EU law, regards the fixing of a minimum resale price, as well as the fixing of a specific resale price and the prohibition of passive sales (absolute territorial protection) as anti-competitive by object.

In Case *Vj-171/2002/15 MOL*, the Competition Council (CC) held that the fixing of the resale price or of a minimum resale price is, according to competition law practice, evidently anti-competitive.[15] This decisional practice has not changed; in Case *Vj-7/2008/178 Castrol Hungária*, the CC confirmed that it is anti-competitive by object and violates Section 11 HCA if the enterprise fixes the minimum or concrete final or consumer price; namely, in this case the trader, due to the restraints on pricing policy, is restricted in using the most important tool of competition.[16]

It is to be noted that in Case *Vj-164/2006 Büki Ásványvíz* the HCO considered a vertical price fixing scheme not to infringe Section 11 HCA. Here, the producer fixed no generally applicable resale price but agreed with the distributors individually. The decision's reasoning suggests that resale price fixing does not violate competition rules automatically and without exception. The HCO held that although it regards horizontal price-fixing as the most serious restriction of competition, this case centred around vertical price-fixing, which required a more complex analysis, due to the potential efficiency arguments. The HCO found that in this matter it was probable that the enterprise's conduct did not aim at switching off price competition and had no such effects, either. First, only a few of the contracts contained resale price fixing clauses. Second, the supplier established no uniform resale price of general application; the resale price was determined on an individual basis, taking into account the market circumstances and there were huge differences between the individual prices (the lowest price was HUF 260, while the highest was HUF 850). The HCO found that the enterprise did not intend to influence the uniform

[11] Case *Vj-64/2000 Délhús and others*; Case *Vj-92/2003 Mentők és Betegszállítók Országos Egyesülete*.

[12] Case *Vj-74/2004 Construm és Royal Bau*, para 89.

[13] See Case *Vj-154/2002 Baucont, Klíma-Vill. és Középületépítő.*

[14] Paras 81 and 83.

[15] Para 52. See Case *Vj-47/2004 Magyar Könyvkiadók és Könyvterjesztők Egyesülése*, para 101.

[16] Para 47.

market price. It happened that within the same settlement one of the traders had a fixed price, while the rest did not. The HCO noted that although selective resale price fixing may fall foul of competition law, as, for instance, it may be susceptible of driving rivals out of the market, no anti-competitive consequences were proved in the proceeding.[17] It is to be noted that in this case the HCO examined the arrangement of resale price fixing under the general prohibition on restrictive agreements (Section 11 HCA) and not under the individual exemption (Section 17 HCA) and came to the conclusion that it did not violate competition law.

The decision in Case *Vj-164/2006 Büki Ásványvíz* clearly suggests a more lenient approach towards resale price fixing, as the HCO in fact regarded this arrangement as not being anti-competitive by object and considered that an effects-analysis would be warranted. However, this trend was not followed subsequently, and, as noted above, in Case *Vj-7/2008/178 Castrol Hungária*, the HCO reiterated the old rule that resale price fixing *per se* violates the general prohibition on restrictive agreements (i.e. Section 11 HCA).

It is to be noted that notwithstanding the HCO's above decisional practice, Hungarian competition law's treatment of resale price fixing is not fully in line with EU competition law. While under EU competition law resale price fixing falls out of the scope of the *de minimis* rule (as stated in the Commission's de minimis notice), under Hungarian competition law vertical price fixing is still covered: if the market share of the parties is less than 10 %, vertical price fixing falls outside the scope of the prohibition of anti-competitive agreements.[18]

In Case *Vj-156/2004 Unilever and others*, the HCO held, referring to EU competition law, that the exclusion of passive sales (absolute territorial protection) is, in fact, *per se* anti-competitive: it violates the general prohibition on restrictive agreements automatically and cannot benefit from an individual exemption.[19] The adoption of the *Consten and Grundig* doctrine in Hungarian competition law is criticized in the scholarship; in EU competition law the most important argument behind the harsh treatment of absolute territorial protection is the purpose of market integration (single market imperative[20]), while this purpose is not part of Hungarian national competition law.[21] Furthermore, under EU competition law, absolute territorial protection falls out of the scope of the *de minimis* rule, as it is regarded as hard-core. On the contrary, under Hungarian competition law absolute territorial protection is covered by the safe harbour of agreements of minor importance: if the market share is less than 10 %, vertical absolute territorial protection falls outside the scope of the prohibition of anti-competitive agreements.[22]

---

[17] Para 75.

[18] Section 13(2) CA.

[19] Paras 88 and 93–94.

[20] Richard Whish and David Bailey. 2012. Competition Law. Oxford: OUP. 51.

[21] Nagy, Csongor István, 2006. Kartelljogi Kézikönyv. A közösségi és a magyar kartelljog kézikönyve. Budapest: HVG-Orac. 241; Nagy, Csongor István. 2013. EU and US Competition Law: Divided in Unity? Farnham and Burlington: Ashgate Publishing. 163–164.

[22] Section 13(2) HCA.

As noted above, in its decisional practice, the HCO worked out the doctrine of 'presumably anti-competitive agreements'. This is a peculiar Hungarian competition law concept, which has no counter-part in EU competition law.[23] Section 11(1) HCA, as a general principle, prohibits all anti-competitive agreements, while Section 11(2) HCA contains an illustrative list. In Case *Vj-21/2005 Albacomp, Synergon and ORACLE*, the HCO established: the legislator presumed that the agreements listed in Section 11(2) HCA were illegal, thus, in such cases no detailed demonstration is required to establish anti-competitiveness.[24] This proposition was confirmed in Case *Vj-7/2008/178 Castrol Hungária*.[25] Accordingly, the following agreements are presumed to be anti-competitive:

- direct and indirect fixing of the purchase or sales prices or other business conditions;
- limitation or control of the production, distribution, technical development or investments;
- division of input sources, restriction of the choice from them, and exclusion of a particular circle of business partners from purchasing a particular product;
- division of the market, exclusion from sales, restriction of the choice between marketing possibilities;
- hindering of market entry;
- discrimination between business partners as to transactions of the same value or character, including the application of prices, payment deadlines, discriminatory sales or purchase conditions or methods that may cause a competitive disadvantage to certain business customers; and
- making the conclusion of the contract subject to the acceptance of obligations that, by their nature or due to customary contractual practice, do not belong to the contract's subject-matter.

As noted above, if an agreement is neither hard-core, nor listed in Section 11(2) HCA, the HCO will examine on a case-by-case basis whether it is anti-competitive by nature and, as such, anti-competitive by object.

Accordingly, before the CJEU's ruling in *Allianz*, Hungarian competition law's grasp of anti-competitive object had been considerably wider and more obscure than its counter-part in EU law. This was regarded as an unfortunate tendency, given that the character of having an anti-competitive object has serious repercussions. The wide grasp of object type agreements may also go counter to the logic and *raison d'être* of this concept. Competition effects-analysis is time-consuming, costly and, last but not least, uncertain. Competition law cannot provide a more predictable standard in any of the leading competition law regimes of the globe. However, as a general principle, it tries to distinguish clear-cut cases from the uncertain ones. Agreements of minor importance and those covered by a block exemption are the

[23] Nagy, Csongor István, 2006. Kartelljogi Kézikönyv. A közösségi és a magyar kartelljog kézikönyve. Budapest: HVG-Orac. 352–353.

[24] Para106.

[25] Para 45.

ones that are clearly not contrary to the law. Agreements anti-competitive by object are those agreements that are clearly contrary to the general prohibition on restrictive agreements (albeit theoretically also these agreements may benefit from an exemption).

The merit of the concept of anti-competitive object is that market context needs not be examined. Of course, the context is relevant from the perspective of the agreement's interpretation; however, this is the maximum function it may have. If the detailed analysis of the market context (definition of the relevant market, calculation of the market shares etc.) cannot be saved because it can be established only on the basis of this context whether the agreement has an anti-competitive object, the essence of this concept is lost.

As noted above, the HCO's endeavour is understandable: the competition authority is tempted to jam-pack the bin of anti-competitive by object as much as possible, since in such cases it does not have to bother itself with proving that the agreement has anti-competitive effects. However, if the definition of object type agreements is too wide and obscure, leaving the competition authority a very wide playing field, its function becomes frustrated and firms will not be able to identify those agreements that may be automatically condemned.

This problematic decisional practice culminated in Case *Vj-51/2005/184 Allianz, Generali and others*,[26] where the HCO investigated, among others, agreements concluded by two Hungarian leading insurance companies (Allianz and Generali) with motor vehicle insurance brokers. Albeit the contracting practices of the two insurance companies were similar, apart from this parallel behaviour, there was no evidence indicating any horizontal collusion between them. The agreements provided that if the insurer's products made up a certain proportion of the products the insurance broker sold, the broker received a higher remuneration. Under Hungarian insurance law, there are three types of insurance intermediaries: brokers, multiple agents and agents. Agents (whether simple or multiple) act on behalf of the insurance company, while brokers are the advisors of the client and not the agents of the insurer. Brokers are independent insurance counsels, who have to give impartial and professional advice to the client. However, according to general industry practice, brokers' remuneration is paid by the insurer and not by the client. Since the remuneration paid by the insurers may vary, it is not easy to reconcile this practice with the circumstance that the broker is the client's adviser and not the insurer's agent. Linking the level of remuneration to the number of insurance products sold catalyses this problem and raises serious issues of conflict of interest.

In some of the agreements, the insurers specified a minimum number or percentage of car insurance policies to be sold over a given period of time and linked the remuneration to this target. In other agreements, concluded with repair shops, the

[26] For a detailed overview on the case see Cseres, Katalin J. & Szilágyi, Pál. 2013. The Hungarian Car Insurance Cartel Saga. In Landmark Cases in Competition Law – around the World in Fourteen Stories, ed. Rodger, Barry, 145. the Hague: Wolters Kluwer.

remuneration was paid in the form of a higher hourly repair charge. Repair shops have a twofold function. First, they repair cars, a part of which is covered by an insurance policy; the reparation of these vehicles is financed by the insurance companies. Second, they also act as insurance brokers, intermediating between clients and insurance companies. In the agreements between the insurers and the repair shops, the hourly repair charge depended on the number of insurance products sold by the repair shop. The HCO held that both above groups of agreements are anti-competitive by object because they cause a serious conflict of interest and interfere with the requirement of impartial and professional advice imposed by Hungarian insurance law on insurance brokers.

The Supreme Court requested a preliminary ruling from the CJEU[27] under the Treaty on the Functioning of the European Union solely concerning the agreements with the repair shops.[28] Although the question related to EU competition law, the Supreme Court advanced that Section 11 HCA and Article 101(1) TFEU had to be given the same interpretation, because they were substantially connected and Section 11 adopted the provision of Article 101(1) almost verbatim. Hence, the application of Section 11 HCA made the interpretation of Article 101(1) TFEU necessary.

AG Cruz Villalón came to the conclusion[29] that the bilateral agreements between the insurers and the repair shops were not anti-competitive by object, unless there was a horizontal agreement or concerted practice.[30] The CJEU, however, did not accept AG Cruz Villalón's opinion and ruled that the agreements between the insurance companies and the repair shops, stipulating that the degree of the remuneration paid by the insurer depends on the number and percentage of insurance products the dealer-broker sells as intermediary, "can be considered to be a restriction of competition 'by object' within the meaning of that provision, where, following a concrete and individual examination of the wording and aim of those agreements and of the economic and legal context of which they form a part, it is apparent that they are, by their very nature, injurious to the proper functioning of normal competition on one of the two markets concerned."[31]

The CJEU's ruling in *Allianz, Generali and others* endorsed the HCO's decisional practice blurring the line between clear-cut *per se* rules and evaluation based on effects-analysis. This has been probably the first case where Hungarian competition law had a significant impact on the development of EU antitrust law.

---

[27] Case *Kfv. IV.37.077/2010/11.*(Supreme Court).

[28] Case C-32/11 *Allianz, Generali and others v GVH*, not published yet.

[29] Opinion of AG Cruz Villalón in Case C-32/11 *Allianz, Generali and others v GVH*, not published yet.

[30] Para 100.

[31] Para 51.

## 4.3 *Allianz* and *Cartes bancaires*: Hungarian Competition Law Re-shapes a Fundamental Notion of EU Antitrust Law

In *Allianz*, the ECJ held that it has to be established on a case-by-case basis, as a result of an individual abbreviated assessment, whether an agreement has an "anti-competitive object".

> In order to determine whether an agreement involves a restriction of competition 'by object', regard must be had to the content of its provisions, its objectives and the economic and legal context of which it forms a part (…). *When determining that context, it is also appropriate to take into consideration the nature of the goods or services affected, as well as the real conditions of the functioning and structure of the market or markets in question.*[32]

Accordingly, the agreement's context has to be taken into account and in the frame of this, a truncated effects-analysis has to be carried out, which extends to the following factors: nature of the goods (services), "the real conditions of the functioning" of the market and the structure of the market; the "court should in particular take into consideration the structure of that market, the existence of alternative distribution channels and their respective importance and the market power of the companies concerned."[33]

When carrying out an effects-analysis, courts and competition authorities often use proxies (e.g. market power, market structure) of (actual or potential) negative effects. This may be due to the circumstance that the effects have not come along and it needs to be established whether they may emerge (potential effects); sometimes, the effects have already taken place but no proper market data is available, so certain circumstances are used as surrogates of anti-competitive impact (circumstantial evidence of actual effects).[34]

In para 48 of the ruling, the CJEU reiterated the above principles (case-by-case assessment and truncated market analysis) and confirmed that the analysis extends, in particular, to market structure, the parties' market power (and presumably also to the share of other market operators) and the examination of alternative distribution channels.

> 48. Furthermore, those agreements would also amount to a restriction of competition by object in the event that the referring court found that it is likely that, *having regard to the economic context, competition on that market would be eliminated or seriously weakened following the conclusion of those agreements. In order to determine the likelihood of such a result, that court should in particular take into consideration the structure of that market, the existence of alternative distribution channels and their respective importance and the market power of the companies concerned* (emphasis added).

---

[32] Para 36 (emphasis added).

[33] Para 48.

[34] Nagy, Csongor István. 2013. The Distinction between Anti-competitive Object and Effect after Allianz: The End of Coherence in Competition Analysis? World Competition 36(4): 541–564, 559.

The CJEU confirmed the *Allianz* ruling in *Cartes bancaires*, where French banks established an economic interest grouping with the purpose to ensure the interoperability of the members' systems for card payment and cash withdrawals. The grouping adopted various measures to stimulate members to engage in acquiring activity, thus maintaining the balance of the system and handling external economic effects.

The CJEU stated that the concept of anti-competitive object is an exception and not the rule, thus, its scope has to be conceived restrictively and should extend solely to the most serious mischiefs of competition law which are, "by their very nature", "harmful to the proper functioning of normal competition",[35] and where the anti-competitive implications are sufficiently clear.

> The concept of restriction of competition 'by object' can be applied only to certain types of coordination between undertakings which reveal a sufficient degree of harm to competition that it may be found that there is no need to examine their effects.[36]

Although in *Cartes bancaires* the CJEU established that anti-competitive object has to be grasped restrictively and found that the arrangement at stake did merit an effects-analysis, it did not overrule *Allianz* and it expressly confirmed the proposition that a limited effects-analysis has to be carried out on a case-by-case basis in order to ascertain whether the agreement is anti-competitive by object or not.[37]

> When determining that context, it is also necessary to take into consideration the nature of the goods or services affected, *as well as the real conditions of the functioning and structure of the market or markets in question*.[38]

It is noteworthy that this seems to be irreconcilable with the Court's statement in para 57: a restriction of competition by object "reveals in itself a sufficient degree of harm to competition." If such an arrangement is in itself anti-competitive, the inspection of the structure of the market seems to be obviously redundant.

## 4.4 Comparative Outlook: The Century-Long Wisdom of US Antitrust Law

A quick comparison to US antitrust law reveals that on the other side of the Atlantic, automatic condemnation (*per se* illegality) is a category-building doctrine, which is not based on a case-by-case assessment and involves no market analysis. This is just as the old concept of anti-competitive object operated.[39]

---

[35] Para 50.

[36] Para 58. See also para 49.

[37] Nagy, Csongor István. 2015. The new concept of anti-competitive object: a loose cannon in EU competition law. European Competition Law Review 36(4): 154–159.

[38] Para 53 (emphasis added).

[39] This section of the paper is based on Nagy, Csongor István. 2013. EU and US Competition Law: Divided in Unity? Farnham and Burlington: Ashgate Publishing.

Under US antitrust law, certain agreements are automatically condemned (*per se* illegality), as they always or almost always bring about anti-competitive consequences[40] without any reasonable chance for redeeming virtue. *Per se* illegality is justified by procedural convenience[41] and legal certainty: such agreements need not be analysed in detail each time they emerge. Nevertheless, the general rule is rule of reason analysis (that is, effects-analysis),[42] and *per se* illegality is confined to arrangements that were specifically classified as such.[43] Automatic condemnation is not meant to ease the life of agencies and courts but it covers only blatantly anti-competitive agreements. "*Per se* rules of illegality are appropriate only when they relate to conduct that is manifestly anticompetitive."[44] In the *per se* "category are agreements whose nature and necessary effect are so plainly anticompetitive that no elaborate study of the industry is needed to establish their illegality – they are 'illegal *per se*.'"[45]

Perhaps, one of the first comprehensive explanations of the rationale of *per se* illegality is the Supreme Court's reasoning in *Northern Pacific*[46]:

> [T]here are certain agreements or practices which because of their pernicious effect on competition and lack of any redeeming virtue are conclusively presumed to be unreasonable and therefore illegal without elaborate inquiry as to the precise harm they have caused or the business excuse for their use. This principle of per se unreasonableness not only makes the type of restraints which are proscribed by the Sherman Act more certain to the benefit of everyone concerned, but it also avoids the necessity for an incredibly complicated and prolonged economic investigation into the entire history of the industry involved, as well as related industries, in an effort to determine at large whether a particular restraint has been unreasonable – an inquiry so often wholly fruitless when undertaken.[47]

---

[40] See *Broadcast Music, Inc. v Columbia Broadcasting System, Inc.*, 441 U.S. 1, 19–20 (1979).

[41] *U.S. v Topco Associates, Inc.*, 405 U.S. 596, 609–610 (1972); *Arizona v Maricopa County Medical Soc.*, 457 U.S. 332, 343–344 (1982); *Northwest Wholesale Stationers, Inc. v Pacific Stationery and Printing Co.*, 472 U.S. 284 (1985); *Arizona v Maricopa County Medical Soc.*, 457 U.S. 332, 343 (1982).

[42] In *Sylania*, the Supreme Court, with reference to *Standard Oil*, held that "since the early years of this century a judicial gloss on this statutory language has established the 'rule of reason' as the prevailing standard of analysis." *Continental T. V., Inc. v GTE Sylvania Inc.*, 433 U.S. 36, 49 (1977).

[43] *Northwest Wholesale Stationers, Inc. v Pacific Stationery and Printing Co.*, 472 U.S. 284, 289 (1985).

[44] *Continental T. V., Inc. v GTE Sylvania Inc.*, 433 U.S. 36, 49–50 (1977).

[45] *National Soc. of Professional Engineers v U. S.*, 435 U.S. 679, 692 (1978).

[46] *Northern Pac. Ry. Co. v U.S.*, 356 U.S. 1 (1958).

[47] Id. at 5. *See Broadcast Music, Inc. v Columbia Broadcasting System, Inc.*, 441 U.S. 1, 19–20 (1979) ("[I]n characterizing (…) [a] conduct under the *per se* rule, our inquiry must focus on whether the effect and, here because it tends to show effect (…), the purpose of the practice are to threaten the proper operation of our predominantly free-market economy – that is, whether the practice facially appears to be one that would always or almost always tend to restrict competition and decrease output, and in what portion of the market, or instead one designed to 'increase economic efficiency and render markets more, rather than less, competitive.'") *National Collegiate Athletic Ass'n v Board of Regents of University of Oklahoma*, 468 U.S. 85, 103–104 (1984) ("*Per se* rules are invoked when surrounding circumstances make the likelihood of anticompetitive conduct so great as to render unjustified further examination of the challenged conduct.")

The *per se* approach is exceptional[48] and "there is a presumption in favour of a rule-of-reason standard; departure from that standard must be justified by demonstrable economic effect (...) rather than formalistic distinctions".[49] While clear-cut rules have their inherent merits (e.g. legal certainty, judicial convenience, deterrence), these obvious benefits do not justify the extensive use of the *per se* approach. *Per se* illegality is not a question of trade-off between the judicial costs of the rule of reason analysis and the chances that agreements of a particular kind may escape Section 1 scrutiny based on reasonable arguments. The only reason to pronounce a particular group of arrangements to be *per se* illegal is that they have manifest anti-competitive effects with no or negligible chance for any pro-competitive value.[50] This was made clear by the Supreme Court, *inter alia*, in *Slyvania*:

> *Per se* rules thus require the Court to make broad generalizations about the social utility of particular commercial practices. The probability that anticompetitive consequences will result from a practice and the severity of those consequences must be balanced against its pro-competitive consequences. Cases that do not fit the generalization may arise, but a *per se* rule reflects the judgment that such cases are not sufficiently common or important to justify the time and expense necessary to identify them. Once established, *per se* rules tend to provide guidance to the business community and to minimize the burdens on litigants and the judicial system of the more complex rule-of-reason trials (...) but those advantages are not sufficient in themselves to justify the creation of *per se* rules. If it were otherwise, all of antitrust law would be reduced to *per se* rules, thus introducing an unintended and undesirable rigidity in the law.[51]

Antitrust law's commitment in favour of the rule of reason approach entails that the creation of a *per se* illegality category requires long-standing judicial

---

[48] See *Northwest Wholesale Stationers, Inc. v Pacific Stationery and Printing Co.*, 472 U.S. 284, 289–291 (1985); *Business Electronics Corp. v Sharp Electronics Corp.*, 485 U.S. 717, 723–724 (1988); *FTC v Indiana Federation of Dentists*, 476 U.S. 447, 458–459 (1986) ("[W]e have been slow to extend *per se* analysis to restraints imposed in the context of business relationships where the economic impact of certain practices is not immediately obvious"); *National Collegiate Athletic Ass'n v Board of Regents of University of Oklahoma*, 468 U.S. 85, 103–104 (1984) ("*Per se* rules are invoked when surrounding circumstances make the likelihood of anticompetitive conduct so great as to render unjustified further examination of the challenged conduct"); *National Soc. of Professional Engineers v U.S.*, 435 U.S. 679, 692 (1978) ("There are, thus, two complementary categories of antitrust analysis. In the first category are agreements whose nature and necessary effect are so plainly anticompetitive that no elaborate study of the industry is needed to establish their illegality-they are 'illegal *per se*.'")

[49] *Business Electronics Corp. v Sharp Electronics Corp.*, 485 U.S. 717, 726 (1988).

[50] Nagy, Csongor István. 2013. EU and US Competition Law: Divided in Unity? Farnham and Burlington: Ashgate Publishing. 98.

[51] *Continental T. V., Inc. v GTE Sylvania Inc.*, 433 U.S. 36, 50 fn 16 (1977). *See also Arizona v Maricopa County Medical Soc.*, 457 U.S. 332, 344 (1982) ("Once experience with a particular kind of restraint enables the Court to predict with confidence that the rule of reason will condemn it, it has applied a conclusive presumption that the restraint is unreasonable. As in every rule of general application, the match between the presumed and the actual is imperfect. For the sake of business certainty and litigation efficiency, we have tolerated the invalidation of some agreements that a fullblown inquiry might have proved to be reasonable."); *Leegin Creative Leather Products, Inc. v PSKS, Inc.*, 127 S.Ct. 2705, 2718 (2007) (Emphasizing that administrative convenience is, in itself, not sufficient to justify the creation of a *per se* rule.)

experience. The mechanism is the following. Courts should not make quick judgements regarding particular types of restraints but they are expected to carry out a detailed analysis without begrudging the judicial resources. Nevertheless, if the multitude of benevolent antitrust analyses of a particular type of arrangement coherently leads to condemnation, such an experience may justify the judicial reflex of outright prohibition.[52] "Once experience with a particular kind of restraint enables the Court to predict with confidence that the rule of reason will condemn it, it has applied a conclusive presumption that the restraint is unreasonable."[53] Accordingly, the Supreme Court is "slow (…) to extend *per se* analysis to restraints imposed in the context of business relationships where the economic impact of certain practices is not immediately obvious".[54]

## 4.5 Conclusions: The Repercussion of the New (Elusive) Doctrine of Anti-competitive Object

In *Allianz*, the CJEU committed two fundamental flaws. First, it disregarded that the doctrine of anti-competitive object was designed to operate through category-building and is not meant to be applied to flesh-and-blood cases on a case-by-case basis. The repercussion of this is that the concept of anti-competitive object became a loose cannon in EU competition law[55]: The CJEU converted a clear-cut rule into the sword of Damocles: the case-by-case assessment abolished predictability, while the consequences of automatic condemnation remained tremendous. Second, it held that, in this regard, no full-fetched examination is required but a perfunctory analysis is sufficient. This increases the risk of false positives: intuition would suggest that as characterization as an agreement that is anti-competitive by object carries the most devastating consequences, this should be based on the most careful analysis. According to *Allianz*, the analysis required concerning anti-competitive object is much less detailed than the analysis to be carried out in case of effect type agreements, though the latter are treated more leniently than object type arrangements.

Very probably, the first 'regulatory victim' of *Allianz* is the safe harbour of agreements of minor importance: the concept of *de minimis* was degraded from a safe harbour to a 'simple' harbour. The old De Minimis Notice[56] was a valuable tool, since it was explicit: agreements not exceeding the market share thresholds set out

[52] Nagy, Csongor István. 2013. EU and US Competition Law: Divided in Unity? Farnham and Burlington: Ashgate Publishing. 99.

[53] *Arizona v Maricopa County Medical Soc.*, 457 U.S. 332, 344 fn 14 (1982).

[54] *FTC v Indiana Federation of Dentists*, 476 U.S. 447, 458–459 (1986).

[55] See Nagy, Csongor István. 2015. The new concept of anti-competitive object: a loose cannon in EU competition law. European Competition Law Review 36(4): 154–159.

[56] Commission Notice on agreements of minor importance which do not appreciably restrict competition under Article 81(1) of the Treaty establishing the European Community (de minimis) [2001] OJ C 368/13.

in the Notice and not coming under one of the hard-core categories of the Notice's exhaustive list were guaranteed legality. The scheme was closed and predictable: if someone went through this check-list, he could be sure that the agreement would definitely benefit from the safe harbour (provided, of course, the relevant market share threshold was not exceeded). The new De Minimis Notice discarded the exhaustive list and provides, in line with *Allianz*, that anti-competitive object has to be established on a case-by-case basis.[57] Although the Notice comprises an illustrative list of hard-core restraints, it contains no list or clear-cut rule on agreements excluded from the benefit of agreements of minor importance. As the value of the *de minimis* rule relies in the positive formulation of what is not caught in the net of Article 101(1) TFEU, this deprives the new Notice much of its use and value. If an arrangement is not covered by the illustrative list, it has to be assessed on a case-by-case basis whether it can benefit from *de minimis* or not; it is exactly this kind of analysis a safe harbour should avoid.[58]

The elusive concept created in *Allianz* puts the consistent application of EU competition law at danger. Procedure and institutional framework do have implications as to substantive law. EU competition law is enforced in a decentralized system, by various national competition authorities and courts of varying experiences and knowledge. Since the application of competition law is, in general, fact-intensive, clear-cut rules are extremely precious not only for enterprises (and their counsels) but also for national authorities and courts. For the effectiveness of the decentralized system, it is essential to preserve the EU institutions' primacy to interpret EU competition law (which is, in case of the CJEU, in fact a monopoly). Therefore, it would be advisable to give, as far as possible, a uniform definition to legal concepts; otherwise, the uniform and consistent application of EU competition law would be unnecessarily endangered. Since it is inevitable to afford national authorities and

[57] Paras 2, 8 and 13 ("13. In view of the clarification of the Court of Justice referred to in point 2, this Notice does not cover agreements which have as their object the prevention, restriction or distortion of competition within the internal market. The Commission will thus not apply the safe harbour created by the market share thresholds set out in points 8, 9, 10 and 11 to such agreements. For instance, as regards agreements between competitors, the Commission will not apply the principles set out in this Notice to, in particular, agreements containing restrictions which, directly or indirectly, have as their object: a) the fixing of prices when selling products to third parties; b) the limitation of output or sales; or c) the allocation of markets or customers. Likewise, the Commission will not apply the safe harbour created by those market share thresholds to agreements containing any of the restrictions that are listed as hardcore restrictions in any current or future Commission block exemption regulation, which are considered by the Commission to generally constitute restrictions by object." [Emphasis added]).

[58] Nagy, Csongor István. 2015. The new concept of anti-competitive object: a loose cannon in EU competition law. European Competition Law Review 36(4): 154–159, 158. Although the Commission adopted a guidance on the interpretation of anti-competitive object for the purpose of the application of the De Minimis Notice (Guidance on restrictions of competition 'by object' for the purpose of defining which agreements may benefit from the De Minimis Notice. SWD(2014) 198 final.), this contains, likewise, only an illustrative list. The Guidance "is without prejudice to any developments in the case law and in the Commission's decisional practice" and "does not prevent the Commission from finding restrictions of competition by object that are not identified below". Id. 5.

courts a considerable give as to effects-analysis, this highly appreciates the value of a uniform and clear-cut concept of anti-competitive object.

Furthermore, the elusive concept created in *Allianz* throws undue temptation in the way of national competition authorities and courts. It is more than questionable whether they will be able to resist the temptation of automatic condemnation and will apply the general doctrine in a restrictive manner (as the CJEU did in *Cartes bancaires*). Hungarian competition law, where this concept originates from, confirms this fear. It is noteworthy that in the follow-on judgment in *Allianz* the Hungarian Supreme Court regarded the CJEU's ruling as a permission to condemn – it did not engage even in the truncated analysis required by the CJEU; it quickly established anti-competitive object and decorated the final judgment with a perfunctory reasoning instead of engaging in a detailed analysis.[59] This peril was clearly perceived by AG Wahl in *Cartes bancaires*, who put this very distinctly: a precautionary approach "is all the more necessary because the analytical framework that the Court is led to identify will be imposed both on the Commission and on the national competition authorities, whose awareness and level of expertise vary".[60]

[59] Case Kfv.II.37.268/2013/8.

[60] Para 59.

# Chapter 5
# Public Investments and the Application of Articles 101 and 102 TFEU

Simona Gherghina

## 5.1 Introduction

This analysis[1] of the application of core competition rules, i.e. those included in Articles 101 and 102 TFEU, to activities related to public investment, builds on the partially explored domain of the interaction between competition rules and public procurement regulations,[2] but it also refers to the impact of these rules beyond the pre-contractual, procurement, stage by examining their effects during the implementation stage of the contract.

Given that the contracts awarded for the achievement of public investment are qualified as administrative contracts in the legal systems that recognise this typology,[3] or as government contracts,[4] this chapter seeks to contribute to the

[1] This research was supported by a grant of the Romanian Ministry of Education CNCS-UEFISCDI, project number PN-II-RU-PD-2012-3-0103, "*Financing public investments: between budgetary and legal limitations and the public interest imperative*".

[2] Several authors have dedicated studies to this interaction between public procurement and competition law: Catriona Munro, *Competition Law and Public Procurement: Two Sides of the Same Coin?*, (2006) 6 Public Procurement Law Review, Albert Sánchez-Graells, *Public Procurement and the EU Competition Rules*, first edition, Hart Publishing, 2011, Grith Skovgaard Olykke, *How Does the Court of Justice of the European Union Pursue Competition Concerns in a Public Procurement Context?*, (2011) 6 Public Procurement Law Review, Albert Sánchez-Graells, *Public Procurement and the EU Competition Rules*, second edition, Hart Publishing, 2015.

[3] Such as the French, Spanish, Italian, Belgian, German, Romanian legal systems.

[4] Especially in the United Kingdom and the United States of America. Anne C.L. Davies, *The Public Law of Government Contracts*, Oxford University Press, 2008.

S. Gherghina (✉)
Faculty of Law, University of Bucharest, Bucharest, Romania
e-mail: simona.gherghina@drept.unibuc.ro





A. Almăşan, P. Whelan (eds.), *The Consistent Application of EU Competition Law*, Studies in European Economic Law and Regulation 9,
DOI 10.1007/978-3-319-47382-6_5

scholarly debate on the application of competition rules in an area traditionally reserved to administrative and, more generally, public law.[5]

The point of reference for this study is represented by the activities conducted by public or private entities for the purpose of carrying out public investments. In the absence of a comprehensive legal definition,[6] the term public investment should be defined, at least from a legal perspective, by reference to its intended result, that is assets to be owned by the state or by local communities[7] or by public undertakings acting on behalf of the state or of local authorities, prior to, or upon the termination of the contract establishing the terms of their construction or rehabilitation. Such assets are the common and constant result of investment actions initiated by public authorities in the performance of their legal duties. Their construction, rehabilitation, extension or operation is necessary for the provision of public services in the broader sense or for any other purpose related to the public interest. Consequently, as part of their general obligation to ensure good administration, public authorities undertake the actions intended to procure such assets in an operational state.

Based on this assumption, public investment includes all actions undertaken by public authorities in the performance of their legal obligations related to the construction, rehabilitation, extension or operation of assets that will be owned by the state or by administrative-territorial units, or by public undertakings acting on behalf of the state or of local authorities. Whether such assets belong to the public or private domain of the state or of the administrative-territorial unit is irrelevant for the purposes of this definition. The same applies to the source of their financing, which is not in any case limited to public spending, but may also include private financing.[8]

Public investments may be achieved by using private financing, with public authorities delegating to private entities the financing and construction of assets that will become the property of the state or of local communities (administrative-territorial units) prior to, or the latest upon the termination of, the contract entered with the private entity. The private investor is allowed to exploit and operate the asset for the purpose of recovering the investment plus a reasonable profit but, in most cases, it will not continue to own the asset after the termination of the contract. This basic structure may take various legal forms, such as concession contracts for

[5] For accounts on competition concerns from a public law perspective, Sophie Nicinski, *Droit Public des Affaires*, L.G.D.J., Paris, 2014, Stéphane Braconnier, *Droit public de l'économie*, Presses Universitaires de France, Paris 2014, Jean-Yves Chérot, *Droit public économique*, 2e éd., Economica, Paris, 2007, Christopher Bovis, *The State, Competition and Public Services*, in Patrick Birkinshaw, Mike Varney (eds.), *The European Union Legal Order after Lisbon*, 2010, Kluwer Law International, p. 137–153.

[6] And, as concerns Romania, the absence of relevant jurisprudence.

[7] According to the Constitution of Romania, the public domain property belongs either to the state or to the administrative-territorial units (local communities). Both the state and administrative-territorial units have legal personality.

[8] John Kitsos, *Construction Investments in Public Works through Public Private Partnerships*, European Procurement and Public Private Partnership Law Review no. 3/2014, p. 202–208.

works and services, service delegation contracts regarding public utilities, or, more generally, public-private partnership contracts.[9]

Irrespective of whether the asset resulting from and representing the public investment was financed from public or private funds, its exploitation is further ensured either by a public entity or by the private investor by delivering mainly services but also goods to the market (users). Most of these services can be qualified as public services because their delivery to the public is part of the general role of public authorities.

In most cases, the assets qualified as public investment result from works performed according to an underlying contract whereby the beneficiary is the public or private entity entrusted by law with the achievement of the respective public investment.[10] If such a contract is financed from public funds and the price for the works performed is paid by the beneficiary, the contract will be most likely a works public contract, and maybe ancillary goods and services public contract. In the case of private financing of public investment, the contract entered into by the public beneficiary[11] may be a works and/or services concession or, more generally, a public-private partnership[12] or a specific service delegation contract for public utilities. Thus, a common element of the activities resulting in the achievement of public investment, irrespective of the public or private financing involved, is the presence, in the broader sense, of public procurement procedures, that include both procurement of goods, works and services (as defined by Directive 2014/24/EU on public procurement) and concessions of works and services (as defined by Directive 2014/23/EU on the award of concession contracts). Some contracts fall outside the scope of the procurement and concession directives, but even in this case they are awarded following a procedure that has to comply with general principles in the Treaty on the Functioning of the European Union (TFEU).[13]

---

[9] For an overview of the regulations and practice of public-private partnerships in several countries, see Francois Lichère (ed.), *Public-Private Partnership: International Academy of Comparative Law XVIIIth Congress*, Bruylant, 2011, Anthony Wall, *Public-Private Partnerships in the USA. Lessons to be Learned for the United Kingdom*, Routledge, 2013, Christopher Bovis, *Public-Private Partnerships in the European Union*, Routledge, 2013, Piet de Vries, Ettienne Yehoue (eds.), *The Routledge Companion to Public-Private Partnerships*, Routledge, 2013, Geert Dewulf, Anneloes Blanken, Mirjam Bult-Spiering, *Strategic Issues in Public-Private Partnerships*, second edition, Wiley-Blackwell 2012.

[10] Yves Gaudemet, *Traité de droit administratif*, vol. 2, *Droit administratif des biens*, L.G.D.J., Paris, 2008, p. 451.

[11] The reference to "public beneficiary" includes those instances in which a publicly owned company or another public undertaking controlled by the state or by local authorities that is qualified as a private entity according to the national rules, is entrusted with the performance of public investments in accordance with the applicable law.

[12] Described, in the broad sense, in the European Commission Green Paper on public-private partnerships and community law on public contracts and concessions COM (2004) 327 final.

[13] Even if they are outside the application domain of the procurement or concession directives, these contracts are awarded by a procedure that is compliant with the general principles stipulated in the TFEU, namely equal treatment, transparency, mutual recognition and proportionality, as detailed in the Commission Interpretative Communication on the Community law applicable to

In legal doctrine, the debate on the application of competition rules within the framework of public procurement procedures, as provided at EU or national levels, focuses primarily on its narrow scope due to the limited application of the concept of "undertaking" to contracting authorities.[14]

In addition, even if the public investment contracts are below the thresholds provided by the directives for their application, this is not sufficient reason to automatically exclude such contracts and related award procedures from the application of competition rules.[15]

Moreover, the incidence of the rules stipulated in Articles 101 and 102 TFEU with the matters related to public investments may not be limited to procurement procedures, as a pre-contractual step, but may also occur during the performance of the contract, especially in respect of certain contractual clauses as well as of contract amendments, such as an extension of the object or of the contract duration. Nevertheless, the contractual terms and provisions are mostly determined during the procurement stage, yet they may be treated separately from the procedural steps within this stage.

This chapter proposes a discussion on the relevance of core competition rules, comprised in Articles 101 and 102 TFEU, to both the award by public entities of public investment contracts and the performance of such contracts. Given that elements such as the provision in the new 2014 Public Sector Directive of a competition principle for procurement procedures and the application of competition rules in Articles 101 and 102 of TFEU solely to "undertakings" are common to the aspects discussed, this chapter examines these aspects in relation to public investment projects. The first section addresses the general aspects of competition as a principle of procurement procedures, the second is concentrated on the presence of undertakings in public investment activities, in the sense derived from the ECJ case law, whilst the following two sections are considering some of the most important instances of application of Articles 101 and 102 TFEU to activities related to public investment.

---

contract awards not or not fully subject to the provisions of the Public Procurement Directives (2006/C 179/02). The ECJ has restated this principle in case C-324/98 *Telaustria and Telefonadress* [2000] ECR I-10745, case C-231/03 *Coname* [2005] ECR I-7287, case C-458/03 *Parking Brixen* [2005] ECR I-8585, case C-324/07 *Coditel Brabant* [2008] ECR I-8457. Carina Risvig Hansen, *Contracts not Covered, or not Fully Covered, by the Public Sector Directive*, Djøf Publishing, 2012, p. 121–144, Dacian Dragoş, Robert Caranta (eds.), *Outside EU Procurement Directives – Inside the Treaty?*, Djøf Publishing, 2012, Sue Arrowsmith, *The Law of Public and Utilities Procurement. Regulation in the EU and UK*, vol. 1, third edition, Sweet&Maxwell, 2014, p. 245–250, Pedro Telles, *The Good, the Bad, and the Ugly: The EU's Internal Market, Public Procurement Thresholds, and Cross-border Interest*, (2013) 1 Public Contract Law Journal, pp. 12–17, Piotr Bogdanowicz, *Cross-border Interest and concession Contracts: a Critical Approach*, European Procurement and Public Private Partnership Law Review 2/2015, p. 83–91.

[14] Sue Arrowsmith, *The Law of Public and Utilities Procurement. Regulation in the EU and UK*, *op. cit.*, p. 324–331, Albert Sánchez-Graells, *Public Procurement and the EU Competition Rules*, *op. cit.*, p. 135.

[15] Sue Arrowsmith, *The Law of Public and Utilities Procurement. Regulation in the EU and UK*, *op. cit.*, p. 334.

## 5.2 Competition as a Principle of Procurement Procedures

The relationship between procurement procedures and competition rules was presented as being two-fold: procurement procedures seek to ensure competition but procurement also has effects on competitive markets.[16] Moreover, the effectiveness of public procurement procedures and the achievement of their objectives related to "value for money"[17] are better served if such procedures are developed in fully competitive markets.[18]

Explicit provisions aimed to ensure that procurement procedures do not affect competition were included in the 2004 Public Sector Directive, which expressly prohibited the use of specific procurement methods in a manner that may hinder, limit or distort competition, such as the use of framework agreements,[19] dynamic purchasing systems[20] and electronic auctions.[21] These provisions applied to all procedures subject to the Directive (i.e. those procedures with a value above the thresholds established for determining the application domain of the directive), whilst such thresholds are irrelevant to the application of competition rules. This technical intersection of application domains of public procurement and competition rules extends the common element already shared by the two sets of rules, namely their common aim related to the creation of the internal market. Coherence of the two sets of rules is thus important to ensure their effectiveness.[22]

The 2014 Public Sector Directive contributes to the expansion of the common application domain by incorporating an explicit principle of competition in its Article 18(1), which stipulates that "The design of the procurement shall not be

[16] Albert Sánchez-Graells, *Prevention and Deterrence of Bid Rigging: A Look from the New EU Directive on Public Procurement*, in G. Racca and C. Yukins (eds), *Integrity and Efficiency in Sustainable Public Contracts*, Bruylant, Brussels, 2014, p. 2, available at SSRN: http://ssrn.com/abstract=2053414 (last accessed on July 20, 2015).

[17] As emphasized in the OECD paper "Public Procurement: The Role of the Competition Authorities in Promoting Competition" DAF/COMP/(2007) 34, "The primary objective of an effective procurement policy is the promotion of efficiency, i.e. the selection of the supplier with the lowest price or, more generally, the achievement of the best "value for money". It is therefore important that the procurement process is not affected by practices such as collusion, bid rigging, fraud and corruption. Anticompetitive conduct affecting the outcome of the procurement process is a particularly pernicious infringement of competition rules. Through bid-rigging practices, the price paid by public administration for goods or services is artificially raised, forcing the public sector to pay supra-competitive prices. These practices have a direct and immediate impact on public expenditures and therefore on taxpayers resources."

[18] William Kovacic, Robert Anderson, *Competition Policy and International Trade Liberalisation: Essential Complements to Ensure Good Performance in Public Procurement Markets*, (2009) 2 Public Procurement Law Review, p. 67–101.

[19] Article 32(2) of the 2004 Public Sector Directive.

[20] Article 33(7) of the 2004 Public Sector Directive.

[21] Article 55(8) of the 2004 Public Sector Directive.

[22] Grith Skovgaard Olykke, *How Does the Court of Justice of the European Union Pursue Competition Concerns in a Public Procurement Context?*, (2011) 6 Public Procurement Law Review, p. 179–192.

made with the intention of excluding it from the scope of this Directive or of artificially narrowing competition". These provisions include the presumption that "Competition shall be considered to be artificially narrowed where the design of the procurement is made with the intention of unduly favouring or disadvantaging certain economic operators". However, this competition principle is not included in the 2014 Concessions Directive. This incongruence may lead to differences in the way the competition rules are construed within the award procedures that may be envisaged for the contracts underlying public investments, as those qualified as public contracts shall fall within the ambit of the Public Sector Directive and those qualified as concessions shall be awarded in accordance with the Concessions Directive.[23] Nevertheless, irrespective of the absence of an explicit reference in the Concessions Directive to the incidence of the competition principle throughout the award procedures, such incidence may not be plainly excluded.

Even the wording of the competition principle in the 2014 Public Sector Directive was criticised for generating confusion between the anti-competitive behaviour and corruption, as well as for introducing the subjective element of "intention", which would require further jurisprudential efforts in providing objective criteria for its identification.[24]

It should be noted that the principle of competition included in Article 18(1) of the 2014 Public Sector Directive is centred on the activity of the authorities organising and conducting the procurement procedures because they are responsible for "the design of the procurement". The procuring authorities have the obligation to ensure that the procedures they have selected guarantee an effective competition. The organisation of a procurement procedure by a contracting authority in a manner that restricts competition may be either the result of corruption[25] or of an infringement of the principle of equality.[26] Most likely, any intervention of a contracting authority in the design of a procurement aiming at artificially narrowing the competition that does not result from corruption would be either the result of an agreement with one or more favoured bidders, or of an abuse of dominant position.

The presence of "intention" as an element of the breach by the contracting authority of its obligation stated in Article 18(1) of the 2014 Public Sector Directive may be thus seen as derived from, and evidence of, the existence of an agreement or of a unilateral decision that should be treated as leading to an artificial narrowing of competition. However, the rules included in Articles 101 and 102 of TFEU are not directly applicable unless the contracting authority is qualified as an undertaking,

---

[23] The distinction criterion between public contracts and concession contracts, expressly provided by the 2014 Concessions Directive (Article 5 para. 1), is the undertaking by the private contractor (concessionaire) of the operational risk of the contract.

[24] Albert Sánchez Graells, *Public Procurement: A 2015 Updated Overview of EU and National Case Law*, e-Competitions, 2015, available at SSRN: http://ssrn.com/abstract=2613076 (last accessed on July 24, 2015).

[25] Peter Trepte, *Transparency and Accountability as Tools for Promoting Integrity and Preventing Corruption in Procurement: Possibilities and Limitations*, OECD Paper 2005.

[26] Omer Dekel, *The Legal Theory of Competitive Bidding for Government Contracts*, Public Contract Law Journal, 37(2) 2008, p. 253–260.

and such limitation of the application domain of the competition rules shall also be a limitation to the scope of the competition principle within public contracts award procedures.

The text of the principle addressed in Article 18(1) of Directive 2014/24 only considers the result, i.e. the artificial narrowing of competition, and not the qualification of the contracting authority as an "undertaking". Consequently, it is most likely to apply to situations which would otherwise fall within the ambit of Article 101 of TFEU or, as the case may be, Article 102 TFEU, should the contractor be an undertaking as defined by the ECJ case law. This may serve as an argument for a future correction of the limitation provided in the definition of an undertaking applied to public entities established by such case law, in addition to the already expressed criticism of this definition.[27]

Notwithstanding any further clarification of its elements and scope for application, the explicit statement of the competition principle establishes an obligation for contracting authorities to carefully consider the impact of the specific details of the procurement procedure they establish may have on competition, both within the procedure and in the relevant market.

## 5.3 The Presence of Undertakings in Public Investment Activities

The works and services needed for the operation and completion of public investments are acquired either by public procurement or the award of concessions by those public entities delegated with the achievement of public investments. Their qualification as "undertakings" for the purpose of application of competition rules is a crucial element in determining the application of such rules to activities related to public investment as both, Article 101 TFEU, prohibiting anti-competitive agreements and Article 102 TFEU, prohibiting the abuse of a dominant market position, apply only to undertakings.

Concerning the other common requirement for the application of the competition rules, i.e. the effect on the trade between Member States, clearly some of the activities related to public investments are likely to have a European dimension,[28] because the works usually required for their achievement are significant and major construction companies from various Member States are interested in such projects. The services provided to the public during the operation of the resulting assets (public investments) also require extensive expertise and therefore the market for such

---

[27] Sue Arrowsmith, *The Law of Public and Utilities Procurement. Regulation in the EU and UK, op. cit.*, p. 330–331.

[28] The ECJ interpreted extensively the requirement of an effect on interstate trade for the application of the competition rules stipulated in the Treaty (e.g. case C-56/64 *Consten and Grunding v. Commission* (1966)) and the European Commission Guidelines on the Effect on Trade Concept in Arts 81 and 82 of the Treaty (2004), OJ C 101/81.

services is likely to attract major international groups of companies. Contracts below thresholds in the public procurement directives may also be of cross-border interest, as stated by settled ECJ case law.[29]

Well-established, although disputed, case law of the European Court of Justice has determined that an entity may be qualified as an "undertaking" if it performs an economic activity, regardless of its status and the way in which it is financed.[30] The generality of the reference to "an economic activity" requires a further case-by-case analysis of the activities performed by public sector entities. Moreover, as stated by the ECJ[31] "the notion of undertaking is a relative concept in the sense that a given entity might be regarded as an undertaking for one part of its activities while the rest fall outside the competition rules". Consequently, the assessment is to be made in respect to a particular activity of an entity.[32]

The ECJ undertook this analysis in a number of cases and drew a distinction between activities that are of an economic nature and those pursuing a social objective and, more generally, related to the exercise of public power. These economic activities were described in relation to the delivery of goods and services on a given market and not to the business of purchasing.[33] Moreover, in applying the concept of undertaking to a public sector buyer the ECJ considered the use of the purchased goods in order to assess the economic character of such purchasing activity. In *FENIN*, the Court stated that "the nature of the purchasing activity must be determined according to whether or not the subsequent use of the purchased goods amounts to an economic activity".[34] However, in its judgment in *Selex*[35] the ECJ confirmed that the scope of the *FENIN* judgment is not confined to the area of social security, but may be used in any procurement activity.[36] Consequently, if a public sector entity does not use the goods or services purchased for the purpose of selling those goods or services to the public, the economic activity cannot be qualified as an "undertaking" for the purposes of competition law and its procurement activities are not included in the application domain of competition rules.

According to case law, the type of activity performed by the public buyer becomes the most important criterion for determining the application of competition law to the procurement activities of such entity. However, despite offering an analysis of the economic or social character of the activity for which the goods or

---

[29] See note 13 above.

[30] Case C-41/90, *Höfner & Elser v. Macrotron* [1991], ECR I-1979, para. 21.

[31] Case C-475/99, *Ambulanz Glöckner* [2001], ECR I-8089, para. 72.

[32] Alison Jones, Brenda Sufrin, *EC Competition Law*, second edition, Oxford University Press, 2004, p. 741.

[33] Case T- 319/99 *FENIN v. Commission* [2003] ECR II-357, para. 37, C-205/03 (on appeal) ECR I-6295, para. 25.

[34] C-205/03, *FENIN v. Commission*, para. 26.

[35] C-113/07P *Selex Sistemi Integrati SpA v. Commission* [2009] ECR I-2207.

[36] Julian Nowag, *Case C-113/07P Selex Sistemi Integrati SpA v. Commission [2009] ECR I-2207: Redefining the Boundaries between Undertaking and the Exercise of Public Authority*, European Competition Law Review, 2010, p. 485.

services were purchased by a public sector entity, the Court did not make a clear distinction between economic activities and the exercise of public powers that may be performed by public entities. Instead of establishing a general criterion for such distinction, the Court upheld the individual approach in which the analysis was based on the activity concerned, irrespective of the legal status of the entity performing that activity. This functional, anti-formalist approach[37] promoted by the ECJ case law is centred on the activity rather than on the intrinsic characteristics of the entity, and only considers the relevant activity and not the overall powers of that entity.

Thus, from a competition law perspective, and for the purpose of determining if it qualifies as an undertaking in this respect, a public entity may be engaged both in economic activities and in activities related to the exercise of public power and therefore it may be an undertaking in respect of some activities, but not in respect of others.[38] Here it is significant to note that the ECJ judgment in *Selex* attempted to identify whether the activities were economic (within the ambit of competition law) only after examining whether the activities deemed as economic could be separated from those activities consisting in the exercise of public authority. Yet, this pragmatic approach fails to provide clear criteria or a coherent methodology for the administration of the eliminatory test of separability.[39]

However, the functional approach in the ECJ case law has been criticized for not providing the criteria for a clear delimitation of such activities[40] and thus, the application domain of EU and national anti-trust rules remains uncertain.[41]

In terms of the identification of an economic activity performed by a public entity, the ECJ case law has determined that an activity has an economic character if it is performed under market conditions, meaning that it is developed in a market where private competitors are present.[42] At least two presumptions are used by the Court's reasoning: if an entity is organized as a profit-making structure or if it operates in a market where it competes with private entities, then it may be presumed that the activity of such entity is not a result of the exercise of public power. However, those situations where the qualification of a public entity as an undertaking is

[37] Albert Sánchez-Graells, *Distortions of Competition Generated by the Public (Power) Buyer: A Perceived gap in EC Competition Law and Proposals to Bridge It*, University of Oxford Centre for Competition Law and Policy, Working Paper CCLP (L) 23, 2009, p. 29, available at https://www.law.ox.ac.uk/sites/files/oxlaw/cclp_l._23.pdf. (accessed on September 27, 2015).

[38] Opinion of Advocate General Jacobs in Case C-475/99, *Ambulanz Glöckner* [2001].

[39] Ronit Kreisberger, *FENIN: Immunity from Competition Law Attack for Public Buyers?*, (2006) 6 Public Procurement Law Review, NA 214–216, Julian Nowag, *Case C-113/07P Selex Sistemi Integrati SpA v. Commission [2009] ECR I-2207: Redefining the Boundaries between Undertaking and the Exercise of Public Authority, op. cit.*, p. 485.

[40] Sue Arrowsmith, *The Law of Public and Utilities Procurement. Regulation in the EU and UK, op. cit.*, p. 329–331.

[41] Catriona Munro, *Competition Law and Public Procurement: Two Sides of the Same Coin?*, (2006) 6 Public Procurement Law Review, p. 352–361.

[42] Joined cases C-264/01, C-306/01, C-354/01 and C-355/01, *AOK Bundesverband v. Ichtyol-Gesellschaft Cordes* [2003], ECR I-2493, para. 56.

required are not that simple to assess. Except for public undertakings organized as commercial companies, the others are not profit-seeking but organized for a purpose that is part of the general interest. Even in the case of commercial companies, some of those operate in areas that are usually circumscribed to the general interest rather than to purely commercial activities, for example energy producers, distributors or sellers, utilities companies, public assets management (construction and administration of the national road and rail infrastructure, exploitation of mineral resources, administration of inland rivers and lakes, administration of public ports or airports, administration of public domain assets such as airspace etc.).

When such commercial companies have private competitors, the second presumption may be activated and they may be qualified as undertakings for the purposes of the application of competition rules in Articles 101 and 102 TFEU. In certain cases, such as the administration of the national road infrastructure in Romania, which is ensured by a commercial company, neither of the two presumptions is clearly met. Despite its legal form, this commercial company is completely dependent on functional, managerial and financial perspectives of the Ministry of Transport because its policies and activities are directed to the proper administration of the road infrastructure irrespective of any profit considerations. The only direct "competitors" of such public undertaking would be the local public authorities, at the levels of administrative-territorial units, because they own and manage the local roads.[43]

The decisions of the Court highlight the importance of the principle of solidarity in establishing the social character of an activity by stating that if an activity, seemingly of economic nature, is based on the principle of solidarity and is supervised by the state, the entity performing such activity will not be qualified as an undertaking.[44] However, this important role was granted to the principle of solidarity in cases related to the social security systems, which were most often qualified as activities pertaining to a social, non-economic scope rather than as purely economic activities. With regard to social security systems, the principle of solidarity is recognized as a basis for their structuring. But for entities acting in different areas, the identification of the existence of a principle of solidarity within their core structure may prove to be difficult and thus the application of this criterion may not be straightforward. In addition, there may be cases where the activities performed by public authorities may serve both social and economic purposes,[45] the delimitation of which may also be difficult as some cases may be placed in a grey area between

[43] Unlike national roads, which are owned by the state and administered by the Ministry of Transport via a special road infrastructure company. Due to this separation of ownership, the construction of national roads is financed from the state budget, through funds transferred for this purpose to the national company entrusted with road administration, whilst the construction of local roads is financed directly from the budget of the local community that will own them.

[44] C-218/00 *Cisal* [2002], ECR I-691, para. 38–42, C-350/07 *Kattner Stahlbau* [2009], ECR I-1513, paras. 44–59. Malcolm Ross, *Promoting Solidarity: From Public Services to a European Model of Competition?*, Common Market Law Review 44: 1057–1080, 2007.

[45] Sue Arrowsmith, *The Law of Public and Utilities Procurement. Regulation in the EU and UK, op. cit.*, p. 331.

services of general economic interest and non-economic services of general interest.[46]

Because it is entirely dependent on the qualification of the activities placed downstream the actual procurement process, some authors argue that the application domain of Articles 101 and 102 TFEU may be extended if, for the purpose of qualifying an activity of a public entity, only the procurement phase is taken into consideration, as proposed by certain authors.[47] The exclusion of the procurement activities not ancillary to an economic activity, performed by the public entity that organized them, is not derived from visible economic reasoning and has been criticised as an unjustified gap in the EU competition law system.[48]

Whilst concentrating on the activity of a public authority as a provider of goods and services to a specific market, the interpretation offered by the *FENIN-Selex* case law fails to consider the potential distortions of competition that could be generated by the activity of a public entity whilst acting as a buyer. It is significant that this ECJ ruling contradicts the previous jurisprudence in several Member States: United Kingdom, France, Germany, the Netherlands and Spain.[49]

In view of this jurisprudence and of the criteria it has established for the identification of an undertaking, thus determining the applicability of competition rules to its economic activities, the various entities that may perform activities related to public investments are to be analysed on a case-by-case basis. Given that such activities are commonly related to construction[50] (including rehabilitation) of immovable assets, the relevant element for the qualification of such activities as economic or related to the exercise of public authority is most likely the purpose envisaged for the asset resulting from the public investment. This delimitation should be made according to the use of the assets to deliver services of an economic nature to the general public or activities related to the exercise of public authority, with due consideration given to the difficulties of such delimitation.[51]

The potential qualification of the provision of public services as an economic activity may be extended to include the use of the underlying assets. Even if this extension is accepted, the activity subject to analysis should be the actual performance of services to the general public.

---

[46] Ulla B. Neergaard, *Services of General Economic Interest: The Nature of the Beast*, in Markus Krajewski, Ulla Neergaard, Johan van den Gronden (eds.), *The Changing Legal Framework for Services of General Interest in Europe – Between Competition and Solidarity*, 2009, p. 39.

[47] Albert Sánchez-Graells, *Distortions of Competition Generated by the Public (Power) Buyer: A Perceived gap in EC Competition Law and Proposals to Bridge It*, University of Oxford Centre for Competition Law and Policy, Working Paper CCLP (L) 23, 2009, p. 47, available at https://www.law.ox.ac.uk/sites/files/oxlaw/cclp_l._23.pdf. (last accessed on September 27, 2015).

[48] *Idem*, p. 44–46.

[49] Albert Sánchez-Graells, *Public Procurement and the EU Competition Rules*, second edition, Hart Publishing, 2015, p. 159–161.

[50] Yves Gaudemet, *Traité de Droit Administratif. Droit Administratif des Biens*, *op. cit.*, p. 453.

[51] Ulla B. Neergaard, *Services of General Economic Interest: The Nature of the Beast, op. cit.*, p. 20–28.

In cases where public investment activities are concentrating both construction and operation activities, the construction period of the asset has a continuous influence on the services provided within its operation, particularly when the financing of the construction was made from private sources by a concession-type agreement.[52] In this type of contracts, the construction period and the operation period are part of the same contractual and financial structure. The initial contract covers both periods and includes clauses related to services performed during the operation of the assets. Because the concessionaire (usually the private partner in this type of contracts) is a private profit-seeking entity, the activity of the concessionaire and, more generally, the structure of the contract and of the public investment project were designed to include both elements related to the public interest and to the recovery by the private entity of its investment, plus a reasonable profit.

Undoubtedly, the private entity engaged in such public investment project will be an undertaking for the purpose of competition law.

However, the question whether a public entity performing investment activities is an undertaking largely depends on the moment when the contract underlying such activities is signed, irrespective of whether it is a public contract (procurement of works and/or services) or a concession contract (of works and/or services). The moment of signature is the culmination of procurement procedures and represents a pre-contractual step. All types of contracts mentioned above, i.e. procurement of works and/or services and concession of works and/or services are falling under the new directives 2014/23/EU and 2014/24/EU, provided that their value is above the threshold, which is usually the case for public investments. Even in the case of contracts falling outside the scope of the directives, the execution of the contract is preceded by an award procedure.[53]

According to the ECJ jurisprudence, the procurement phase in itself is not relevant to the qualification of the contracting authority as an undertaking. The purpose of procurement in the case of public investments is to obtain an asset intended to be used for the provision of public services, therefore the procurement and the provision of services are to be analysed together. If, during the exploitation/operation of the asset resulting from the public investment, the services are provided in a market context and an exclusive social purpose or the exercise of public power are not identifiable, the contracting authority can be qualified as an undertaking.

---

[52] This comprehensive type of contractual arrangements structured on the basis of a concession, i.e. the right granted to the private partner to exploit the asset and recover its investment plus a reasonable profit, includes not only works and services concessions, but also public-private partnerships and delegated management of utilities.

[53] Sue Arrowsmith, *The Law of Public and Utilities Procurement. Regulation in the EU and UK*, *op. cit.*, p. 245–250, Piotr Bogdanowicz, *Cross-Border Interest and concession Contracts: A Critical Approach*, European Procurement and Public Private Partnership Law Review 2/2015, p. 83–91, Charles Clarke, *CJEU Holds Against the Direct Awarding of Concession Contracts That Have a Potential Cross-Border Interest*, European Procurement and Public Private Partnership Law Review 4/2014, p. 258–263, Adrian Brown, *The Application of EU Treaty Principles to the Grant of a Service Concession for the Use of the Publicly-Owned Cable Networks in Belgium: Case C-221/12 Belgacom*, (2014) 2 Public Procurement Law Review, p. 50.

As a result of the possibility of public or private financing of public investments, a distinction should be made whether the rationale is still valid for services provided by the contracting authority as well as for those provided by the private partner or concessionaire. It is generally accepted that in works and services concessions the operation of the asset(s) built by the concessionaire and the performance of the services included in this operation are conducted by the concessionaire under the supervision of the contracting (concession-granting) authority.

Even if the public entity does not perform the services directly, it retains a major influence on their delivery because the contract establishes the levels of service that have to be met by the concessionaire, as well as any tariff amendments to be approved by the conceding authority, according to specific contractual mechanisms. Moreover, the performance by the concessionaire of the levels of service is continuously monitored by the concession-granting authority, which is entitled to apply penalties for failure to comply with such levels of service and even to unilaterally terminate the contract in case of significantly material non-compliance.

In the context of a concession-type contract, because the terms and conditions of the performance of services following the completion of the public investment are almost entirely provided by the contract whose content was determined during the procurement phase, and thus the contracting authority has an extensive influence on the performance of services, the fact that the contracting authority is not further involved in the actual provision of the service other than in a supervisory capacity, is not a sufficient reason to exclude it entirely from the application of competition rules. The role of the conceding authority cannot be simply limited, in this type of contractual arrangements, to the exercise of public authority because most of the monitoring and control activities are included in the contract. The rationale of the ECJ rather limited jurisprudence related to the application of competition law to concession contracts may not be applicable in this case.

The Court has decided in *Bodson*[54] that Article 85 of the EEC Treaty (now Article 101 TFEU) does not apply to "contracts for concessions concluded between communes by local communities acting in their capacity as public authorities and undertakings entrusted with the operation of a public service". Consequently, the concession contract concluded between a local authority and a private undertaking for the operation of certain funeral services was not deemed as an agreement between undertakings. The main element of this qualification appears to be the assumption made by the Court that, for a public authority, the granting of a concession is an act of public power and not an economic activity.

However, considerations of general interest and of economic purpose are mixed in the activity of public entities entrusted with the achievement of public investments. An asset resulting from a public investment fulfils a general interest purpose and the use of such asset for provision of public services will do the same, an outcome expected by the public as a normal outcome of the activity of public authorities. When the framework for the provision of services by the concessionaire is set

[54] C-30/87 *Bodson* [1988], ECR 2479, paras. 17–18.

by contract,[55] the public authority has an almost decisive influence on such rules and also retains a continuous supervision and control role in respect of levels of service. This level of involvement is certainly aimed at serving the general interest and ensuring that the objectives of public services are met.

In certain cases, the concession may be structured in a way that allows the public authority to share with the concessionaire the profit resulting from the operation of the concession. The public authority may be a shareholder of the concessionaire's project company[56] or the concession contract may include various financial clauses such as sharing of profits resulting from loan refinancing,[57] payment of variable concession fees determined as a percentage of either profit or revenues etc. This type of financial arrangements included in the concession contract may result in economic gains for the public authority well beyond the achievement of the general interest objectives attached to the performance of the public service or generally to the operation/exploitation of a public asset by a concessionaire.

Consequently, such financial arrangements may be a sufficient argument for the qualification at least of this part of the activity performed by the public authority, within the framework of the procurement and performance of a concession agreement, as an economic activity. First, such overall involvement of the public (conceding) authority in a concession process is complex and includes several types of activities. This is in line with the ECJ findings in *Selex*, where it is stated that the various activities undertaken by an entity have to be analysed individually.[58] Second, although the services are formally provided to the public (market) by the concessionaire, the public authority has a direct interest in the economic result of such economic activity.

---

[55] The Romanian law and legal doctrine use the distinction (originated in French law) between two separate areas of a concession contract: the regulatory part and the negotiated part. Those clauses set by the public authority and which define the mandatory conditions for the administration of a public domain, achievement of works and/or the provision of public services, being usually included in the tender documents, are qualified as the regulatory part of the contract. All other clauses, resulting from the agreement of the parties, and usually related to details and other aspects not included in the regulatory part, represent the negotiated part of the contract. The main effect of such a division is the right generally recognized to the public authority to unilaterally modify the regulatory part of the contract. This approach has changed in respect of concession contracts subject to procurement regulations, given the ECJ jurisprudence related to the modification of contracts during their performance. Unilateral amendments by the public authority of the regulatory part of the concession contracts are acceptable only if the reasons and the scope for such amendments are clearly provided by the procurement documents and the contract.

[56] The relatively often use, in certain domains, of the financial structure by which the conceding authority becomes a shareholder to the project company of the concessionaire, generally referred to as an institutionalized public-private partnership is recognized in the *Green Paper on Public-Private Partnerships and Community Law on Public Contracts and Concessions* COM (2004) 327 final. The impact of the procurement rules on its application is detailed in the *Commission Communication on the Application of Community Law on Public Procurement and Concessions to Institutionalized Public-Private Partnerships (IPPP)*, COM(2007) 6661.

[57] EPEC "Guide to Guidance. How to Prepare, Procure and Deliver PPP Projects", http://www.eib.org/epec/resources/guide-to-guidance-en.pdf (accessed on September 14, 2015).

[58] C-113/07P *Selex Sistemi Integrati SpA v. Commission* [2009], note 35 above.

Moreover, if the public authority is a shareholder in the project company, together with the concessionaire and, based on such shareholding, it has a direct influence over the decisions of the project company as the provider of services, it may be deemed that the public authority has a participation that is similar to that of the concessionaire in the operation of the economic activity. The fact that, in these types of financial arrangements, the public authority usually has a minority shareholding is irrelevant for the purpose of this analysis as there is no justification, from the perspective of the pursuit of the general interest, for the participation, with any percentage, as a shareholder of the project company. In most cases, the general interest may be similarly well served by the regulatory, supervision and control roles generally undertaken by the conceding authority. In this context, the public authority's participation as a shareholder of the project company is explained by purely financial considerations. The explicit pursuit of profit by the project company is also an argument which added to those detailed above may uphold the qualification of the activities of the public authority as being of an economic nature similar to the interpretation provided by the ECJ jurisprudence. Consequently, both the procurement and the performance of such concession contract should be subjected to the application of the competition rules included in Articles 101 and 102 TFEU.

## 5.4 The Application of Article 101 TFEU

Provided they are qualified as undertakings, public entities achieving public investments may be affected by the prohibitions stated by Article 101 TFEU when the contracts they enter for this purpose tie up the market for a service or in respect of certain goods in a restrictive manner.[59] The understanding of the fact that the prohibitions stated by Article 101 TFEU (or by its national equivalent for the agreements not having an effect on the trade between Member States) are applicable to such contracts is important for both the public entity conducting such activities and the private entities becoming parties to the contracts because the failure to observe such prohibitions may result in that contract being automatically void.

In the context of public investments activities, Article 101 TFEU covers both actions initiated by the public entity and collusive practices on the bidders' side. The agreements initiated by the public entity may include those that stipulate excessive contract duration or the extension of the scope of the contract, whilst collusive practices are used on a large scale in relation to public works, being also facilitated by transparency requirements in the public procurement directives, framework agreements and the division of contracts into lots.[60]

[59] Sue Arrowsmith, *The Law of Public and Utilities Procurement. Regulation in the EU and UK*, *op. cit.*, p. 332.

[60] *Idem*, p. 333, Albert Sánchez-Graells, *Public Procurement and the EU Competition Rules*, second edition, *op. cit.*, p. 355–363, Albert Sánchez-Graells, *The Difficult Balance between Transparency and Competition in Public Procurement: Some Recent Trends in the Case Law of the*

### 5.4.1 Excessive Contract Duration

Excessive contract duration is likely to lead to distortions of competition and thus breach the prohibitions stipulated in the TFEU or in domestic regulations, mostly in cases of concession-type structures used for the private financing of public investments.

It is unlikely that such issue arises in public works contracts entered into by public entities, following the procurement of works procedures. The duration of such public contracts is generally set in relation to the specific circumstances of the respective construction or rehabilitation works and is influenced by the need of the public beneficiary to receive the resulting assets and begin the operation of these assets. On the contrary, in case of concession-type contractual structures, including concession contracts, public-private partnership contracts and the contracts of service delegation of public utilities, contract duration is set by the public authority as an important element of the procurement procedure. The offers submitted by the tenderers are taking into consideration, amongst other issues, the estimated contract duration.

Given that in the case of concession-type arrangements the contract performance is divided into two periods, namely the construction and the operation phases, the excessive duration may be addressed only in respect of the operation. The parties to the contract have divergent interests during this phase because the private investor is interested in the longest duration possible whilst the public entity is presumed want to regain full control and ownership over the asset. Yet, in practice the interests of the parties may end up being quite convergent, as the operation of the asset by the concessionaire releases the public entity from the obligation of operating the asset itself.

The 2004 procurement directives do not provide expressly rules concerning the duration of contracts, but the ECJ case law stated that, in principle, a contract cannot be entered into for an indefinite period.[61] Amongst the grounds for its finding that the grant of concessions for an unlimited duration is contrary to the EU legal order, the Court mentions the need to guarantee competition.[62] However, Romanian regulations regarding concession contracts and the contracts of service delegation of utilities provide various rules concerning the determination of the duration of such contracts. No such rules have been adopted for public-private partnership contracts. Having failed to adopt a unitary solution, the Romanian legislator sets particular rules for each type of contract.

---

*European Courts and a Look at the New Directives* (November 2013), University of Leicester School of Law Research Paper No. 13-11, available at SSRN: http://ssrn.com/abstract=2353005 (accessed on August 25, 2015), Carmen Estevan de Quesada, *Competition and transparency in public procurement markets*, (2014) 5 Public Procurement Law Review, p. 229–244.

[61] Case C-454/06 *pressetext Nachrichtenagentur* [2008], ECR I-4401, para. 73, case C-451/08 *Helmut Müller GmbH v. Bundesanstalt für Immobilierenaufgaben* [2010], ECR I-2673, para. 79.

[62] Case C-451/08 *Helmut Müller*, para. 79.

As concerns works and services concession contracts, the previous Methodological Norms for the award of concession contracts[63] stipulated three criteria to be collectively observed by the public entity granting the concession when determining the duration of the contract: (i) avoid an artificial restriction of access to competition, (ii) ensure a minimum profit as a result of operating an asset during a given period and (iii) ensure a reasonable price level for services performed during the contract and the costs of which are borne by the final users. Similar criteria are restated by the draft of the methodological norms that will be used for Law no. 100/2016 on concession contracts, which transposed the Concession Directive into Romanian law.

The special laws regulating the contracts of service delegation of utilities set a different rule, based primarily on a maximum allowed duration. According to the provisions of Law no. 51/2006 on public utilities services,[64] the duration of the delegation contract is determined by taking into account the time needed to recoup the investments made by the operator and the maximum limit has two levels: an initial period of maximum 35 years, which could be extended once so that the total duration of the contract does not to exceed 49 years.[65] The extension of the contract may only take place if the local authority requires the operator to perform investments that could only be recouped during the remaining term of the contract by "excessively" increasing the tariffs related to the service. A similar system is provided by French law.[66]

The special laws applicable to different types of public utility services bring additional nuances to the general rules in Law no. 51/2006 on public utilities services, as concerns the modality of establishing the contract duration. Law no. 101/2006 regarding the waste collection service of localities resumes the solution in Art. 15 of Law no. 51/2006 but adds in paragraph 2 that the request for an extension and for new investments is to be made by the local authority based on a technical-

---

[63] Approved by the Government Decision no. 71/2007, repelled by Law no. 100/2016 transposing the Concessions Directive.

[64] According to its Article 31 paragraph (3) "The duration of a contract of delegation cannot be longer than 35 years, to be determined by taking into consideration the duration needed for the amortization of the investments assumed by the operator/regional operator under the delegation contract. The duration may be extended under the same contractual conditions whenever the local public authority requires that the operator, for the proper performance of the service, makes investments that could only be recouped in the remaining term of the contract by an excessive increase in tariffs and taxes. The extension can be agreed as long as the maximum duration of the contract does not exceed 49 years.

(4) The extension is approved in accordance with paragraph (3) by the deliberative authorities of administrative-territorial units. The delegation contract is extended, in conformity with the law, by an addendum signed between the operator and the administrative territorial unit, or, as the case may be, the regional operator and the inter-community development associations working in the area of the public utility services, based on the received mandate."

[65] In France, the Constitutional Council decided in 1993 by decision no. 92–316 that establishing, through general rules, the maximum duration of contracts for public services delegation would violate the principle of unfettered administration by local authorities. However, a number of special regulations have introduced maximum limits for certain types of public property or public services concessions (water, sewerage).

[66] Laurent Richer, *La Concession en Débat*, L.G.D.J.; Paris, 2014, p. 202.

economic substantiation intended to ensure the proper execution of the service, as well as a statement that new investments may be required by the amendment of the EU/national legislation or local management waste strategy.

The difference between the two solutions for the regulation of the duration of similar contracts could be explained by the fact that whilst concessions are subject to the procurement directives and to the ECJ jurisprudence in respect of their interpretation, contracts of service delegation for public utilities are placed outside the scope of the directives as they are qualified as services concessions.[67] When deciding to transpose the directives and to include in the scope of the national procurement regulations not only the works concessions but also services concessions, the Romanian legislator has excluded the concession of public utilities, i.e. contracts for service delegation of public utilities based on the French model.

The diversity of the solutions adopted by the Romanian legislator in regulating the duration of the concession, public-private partnership and service delegation contracts finds an element of unity and, therefore, is subject to fairly significant changes, further to the transposition of Concessions Directive 2014/23/EU into Romanian law. At least the contracts that will fall under this regulation, namely works concession contracts, services concession contracts, public-private partnership contracts and service delegation contracts will be subject to the provisions of the Directive on the duration of the contract.[68] Therefore, the regulations applicable to such contracts should reflect these norms.

According to Article 18 of the Concessions Directive,[69] the duration of the concession should be established by the contracting authority or contracting entity, based on the works or services covered by the contract, with a maximum of 5 years duration being accepted in situations where the duration of the concession is not justified by the investments made by the concessionaire. For any duration of the contract exceeding 5 years, the duration of the concession must be established according to the criterion of recoupment of the investments made by the concessionaire and a reasonable profit on invested capital. The Concession Directive states that the investments envisaged for determining the duration of the contract include both "initial investments", as well as "investments throughout the concession".

In view of the absence of explicit limitations regarding contract duration in the 2004 Public Sector Directive as well as of limitations that may be included in

---

[67] Christopher Bovis, *EU Public Procurement Law*, Edward Elgar, 2012, p. 447, Jean-Yves Chérot, *Droit public économique*, 2nd ed., Economica, 2007, p. 679–681.

[68] Sophie Nicinski, *La Délégation de Service Public et le Temps*, Actualité Juridique Droit Administratif 2013, p. 1441.

[69] "(1) The duration of concessions shall be limited. The contracting authority or contracting entity shall estimate the duration on the basis of the works or services requested.

(2) For concessions lasting more than five years, the maximum duration of the concession shall not exceed the time that a concessionaire could reasonably be expected to take to recoup the investments made in operating the works or services together with a return on invested capital taking into account the investments required to achieve the specific contractual objectives.

The investments taken into account for the purposes of the calculation shall include both initial investments and investments during the life of the concession."

national regulations, the inclusion in a concession contract of a duration that could be interpreted as excessive could be qualified as an infringement of Article 101 TFEU. However, the absence of any clear criteria for determining a duration as being excessive was likely to render such qualification quite difficult. The stipulation of specific limitations to contract duration in the new 2014 Concession Directive, and the criterion stated in the same Article 18 for the determination of duration, may bring additional clarification. Based on Article 18(2) of the Concessions Directive, the assessment of contract duration should consider the financial structure of the contract and the possibility[70] granted by the contract to the concessionaire to recoup the investments and the operating costs, together with a return on capital. The same criterion is described by the Preamble of the Concessions Directive (paragraphs 18–20 and 52), and also stated in the second paragraph of Article 5(1). Although these texts refer primarily to the operating costs and the costs related to investments undertaken by the concessionaire, paragraph 52 of the Preamble is elaborating on the criteria for determining the duration of the concession as well as on the potential anti-competitive effects of a long duration:

> The duration of a concession should be limited in order to avoid market foreclosure and restriction of competition. In addition, concessions of a very long duration are likely to result in the foreclosure of the market, and may thereby hinder the free movement of services and the freedom of establishment. However, such a duration may be justified if it is indispensable to enable the concessionaire to recoup investments planned to perform the concession, as well as to obtain a return on the invested capital. Consequently, for concessions with a duration greater than five years the duration should be limited to the period in which the concessionaire could reasonably be expected to recoup the investment made for operating the works and services together with a return on invested capital under normal operating conditions, taking into account specific contractual objectives undertaken by the concessionaire in order to deliver requirements relating to, for example, quality or price for users. The estimation should be valid at the moment of the award of the concession. It should be possible to include initial and further investments deemed necessary for the operating of the concession in particular expenditure on infrastructure, copyrights, patents, equipment, logistics, hiring, training of personnel and initial expenses. The maximum duration of the concession should be indicated in the concession documents unless duration is used as an award criterion of the contract. Contracting authorities and contracting entities should always be able to award a concession for a period shorter than the time necessary to recoup the investments, provided that the related compensation does not eliminate the operating risk.

The extension of the contract duration initially set in the concession contract is an important modification and for contracts falling within the scope of the Public Sector Directive the relevant ECJ jurisprudence applies.[71] However, for contracts

---

[70] But not the guarantee thereof, as stated in recital 18 of the Preamble to the Concessions Directive.

[71] In case C-454/06 *pressetext*, note 61 above, the ECJ held that an amendment to a contract during its execution can be considered to be significant when it introduces conditions which, had they been included in the initial award procedure, would have allowed the acceptance of other bidders than those admitted initially or would have allowed to accept another offer than that originally accepted (par. 35). The Court also determined that an amendment can be regarded as significant when it changes the economic balance of the contract in favour of private co-contractor in a manner which was not envisaged in the original contract (par. 37). The findings were restated in future

falling outside the scope of the procurement regulations at the time of their execution, such as service delegation contracts which were not regulated by the 2004 Public Sector Directive, the rationale for preventing extensions of contract duration derived from the directive were not applicable. Any solutions to this issue were found in the national limitations in this respect, if any.

In 2008, the Romanian Competition Council conducted an inquiry into the contracts on the basis of which the municipalities of all six districts of Bucharest delegated to private companies the waste collection and management utilities. The investigation was aimed at identifying potential distortions of competition rules induced by the district councils through the service delegation contracts investigated, with a focus on the duration of these contracts. Following this investigation, the Competition Council issued in 2009 a decision[72] which stated that all six district municipalities acted in an anti-competitive manner when establishing the duration of the delegation contracts of waste collection and management activities entered into with private operators and identified three types of anti-competitive behaviour. Some municipalities extended the contract with the existing operator after the expiry of the initial contract duration without organizing any tender procedure. Other municipalities delegated the public service following a tender, but the contract was entered into for 25 years without properly identifying the investment to be performed by the operator. Yet, in other cases, a procedure was organized for the delegation of the service for 25 years without any specific investment obligation included in the tender documents, but the procedure was not completed and no contract was entered into prior to the publication of the decision of the Competition Council.

In the cases where the contract was extended after the expiry of its initial duration, the Competition Council required municipalities to organize competitive procedures for the award of new service delegation contracts. In such cases, the competition was affected by a breach of the applicable procurement provisions and the role of the Competition Council in restoring the legality was made possible by the fact that the procurement authorities are not intervening in procedures falling outside the scope of the Romanian legislation transposing the procurement directives. If the service delegation of public utilities are excluded from the ambit of the main procurement regulations transposing the prevailing directives, it becomes evident that the Romanian legislator has failed to provide an institutional framework for the supervision of competitive award procedures organized for such contracts.

A regulatory authority was created for the supervision of public service activities, but its powers are limited to overseeing the activity of the operators and of local authorities regarding the actual performance of the public services rather than the

---

cases, as C-423/07 *Commission v. Spain* [2010], ECR I-2439, C-91/08 *Wall AG v. Stadt Frankfurt am Main, Frankfurter Entsorgungs und Service GmbH* [2010], ECR I-2815. Gabriella Racca, Roberto Cavallo Perin, *Material Amendments to Public Contracts during their Terms: From Violation of Competition to Symptoms of Corruption*, European Procurement and Public Private Partnership Law Review, 4/2013, p. 54–58.

[72] Decision no. 58/2009 of the Romanian Competition Council, http://www.consiliulconcurentei.ro/uploads/docs/items/id2906/decizie_de_publicat.pdf, (accessed on September 7, 2015).

contract award procedures.[73] Consequently, in the absence of any challenge by an interested party of the flaws of an award procedure, also given the fact that the procurement authority could not intervene in a case outside its area of competences, the anti-competitive effects of the failure to organize a competitive award procedure were assessed by the Competition Council. Although the issue of competition within award procedures is normally absorbed into the regulation of such procedures, as one of its main objectives, in such case the Competition Council did not simply challenge the breach of the existing special legal provisions concerning the award of service delegation contracts, but merely identified the anti-competitive effects of the breach, without naming it as such.[74]

However, particularly intriguing is the analysis by the Competition Council of contracts entered into or planned to be entered into for 25 years, in which the public authority provides no justification of such duration in terms specifically related to the investments expected to be performed by the operator within the public utility system. In its decision, the Competition Council required the relevant district municipalities to re-examine the duration of the service delegation contract and to set it in strict correlation with the amortization of investments (art. 4 of the decision). The decision reaffirms the general criteria for the duration of all service delegation contracts stipulated in Law no. 51/2006 on public utility services (Article 31, paragraph. 3), namely: "The duration of a contract of delegation cannot be longer than 35 years, to be determined by taking into consideration the duration needed for the amortization of the investments assumed by the operator/regional operator under the delegation contract.". This criterion for the determination of the duration in relation to the amortization of the investments undertaken by the private operator is also inspired from French law Sapin.[75]

The legal reasoning of this decision of the Romanian Competition Council is based on a specific provision of the Romanian law which prohibits any actions of a public authority that generate, or may result in, anti-competitive effects. According to Article 8[76] of the Competition Law no. 21/1996,

[73] The National Authority for the Regulation of Public Utility Services (ANRSC) is regulated by the same Law no. 51/2006 on public utilities services and is organized as a separate, but not independent, entity within the Ministry of Regional Development and Public Administration.

[74] This lack of reference to the breach of existing provisions in the law concerning the award of delegated management contracts may be explained by the intention to avoid any further challenge to the Competition Council decision on the grounds that its rationale refers to issues outside its supervisory powers (in this case, the assessment of the legality of the contract extension without an award procedure). Consequently, the Council may have preferred to rely exclusively on considerations limited to its powers, i.e. regarding the anti-competitive effects of the contract extension in such cases.

[75] Loi no. 93–122 du 29 janvier 1993 relative à la prévention de la corruption et à la transparence de la vie économique et des procédures publiques.

[76] Prior to the republication of the law in 2014, i.e. at the date of the publication of Decision No. 58/2009, this article was numbered as article 9.

Are prohibited any actions or inactions of central or local public authorities or institutions or of entities to which they may delegate their powers, which are restricting, impeding on or distorting the competition, such as:

(a) the limitation of freedom of trade or of autonomy of undertakings, exercised in compliance with [existing] legal provisions;
(b) the establishment of discriminatory conditions for the activity of undertakings.

If a decision adopted by the Competition Council ordering the reinstatement of the competitive environment is not observed by the public authorities concerned, the Council may file in the Court of Appeal a request for the invalidation of the (non-legislative) act that affected the competition.

Being a national expression of the State Action Doctrine[77] expressed by settled case law of the ECJ,[78] these provisions relieve the Competition Council from the duty to assess whether the public authority that entered into a contract resulting in anti-competitive effects is an undertaking for the purpose of Article 101 TFEU.

Except for this qualification, all other conditions for the application of the prohibition established by Article 101 TFEU are met. In addition, in this case the public authority is entering into an agreement with undertakings, thus acting in a contractual manner. Despite the difference between the two provisions regarding the role played by the qualification of the public authority as an undertaking, the similarities cannot be denied. Where actions having anti-competitive effects take the form of agreements entered into by public authorities, the failure to qualify them as undertakings impedes the application of Article 101 TFEU. In this case, is this specific provision of the Romanian Competition Law that makes irrelevant such qualification of the public authority, still compatible with EU competition law,[79] given that it may be deemed to extend its application domain?

According to Article 3(2) of the Regulation 1/2003, Member States may apply stricter national rules which prohibit or sanction unilateral conduct engaged in by undertakings. Yet, an extension of prohibitions by national rules to agreements entered into by entities that may not qualify as undertakings according to ECJ case law, would result in an expansion of the application domain of the competition rules provided by Articles 101 and 102 TFEU. Whilst the latter is tolerated by EU law, the extension in respect of Article 101 TFEU is prohibited by the first phrase of the same Article 3(2) of the Regulation 1/2003.[80]

---

[77] Albert Sánchez-Graells, *Public Procurement and the EU Competition Rules*, second edition, *op. cit.*, p. 147–149.

[78] The elements of the State Action Doctrine were formulated in the ECJ decision in case C-267/86 *Van Eycke* [1988], ECR 4769, para. 16, and further restated in case C-339/89 *Alsthom Atlantique* [1991] ECR I-107, case C-332/89 *Marchandise* [1991] ECR I-1027, and more others.

[79] The 2014 OECD Report "Competition Law and Policy in Romania. A Peer Review" considers this article as a "particularly effective tool" (page 45) http://www.oecd.org/daf/competition/Romania-Competition-Law-Policy-2014-EN.pdf (accessed August 6, 2015).

[80] Albert Sánchez-Graells, *Public Procurement: A 2014 Updated Overview of EU and National Case Law 2014, e-Competitions 2014*, p. 9, available at SSRN: http://ssrn.com/abstract=1968371 (accessed on August 27, 2015).

Consequently, the provisions of Article 8 of the Romanian Competition Law may be deemed as compatible with the EU law in respect of Article 101 TFEU, only if they refer to unilateral conduct undertaken by public authorities. Also, the prohibition stipulated in Article 8 of the Romanian Competition Law may be compatible with the application of Article 102 TFEU.

Of course, if the Competition Council had examined the application of Article 101 TFEU to service delegation contracts entered into for an unreasonable duration, it would have had to verify whether the municipality that entered into the contract may be qualified as an undertaking in light of the criteria set by the *FENIN/Selex* case law.

However, because the result of the application of Article 101 TFEU is similar to that of the application of Article 8 of the Competition Law, i.e. the potential annulment by the court of the agreement, whilst the application of Article 101 is more difficult than the use of the domestic law provision due to the test of "downstream economic activity", the choice of legal rule seems to favour the simpler route.

From the perspective of the legal regime of public investments, the decision of the Competition Council upholds the necessity to stipulate clearly the investment obligations undertaken by the private partners in contracts regarding the private financing of public investments (such as concession contracts, public-private partnership contracts and service delegation contracts). Such description of the investment obligations of the private partners should be included both in the award documents and in the body of the contract. If the contract does not stipulate the obligation of the operator to perform certain investments,[81] there will be no criterion for determining the duration of the contract. However, for the contracts subject to the new Concessions Directive, if the duration is less than 5 years it does not have to be justified by the investments undertaken by the private partner. It follows that, in line with Article 18 of the Concessions Directive, a concession-type contract that does not stipulate the obligation of the private partner to perform an investment may be concluded for a period of maximum 5 years.

In any case, establishing the duration of long-term contracts is a crucial element of the effort to ensure the validity of the contractual structure, as the failure to determine the duration is likely to generate not only a breach of the rules included in Article 101 TFEU but also disputes related to the presence of state aid.[82]

---

[81] The contractual obligation to invest may be stated either directly, by describing the actual works to be completed, or indirectly, by setting certain level of services and specific deadlines for compliance with each of them. Such compliance and further maintenance of the levels of services requires an amount of investment that is not prescribed by the contract, but was estimated by the bidders as a basis for their offered tariffs. This structure was used in the concession contract for the water and sewerage services in Bucharest, entered for 25 years starting from 2000 http://www.apanovabucuresti.ro/!res/fls/contract-de-concesiune.pdf (last accessed September 3, 2015).

[82] In this respect, the decision of the European Commission in case N-264/2002 *London Underground*, stated that a 30 years duration for a public-private partnership contract concerning the upgrading and maintenance of the London underground infrastructure was necessary and proportionate as it ensured the recoupment of the investments undertaken by the private partner.

### 5.4.2 Amendments to Existing Contracts

Another type of agreements potentially affecting competition are those entered into as amendments to existing contracts for the purpose of extending their scope, alone or in conjunction with an extension of the duration. The absence of any reference to contract amendments in the 2004 Public Sector Directive was replaced by the explicit provisions concerning the modification of concession contracts included in the 2014 Public Sector and Concessions Directives. Such provisions are structured along reasoning stated by the ECJ case law, especially its decision in *pressetext* case.[83] Consequently, the principles developed by such jurisprudence continue to be applicable to the interpretations of the provisions in the new directives. Moreover, the principles stated by the ECJ jurisprudence, which build on the principles of equal treatment and transparency derived from TFEU,[84] are also applicable to works or concession contracts that are excluded, or below the threshold, in the Directives.[85]

Article 43 of the Concessions Directive continues to apply the materiality test[86] to determine whether the contract amendments are acceptable or require a new tender procedure for the new contract, including the amendments. Thus, contracts may be modified without a new award procedure when such modifications are deemed not substantial and they meet the criteria for identification stipulated in paragraphs 1[87] and 2.[88] Paragraph 4 stipulates the cases in which a modification is deemed to be substantial. However, the cases of permitted amendments listed in paragraphs 1 and 2 are exclusive as paragraph 5 of Article 43 provides that any modification that does

[83] Case C-454/06 *pressetext*, note 61 above. The Court held that compliance with the transparency and equal treatment principles requires that changes to an existing contract are to be considered, a new contract if the changes are materially different from the provisions of the original contract and thereby demonstrate that it was the intention of the parties to renegotiate the basic elements of the contract. (para. 34).

[84] Sune Troels Poulsen, *The Possibilities of Amending a Public Contract Without a New Competitive Tendering Procedure under EU law*, (2012) 5 Public Procurement Law Review, p. 168.

[85] C-91/08 *Wall*, note 71 above.

[86] Kristian Hartlev, Morten Wahl Liljenbøl, *Changes to Existing Contracts Under the EU Public Procurement Rules and the Drafting of Review Clauses to Avoid the Need for a New Tender*, (2013) 22, 2, Public Procurement Law Review, p. 54–57. Rafael Dominguez Olivera, *Modification of Public Contracts. Transposition and Interpretation of the new EU Directives*, European Procurement and Public Private Partnership Law Review 1/2015, p. 45–47.

[87] Paragraph 1 stipulates a number of cases in which the concession contract may be modified without a new award procedure: (a) modifications provided by revision clauses, (b) additional works and services that have become necessary and where a change of concessionaire cannot be made for economic or technical reasons or due to significant inconvenience or substantial duplication of costs for the contracting authority, (c) unforeseeable circumstances, (d) replacement of the concessionaire in limited circumstances and (e) modifications that are not substantial.

[88] According to paragraph 2, contract amendments with a value below both, the threshold for the award of concession contracts and 10 % of the initial value of the contract which do not change the overall nature of the initial contract, may be implemented without re-tendering. Such thresholds are applicable to all cumulated changes to the contract.

not meet such criteria requires a new award procedure. A similar structure is provided by Art. 72 of the 2014 Public Sector Directive.

Yet, a surprising detail was revealed by a report issued by the Romanian Competition Council following a sectoral investigation conducted in 2013 regarding the road infrastructure construction works market.[89] Most contracts for works or services entered into by the contracting authority were amended, with a significant number of such amendments being made in respect of additional works, thus increasing the total contractual value. Some of the amendments extending the object of the contract, thus increasing its total value, were made in compliance with relevant procurement regulations (i.e. the conditions for including additional works or services to the initial ones were met, and the value of the contract was not increased by more than 50 % and 20 %, respectively, of the initial value[90]), but some exceeded the acceptable limitation of increases in contractual value.

The Competition Council noted that, in such cases, the value of additional works is negotiated directly between the parties to the contract without the intervention of any market competition element. Irrespective of their conformity with the procurement regulations, such amendments are likely to distort competition and generate dysfunctionalities in the market. Yet, the Council resolved to simply recommend that this practice should be avoided.

This type of contract amendment by increasing the contract value due to additional works, especially when such works are deemed as imposed by unforeseen circumstances, is pervasive and may be seen as responsible for low offers submitted by bidders within contract award procedures with an expectation for further increases of the contract price by means of such amendments. No extensive criteria for the identification of foreseeability of specific circumstances by the contracting authority were laid down by the ECJ,[91] whilst the impact of such situations was accepted by the European Commission for changes to tender conditions in an ongoing procedure (in *London Underground* state aid decision, where changes required

---

[89] http://www.consiliulconcurentei.ro/uploads/docs/items/id8693/raport.pdf (last accessed August 9, 2015).

[90] By the end of 2011 the limit to any increase of the contractual value by amendments was reduced to 20 %, from 50 % as provided by the initial (2006) national procurement regulations.

[91] Although the Court was reluctant in easily accepting the unforeseeable character of external circumstances that caused amendments to the contract and imposed on contracting authorities the duty of thoroughly assessing any potential need for amendments. In case C-496/99 *Commission v. CAS Succhi di Frutta Spa* [2004], ECR I-3801, the Court held that the contracting authority should have included a revision clause in the award documentation, whilst in case C-318/94 *Commission of the European Communities v Germany* [1996] E.C.R. I-01949, the Court did not accept that it was not foreseeable for a contracting authority that a newly built ship could not be moved from the shipyard to the sea and that required an extension of an existing contract to works for deepening the sea-communication canal. However, in case C-24/91 *Commission of the European Communities v Spain* [1992] E.C.R. I-1989, the Court accepted that a works contract awarded for the construction of new university buildings was extended to additional new buildings as a result of an unexpected increase in the number of incoming new students.

by a risk of terrorist attacks were accepted[92]) and also as a principle, in the context of long-term contracts (public-private partnerships[93]). Although corruption plays a significant role in sustaining the approach of low bids followed by contract amendments, contract modification is still an area of anti-competitive behaviour, requiring careful scrutiny by both procurement and competition authorities.

### *5.4.3 The Joint Award of Contracts by Local Authorities*

The Law no. 215/2001 on local public administration allows the local authorities from different administrative-territorial units to act together for the completion of public investments or the provision of public services, by creating so-called inter-community development associations ("IDA"). Registered as a non-profit organization, the association decides for its members – which are local communities (administrative-territorial units) in matters related to public services or public investment. Although the contracts for the operation of the public investment or the provision of a public service are entered into by the IDA, the resulting assets are owned by the administrative-territorial unit established by law or agreed by the members of the IDA.[94] The assets are used for the provision of services to all local communities that are members of the association. Within the IDA, the decisions are made following the vote of the representatives of all its members, which have equal voting rights, with all procurement procedures organized and conducted by the IDA for the benefit of its members. Most likely inspired by the idea of central purchasing bodies and adapted for the procurement of utilities services for local communities, the IDAs are used in practice usually for water and sewerage, waste collection and public transportation services.

If all the members of an IDA are qualified as undertakings and, within the framework of procurement procedures, have an anti-competitive behaviour, this situation would fall under the rules established by Article 101 TFEU. Even in the absence of their qualification as undertakings, the local authorities involved in an IDA would fall within the ambit of Article 8 of the Romanian Competition Law if they pursue any action or inaction having anti-competitive effects.

Moreover, the IDA itself may be qualified as an undertaking if procuring goods, works and services that are used to deliver public services on behalf of its members.[95] Whether such public services are "economic activities" for the purpose of the *FENIN/Selex* case law, is a matter to be determined on a case by case basis, but some of these services are provided in a noticeably competitive market, such as

---

[92] Sue Arrowsmith, *The Law of Public and Utilities Procurement. Regulation in the EU and UK*, *op. cit.*, p. 590.

[93] Green Paper on public-private partnerships and community law on public contracts and concessions, COM (2004) 327 final, para. 49.

[94] One asset cannot have more than one owner which is an administrative-territorial unit.

[95] James Chard, Gustaf Duhs, John Houlden, *Body Beautiful or Vile Bodies? Central Purchasing in the UK*, (2008) 2 Public Procurement Law Review, NA 26–34.

public transport. The fact that the IDAs are organized as non-profit entities is potentially irrelevant for their qualification as undertakings.

### 5.4.4 Bid Rigging

Despite a number of significant cases where bid rigging during public procurement procedures related to public works was sanctioned by the European Commission and especially by national competition authorities,[96] there are significant difficulties in detecting and proving various types of bid rigging cases.[97] They occur most often in the context of framework agreements and of division of construction works into lots.

*Framework Agreements* A common practice among contracting authorities, allowed by procurement regulations, which may be extended in the public works sector and leads to bid rigging is the use of framework agreements entered into with several providers. Based on such framework agreements, the subsequent contracts are re-tendered amongst the selected providers and this repeated procedure is likely to encourage bid rigging in various forms.[98] Framework agreements are regulated by Article 33 of the 2014/24 Public Sector Directive. Due to the benefits they may generate for contracting authorities, framework agreements[99] are used not only for procurement of general goods or services, but also in the construction sector[100] and in the road infrastructure construction and maintenance,[101] which are relevant to this analysis.

---

[96] Albert Sánchez-Graells, *Public Procurement: A 2014 Updated Overview of EU and National Case Law*, e-Competitions, 2014, *op. cit.*, p. 5–6. Albert Sánchez-Graells, *Prevention and Deterrence of Bid Rigging: A Look from the New EU Directive on Public Procurement*, in G Racca, C Yukins (eds), *Integrity and Efficiency in Sustainable Public Contracts*, Bruylant, Brussels, 2014, p. 6–8, available at SSRN: http://ssrn.com/abstract=2053414 (accessed on September 12, 2015).

[97] Alberto Heimler, *Cartels in Public Procurement*, Journal of Competition Law & Economics, 2012, p. 11–23, available at SSRN: http://ssrn.com/abstract=2336030 (accessed on September 17, 2015), Marsela Maci, *Bid Rigging in the EU Public-Procurement Markets: Some History and Developments*, European Competition Law Review, 2011, 32(8), p. 406–413.

[98] The various forms of bid rigging are described in the OECD Guidelines for fighting bid rigging in public procurement, published in 2009: http://www.oecd.org/competition/cartels/42851044.pdf (accessed on July 31, 2015). As stated by OECD in its 2007 paper on "Public Procurement: The Role of the Competition Authorities in Promoting Competition" DAF/COMP/(2007) 34, "The formal rules governing public procurement can make communication among rivals easier, promoting collusion among bidders. While collusion can emerge in both procurement and ordinary markets, procurement regulations may facilitate collusive arrangements."

[99] Sue Arrowsmith, *The Law of Public and Utilities Procurement. Regulation in the EU and UK*, *op. cit.*, p. 333.

[100] Peter Arden, *Legal Regulation of Multi-Provider Framework Agreements and the Potential for Bid Rigging: A Perspective from the UK Local Government Construction Sector*, (2013) 22(4), Public Procurement Law Review, p. 172–174.

[101] http://www.consiliulconcurentei.ro/uploads/docs/items/id8693/raport.pdf (accessed on July 31, 2015). Data regarding the pervasiveness of bid rigging in construction sector are presented in the OECD report "Policy Roundtable on the Construction Industry", 2008, http://www.oecd.org/regreform/sectors/41765075.pdf (accessed on July 31, 2015).

One frequently mentioned effect that framework agreements may have on competition is the facilitation of collision between transparency and the rules for entering into subsequent contracts.[102] According to both the 2004 and 2014 Public Sector Directives, if a framework agreement is concluded for a maximum period of 4 years and is not open to new parties, with all subsequent contracts being allotted to existing parties, a variety of mechanisms may be used for such allotment, with some of those including a re-opening of competition.[103] To reduce the risk of collusion, a variety of call-off methods was recommended as a mechanism for creating uncertainty amongst bidders.[104]

Generally, the transparency obligations imposed on contracting authorities by both the 2004 and 2014 Public Sector Directives may impact on the effective competition within the procurement procedures and may increase the risk of cartelisation of procurement markets.[105] Despite various reiterations, in the OECD documents,[106] of the negative effects that may result from the tension between the transparency provisions aimed at preventing corruption in procurement procedures and the competition imperatives seeking to prevent the collusion of bidders, the ECJ has determined that the obligation of transparency is fulfilled when detailed information is provided in respect of the tender evaluation process, provided that it enables the tenderer to identify the characteristics and relative advantages of the best ranked tenderer's offer.[107]

In its 2013 Report on a sectoral investigation regarding the road infrastructure construction works market,[108] the Romanian Competition Council explains, in fairly general terms, the potential anti-competitive effects of framework agreements, mainly in terms of their duration. Under Romanian (and EU) procurement regulations, framework agreements may be generally concluded for a duration of up to 4 years, which makes them really attractive if their object relates to works and services (such as maintenance) in the area of road infrastructure. However, duration is not the only element of framework agreements that may facilitate collusive practices because their value, together with the absence of clear rules for the allocation

[102] Peter Arden, *Legal Regulation of Multi-Provider Framework Agreements and the Potential for Bid Rigging: A Perspective from the UK Local Government Construction Sector, op. cit.*, p. 173.

[103] Sue Arrowsmith, *The Law of Public and Utilities Procurement. Regulation in the EU and UK, op. cit.*, p. 335.

[104] Peter Arden, *Legal Regulation of Multi-Provider Framework Agreements and the Potential for Bid Rigging: A Perspective from the UK Local Government Construction Sector, op. cit.*, p. 173.

[105] Albert Sánchez-Graells, *The Difficult Balance Between Transparency and Competition in Public Procurement: Some Recent Trends in the Case Law of the European Courts and a Look at the New Directives*, 2013, *op. cit.*

[106] Recommendation of the OECD Council on Fighting Bid Rigging in Public Procurement, 2012, http://www.oecd.org/daf/competition/RecommendationOnFightingBidRigging2012.pdf (accessed on August 2, 2015) Competition and Procurement: Key Findings, OECD 2011, http://www.oecd.org/daf/competition/sectors/48315205.pdf (accessed on August 2, 2015).

[107] C-629/11 *P Evropaïki Dynamiki v. European Commission* [2012], EU:C:2012:617, para. 30.

[108] http://www.consiliulconcurentei.ro/uploads/docs/items/id8693/raport.pdf (accessed on August 2, 2015).

of subsequent contracts, may also contribute to the occurrence of such practices.[109] Framework agreements may be covered by the rules included in Article 101 TFEU irrespective of the fact that these agreements are not binding but serve only to set the terms of future contracts to be entered into by the parties.[110]

In addition, the 2013 Report of Romanian Competition Council only draws attention to the potential for bid rigging generated by the use of joint bids on a large scale,[111] although joint bid submissions are allowed by the procurement regulations.

*Division into Lots* A specific feature of the award of public works contracts in respect of road and highways infrastructure in Romania, including construction, rehabilitation and maintenance works, is their usual division into lots, which are awarded by the same contracting authority. Generally, the lots have a similar object, with any variations being the result of the circumstances related to their actual location. The main benefit of this practice is the relatively concomitant progress of works, which allows the contracting authority to commission the completed road at a specific date. Because the lots are more or less equal and the dates for the commencement of works are close in time, if not simultaneous, the completion dates for the different lots of a road are likely to be very close in time, depending on the presence of specific circumstances for certain lots.

As all lots are awarded at the same time by the same contracting authority and most bidders usually submit bids for all lots, there may be a temptation for collusion amongst bidders that would enable each of them to obtain at least a lot.[112] Consequently, the number of lots should be determined to be higher than the number of expected bidders. In addition, clear criteria and rules should in place for the award of several lots to one bidder as well as for instances when not all lots were awarded.[113]

The 2014 Public Sector Directive allows contracting authorities to limit the number of lots awarded to one bidder,[114] provided that such limitation is stipulated in the tender documents together with the "objective and non-discriminatory criteria or rules they intend to apply to determine which lots will be awarded where the application of the award criteria would result in one tenderer being awarded more lots

[109] William Kovacic, Robert Anderson, *Competition Policy and International Trade Liberalisation: Essential Complements to Ensure Good Performance in Public Procurement Markets*, (2009) 2, Public Procurement Law Review, p. 90.

[110] Sue Arrowsmith, *The Law of Public and Utilities Procurement. Regulation in the EU and UK*, *op. cit.*, p. 333.

[111] http://www.consiliulconcurentei.ro/uploads/docs/items/id8693/raport.pdf (accessed on August 2, 2015).

[112] Stefan Weishaar, *2014 Procurement Reforms and Bid Rigging: Mixed Blessings or Our Happily Ever After?*, in Sarah Schoemaekers, Wouter Devroe, Niels Philipsen (eds.), *State Aid and Public Procurement in the European Union*, Intersentia, 2014, p. 111.

[113] Albert Sánchez-Graells, *Prevention and Deterrence of Bid Rigging: A Look from the New EU Directive on Public Procurement*, *op. cit.*, p. 12–16.

[114] Article 46(2) of the Directive 2014/24.

than the maximum number". It is unclear whether or not this limitation is a facilitator of collusive agreements because the aim of such agreements, for example to secure a lot for each tenderer, is rendered even more desirable as one tenderer is allowed to obtain a limited number of contracts despite being allowed to bid for all. A new rule regarding the award of lots is provided in Article 46(3) of the 2014 Public Sector Directive, which allows Member States to include in their national regulations the possibility of combining several or even all lots in those cases where more than one lot is awarded to a single tenderer. The procurement documentation should include specific reference to this possibility of awarding the contracts for several lots, together with details concerning the lots or groups of lots that may be combined.

The new rules concerning the division into lots included in the 2014 Public Sector Directive may contribute to a reduction of collusive practices in procurement procedures, provided that the relevant economic considerations and recommendations are also observed in designing such division.[115]

In addition, the economic crisis and the continued reduction in public investments are perceived as circumstances that increase the risk of collusion amongst companies facing economic difficulties and severely reduce the number and value of public works contracts awarded.[116] In Romania, the absence of relevant case law could be seen as an indicator of the difficulties in proving actual collusive practices,[117] despite cases of significant bid rigging practices uncovered and fined in other Member States.[118]

## 5.5 Exclusion of Bidders

Given that the award of public investment contracts will largely fall within the ambit of procurement regulations, the implementation of the new rules introduced in Directive 2014/24/EU may reduce the incidence of bid rigging on these procedures.

[115] Such as the OECD Recommendations and Guidelines for fighting bid rigging in public procurement.

[116] Peter Arden, *Legal Regulation of Multi-Provider Framework Agreements and the Potential for Bid Rigging: A Perspective from the UK Local Government Construction Sector, op. cit.*, p. 178–179.

[117] From 2010, when a special unit dedicated to bid rigging inquiries was created within the Romanian Competition Council, to 2014 a number of 12 investigations were conducted and only two resulted in decision (no. 71/2012 and no. 72/2012) that fined in each case two companies (different from one case to the other for bid rigging a tender organized for construction of gas distribution networks (although several other companies were inquired).

[118] Notably in the road construction sector infringement decisions against bid cartels were made in the United Kingdom, the Netherlands and France. However, it appears to be a discrepancy between the understanding of bid rigging cases by competition authorities and respectively by the courts, as the latter have reduced the fines applied by the competition authorities on the grounds that some of the bid rigging instances were not qualified as such (especially cover bids and bid suppressions). For an overview, Albert Sánchez-Graells, *Prevention and Deterrence of Bid Rigging: A Look from the New EU Directive on Public Procurement, op. cit.*, p. 6–8.

The provisions of Article 57(4)(d) and of Article 57(5), respectively, could provide contracting authorities with effective legal tools for excluding tenderers against which there is sufficient circumstantial evidence of being engaged in collusive arrangements. The use of these tools by the contracting authorities (and also by other participants to the procurement procedure) may lead to a more effective prevention of collusive tendering, as the sanctions applicable to those involved in such practices would not be just those stipulated by competition regulations but also the exclusion for a specific period from participation to public markets.[119]

The provisions in Article 57 of the Public Sector Directive 2014/24 generally cover the grounds for exclusion that may be used by contracting authorities during procurement procedures. Paragraph (4)(d) of this Article states that "contracting authorities may exclude or may be required by Member States to exclude from participation in a procurement procedure any economic operator" if "the contracting authority has sufficiently plausible indications to conclude that the economic operator has entered into agreements with other economic operators aimed at distorting competition." The exclusion grounds related to the anticompetitive behaviour of bidders are provided by the Directive as discretionary rather than mandatory grounds, but Member States may transpose these provisions by setting them as mandatory grounds for exclusion ("may be required by Member States to exclude").

The scope of such exclusion remains to be determined, due to the obvious difference between the text of the Directive and that of Article 101 TFEU. The provision in Article 57(4)(d) of the 2014 Public Sector Directive refers to the fact that the economic operator subject to exclusion from the procedure "has entered into agreements" (emphasis added) and therefore seems to refer to at least one of the modalities of anti-competitive behaviour prohibited by Article 101 TFEU (which also refers to "decisions or concerted practices"). In addition, the ground for exclusion provided by Article 57(4)(d) refers only to agreements aimed at distorting competition, whilst Article 101 TFEU refers to agreements seeking, or resulting in "the prevention, restriction or distortion of competition".

Based on a literal interpretation, arguments have been made for a restrictive determination of the scope of Article 101, limited to the participation of economic operators to agreements aimed at distorting competition.[120] In another opinion, the exclusion should refer at least to all types of anticompetitive conduct covered by Article 101(1) TFEU.[121] Because the legal text stipulates a limitation of rights, it should be interpreted in a restrictive manner, by using the literal interpretation of the text and considering any enumeration as being exhaustive (limitative).[122]

However, the rules of implementation of the exclusion of economic operators from procurement procedures are adopted at national level, which could lead to a

[119] *Idem*, p. 17–21.

[120] Hans-Joachim Priess, *The Rules on Exclusion and Self-Cleaning under 2014 Public Procurement Directive*, 2014, 23 (3) Public Procurement Law Review, p. 112–123.

[121] Albert Sánchez-Graells, *Public Procurement: A 2015 Updated Overview of EU and National Case Law, op. cit., p.* 8.

[122] C-465/11 *Forposta and ABC Direct Contact* [2012], EU:C:2012:801, para. 38.

variety of solutions and thus to a non-uniform application of the criteria for exclusion.[123] Article 57(7) stipulates that where the exclusion is decided on grounds related to anticompetitive conduct, the maximum exclusion period cannot exceed 3 years from the date of the relevant event, except for the case when the exclusion period is explicitly set by a final court decision.

In addition to the possibility of excluding an economic operator involved in collusive practices prior to the procedure, Article 57(5) extends this possibility to the case in which the contracting authority has sufficiently plausible indications that such collusive conduct takes place during the current procedure.[124] The possibility of exclusion is thus widened by this new rule and refers to both past and current breaches of competition regulation.

However, the exclusion and subsequent debarment of a potential contractor/bidder in cases where there are few competitors in the specific market may lead to the ineffectiveness of the procurement procedure.[125] In such cases, the "self-cleaning" provisions in Article 57(6) of the 2014 Public Sector Directive may allow contracting authorities to accept participation to the procedure to those potential bidders that have paid, or undertaken to pay, compensation for any damage caused by the criminal offence or misconduct, clarified the facts and circumstances in a comprehensive manner by actively collaborating with the investigating authorities and taken concrete technical, organisational and personnel measures that are appropriate to prevent further criminal offences or misconduct.

Further deterrence of collusive agreements may be determined by the fact that, following the entry into force on February 1, 2014 of the new Romanian Criminal Code, "the agreement between bidders to distort the award price" is a criminal offence that may be punished with imprisonment from 1 to 5 years,[126] whilst no significant practice is in place. Participation to a cartel can also be a criminal offence in Germany[127] as well as in the United Kingdom under the Enterprise Act 2002, yet without any significant investigation conducted to date on these grounds.[128]

To ensure an effective implementation of both competition and public procurement rules and thus increase competition in the public procurement markets, it was proposed that there should be a direct involvement of the competition authorities in

---

[123] Hans-Joachim Priess, *The Rules on Exclusion and Self-Cleaning under 2014 Public Procurement Directive, op. cit.*, p. 123.

[124] According to Article 57(5), "At any time during the procedure, contracting authorities may exclude or may be required by Member States to exclude an economic operator where it turns out that the economic operator is, in view of acts committed or omitted either before or during the procedure, in one of the situations referred to in paragraph 4."

[125] Jennifer S. Zucker, *The Boeing Suspension: Has Increased Consolidation Tied the United States Department of Defence's Hands?*, (2004), 13 (5), Public Procurement Law Review, p. 260.

[126] Article 246 of the Romanian Criminal Code (Law no. 286/2009).

[127] David Edward, Robert Lane, *European Union Law*, Edward Elgar, 2013, p. 750.

[128] Catriona Munro, *Competition Law and Public Procurement: Two Sides of the Same Coin?*, *op. cit.*, p. 359. Imelda Maher, Oana Ştefan, *Competition Law in Europe: The Challenge of a Network Constitution*, in Dawn Oliver, Tony Prosser, Richard Rawlings, *The Regulatory State. Constitutional Implications*, Oxford University Press, 2010, p. 178.

public procurement procedures.[129] Such involvement is considered to include decisions concerning the enforcement of rules against bid riggers, the assessment of the expertise of competition authorities in these matters as well as a more general oversight of activities conducted by contracting authorities that may have anti-competitive effects.

## 5.6 The Application of Article 102 TFEU

The cases in which public entities entrusted with the performance of public investments are subject to the application of Article 102 TFEU are likely to occur less often than potential breaches of Article 101 TFEU. Such cases shall occur where contracting authorities conducting public investments exercise a dominant position in a specific market.

Once the difficult test of qualifying such entities as "undertakings" is passed, because such undertakings are, in most cases, contracting authorities or contracting entities for the purpose of public procurement directives, most contracts will be awarded following competitive procedures. The existence of tender procedures renders less likely allegations of unreasonable purchase price, unless the price in the offer is further reduced by negotiations with the bidders[130] as well as allegations concerning unusual unbalanced contractual provisions.[131]

Amongst unbalanced contractual provisions the practice has revealed those related to late payments,[132] but following the Directive 2011/7 on combating late payment in commercial transactions, transposed into the Romanian legal system by Law 72/2012, any contractual provision stipulating a payment due date that is longer than the maximum terms allowed[133] shall be null and void.

Nevertheless, late payments by the contracting authority may occur in violation of the contract terms,[134] and the practice of works contracts concluded by the Romanian authorities is relevant in this respect. This continued practice has led to

---

[129] Albert Sánchez-Graells, *Public Procurement and Competition: Some Challenges Arising from Recent Developments in EU Public Procurement Law*, in Christopher Bovis, *Research Handbook on EU Public Procurement Law*, forthcoming (2016), available at SSRN: http://ssrn.com/abstract=2206502 (last accessed on September 29, 2015), p. 36.

[130] Sue Arrowsmith, *The Law of Public and Utilities Procurement. Regulation in the EU and UK, op. cit.*, p. 336–337.

[131] Jennifer Skilbeck, *Just When Is a Public Body an "Undertaking"? Fenin and BetterCare Compared*, (2003) 4, Public Procurement Law Review, NA75–77, Catriona Munro, *Competition Law and Public Procurement: Two Sides of the Same Coin?, op. cit.*, p. 358.

[132] Case T- 319/99 *FENIN v. Commission* [2003], note 33 above.

[133] Under law 72/2012, contracting authorities may not include in contracts to which they are party payment delays longer than 30 days, except for cases where payment delays are set at a maximum of 60 days from the date of delivery by the private contractor of goods, works and services.

[134] Sue Arrowsmith, *The Law of Public and Utilities Procurement. Regulation in the EU and UK, op. cit.*, p. 337.

the accumulation of arrears in the public budgets, which seriously hindered the inclusion of further expenditure in the budgets upon their approval, as most available budgetary resources had to be directed for payment of arrears. The solution[135] adopted by the legislator was the limitation of goods, services and works received under ongoing public contracts only to those that may be paid for under the current budget lines. For implementing this solution, upon the approval of the prevailing budgets the contracting authorities are required to notify their contractors on the budgeted amounts available and further adjust the contracts accordingly in respect of deliverables and payments. The mere existence of detailed rules aimed at solving the issue of arrears is an indication of its pervasiveness. Whilst the arrears are defined by law as debts overdue for more than 90 days after their due date, the applicable rules shall not concern payment delays of less than 90 days. In addition, such restrictions provided by law for preventing accumulation of arrears are only applicable to public entities financed from public budgets but not to public undertakings. Consequently, this practice of late payments may further trigger application of article 102 TFEU to contracts entered for performance of public investments.

## 5.7 Conclusions

Core competition rules comprised in Articles 101 and 102 TFEU may be incident on activities performed by the public entities (public authorities and public undertakings) for the achievement of public investments, both in respect of the procurement procedures conducted for the award of underlying contracts and in respect of the actual contract performance. Irrespective of the public or private financing of public investments, the competition principle will apply to the design of all procurement procedures, including those conducted under the 2014 Concessions Directive as well as those related to contracts excluded from the ambit of the EU procurement directives.

As a preliminary condition for the application of Articles 101 and 102 TFEU to both the award and the performance of contracts entered for the achievement of public investments, the qualification of public entities as undertakings in the sense upheld by the ECJ case law may lead to specific outcomes due to the particular structure of concession-type contracts. In such contracts, the influence of the public entities on the actual performance of the services to the public continues after the contract execution, in terms of supervision and monitoring of compliance with the levels of services and even by participation to the financial results. Consequently, there are arguments for qualifying the activity of the public entity as being of an

[135] As provided by Article 431(2) of the Public Finances Law (no. 500/2002, as further amended), and by Article 41 of the Local Public Finances Law (no. 273/2006, as further amended).

economic nature and therefore lead to the conclusion that the procurement of such services and works that will be the infrastructure for public services falls within the ambit of competition law. Furthermore, during the performance of both public contracts and concession contracts related to the achievement of public investments, various cases of application of core competition rules may occur.

The impact of competition law rules on public investment projects is a common element of both public and private financing structures. Amongst the contracts entered into by public entities, concession and related contracts are those that are most likely to generate distortions to competition, especially due to their long duration and the need to adapt the contract to maintain the economic balance. Consequently, competition law rules, as provided by national law, but mostly by the EU law (including the relevant ECJ jurisprudence) are an important part of the legal regime of public investments.

# Part III
# Jurisdictional Challenges to the Consistent Application of Articles 101 and 102 TFEU

# Chapter 6
# European Cartel Criminalization and Regulation 1/2003: Avoiding Potential Problems

**Peter Whelan**

## 6.1 Introduction

In recent years, debate has been ongoing within Europe concerning the introduction and maintenance of criminal (i.e., custodial) sanctions for cartel activity. This debate has been and continues to be a lively and interesting one. Many issues have been considered in the literature; they include, for example: the necessity and appropriateness of such sanctions; the effectiveness of such sanctions in achieving deterrence; the relevance of public views on the morality of cartel activity; the issue of human rights; difficulties associated with international enforcement cooperation; and the interaction between criminalisation and (administrative) leniency programmes. Clearly, this debate is far from academic. In fact one can detect a growing tendency within the EU to criminalise 'hard core' cartel activity. In this context, it is frequently argued (although far from universally accepted) that this type of enforcement is superior to administrative enforcement in achieving the deterrence of 'hard core' cartel activity. It is submitted that, while the criminalisation of cartels has some merit in theory, it also engenders significant theoretical, legal and practical problems that need to be overcome if criminalisation is to be as effective as claimed.[1] One of the major challenges in this context is the challenge of respecting the dictates of EU law, in particular those contained within Regulation 1/2003, the EU Regulation that implements the EU competition law rules contained within Articles 101 and 102 of the Treaty on the Functioning of the European Union

[1] See Whelan, P., *The Criminalization of European Cartel Enforcement: Theoretical, Legal, and Practical Challenges*, Oxford University Press, 2014.

P. Whelan (✉)
School of Law, University of Leeds, Leeds, UK
e-mail: p.whelan@leeds.ac.uk



A. Almăşan, P. Whelan (eds.), *The Consistent Application of EU Competition Law*, Studies in European Economic Law and Regulation 9,
DOI 10.1007/978-3-319-47382-6_6

('TFEU').[2] Indeed, as will be demonstrated below, that particular implementing Regulation, if applicable to cartel criminalisation within an EU Member State, can arguably have a significant impact on the content and operation of the national criminal cartel offence.

This chapter analyses in detail the potential impact of Regulation 1/2003 on the design and operation of a national criminal cartel offence and the extent to which there is scope to avoid such an impact in this context. It is divided into two sections. Section 6.2 makes the assumption that Regulation 1/2003 applies to the enforcement of a given national cartel offence and examines how it can impact upon the definition and the operation of the national criminal cartel offence. In doing so, it demonstrates both: how Regulation 1/2003 can be used to ensure a level of consistency in national criminal cartel enforcement; and how the pursuance of such consistency through the use of Regulation 1/2003 can have negative implications in the context of *criminal* antitrust enforcement. Section 6.3 analyses the assumption made in the earlier section and, in the process, examines how the national criminal cartel offence can be designed so as to reduce the scope for any (negative) impact of Regulation 1/2003. Taken together, these sections provide concrete advice to those European legislators that wish to implement a successful policy of cartel criminalisation while respecting the dictates of EU law.

## 6.2 Regulation 1/2003's Potential Impact on the Definition and Operation of the National Criminal Cartel Offence

Regulation 1/2003 was adopted in order *inter alia* to decentralise the enforcement of EU competition law and to clarify the relationship between the enforcement of EU competition law and the enforcement of national competition law. Regulation 1/2003 abolished the centralised notification and authorisation system established under Regulation 17/62 and replaced it with a system whereby Articles 101 and 102 TFEU would be directly applicable in full,[3] with the Commission, the NCAs and the national courts having the power to apply those particular provisions of EU law.[4] The main underlying rationales for the 'modernisation' of EU competition law through Regulation 1/2003 were to increase the application of Articles 101 and 102 TFEU at Member State level and to allow the Commission to prioritise its resources in those particular areas of competition policy where it can contribute significantly to the enforcement of the EU competition law rules.[5] Regulation 1/2003 provides

[2] *Council Regulation (EC) No 1/2003 of 16 December 2002 on the Implementation of the Rules on Competition Laid Down in Articles 81 and 82 of the Treaty* ('Regulation 1/2003'), [2003] OJ L1/1.

[3] Regulation 1/2003, Recital 4 and Article 1.

[4] See, e.g., *ibid.*, Articles 4, 5 and 6.

[5] De Smijter, E. and Kjølbye, L., 'The Enforcement System under Regulation 1/2003', in Faull, J. and Nikpay, A. (eds), *The EC Law of Competition*, 2nd Edition, Oxford University Press, Oxford, 2007, 89–91.

some scope for a potential (problematic) impact on the definition of the national criminal cartel offence as a result of its Article 3. The actual operation of the national criminal cartel offence can also arguably be (negatively) influenced as a result of, *inter alia*, Articles 11(6) and 35 of the Regulation.[6]

## 6.2.1 Impact on Definition: Article 3

Article 3(1) of Regulation 1/2003 provides that when the NCAs or national courts apply 'national competition law' to agreements, decisions by associations of undertakings or concerted practices[7] within the meaning of Article 101(1) TFEU *which may affect trade between Member States* within the meaning of that provision, they shall also apply Article 101 TFEU to such agreements etc. As a result, when there is no effect on trade, Member States may apply their national competition laws without applying Article 101 TFEU; but when there is an actual or potential effect on trade and Member States are applying their national competition law to the agreement etc. then they must also apply Article 101 TFEU to that agreement etc. This particular rule ensures that parallel application of both EU competition law and national competition law is legally possible following the adoption of Regulation 1/2003,[8] just like it had been under Regulation 17/62.[9] It also ensures that 'the EU competition rules are applied to all cases within their scope and are not avoided by applying only national law'.[10] According to Recital 8 of Regulation 1/2003, Article

[6] Other articles of Regulation 1/2003 also have the potential to impact negatively upon the operation of the criminal cartel offence, such as the article imposing an obligation on the NCAs to inform the Commission in writing after commencing the first formal investigative measure in applying Article 101 TFEU: Article 11(3). However, it is submitted that Articles 11(6) and 35 provide a sufficient illustration of the potential (problematic) impact of Regulation 1/2003 for present purposes. In addition, there may be disadvantages for the criminalized regime if Regulation 1/2003 *does not apply*; for example: 'it would not be possible to use Articles [*sic.*] 12 or 22 of the Regulation as a legal basis for exchanging information with and/or requesting or granting assistance in investigations to other competition authorities': Lowe, P., 'Preventing and Sanctioning Anticompetitive Conduct: Effective Use of Administrative and Criminal Sanctions, Leniency Programmes and Private Action in the EU', in Hawk, B. (ed.), *International Antitrust Law & Policy: Fordham Corporate Law 2006*, Juris Publishing, 2007, 97. This point is not developed here however as the aim of this section is to analyse the *negative* impact of Regulation 1/2003 on the enforcement of the national criminal cartel offence.

[7] In the remainder of this chapter, the phrase 'agreements, decisions by associations of undertakings or concerted practices' has been shorted to 'agreements etc.'.

[8] De Smijter and Kjølbye (n. 5), 96.

[9] See Case 14/68, *Walt Wilhelm v. Bundeskartellamt* [1969] ECR 1, [9] (where it was held that national competition law enforcement could occur so long as it did not 'prejudice the full and uniform application of Community law or the effects of measures taken or to be taken to implement it').

[10] Rose, V. and Bailey, D. (eds), *Bellamy & Child – European Union Law of Competition*, 7th Edition, Oxford University Press, Oxford, 2013, 64. See also Wils, W., *Principles of European Antitrust Enforcement*, Hart Publishing, Oxford, 2005, 41.

3(1) helps to ensure 'the effective enforcement of the Community competition rules and the proper functioning of the cooperation mechanisms contained in this Regulation'.

From Article 3(1) of Regulation 1/2003 it is clear that the concept of 'effect on trade' plays a central role in determining the jurisdictional extent of EU competition law: it is the concept that draws the 'boundary line' between national competition law enforcement where EU competition law does not play a part and national competition law enforcement where EU competition law must play a part.[11] Given that the concept of 'effect on trade' has only a jurisdictional role to play, it 'has been interpreted broadly, although it is accepted that the EU has no jurisdiction over cases in which the effects of an agreement … are confined to one Member State'.[12] According to the Court of Justice, to establish the requisite effect on trade 'it must be possible to foresee with a sufficient degree of probability on the basis of a set of objective factors of law or of fact that the agreement in question may have an influence, direct or indirect, actual or potential, on the pattern of trade between Member States'.[13] According to Marco Colino, as a practical issue 'it will not be difficult to show that most transactions of any real size are capable of affecting trade between Member States', and that an 'extreme reading' of the Court of Justice's pronouncements on this concept 'would permit the application of EU law to almost any situation'.[14]

Article 3(2) of Regulation 1/2003 contains the so-called 'convergence rule' whereby the application of national competition law may not lead to the prohibition of agreements etc. which may affect trade between Member States but which do not restrict competition within the meaning of Article 101(1) TFEU, which fulfil the conditions of Article 101(3) TFEU or which are covered by a Regulation for the application of Article 101(3) TFEU (a so-called 'block exemption Regulation'). This effectively means that if there is an effect on trade and national competition law is being applied alongside EU competition law, then national competition law cannot treat agreements etc. more strictly than EU competition law. Article 3(2) is a 'directly applicable rule that can be relied on before national courts, which implies that any measure adopted in breach of that rule would be inapplicable and unenforceable'.[15] The decentralisation of the enforcement of the EU competition law rules is therefore 'compensated with the obligation imposed on national courts to set aside divergent national rules where the jurisdictional criteria of Community

[11] Case 22/78, *Hugin Kassaregister AB and Hugin Cash Registers Ltd v. Commission* [1979] ECR 1869, [17].

[12] Jones, A. and Sufrin, B., *EU Competition Law: Text, Cases and Materials*, 4th Edition, Oxford University Press, Oxford, 2011, 178.

[13] Case 56/65, *Société La Technique Minière Ulm v. Maschinenbau* [1966] ECR 235, 249.

[14] Marco Colino, S., *Competition Law of the EU and UK*, 7th Edition, Oxford University Press, Oxford, 2011, 52–53.

[15] European Commission, *Commission Staff Working Paper Accompanying the Communication from the Commission to the European Parliament and the Council – Report on the Functioning of Regulation 1/2003*, SEC(2009) 574 final, Brussels, 29 April 2009, 49.

law are met'.[16] The idea here is that Article 3(2) 'eliminates legal uncertainty coming out of concurrent application of national and Community law and directly contradicts fears of renationalisation' of competition law rules in the EU.[17] That said, Article 3(2) does not prevent stricter national competition laws from being applied to unilateral conduct, and there are further exceptions provided in Article 3(3).[18]

Assuming that Regulation 1/2003 applies to the criminal cartel offence, it is arguable that Article 3(1) and Article 3(2) can influence the content of a national criminal cartel offence, if only in those circumstances where there is an effect on trade due to the cartel in question. The argument runs as follows. If there is an effect on trade between Member States due to the cartel which forms the substance of the criminal prosecution then the national authority enforcing the cartel offence must also apply Article 101 TFEU: Article 3(1). In doing so, the national authority cannot allow for the application of the national cartel offence to result in a stricter prohibition of the cartel than would occur under Article 101 TFEU: Article 3(2). If the (criminal) cartel in question would not have violated the prohibition in Article 101(1) TFEU, would have fulfilled the criteria of Article 101(3) TFEU or would have been covered by a block exemption then it could not form the subject matter for the national criminal sanction. EU law, in other words, can ensure that the national cartel offence is restricted in its application when there is an effect on trade: the scope of the national cartel offence can be affected.

This particular argument, if accepted, is problematic for national criminal cartel enforcement for a number of reasons. First, it makes the concept of 'effect on trade' relevant in a criminal trial. If EU competition law would be less strict in terms of prohibiting the cartel than the national cartel offence it would be in the interests of the defendant to argue that her cartel had an actual or potential effect on trade in the hope that the criminal judge would apply the 'convergence rule' in Article 3(2) in her favour. In fact, given how broadly this concept is defined, it is not unlikely that a defendant would try to rely upon it to secure a more lenient treatment in the criminal courts. This should be avoided. Indeed, the undesirability of having the effect on trade criterion analysed in a court of law was one of the reasons why the parallel application for national and EU competition law is allowed[19] and why the Commission's original legislative proposal for exclusive application of Article 101 TFEU to agreements etc. having an effect on trade was not followed.[20] Second, it

---

[16] Boskovits, K., 'Modernization and the Role of National courts: Institutional Choices, Power Relations, and Substantive Implications', in Lianos, I. and Kokorris, I. (eds), *The Reform of EC Competition Law: New Challenges*, Kluwer Law International, Amsterdam, 2010, 99.

[17] Pijetlovic, K., 'Reform of EC Antitrust Enforcement: Criticism of the New System is Highly Exaggerated' (2004) 25(6) European Competition Law Review 356, 360.

[18] Article 3(3) will be considered below when the assumption that Regulation 1/2003 applies to cartel offence is considered; see Section 6.3, *infra*.

[19] See De Smijter and Kjølbye (n 5), 98.

[20] See European Commission, *Proposal for a Council Regulation on the implementation of the rules on competition laid down in Articles 81 and 82 of the Treaty and amending Regulations (EEC) No 1017/68, (EEC) No 2988/74, (EEC) No 4056/86 and (EEC) No 3975/87*, COM(2000) 582 final, Brussels, 27 September 2000, Article 3.

opens the way for economic arguments to be made in the context of a criminal trial, something that the legislator may have been keen to avoid in drafting the criminal cartel offence in such a way that it does not require a finding of a violation of Article 101 TFEU. In particular it brings in the Article 101(3) 'defence' through the back-door (if it is not expressly contained in the national criminal cartel offence).[21] Harding and Joshua seem to acknowledge this type of problem when they posit that with the enforcement of the UK Cartel Offence 'there is still some possibility that the defence in criminal proceedings could exploit a potential "Euro-defence" (i.e. raise some doubt as to whether there was a violation of Article 101)'.[22] Finally, by allowing Regulation 1/2003 to dictate the content of the cartel offence (in particular, by requiring it to provide a defence in the form of Article 101(3) TFEU) the criminalized jurisdiction may be restricted in its ability to generate a moral norm against cartel activity in the hope that cartelists will internalise the norm, thereby reducing the cost of criminal cartel enforcement. When a defence along the lines of Article 101(3) TFEU is provided it may well foster an (arguably already existing) perception among EU citizens that competition law enforcement (including its criminal variant) is about 'satisfying somewhat technical and arcane regulations rather than about preventing conspiracies that cost EU consumers large amounts of money'.[23] The existence of Article 101(3) TFEU as a defence in a criminal cartel regime communicates the message that the criminality of cartel activity (in particular its moral wrongfulness) is ambiguous.

### 6.2.2 *Impact on Operation: Article 11(6) and Article 35*

Article 11(6) of Regulation 1/2003 contains the European Commission's power to withdraw a case from the national competition authorities. The provision stipulates that the 'initiation by the Commission of proceedings for the adoption of a decision under Chapter III [of Regulation 1/2003] shall relieve the competition authorities of the Member States of their competence to apply' Articles 101 and 102 TFEU. It further provides that if an NCA is 'already acting on a case, the Commission shall only initiate proceedings after consulting' with that NCA. As noted in Recital 35 of Regulation 1/2003, the effects of Article 11(6) apply to all NCAs (which can include courts), but there is an exception to the general rule: 'where a prosecuting authority

---

[21] *Cf.* Furse, M., *The Criminal Law of Competition in the UK and in the US: Failure and Success*, Edward Elgar, Cheltenham, UK and Northampton, MA, USA, 2012, 122.

[22] Harding, C. and Joshua, J., *Regulating Cartels in Europe*, 2nd Edition, Oxford University Press, Oxford, 2010, 348. Admittedly, while their comment is located in a section in their book entitled 'Problems at the interface with European law', it may be explained on the basis that a Euro-defence could be understood as flowing merely from the use of the definitional element of 'dishonesty' in the UK Cartel Offence (rather than from Articles 3(1) and (2) of Regulation 1/2003). Either way, their anxiety about the existence of a Euro-defence is equivalent in nature to that identified above.

[23] Massey, P., 'Criminal Sanctions for Competition Law: A Review of Irish Experience' (2004) 1(1) Competition Law Review 23, 32.

brings a case before a separate judicial authority, Article 11(6) should apply to the prosecuting authority subject to the conditions of Article 35(4)'. Article 35(4) therefore ensures that Member States can arrange their national procedures 'so as formally to avoid the Commission withdrawing a case from a national court in circumstances where cases are brought before the court by a prosecutor'[24] (as a criminal cartel case would surely be). In addition, Article 11(6) does not apply to courts if they are acting as review courts: Article 35(3). Guidance on the operation of Article 11(6) is provided in the Commission Notice which is dedicated to the issue of cooperation with the NCAs.[25]

The existence of Article 11(6), which is generally understood to be 'central to the functioning of Regulation 1/2003',[26] can be rationalised on the basis of the consistent application of the EU competition law rules: '[i]f the competition rules are to be applied consistently and, at the same time, the network [i.e., the ECN] is to be managed in the best possible way, it is essential to retain the rule that the competition authorities are automatically relieved of their competence if the Commission initiates its own proceedings'.[27] From a reading of the Regulation as a whole (including Article 3(1) thereof) it is clear that Article 11(6) relieves the NCA not only of its power to enforce EU competition law but also of its power to enforce national competition law.[28] However, following the conclusion of the Commission's proceedings, there is a revival of the relevant NCA's jurisdiction to apply both EU competition law and its national law,[29] subject to the obligation in Article 16 of Regulation 1/2003 not to adopt a decision which runs counter to the findings of the Commission.[30] The ability of the Commission under Article 11(6) to restrict the competence of the NCAs to enforce competition law is 'a powerful weapon' and one which gives the Commission 'considerable leverage over an NCA when it disapproves of the decision it is about to adopt'.[31] That said, to this author's knowledge Article 11(6) has not been used to date to 'correct' the approach of a Member State.[32]

If Regulation 1/2003 applies to the enforcement of a national cartel offence then Article 11(6) of the Regulation has the potential to influence the operation of that

---

[24] De Smijter and Kjølbye (n. 5), 162. It seems in fact that Article 35(4) 'was introduced to accommodate the sensitivities of certain Member States where the first decision-maker is a court': *ibid.*

[25] See European Commission, *Commission Notice on Cooperation within the Network of Competition Authorities*, [2004] OJ C101/03, [50]–[57].

[26] Whish, R. and Bailey, D., *Competition* Law, Oxford University Press, Oxford, 2012, 265.

[27] Regulation 1/2003, Recital 17.

[28] Case C-17/10, *Toshiba Corp v. Czech Competition Authority*, Judgment of 14 February 2012, ECLI:EU:C:2012:72, [72] *et seq.*

[29] See *ibid.*, [79]–[80].

[30] Rose and Bailey (n. 10), 1173.

[31] Jones and Sufrin (n. 12), 1162.

[32] See also European Commission, *Commission Staff Working Paper Accompanying the Communication from the Commission to the European Parliament and the Council – Report on the Functioning of Regulation 1/2003*, SEC(2009) 574 final, Brussels, 29 April 2009, 76–77.

national offence.[33] Specifically the Commission, in theory at least, would hold the power to relieve the prosecuting authority of its competence to lead a criminal cartel prosecution in front of a criminal court, in effect bringing the national criminal proceedings to an end. This is a relatively uncomplicated conclusion, provided of course that the assumption is correct that Regulation 1/2003 applies to the enforcement of the national cartel offence in the first place. However, when *private* criminal prosecutions are allowed under the national regime the situation becomes more complicated. Indeed, it might be argued that it is at least questionable whether Article 11(6) could bring the national criminal proceedings to a close when a private criminal prosecution is at issue concerning the national cartel offence: the private prosecutor would not exactly be a 'competition authority' in the literal sense of the phrase and would therefore not be subject to the dictates of Article 11(6), which relieves the *competition authorities of the Member States* of their competence to apply Article 101 TFEU. It would all depend on whether: (i) the criminal court would be deemed to be a national competition authority for the purposes of Article 11(6) of Regulation 1/2003; and (ii) and whether Article 35(4) of that Regulation would be applicable in the context of a private prosecution. The criminal court could certainly be a national competition authority, as Article 35(1) of the Regulation provides that the designated authorities 'may include courts'. Whether a given national criminal court would be a designated national competition authority would of course depend on the actions of the Member State in question regarding its designation of its national competition authorities.[34] In addition, it seems very likely, given its wording, that Article 35(4) would not be relevant, therefore allowing for Article 11(6) to apply directly to the criminal court in the context of a private prosecution (provided that the court were a designated authority for the purpose of that, latter Article). Article 35(4) essentially provides that where the 'authority' prosecuting the case is separate from the judicial authority deciding the case then the direct effects of Article 11(6) shall be limited to that authority prosecuting the case. But Article 11(6), as was noted, only applies to the 'competition authorities of the Member States'. Relying upon this fact, one can argue that the term 'authority' in Article 35(4) actually means a (public) national competition authority, and therefore that Article 35(4) has no bearing on the operation of Article 11(6) in the context of a private criminal investigation. To this author, this seems the most sensible interpretation.

The argument that Article 11(6) can influence the operation of a criminal cartel offence may not be a mere academic argument. Its effects can possibly be detected in the approach to criminal cartel enforcement adopted in Ireland, a jurisdiction

[33] Wils appears to agree: Wils, W., 'Is Criminalization of EU Competition Law the Answer?', in Cseres, K., Schinkel, M. and Vogelaar, F. (eds), *Criminalization of Competition Law Enforcement: Economic and Legal Implications for the EU Member States*, Edward Elgar Publishing, Cheltenham, 2006, 73.

[34] If the criminal court is not a 'designated' competition authority under Regulation 1/2003 another issue arises: the issue as to whether the criminal court could in fact enforce Article 101 TFEU at all. This issue is considered directly below.

with a criminal cartel offence that is clearly based upon the specific wording of Article 101(1) TFEU. Massey and Cooke note that Irish criminal cartel enforcement has focused entirely on relatively localised businesses, and that this particular enforcement policy is unlikely to change for a number of reasons, chief of which is the potential impact of Regulation 1/2003 when larger, perhaps EU-wide cartels are prosecuted.[35] While Massey and Cooke do not mention Article 11(6) and instead focus their energies on highlighting that Article 3 of Regulation 1/2003 will require the enforcement of Article 101 TFEU alongside the national cartel offence contained in Section 4 of the Competition Act 2002 (if there is an effect on trade between Member States), their analysis can nonetheless be extended to Article 11(6). In short, the focus on domestic cartels could well be explained by a desire to avoid the cooperation mechanisms in Regulation 1/2003 (which come into play as a result of Article 3 thereof), including the specific cooperation mechanism contained in Article 11(6).

Another provision of Regulation 1/2003 that can impact upon the operation of a national cartel offence is Article 35(1). That particular Article provides that the 'Member States shall designate the competition authority or authorities responsible for the application of [Articles 101 and 102 TFEU] in such a way the provisions of [Regulation 1/2003] are effectively complied with'. The argument here is that if the criminal courts are not in fact designated as competition authorities for the purposes of Regulation 1/2003, and EU competition law must be applied if the national cartel offence is being enforced (due to the existence of an effect on trade), then those criminal courts will not have the jurisdiction to apply EU competition law and therefore will not have the jurisdiction to apply the national cartel offence. This type of argument was presented by counsel in the prosecution by the UK Office of Fair Trading of BA executives accused of fixing fuel surcharges on long haul flights contrary to Section 188 of the Enterprise Act 2002.[36] It relies upon the assumption that only those national competition authorities and/or national courts designated as competition authorities for the purpose of Regulation 1/2003 have the competence to enforce the provisions of EU competition law. The Court of Appeal in the *IB* case rejected the defendants' argument that the Crown Court did not have the jurisdiction to rule on whether the UK Cartel Offence was committed due to the fact that the Crown Court had not been designated as a competition authority for the purposes of Regulation 1/2003.[37] In so ruling, the Court of Appeal noted that there was nothing in the Regulation itself which states that only a designated competition authority has the competence to enforce EU competition law and that it 'makes excellent sense' for the directly-effective Regulation to enable the Member States to enforce the EU

---

[35] Massey, P. and Cooke, J., 'Competition Offences in Ireland: The Regime and Its Results', in Beaton-Wells, C. and Ezrachi, A. (eds), *Criminalising Cartels: A Critical Interdisciplinary Study of an International Regulatory Movement*, Hart Publishing, Oxford, 2011, 128. See also Furse (n. 21), 187.

[36] *IB v. The Queen* [2009] EWCA Crim 2575, [19].

[37] *Ibid.*, [38].

competition law rules without the need for domestic legislation.[38] While this appears to be a sensible approach to the issue, it is obviously not the end of the matter for European antitrust criminalization. Only a ruling from the Court of Justice in a preliminary reference request would put this question to rest once and for all. If it were required to rule on this issue, it would be advised to follow the lead of the Court of Appeal, particularly if it wished to see national criminal cartel enforcement develop without complicating matters by requiring the designation of the Member States' criminal courts as national competition authorities.

## 6.3 Dealing with the Potential Impact Through Legislative Drafting

To minimise the problematic impact of Regulation 1/2003 on the content and the operation of the national criminal cartel offence one could, from the outset, base the criminal cartel offence completely on the cartel prohibition in Article 101(1) TFEU and allow for a defence based on Article 101(3) TFEU. In other words one could link the cartel offence to the EU-level cartel prohibition, thereby avoiding the operation of the 'convergence rule' in a criminal trial. This would ensure that from the very creation of the criminal cartel offence one can be certain of its elements and of any potential defence to its commission. Regulation 1/2003, then, would not throw up nasty surprises for the prosecution in the context of a criminal trial, such as providing for the introduction of the defence of Article 101(3) TFEU through the backdoor when an effect on trade between Member States can be identified. This of course brings with it the disadvantage of dealing with such a defence in a criminal trial. It introduces the potential, then, for economic evidence to be considered as part of the criminal trial, something that legislatures can be keen to avoid.[39] Indeed, creating a national 'stand-alone' criminal cartel offence (applicable to individual cartelists) which does not include an exemption/exception-type defence acknowledges in effect that Article 101 TFEU 'is ill-suited to form the basis of a criminal charge'[40] and helps to ensure that the criminal cartel offence is underpinned by moral norms which are simple and unequivocal, i.e. of the 'thou shall not' variety, thereby facilitating educative efforts.[41] In fact, for related reasons, Ireland has been criticised for not adopting such an approach when it introduced criminal antitrust sanctions.[42] To avoid any argument concerning lack of competence based on Article 35(1) of Regulation 1/2003, the criminalized jurisdiction would also be advised to

---

[38] *Ibid.*

[39] See, e.g.: BIS, *Growth Competition and the Competition Regime: Government Response to Consultation*, March 2012, [6.9]; and DTI, *A World Class Competition Regime*, Cm 5233, July 2001, [7.30].

[40] Joshua, J., 'Flawed Thinking About Price Fixers', *Financial Times*, London, 2 August 2001.

[41] See Stucke, M., 'Morality and Antitrust' [2006] Columbia Business Law Review 443, 527.

[42] Massey (n. 23), 38.

designate the criminal courts as national competition authorities for the purposes of the Regulation. Of course, all of these measures are also inherently limited in that they do not remove the (theoretical) possibility for the Commission to use Article 11(6) to take jurisdiction over the criminal cartel case from the criminal court.

Central to the potential impact of Regulation 1/2003 is the concept of effect on trade. Where there is no effect on trade between Member States due to the cartel under investigation then the EU competition law rules will not be applied (even if Regulation 1/2003 itself applies to the enforcement of the national cartel offence) and the problems due to the potential application of Regulation 1/2003 could be avoided. If one were very concerned about the negative impact of Regulation 1/2003, one might be inclined to argue for the creation of a criminal cartel offence that only applies to those cartels which do not have an effect on trade. But such an approach would be on very doggy legal ground, so to speak. This is due to the principle of equivalence,[43] a general principle of EU law which, broadly speaking, ensures that the penalties provided under national law for the violation of Article 101 TFEU 'must at least be equivalent in effectiveness and dissuasiveness to the sanctions they provide for comparable violations of their national laws'.[44] Where criminal sanctions for violation of Article 101 TFEU were not available (due to the existence of an effect on trade) and such sanctions would be available under national competition law (albeit only when there is no effect on trade) the criminal cartel law would arguably violate the principle of effectiveness contrary to the dictates of EU law, provided of course that the criminal cartel offence could be understood as a violation comparable to Article 101 TFEU for the purposes of that particular principle. This would only be so, of course, where it can be established that imprisonment for cartel activity is a more effective and dissuasive sanction than the (non-custodial) sanction provided in national law for violation of Article 101 TFEU.[45]

If one wished to avoid the impact of Regulation 1/2003 without running the risk of violating the principle of equivalence one could simply follow the (apparent) Irish enforcement policy and ensure that the cartels that the authority prosecutes are always local in nature and do not have an effect on trade. This would ensure autonomy in practice for the criminalized jurisdiction over the content and the operation of the criminal cartel offence, but unfortunately it would also bring with it a number of problems concerning the achievement of the underlying criminal enforcement objectives. For a start, if business executives are aware of such an enforcement policy then they will be incentivised to engage in cartel activity on a large scale (which ensures an obvious effect on trade) as they will know that criminal sanctions will not be pursued against them. This clearly reduces the deterrent effect of the law.

[43] See, e.g., Case C-231/96, *Edilizia Industriale Siderurgica Srl (Edis) v. Ministero delle Finanze* [1998] ECR I-4951, [36].

[44] Wils (n. 33), 72.

[45] On the effectiveness of imprisonment as a method of achieving the underlying enforcement aims of antitrust law, see Whelan (n. 1), Chapters 3 and 4.

Indeed, as noted during the Committee stage of the passage of the UK Cartel Offence through Parliament:

> [r]unning the risk of sending small offenders to prison or fining them heavily, and of subjecting large offenders to civil rather than criminal sanctions makes a nonsense of the deterrence argument.[46]

Such a policy would also cause problems with the achievement of retribution as the most serious cartels (i.e., those with an effect on trade and, therefore, presumably with the highest degrees of social harmfulness) would not be subjected to criminal punishment, unlike the less serious, localised cartels. Such an enforcement policy would clearly not be ideal. What would be better would be for the criminalized jurisdiction to ensure that Regulation 1/2003 did not apply at all to the enforcement of the national criminal cartel offence.

All of the above discussion of the potential impact of Regulation 1/2003 has proceeded on the assumption that Regulation 1/2003 would apply to the enforcement of the national cartel offence in the first place. It is clear that the impact of Article 3, Article 11(6) or Article 35 will only be felt if the Regulation actually applies to the enforcement of the national criminal cartel offence: if the national cartel offence is not subject to Regulation 1/2003 then of course it is not subject to its Articles, and the problems of the impact of Regulation 1/2003 will not exist. In order to provide an insight into how one should draft a criminal cartel offence in order to avoid the application of Regulation 1/2003 one should of course understand when that particular Regulation would indeed apply to a criminal cartel offence; with this knowledge one can try to shape the national cartel offence so that Regulation 1/2003 does not apply to it, thereby avoiding the problems associated with Articles 3, 11(6) and 35. For this reason, the assumption in question needs to be analysed in detail.

Central to the resolution of the issue as to whether Regulation 1/2003 applies to the enforcement of a national cartel offence are Recitals 8 and 9 and Article 3(3) of the Regulation. Recital 8 provides *inter alia* that Regulation 1/2003 'does not apply to national laws which impose criminal sanctions on natural persons except to the extent that such sanctions are the means whereby competition rules applying to undertakings are enforced'.[47] Recital 9 states that Regulation 1/2003, which has been adopted to implement Articles 101 and 102 TFEU,

> does not preclude Member States from implementing on their territory national legislation, which protects other legitimate interests provided that such legislation is compatible with general principles and other provisions of Community law. In so far as such national legislation pursues predominantly an objective different from that of protecting competition on the market, the competition authorities and courts of the Member States may apply such legislation on their territory.

---

[46] Nigel Waterson MP, House of Commons Debates, 10 April 2002, Column 152. This point is also made in Joshua, J., 'D.O.A: Can the UK Cartel Offence be Resuscitated?', in Beaton-Wells, C. and Ezrachi, A. (eds), *Criminalising Cartels: A Critical Interdisciplinary Study of an International Regulatory Movement*, Hart Publishing, Oxford, 2011, Footnote 83.

[47] For the purpose of this chapter this phrase is referred to as 'the relevant sentence in Recital 8'.

Article 3(3) provides *inter alia* that without prejudice to general principles and other provisions of EU law, Articles 3(1) and 3(2) of Regulation 1/2003 'do not preclude the application of provisions of national law that predominantly pursue an objective different from that pursued by' Articles 101 and 102 TFEU.

One possible reading of these provisions is that a national criminal cartel offence which only applies to individuals and which, therefore, does not apply to undertakings (corporations) is not subjected at all to Regulation 1/2003. This is the position adopted by the Office of Fair Trading ('OFT') (now the Competition and Markets Authority ('CMA')) in its understanding of whether Regulation 1/2003 applies to the enforcement of the UK Cartel Offence,[48] a position that appears to be supported by a number of academics.[49] The argument depends upon a rather restricted and literal interpretation of the relevant sentence in Recital 8. The OFT argued in effect that as the Cartel Offence only targets individuals it is not a means by which competition rules applying to undertakings are enforced;[50] consequently, as a result of Recital 8, Regulation 1/2003 does not apply to it.[51] The point here is that the term 'means whereby competition rules applying to undertakings are enforced' is understood as implying a requirement that undertakings be subjected to the criminal cartel offence alongside individuals. Where undertakings cannot be made subject to criminal proceedings for cartel activity, so the argument runs, the criminal cartel offence cannot be understood as a 'means whereby competition rules applying to undertakings are enforced'. This interpretation has the advantage of simplicity: if one wishes to avoid any impact of Regulation 1/2003 on the operation and the content of the national criminal cartel offence, all one has to do is ensure that it applies to individuals and not to undertakings. However, such an interpretation can be criticised on the basis that it not only ignores the fact that undertakings can in some circumstances be constituted by a mere individual (provided they are carrying out an economic activity),[52] but also that it gives too much importance to what is admittedly merely a Recital (as opposed to an Article) in the Regulation. In addition, this type of interpretation of the applicability of Regulation 1/2003 in this context would clearly not be acceptable to those who wish to see the Commission have the power to influence the operation of competition policy in the Member States (even when it

[48] See OFT, *Modernisation – Understanding Competition Law*, OFT 442, December 2004, [4.21]–[4.22]. See also Bloom, M., 'Response: A Significant Step Forward: The UK Criminalization Initiative' (2002) 17 Antitrust 59, 59, who at the time was the Director of Competition Enforcement at the OFT, commenting on a draft of Regulation 1/2003 (that contained the same phrase as the relevant sentence in Recital 8).

[49] See, e.g.: Riley, A., 'EC Antitrust Modernisation: The Commission Does Very Nicely – Thank You! Part 1: Regulation 1 and the Notification Burden' (2003) 24(11) European Competition Law Review 604, 606–607; and Furse, M. and Nash, S., *The Cartel Offence*, Hart Publishing, Oxford, 2004, 9–10. See, however, Furse's reconsideration of this issue in Furse (n. 21), 124 *et seq.*

[50] OFT (n. 48), [4.21].

[51] *Ibid.*, [4.22].

[52] See, e.g.: IV/29.559, *RAI/UNITEL*, Commission Decision, 15 June 1978, [1978] OJ L157/39 (opera singers); and IV/28.996, *Reuter/BASF*, Commission Decision, 26 July 1976, [1976] OJ L254/40 (individual inventors).

is dictated towards individuals as such rather than undertakings). Indeed in a 2004 letter addressed to the Director General of the Swedish Competition Authority, the then Director General of DG Competition set out the Commission's thinking on the applicability of Regulation 1/2003 to a proposed Swedish national cartel offence and in the process expressly disavowed the interpretation favoured by the OFT, noting that it 'fail[s] to find any support for such conclusion in the Regulation'.[53]

Another possible reading of the relevant provisions in Regulation 1/2003 is provided by Wils, who argues that the relevant sentence in Recital 8

> merely specifies, with regard to national laws which impose criminal sanctions on natural persons, what already follows from Article 3(3) of Regulation 1/2003, namely that Article 3(1) and (2) of this Regulation do not preclude the application of provisions of national law that predominantly pursue an objective different from that pursued by [Articles 101 and 102 TFEU].[54]

What Wils in effect proposes is that one should interpret the relevant sentence in Recital 8 (which he admittedly, and rightly, finds hard to understand[55]) to mean nothing more than that the national criminal cartel offence must have the same predominant objective as Articles 101 and 102 TFEU for Regulation 1/2003 to apply to it.[56] Wils offers four points in support of his broad interpretation of the true meaning of the phrase 'means whereby competition rules applying to undertakings are enforced'.[57] First, the relevant sentence in Recital 8 is located at the end of the first of the two recitals which accompany Article 3 of Regulation 1/2003.[58] Second, the phrase 'competition rules applying to undertakings' in used in the chapter and section headings which cover Articles 101 and 102 TFEU.[59] Third, it is clear from Article 5, read alongside Article 12(3) of Regulation 1/2003, that the Regulation 'applies in principle to all types of penalties which national law may provide for violations of [Articles 101 and 102 TFEU], including criminal sanctions on natural persons'.[60] Finally, the purpose of Article 3 of Regulation 1/2003 (i.e., ensuring that the NCAs or national courts do not circumvent the application of Regulation 1/2003 and, in particular, its cooperation mechanisms) would be undermined if a narrow interpretation of the relevant sentence in Recital 8 were adopted.[61] The European Commission appears to favour Wils's approach. Indeed, it has argued that a Swedish

[53] European Commission, *DG Competition's Reply to Questions Raised by the Swedish Competition Authority with Regard to SOU 2004:131*, Brussels, 29 April 2005, 3.

[54] Wils (n. 33), 74.

[55] Wils (n. 10), 42.

[56] Finding 'difficulty seeing how one could consider that the UK cartel offence predominantly pursues an objective different from that pursued by [Article 101 TFEU]', Wils believes that the UK Cartel Offence should 'be considered a means whereby competition rules to undertakings are enforced': Wils (n. 33), 74.

[57] See Wils (n. 10), 43.

[58] *Ibid.*

[59] *Ibid.*

[60] *Ibid.*

[61] *Ibid.*

proposal to introduce individual criminal cartel sanctions would have the same objective as the enforcement of Article 101 TFEU and that therefore 'the sanctioning of individuals [for cartel activity] would appear to be a means to influence the behaviour of the undertakings', a fact that ensures the applicability of Regulation 1/2003 to the future enforcement of the proposed cartel offence.[62]

There are potential problems, however, with Wils's approach. The first is that Recital 8 and Article 3(3) seem to perform different functions, and therefore interpreting the former of these provisions by relying upon the latter can be questioned. The sentence in Recital 8 – whatever it may mean – actually takes the enforcement of the national cartel offence outside of the scope of Regulation 1/2003 as a whole. Article 3(3) does not do this: if its conditions are fulfilled, it merely takes the enforcement of the criminal cartel offence outside of the scope of Articles 3(1) and 3(2). In practice there may be little difference of course: by removing the requirement to enforce EU competition law, Article 3(3) provides the scope for the national criminal cartel law enforcer to avoid enforcing EU law, thereby ensuring the irrelevance of Regulation 1/2003. Nonetheless, if Recital 8 is indeed to be interpreted in the manner suggested by Wils, one can legitimately inquire why the Regulation should actually contain the statement that Articles 3(1) and 3(2) of Regulation 1/2003 'do not preclude the application of provisions of national law that predominantly pursue an objective different from that pursued by' Articles 101 and 102 TFEU. The answer, however, might lie in the fact that a Recital does not have the same force of law as an Article and that the Article in question is in one respect more extensive than the relevant sentence in Recital 8[63]: it ensures that national laws that predominantly pursue an objective different from that pursued by Articles 101 and 102 TFEU are not subjected to Articles 3(1) and 3(2), *irrespective of whether they impose criminal sanctions on individuals.*

More problematic however, and particularly so for those who wish to draft a criminal cartel offence to ensure that it lies outside of the scope of Regulation 1/2003, is the issue of 'predominant objective'. In fact, Wils's approach begs the question as to what the predominant objective of the provisions of EU competition law actually is. If the predominant objective of EU competition law is to prevent anticompetitive behaviour from occurring in an economy then it would be very difficult to demonstrate that a criminal cartel offence does not pursue the same objective. If so, the application of Regulation 1/2003 to the enforcement of the national cartel offence would be difficult to avoid (when the cartel activity in question affects trade between Member States). However, by having a rather restricted approach to the identification of the predominant objective of EU competition law one can ensure that there is sufficient scope to allow for the creation of a national criminal cartel offence that does not engage the operation of Regulation 1/2003 – even if one adopts Wils's broad approach to the interpretation of the relevant sentence in Recital 8.

---

[62] European Commission (n. 53), 3.

[63] *Cf.* De Smijter and Kjølbye (n. 5), 111.

What is required, then, if one is to follow Wils's interpretation is a definitive statement on what the predominant purpose of the EU competition rules actually is for the purpose of the relevant provisions (Recitals 8 and 9 and Article 3(3)) in Regulation 1/2003. The EU Courts have not provided a ruling on this issue, but there is an English case that can be useful in this context: *IB v. The Queen*.[64] In that particular case the Court of Appeal held that the UK Cartel Offence is not a 'national competition law' within the meaning of Article 3(1) of Regulation 1/2003. In coming to this conclusion the Court held that the test for determining what is a 'national competition law' for this purpose is not 'as broad as whether the law in question pursues the objective of preventing anti-competitive practices'.[65] For it, the mere fact that a national criminal cartel offence is designed to prevent anticompetitive behaviour does not ensure that that particular offence would be considered a 'national competition law' within the meaning of Article 3(1).[66] What is in fact required in order for a criminal cartel offence to be a 'national competition law' is for the enforcement of that criminal offence to have a direct impact on the *validity* of an agreement, decision by an association of undertakings or concerted practice made by an undertaking: imprisonment of an individual must be part of the process of ruling upon the invalidity of an agreement etc. made by an undertaking.[67] When, in enforcing a criminal cartel offence, no decision is required from the criminal court on the validity of the underlying cartel agreement, then, according to the Court of Appeal, that criminal cartel offence would not be a 'national competition law' and therefore would not be subject to Article 3(1) of Regulation 1/2003. In coming to this conclusion, the Court highlighted that the aim of Regulation 1/2003 in directly enforcing EU competition law rules is to avoid 'the risk of "limping" agreements, which are enforceable in one jurisdiction and not in another'.[68]

The ruling of the Court of Appeal on the definition of a 'national competition law' could arguably be used for present purposes in order to inform the test as to what the 'predominant objective' of a criminal cartel offence must be in order for Regulation 1/2003 as a whole to apply to its enforcement.[69] In short, if the criminal

[64] *IB v. The Queen* [2009] EWCA Crim 2575.

[65] *Ibid.*, [35].

[66] *Ibid.*, [24].

[67] See *ibid.*, [34], [35] and [38].

[68] *Ibid.*, [34].

[69] Indeed, the possible link between the term 'national competition law' and the relevant sentence in Recital 8 has been noted in the literature. It has been argued, for example, that if criminal sanctions imposed on natural persons are indeed 'the means whereby competition rules applying to undertakings are enforced' then the relevant provision of national criminal law 'can be classified as belonging to national competition law within the meaning of Article 3': Böge, U. and Bardong, A., 'Article 3: Relationship between Articles 81 and 82 of the Treaty and National Competition Laws', in Hirsch, G., Montag, F. and Jürgen Säcker, F. (eds), *Competition Law: European Community Practice and Procedure – Article-by-Article Commentary*, Sweet & Maxwell, London, 2008, 1546. See also the definition of 'national competition law' put forward in the revised Presidency compromise proposal for a Directive on rules governing national damages actions for infringement of the EU competition law provisions: Council of the European Union, *Proposal for*

cartel offence does not require a ruling on the validity of an agreement etc. entered into by an undertaking, then one can argue that it does not pursue the same predominant objective of the EU competition law rules, and that therefore its enforcement should not be subjected to Regulation 1/2003. This approach would operationalise the interpretation of Recital 8 offered by Wils without allowing for an overly broad definition of the predominant objective of the EU competition law rules (such as the protection of competition on the market). Importantly, such an interpretation of the predominant objective of the EU competition law rules finds some support in Regulation 1/2003 as well as official statements from the Commission. From the first three sentences of Recital 8 of Regulation 1/2003, for example, it is clear that the 'convergence rule' in Article 3(2) is rationalised on the basis of creating a 'level playing field' for agreements etc. within the internal market, as has been confirmed by the Commission itself.[70] The point here is that the objective of creating such a 'level playing field' can only be achieved if the enforcement of competition rules requires a ruling on the validity of the underlying agreement etc. entered into by the undertaking. This type of logic may have found some support in the literature. De Smijter and Kjølbye argue, for example, that a 'criminal offence that applies irrespective of any findings of an infringement on the part of undertakings [which, if Article 101(1) TFEU is involved, inevitably brings with it a ruling on the enforceability of the agreement etc. due to Article 101(2) TFEU] is … deemed not to belong to the sphere of national competition law'.[71] For them, then, criminal sanctions against natural persons will not be the means of enforcing competition rules against undertakings if the criminal offence applies 'irrespective of any finding of an infringement on the part of undertakings'.[72]

This approach is not without its problems however. One can plausibly argue that the predominant objective of Article 101 TFEU is to ensure that a 'level playing field' exists across the EU concerning anticompetitive agreements etc. But one cannot easily do so when the Treaty provision in question is Article 102 TFEU, the provision that prohibits an abuse of a dominant position. The reason for this is that a finding of a violation of Article 102 TFEU by a NCA does not automatically render unenforceable any agreement which is deemed to underlie an abuse of a dominant position.[73] One may well posit that Article 102 TFEU is irrelevant when

---

*a Directive of the European Parliament and of the Council on Certain Rules Governing Actions for Damages under National Law for Infringements of the Competition Law Provisions of the Member States and of the European Union – Adoption of the General Approach*, 17317/13, Brussels, 3 December 2013, Annex, Article 4(2).

[70] European Commission, *Commission Staff Working Paper Accompanying the Communication from the Commission to the European Parliament and the Council – Report on the Functioning of Regulation 1/2003*, SEC(2009) 574 final, Brussels, 29 April 2009, 49.

[71] De Smijter and Kjølbye (n. 5), 111.

[72] *Ibid.*

[73] That is not to say, however, that a party to a contract with a dominant undertaking cannot argue in a civil case that clauses in the contract are prohibited by Article 102 TFEU and are therefore void and unenforceable; see, e.g.: Jones and Sufrin (n. 12), 265; and *English Welsh and Scottish Railway Ltd v. E.ON UK plc* [2007] EWHC 599.

analysing cartel agreements and therefore that its apparent role regarding the declaration of invalidity would also be irrelevant. But this would be missing the point: Article 102 TFEU is relevant when determining what the predominant objective of the EU competition law rules actually is. If one looks at the wording of Article 3(3) of Regulation 1/2003 one can see that it states that Articles 3(1) and (2) do not preclude 'the application of provisions of national law that predominantly pursue an objective different from *that* pursued by Articles [101] *and* [102 TFEU]'.[74] The use of the word 'that' rather than 'those' combined with the use of the word 'and' rather than 'or' to connect Articles 101 and 102 TFEU seems to suggest that there is one predominant objective of the EU competition rules.[75] If so, it is this particular objective which would inform the test to be used when applying Wils's approach to the relevant sentence in Recital 8. Given that Article 102 TFEU does not necessarily rule on the enforceability of agreements etc. (unlike Article 101 TFEU) one may be forced to admit that the relevant objective is wider than the ruling on validity and may in fact be as wide as the 'protection of competition on the market'[76] or 'the maintenance of effective competition within the common market'.[77] If this is so, one is inevitably led back to the problems associated with Wils's original (overly broad) contention concerning the logical implication of his approach to interpreting the relevant sentence in Recital 8.

The legal position on the applicability of Regulation 1/2003 to a national criminal cartel offence has yet to be definitively explained by the Court of Justice. Given the different possible explanations that can be offered regarding its application, it is obvious that a cautious approach to this issue is warranted. Nonetheless, subject to the specifics of the (rational) interpretation of the legal situation that is chosen as being relevant, useful advice can be formulated and provided to national legislators who wish to design criminal cartel offences in such a manner that avoids the potential application of Regulation 1/2003. If one adopts the interpretation of the OFT, all the national legislature has to do to avoid the application of Regulation 1/2003 to the national criminal cartel offence is ensure that undertakings (as opposed to individuals) cannot be subjected to a criminal prosecution for commission of the criminal cartel offence. If one is not swayed by the OFT's argument one could find inspiration from Wils and create a criminal cartel offence that does not pursue the same predominant objective as the EU competition law rules. As noted above, this of course begs the question as to what that predominant objective might be. If one were to take inspiration from the Court of Appeal in the *IB* case concerning this issue, one could design the criminal cartel offence so that it does not inevitably involve a finding by the criminal court on the validity of the underlying agreement etc. that is

[74] Emphasis added.

[75] See also Case 6/72, *Continental Can v. Commission* [1973] ECR 215, [25] ('Articles [101] and [102 TFEU] seek to achieve the *same aim* on different levels, *viz.* the maintenance of effective competition within the same market' (emphasis added)).

[76] See Regulation 1/2003, Recital 9.

[77] Case 6/72, *Continental Can v. Commission* [1973] ECR 215, [11].

entered into by undertakings. As was explained above, such a restrictive approach to the issue of 'predominant objective' can be questioned.

If one wished to have a more robust approach in defining the criminal cartel offence so that it is not subjected to Regulation 1/2003, then in addition to delinking the criminal cartel offence from a finding of invalidity regarding the agreement etc., one could design the offence in such a way that one can plausibly argue that its predominant objective is not 'the protection of competition on the market' or 'the maintenance of effective competition within the common market'. This might be difficult to do, particularly if the rationale for the introduction of criminal cartel sanctions is the achievement of deterrence of anticompetitive behaviour. One possible way of 'engineering' a different predominant objective for the criminal cartel offence to that involving the prevention of anticompetitive behaviour (and with it the protection of the market) would be to create the cartel offence on the basis of an explicit moral concept.[78] According to Lord Bingham, the punishment of immoral (anticompetitive) behaviour can be understood as being conceptually distinct from the punishment of cartel activity for the purposes of enforcing competition rules:

> in a case involving dishonest misstatement in connection with price-fixing, it would be the punishment of the dishonesty not price-fixing which would be the 'objective' of the criminal [cartel] law.[79]

Leading on from this, one could, for example, define the criminal cartel offence in such a manner that it requires the cartelist to 'dishonestly' agree with another to engage in cartel activity. However, such an approach is not without its own significant problems, as demonstrated by the recent reform of the UK Cartel Offence (and with it the removal of the difficult requirement to prove the 'dishonesty' of the defendant in this context). Alternatively, one could create a criminal cartel offence that necessarily captures the moral wrongfulness of cartel activity by creating an express link between cartel activity and the violation of one or more of the norms against stealing, deceiving and cheating.[80] For example, before imposing criminal cartel sanctions, one could require proof that the cartelist intended to mislead customers. Admittedly, such an approach, while operationalizing the justificatory theory of retribution more fully, could easily run counter to the achievement of deterrence: additional definitional elements present *additional* hurdles for antitrust enforcers, and *ceteris paribus*, a given amount of resources will most likely produce fewer successful prosecutions if a criminal cartel offence requires proof of additional definitional elements. Moreover, the 'engineering' process may not work in practice: depending on the rules of legal interpretation in existence in a given jurisdiction, its judicial authorities may look beyond the exact definition in the cartel

[78] See Whelan, P., 'Improving Criminal Cartel Enforcement in the UK: The Case for the Adoption of BIS's "Option 4"' (2012) 8(3) European Competition Journal 589, 599–600.

[79] *Norris v Government of the United States of America and others* [2008] UKHL 16, [51]. See also Furse (n. 21), 126, noting a similar point that was made in *R v. GG plc and others* [2008] UKHL 17.

[80] See Whelan, P. 'Cartel Criminalization and the Challenge of Moral Wrongfulness' (2013) 33(3) Oxford Journal of Legal Studies 535.

offence to green and white papers, consultation documents, responses to consultation documents, legislative debates, draft legislation etc., all of which may reveal that a predominant purpose to the introduction of a criminal cartel offence is in fact to prevent anticompetitive conduct in order to protect the functioning of markets.[81]

## 6.4 Conclusion

One of the most important practical issues which has the potential to undermine the effectiveness of criminal antitrust enforcement is the issue as to how to define the criminal cartel offence. This chapter analysed a very important issues concerning the definition of the criminal cartel offence: the potential (negative) impact of Regulation 1/2003 on the design and operation of a national criminal cartel offence and what can be done to reduce the scope for such impact in this context.

If Regulation 1/2003 applies to the enforcement of the national cartel offence, then there is a clear case that that particular Regulation can impact upon both the definition and the operation of the criminal offence. The definition of the criminal cartel offence could be affected as a result of Article 3 of Regulation 1/2003. Where there is an effect on trade between Member States (and the Regulation applies to the enforcement of the criminal cartel offence) the antitrust enforcers must also apply EU competition law, and in doing so they cannot prohibit agreements under national law which would not be prohibited under EU competition law. Arguably this feature of competition law enforcement restricts the scope of a criminal cartel offence in that (when there is an effect on trade) the criminal offence cannot capture cartel activity which would not have violated the prohibition in Article 101(1) TFEU, would have fulfilled the criteria of Article 101(3) TFEU or would have been covered by a block exemption. This situation is problematic for three reasons: (i) it makes the concept of 'effect on trade' relevant in a criminal trial; (ii) it allows for (potentially confusing) economic arguments to be made in a criminal trial; and (iii) it restricts the ability of a jurisdiction to generate a moral norm against cartel activity, as citizens may perceive the criminal cartel offence as focusing on the technical and arcane regulation of trade rather than on preventing conspiracies that cost consumers significant amounts of money. For their part, Articles 11(6) and 35 have the potential to impact negatively on the operation of the criminal cartel offence. If Regulation 1/2003 applies to the enforcement of the national criminal cartel offence then, under Article 11(6) thereof, the Commission would have the power to relieve the national criminal cartel enforcer of its power to prosecute cartelists for their commission of the criminal cartel offence. There is also the possibility that Article 35(1) of the Regulation could also be used to argue that if the national criminal enforcer is not a designated NCA under Regulation 1/2003 then it would not have

---

[81] See, e.g., the analysis of the Court of Appeal concerning the travaux prěparatoire of the UK Cartel Offence in *IB v. The Queen* [2009] EWCA Crim 2575, [21]–[23].

jurisdiction to prosecute an individual for an alleged commission of the criminal cartel offence.

One could eliminate the possibility for a later 'surprise' restriction of the scope of the national criminal cartel offence by linking the offence to a violation of Article 101(1) TFEU and by providing a defence along the lines of Article 101(3) TFEU. In addition, one can also designate the criminal prosecutor as an NCA under Regulation 1/2003. However, while this approach would avoid certain nasty surprises for the prosecution during a criminal trial, and would avoid arguments centred on a lack of jurisdiction due to Article 35 of Regulation 1/2003, it would also facilitate the introduction of economic evidence in a trial (something that legislators are keen to avoid) and would not deal with the Article 11(6) issue. Alternatively, one could design the criminal cartel offence so that it only applied to situations where there was no effect on trade between Member States. However such an approach would be legally questionable. A policy of only pursuing cases with no effect on trade would be preferable, but such an option brings with it disadvantages in terms of achieving deterrence and/or retribution.

The best option would be to design the criminal cartel offence in such a manner that Regulation 1/2003 would not apply to it at all. This is a difficult thing to do, as it is not exactly clear when the Regulation will and will not apply concerning the enforcement of a national criminal cartel offence. This is due to, *inter alia*, the ambiguous nature of the relevant sentence in Recital 8 of Regulation 1/2003. Two alternative interpretations of when Regulation 1/2003 will not apply were identified: (a) when undertakings (as opposed to individuals) cannot be subjected to a criminal prosecution for commission of the criminal cartel offence; or (b) when the criminal cartel offence does not pursue the same predominant objective as the EU competition law rules. If one is persuaded by the former interpretation then all that one needs to do to avoid the impact of Regulation 1/2003 is ensure that only individuals can be convicted of the criminal cartel offence. If the later interpretation is preferred then one is required: (i) to take a (supportable) decision regarding the predominant objective of EU competition law; and (ii) to design the criminal cartel offence in such a way that its predominant objective can be distinguished from that of the EU competition law rules. One way of doing this might be to argue that the predominant objective of the EU competition rules is 'the protection of competition on the market' and that this is not pursued by the creation of a criminal cartel offence that is linked to an explicit moral concept, such as one of the norms against stealing, deception or cheating.

# Chapter 7
# Regulation Brussels 1 and the Application of Articles 101 and 102 TFEU by National Courts

**Jean-Marc Thouvenin**

## 7.1 Introduction

In a Green Paper dated December 2005 which was devoted to damages actions for breach of EU competition rules,[1] the European Commission wrote the following:

> Jurisdiction of courts to hear cases brought against defendants domiciled in Member States is governed by Regulation 44/2001. Such defendants can either be sued in the courts of the state where they are domiciled or – at the choice of the claimant – in the courts of the state where the harmful event occurred. The place where the harmful event occurred can be either (a) the place where the event giving rise to the damage occurred or (b) the place where the damage itself occurred (at the choice of the claimant). Articles 6, 27 and 28 of the Regulation allow coordination of different, but linked, actions.

This statement is supposed to reflect some of the basic rules adopted under Regulation 44/2001 of 22 December 2000 on jurisdiction and the recognition and enforcement of judgments in civil and commercial matters.[2] It clarifies that, according to EU Law, the right to chose the jurisdiction before which to lodge a claim, between the one of the State where the harmful event occurred, which is often the claimant's national jurisdiction, or the one of the State where the defendant is domiciled, is a privilege duly recognized to complainants in the context of damages actions for breach of the EU antitrust rules.

---

[1] COM(2005) 672 Final.

[2] OJ L 12, 16.01.2001, pp. 1–23; the Regulation has been amended and recast by Regulation (EU) No 1215/2012 of 12 December 2012, OJ L 351, 20.12.2012, pp. 1–32. The new version does not differ to the original one with respect to the provisions mentioned in this contribution, but the Articles have been renumbered. We refer in this contribution to the articles as renumbered.

J.-M. Thouvenin (✉)
Université de Paris Ouest Nanterre La Défense, Nanterre, France
e-mail: jmthouvenin@wanadoo.fr



A. Almăşan, P. Whelan (eds.), *The Consistent Application of EU Competition Law*, Studies in European Economic Law and Regulation 9,
DOI 10.1007/978-3-319-47382-6_7

Is this principle a good one when applied to antitrust matters? Even if no one seems to have doubts, this is debatable, and some criticisms about the options left to complainants to choose the jurisdictions before which to lodge their claims in antitrust matters can be elaborated. To this effect, the main rules of Regulation Brussels 1 will be discussed (Sect. 7.2), separately from its Article 25 related to prorogation of jurisdiction, which deserves a specific comment (Sect. 7.3).

## 7.2 A Critique of *Forum Shopping* in Antitrust Matters Authorized by Regulation Brussels 1

As rightly mentioned by the EU Commission in its 2005 statement, Regulation Brussels 1 grants in civil and contractual litigations a right to claimants to chose the jurisdiction before which to lodge their claims. The complainant can indeed simply opt for the jurisdiction of the defendant. In this regard, Article 4 (1) sets out the general principle that:

> Subject to this Regulation, persons domiciled in a Member State shall, whatever their nationality, be sued in the courts of that Member State.

But this principle, also known as *actor sequitur forum rei*, can be discarded. Indeed, in the words of the European Court, Regulation Brussels 1 puts a "derogation from the fundamental principle laid down" in Article 4,[3] a derogation according to which the plaintiff can opt for other Courts. In this respect, Article 7 states that:

> A person domiciled in a Member State may, in another Member State, be sued:
> 1. (a) in matters relating to a contract, in the courts for the place of performance of the obligation in question;
> …
> 3. in matters relating to tort, delict or quasi-delict, in the courts for the place where the harmful event occurred or may occur.

As a consequence, the victim of a damage in contractual matters or matters relating to tort, delict or quasi-delict is provided with options, as it can freely select between at least two different national jurisdictions before which it will file its case. Moreover, in certain cases, in tort, delict or quasi-delict cases, the claimant can have the choice between three jurisdictions, the one of the domicile of the defendant, or two others, insofar as the notion of "'place where the harmful event occurred or may occur' … is intended to cover both the place where the damage occurred and the place of the event giving rise to it, so that the defendant may be sued, at the option of the applicant, in the courts for either of those places."[4]

According to the European Court in *Bier v. Mines de Potasse d'Alsace*, the *rationale* of this privilege is as follows:

[3] Judgment of the Court of 22 January 2015, *Pez Hejduk v. EnergieAgentur. NRW GmbH*, Case C-441/13, pt. 17.

[4] *Ibid.*, pt. 18.

> This freedom of choice was introduced having regard to the existence, in certain clearly defined situations, of a particularly close connecting factor between a dispute and the court which may be called upon to hear it, with a view to the efficacious conduct of the proceedings.[5]

More recently, the Court confirmed that:

> According to settled case-law, the rule of special jurisdiction laid down in Article [7](3) of that regulation is based on the existence of a particularly close linking factor between the dispute and the courts of the place where the harmful event occurred or may occur, which justifies the attribution of jurisdiction to those courts for reasons relating to the sound administration of justice and the efficacious conduct of proceedings.[6]

The freedom of choice rule is therefore deemed to reflect the principle of good administration of justice, which includes "proximity of the Court to the conflict, efficiency, and cost awareness."[7]

It is fair to say that freedom of choice sounds like a good rule. But if it sounds right "generally", it is not necessarily correct in the context of antitrust matters. In this respect, it should be remembered that the victim's privilege has been adopted as a principle in Europe at a moment where antitrust private litigations were virtually non-existent, so that its relevance has simply not been assessed in the specific context of antitrust damages litigation. Yet, even if it was not its aim when it was adopted, there is no doubt that Regulation Brussels 1 does apply to damages actions for breach of the EU antitrust rules. Indeed, according to Article 1 of the Regulation, it lays down rules governing the jurisdiction of courts in civil and commercial matters, which of course include antitrust civil cases.

Thus, the question that was not addressed when the rule was established is whether this rule makes sense concerning antitrust cases. In my view, this is not so, for three reasons.

First, it is *not* common ground for private international rules validating the choice of jurisdiction principle to be also applicable to antitrust cases. For example, the Hague Convention on Choice of Court Agreements, concluded 30 June 2005, explicitly excludes antitrust matters from its scope of application (Article 2, part. 2, al. h). It has been considered by the signatories that private litigants should not have the right to dispose of the matter for themselves, insofar as it involves the public interest.[8] This reasoning could fit in Europe, as European Competition law is

---

[5] Judgment of the Court of 30 November 1976, *Handelskwekerij G. J. Bier BV v Mines de potasse d'Alsace SA*, Case 21–76, pt. 10–11.

[6] Judgment of the Court of 22 January 2015, *Pez Hejduk v. EnergieAgentur. NRW GmbH*, Case C-441/13., pt. 19.

[7] E. Storskrubb, *Civil Procedure and EU Law: A Policy Area Uncovered*, OUP, 2008, p. 152.

[8] Draft Uniform International Choice of Court Agreement Act, National conference of Commissioners on Uniform State Laws, 2010, at p. 18 (https://lettersblogatory.com/wp-content/uploads/2012/02/UICCAA.pdf).

predominantly regulatory law, even with respect to private damages claims. Indeed, one of the major purposes of such claims remains regulatory.[9]

Second, under the Brussels 1 approach, there is clearly a *principle* – namely that the competent Court is the one of the Member State where the wrongdoer is domiciled – and an *exception* – the competent Court can be the one of the place of performance of the obligation, or the one of place where the harmful event occurred. The European Court confirmed that Article 7 reflects a mere exception that should be interpreted restrictively in *Dumez France v. Hessische Landesbank* (ECJ, 11 January 1990, C-220/88).[10]

By contrast, one could submit that the correct principle to be applied in antitrust matters should be that the competent Court(s) is (are) the Court(s) having jurisdiction on the affected market on which the complainant is active and suffered damages. Indeed, the object of competition law is to protect the openness and efficiency of competitive markets, and an action for damages is considered as nothing but a reinforcement of this protection. This is clearly illustrated by the fact that in the USA, actions for damages for breach of antitrust laws give rise to very special damages, namely treble damages, which are of a punitive nature.

It seems therefore reasonable that actions for damages should be located before the Courts of the market that is affected by the anti-competitive behaviour, in the same manner as national authorities of each member State are competent to address anticompetitive behaviours located on their national markets.[11] This solution would be completely in line with the finding of the Court that:

> the courts for the place where the harmful event occurred or may occur are usually the most appropriate for deciding the case, in particular on the grounds of proximity and ease of taking evidence,[12]

and that:

> [t]hat place fully guarantees the efficacious conduct of potential proceedings, given that the assessment of a claim for damages for loss allegedly inflicted upon a specific undertaking as a result of an unlawful cartel, as already found by the Commission in a binding decision, essentially depends on factors specifically relating to the situation of that undertaking. In

---

[9] H. L. Buxbaum, R. Michaels, "Jurisdiction and Choice of Law in International Antitrust Law – A U.S. Perspective", in *International Antitrust Litigation: Conflict Of Laws And Coordination (Studies In Private International Law)*, J. Basedow, S. Francq, L. Idot, eds., Oxford: Hart Publishing, 2012, p. 244.

[10] This is confirmed, e.g., in Judgment of the Court of 5 June 2014, *Coty Germany BmbH*, Case C-360/12., at pt. 45: "In so far as the jurisdiction of the court of the place where the harmful event occurred or may occur constitutes a rule of special jurisdiction, it must be interpreted restrictively and cannot give rise to an interpretation going beyond the cases expressly envisaged by that regulation".

[11] In cases where more than one Court would be competent under this criteria, a solution inspired by a decision of 7 March 1995, *Shevill*, C-68/93 (action before each Court in which the market is affected, or, as an exception in order to avoid a multiplication of proceedings, before the Court of the location of the defendant) could be contemplated.

[12] Judgment of the Court of 21 May 2015, *Cartel Damage Claims*, Case C-352/13, pt. 40.

> those circumstances, the courts in whose jurisdiction that undertaking has its registered office are manifestly best suited to adjudicate such a claim.[13]

It would also be coherent with the provisions of Regulation Rome II (Reg. 864/2007) according to which:

> [t]he law applicable to a non-contractual obligation arising out of a restriction of competition shall be the law of the country where the market is, or is likely to be, affected. (Article 6, par. 1, al 3).

Third, if applied in antitrust matters, the Brussels 1 approach may lead to incoherent legal decisions on the very same issues. The example of a company located in France, which claims that it has suffered damages in France as a result of an abuse of a dominant position committed by a company active on the European market, but located in a foreign country, can be taken as an illustration. In this particular case, the victim is entitled to lodge at the same time two claims before two different authorities in charge of applying European competition law:

(i) before the competitive authority of France, the Autorité de la concurrence, and, among others,
(ii) before the Court of the State in which the defendant is domiciled.

It is possible in such a situation that one of these two authorities holds that the defendant effectively committed an abuse of a dominant position, while the other holds a completely opposite view, whether because the defendant is not dominating the relevant market, or because it considers that no abusive conduct can be reproached to the defendant. Indeed, Directive 2014/104/EU of the European Parliament and of the Council of 26 November 2014, "on certain rules governing actions for damages under national law for infringements of the competition law provisions of the Member States and of the European Union",[14] expressly recognizes, at Article 9, that if,

> 1. Member States shall ensure that an infringement of competition law found by a final decision of a national competition authority or a review court is deemed to be irrefutably established for the purposes of an action for damages brought before their national courts under Article 101 or 102 of the Treaty or under national competition law ...,

by contrast

> 2. Member States shall ensure that a final decision referred to in paragraph 1 given in another Member State may, in accordance with their respective national law, be presented before their national courts as at least prima facie evidence that an infringement of competition law has occurred and, as appropriate, may be assessed along with any other material brought by the parties.

In the hypothesis under review, this means that the foreign court would certainly have to consider the position of the Autorité de la concurrence as a "*prima facie* evidence", but would not be compelled to hold the same conclusion. This national

[13] *Ibid.*, pt. 53.

[14] OJ L 349, 5.12.2014, p. 1–19.

jurisdiction could request a preliminary ruling from the European Court, in order to secure its own position, but in this case, the objective of the current legal architecture, which is to organize the decentralization of the implementation of European Competition Law, would have failed.

It should be added that there is another risk of jurisdictional incoherence. Indeed, an action for a *declaration of nullity* of a contract that is an infringement of Article 101 TFEU belongs to "contractual matters", not to tort, delict or quasi delict matters. As a consequence, the choice of jurisdiction by the claimant should be based on Article 7(1) of Regulation Brussels 1, not on Article 7(3). Therefore, it is possible that a claim for nullity of a contract is brought before the Court of one State, while the action for damages would be brought before the jurisdiction of another State. Here, again, there would be a risk of incoherent justice.

As can be seen, the situation arising out of the application of Brussels 1 to competition law cases is in sharp contradiction with the principle emphatically proclaimed at point 21 of the preamble of the Regulation Brussel I, as recast, that "in the interests of the harmonious administration of justice it is necessary to minimise the possibility of concurrent proceedings and to ensure that irreconcilable judgments will not be given in different Member States." Nevertheless, it seems clear that these arguments did not convince the EU to rethink its "choice of court" doctrine, insofar as antitrust matters are concerned. In particular, it did not seize the opportunity of the negotiation of the Directive 2014/104/EU of the European Parliament and of the Council of 26 November 2014 to rethink this question. Yet, even if a new doctrine were to be adopted, another question would have to be addressed, namely whether Article 25 of Regulation Brussels 1 is of relevance in antitrust matters.

## 7.3 Does Article 25 of Regulation Brussels 1 Apply to Antitrust Matters?

Art. 25 of Regulation Brussels 1 is related to "prorogation of jurisdiction". It reads as follows:

> 1. If the parties, regardless of their domicile, have agreed that a court or the courts of a Member State are to have jurisdiction to settle any disputes which have arisen or which may arise in connection with a particular legal relationship, that court or those courts shall have jurisdiction, unless the agreement is null and void as to its substantive validity under the law of that Member State. Such jurisdiction shall be exclusive unless the parties have agreed otherwise.

As can be seen, this provision covers disputes "which have arisen or which may arise in connection with a particular legal relationship." Insofar as the Regulation generally applies to antitrust matters, it is necessary to assess the measure in which this article is applicable to cases related to damages that are caused by an infringement of Article 101 TFEU, or of Article 102 TFEU.

### 7.3.1 *Article 25 of Regulation Brussels 1 and Article 101 TFEU*

Situations where a contractual election of court could be applicable can obviously occur in cases of infringement of Article 101 TFEU. This is certainly possible in the context of vertical relations between a seller and a reseller. These relations are normally established on the basis of a contract, and antitrust disputes can arise if the contract contains provisions, e.g. exclusivity provisions, that are in breach of Article 101 TFEU. In this case, it could seem obvious that the prorogation of jurisdiction would apply, so that the court having jurisdiction would be any court, insofar as the parties contractually agreed on it.

Here again, it is submitted that this solution, derived from a purely private international law approach, and which does not take account of the specificity of antitrust laws, is not a reasonable solution, for at least three reasons.

First, antitrust matters should not be at the disposal of litigating parties. The contractual autonomy of the parties, which is an important feature in private international law, should be considered irrelevant in antitrust matters.

Second it should be remembered that, according to the Court in *Bier v. Mines de Potasse d'Alsace* and subsequent case law, if a choice of jurisdiction is provided to complainants by Article 7 of Regulation Brussels 1, it is in regard of a "particularly close connecting factor between a dispute and the court which may be called upon to hear it, with a view to the efficacious conduct of the proceedings."[15] By contrast, there is absolutely no such justification for applying a prorogation of jurisdiction in antitrust matters. Obviously, under Article 25 of Regulation Brussels 1, the choice of court is completely discretionary, so that any court, even a court without any connection at all with the case at stake, could be chosen. This has been confirmed by the European Court in *Castelletti* in 1999.[16] In this case, the question put was whether it was "necessary for the parties to choose a court having some link to the case", and the Court clearly held that for a choice of court provision to be covered by Article 25, "considerations about the links between the court designated and the relationship at issue" are completely irrelevant. But if this is acceptable generally, it is not, one could submit, reasonable in matters involving the public interest, which is the case concerning antitrust.

Third, this could lead to incoherent legal decisions addressing the same antitrust infringement.

Although unreasonable, the relevance of Article 25 with respect to competition litigations has not been discussed until recently, and some clarification in this regard has been brought only in 2015.

[15] Judgment of the Court of 30 November 1976, *Handelskwekerij G. J. Bier BV v Mines de potasse d'Alsace SA*, Case 21–76, pt. 10–11.

[16] Judgment of the Court of 16 March 1999, *Trasporti Castelletti Spedizioni Internazionali SpA v Hugo Trumpy SpA*, Case C-159/97.

Indeed, doubts about the applicability of a prorogation of jurisdiction provision to an action for damages for breach of Article 101 TFEU have been raised by a German court which requested the European Court of Justice to provide a preliminary ruling on the question "whether Article 2[5](1) of Regulation [Brussels 1] and the requirement of effective enforcement of the prohibition of cartel agreements in EU law must, in the case of actions for damages for an infringement of Article 101 TFEU and Article 53 of the EEA Agreement, be interpreted as allowing account to be taken of jurisdiction clauses contained in contracts for the supply of goods where this has the effect of excluding the jurisdiction of a court with international jurisdiction under Article [7](3) and/or Article [8](1) of that regulation".[17]

The Court rejected the idea that antitrust matters should be excluded from the application of a prorogation of jurisdiction provision. It held in particular that:

> the court seised of the matter cannot, without undermining the aim of Regulation [Brussels 1], refuse to take into account a jurisdiction clause which has satisfied the requirements of Article 2[5] of that regulation solely on the ground that it considers that the court with jurisdiction under that clause would not give full effect to the requirement of effective enforcement of the prohibition of cartel agreements by not allowing a victim of the cartel to obtain full compensation for the loss it suffered. On the contrary, it must be considered that the system of legal remedies in each Member State, together with the preliminary ruling procedure provided for in Article 267 TFEU, affords a sufficient guarantee to individuals in that respect (see, by analogy, judgment in *Renault*, C-38/98, EU:C:2000:225, paragraph 23).[18]

Therefore, a prorogation of jurisdiction can, in principle, apply to a claim for damages made by the victim of a cartel that would be in a contractual relation with the defendant. But the Court largely mitigated this holding by stating that:

> A jurisdiction clause can concern only disputes which have arisen or which may arise in connection with a particular legal relationship, which limits the scope of an agreement conferring jurisdiction solely to disputes which arise from the legal relationship in connection with which the agreement was entered into. The purpose of that requirement is to avoid a party being taken by surprise by the assignment of jurisdiction to a given forum as regards all disputes which may arise out of its relationship with the other party to the contract and stem from a relationship other than that in connection with which the agreement conferring jurisdiction was made (see, to that effect, judgment in *Powell Duffryn*, C-214/89, EU:C:1992:115, paragraph 31).
>
> In the light of that purpose, the referring court must, in particular, regard a clause which abstractly refers to all disputes arising from contractual relationships as not extending to a dispute relating to the tortious liability that one party allegedly incurred as a result of the other's participation in an unlawful cartel.
>
> Given that the undertaking which suffered the loss could not reasonably foresee such litigation at the time that it agreed to the jurisdiction clause and that that undertaking had no knowledge of the unlawful cartel at that time, such litigation cannot be regarded as stemming from a contractual relationship. Such a clause would not therefore have validly derogated from the referring court's jurisdiction.
>
> By contrast, where a clause refers to disputes in connection with liability incurred as a result of an infringement of competition law and designates the courts of a Member State

[17] Judgment of the Court of 21 May 2015, *Cartel Damage Claims*, Case C-352/13, pt. 57.
[18] *Ibid.*, pt. 63.

> other than the Member State of the referring court, the latter ought to decline its own jurisdiction, even where that clause entails disregarding the special rules of jurisdiction laid down in Articles 5 and/or 6 of Regulation No 44/2001.[19]

As a consequence of the *Cartel Damage Case* ruling, it is only where a prorogation of jurisdiction clause does "refer to disputes concerning liability incurred as a result of an infringement of competition law" that it is applicable to damages actions for breach of the EU antitrust rules.[20]

### 7.3.2 *Article 25 of Regulation Brussels 1 and Article 102 TFEU*

Concerning Article 102 TFEU, one can ask whether an action for damages based on a violation of that particular provision, brought by a claimant in contractual relationship with the defendant, can be governed by the choice of court provision of this contract.

*A priori*, one can assume that an abuse of a dominant position is a unilateral conduct that is not supposed to be covered by a contractual prohibition existing between the wrongdoer and the victim. In short, it will be quite rare to find situations where an abuse of a dominant position is, in itself, a breach of a contract. It is possible that a contract is the result of an abuse of dominant position; but the latter would not be a breach of the former.

But upon a closer look, this observation appears irrelevant. Indeed, for Article 25 to apply, the dispute must only be in "connection" with a "legal relationship". Therefore, a non-contractual dispute can be covered by a choice of court provision, to the extent that this dispute is in "connection" with a contractual relationship or, more generally, a "legal relationship".

From there, and until the *Cartel Damage Claims ruling*, it was considered that a damages action for breach of Article 102 could quite easily be covered by a choice of court provision.

As an illustration, the Paris Court of Appeal held on 8 April 2014 in the *Ebizcuss v. Apple Case* that a choice of court provision was applicable in a civil case involving an abuse of a dominant position.

According to the facts of this case, a purchase agreement was in force between a large international firm and a small French reseller. The reseller sued the seller, claiming that the latter entered into a discriminating selling policy, advantaging other resellers, and also reducing or postponing the delivery of products. The claim for damages was lodged before a French court. Clearly, the dispute was not about a breach of the purchase agreement, but was focusing on the violation of Article 102 TFEU. Yet, the contract contained the following choice of court provision:

---

[19] *Ibid.*, pt. 68–71.

[20] *Ibid.*, Dispositive, 3).

> This Agreement and the corresponding relationship between the parties shall be governed by and construed in accordance with the laws of the Republic of Ireland and the parties submit to the jurisdiction of the courts of the Republic of Ireland.

On this basis, the defendant argued that the reseller should have lodged its claim before the Irish judge. The reseller opposed that this provision could not cover the antitrust dispute it had engaged in, because the alleged abuse was not a matter addressed by the agreement. But the Court of Appeal held that the provision was broad enough to cover the action, holding that the dispute found its *origin* in the execution of the contract. In other words, the dispute would not have existed if the contract had not existed.

The reseller brought the case to the Court of Cassation, which annulled the ruling of the Court of Appeal on the basis of the *Cartel Damage Claims* ruling,[21] under which only prorogation of jurisdiction provisions that "refer to disputes concerning liability incurred as a result of an infringement of competition law" can apply to antitrust disputes. Indeed, in the current case, the prorogation of jurisdiction provision clearly did not contain any reference to infringement of competition law, so that it could not be of application.

## 7.4 Conclusion

Regulation Brussels 1 was adopted at a moment when damages actions for breach of European Competition Law were virtually inexistent, so that the opportunity to apply it to such matters had never been seriously assessed. Upon analysis, there are quite good arguments that show that it not adapted. The position of the European Court in the *Cartel Damage Claims* is a sign of such misconception. A serious rethinking of the rules regarding the choice of jurisdiction before which a claim for damages suffered as a consequence of a breach of the European competition law is therefore suggested.

---

[21] French *Cour de Cassation*, case n° 1053 of 7 October 2015 (14–16.898), 1st Civil Chamber.

# Chapter 8
# The Arbitrability of Articles 101 and 102 TFEU

**Adriana Almăşan**

## 8.1 Introduction

At one point in time, a debate on the possible private enforcement of the EU competition rules was engendered. The discussion stemmed from the conjecture that the administration of the EU competition rules represented the exclusive prerogative of the Member States and Community authorities. However, this particular limitation in the applicability of the EU rules remained unsustainable after the entry into force of Regulation 1/2003, the Regulation that addressed, *inter alia*, the challenge of applying Community law at national level. Indeed, the broadening effect of the Regulation 1/2003 did not explicitly extend to arbitration matters; however, the Regulation rendered the critique of the direct application in private judgements less vivid. That said, for several reasons, there has been a tendency to challenge the application of the EU competition rules not only in international disputes but also in intra-community arbitration cases as well.

The arbitrability of the EU competition rules may be analysed from different perspectives, due to its terminological plurality. This chapter focuses on the capability of arbitral courts to solve disputes grounded on EU competition substantive law. Such a capability stems from the various restrictions that national jurisdictions have imposed on the parties' election for arbitral resolution. Consequently, the larger sense of the US term of "arbitrability", referring generally to arbitral jurisdiction, has no concern for the subject tackled herein.[1] From this perspective, the term arbitrability implies that some countries are excluded from arbitration.[2]

[1] Julian D. M. Lew, Loukas A. Misteris, Stefan M. Kroll, Comparative International Commercial Arbitration, Kluwer Law International, 2003, 188.

[2] *Ibid*, 189.

A. Almăşan (✉)
Faculty of Law, University of Bucharest, Bucharest, Romania
e-mail: adriana.almasan@drept.unibuc.ro

 
A. Almăşan, P. Whelan (eds.), *The Consistent Application of EU Competition Law*, Studies in European Economic Law and Regulation 9,
DOI 10.1007/978-3-319-47382-6_8

The inclination of the authors towards the application of the Treaty on Functioning of the European Union in arbitral disputes depends in a great measure on the type of infringement; the infringements grounded on Articles 101 and 102 TFEU are the most common submitted to courts.

In front of national arbitration courts, the matter of the arbitrability of competition matters is less complicated. The applicable law being national law, it clearly results that an arbitral court of an EU Member State will apply the *ius congens*, which here includes the Treaty on Functioning of the European Union. The debate on the applicability only arrives in international arbitration. The challenge in applying competition law in international arbitration stems from, *inter alia*, the lack of uniform international regulation on competition. Indeed, despite the general inspiration provided by the United States' Sherman Act, for many legislators worldwide, including the European Union, there is no precise juxtaposition of provisions. In fact, the TFEU provisions in competition matters cannot stand as public policy except in the European Union; hence the arbitral disputes between nationals of other states and nationals of EU Member States engender, on a case-by-case basis, the sensitive issue of determining the applicable law that may not be the law of an EU Member State national.

Another challenge derives from the fact that arbitration confers less protection of statutory rights than judicial courts. In the absence of injunction measures, or any preventive measure, the arbitral tribunal can only provide the comfort of a less lengthy procedure, rendering the final decision in up to ten times less than judicial courts, depending on the judicial system, but not the immediate relief, which often quite needed in competition infringements. Considering that, in some situations, the illicit behaviour may determine substantial losses or even bankruptcy to its victims, time may be essential in availing of an efficient remedy.

The competition law disputes resolved in arbitration might observe several models, in order to develop a specific procedure. Specially tailored arbitral procedures for specific law areas, such as securities' transactions, insolvency (in core and non-core matters), and intellectual property may be of use to this end.[3]

Critics of the applicability of EU competition law in arbitration have argued that private enforcement is unnecessary both as an additional mechanism for enforcement of rules and as a mechanism for achieving corrective justice.[4] The rationale sustaining this point of view derives from the excesses reached especially in the US system and the lack of proper control exercised in that context. Practice reveals, however, a contending perspective, in the sense that disputes in the field of competition are arbitrable, as generally property rights or economic rights are at stake.[5] This was also the argument held in the *Eco Swiss* landmark ruling by the Court of Justice of the European Union, from which stemmed a favourable trend to application in practice.

---

[3] Julian D. M. Lew, Loukas A. Misteris, Stefan M. Kroll, Comparative International Commercial Arbitration, Kluwer Law International, 2003, 206 ff.

[4] Wouter Wils, Principles of European Antitrust Enforcement, Hart Publishing, 2005, 473.

[5] Julian D. M. Lew, Loukas A. Misteris, Stefan M. Kroll, Comparative International Commercial Arbitration, Kluwer Law International, 2003, 200.

## 8.2 Private Enforcement

Private enforcement has at least two meanings. On the one hand, private enforcement occurs whenever the parties elect an alternative method to state judiciary in order to solve a dispute. This sense comprises mediation, conciliation, arbitration and any other "soft" resolution method.

There is another meaning discussed in competition law disputes where private is antithetic with public, and it designates the situation when a court, instead of the National Competition Authority or the European Commission, takes the appropriate measures to reinstate competition rules in the case of infringement. The measures afforded to the national judge are however limited, not including the application of fines, and, depending on jurisdiction, even structural and behavioural actions.

Nonetheless, the awarding of damages remains the prerogative of the national judge, with the administrative authorities lacking capacity to rule on this issue. This entails the conclusion that the NCAs and the European Commission apply EU competition law with different effect than the judicial and arbitration courts, with the former entities not being able to compensate the damages suffered by the complainants, whereas the latter ones lack the investigative powers and the capacity to enforce ancillary behavioural and structural measures.

Undoubtedly, there is a Union right to damages, confirmed by the recent Directive on certain rules governing actions for damages under national law for infringements of the competition law provisions of the Member States and of the European Union.[6] Individuals may "privately" enforce the competition rules by raising the application of Article 101 or 102 TFEU in front of the national court, according to Article 6 of Regulation 1/2003, either as a sword[7] or as a shield by virtue of standalone actions.

There is no condition required to follow a preliminary procedure for the actions afforded in judicial courts by the European Union legislation, such as a complaint in front of the national authority. This rule is also transposed in the national law of the Member States. The actions in court, even though amply promoted by the European Commission and the NCAs by public programs, are not a common practice for the victims in order to get relief for already sanctioned illicit behaviour. Consequently, the scarcity of standalone actions, not preceded by a complaint in front of the NCA, is not unexpected.

Without entering into the specific challenges of the private enforcement itself, the challenges in obtaining pecuniary relief in front of national judicial courts entail,

---

[6] See also *Manfredi v Lloyd Adriatico Assicurazzioni Spa*, Case C259-298/04, providing that domestic procedural rules would apply and compensation would cover both losses incurred and lost profits. For an extended comparative law analysis on the value of damages, please see Ewoud Hondius, Andre Janssen (ed.), Disgorgement of Profits. Gain-Based Remedies throughout the World, Springer, 2015.

[7] Assimakis P. Komninos Arbitration and EU Competition Law in International Antitrust Litigation. Conflict of Laws and Coordination (ed. Jurgen Basedow, Stephanie Francq, Laurence Idot), Hart Publishing, 2012, 194.

among many other issues, the damage and the illicit behaviour assessment, which are both difficult from the evidentiary perspective.

Actions for damages also require that the victims prove imputability; considering that the NCA's or European Commission's decision already establishes the illicit behaviour and the imputability in follow-on actions, the standalone actions raise supplementary important questions diminishing the chances of success in comparison with the follow-on actions. Moreover, the claimant has to quantify the damages, as the investigation authority does not establish the value of damages.[8]

The Commission White Paper and the accompanying Staff Working Paper have added several hints for better administrating the challenges of private enforcement, pursuant to Regulation 1/2003. These include guidance for quantification,[9] the calculation of double damages in hard-core cartel cases, leniency applicants – exempted from joint and several liability or limit to single damage, as well as the impact of admissibility and operation of passing on defence.

Some of the challenges (such as the disclosure of documents grounding the leniency decision) were addressed by the Directive on certain rules governing actions for damages under national law for infringements of the competition law provisions of the Member States and of the European Union. Still the Directive discusses the national courts, and only conditioned by the full assimilation of arbitration tribunals to national courts some of the improvements in merit may be translated into national law without prejudice to EU competition enforcement. All these particularities of private enforcement are common for ordinary courts and arbitration.

Arbitration, being national or international, also presents additional weaknesses in comparison with the judicial courts, most of them deriving from the fact that it holds *iudicium* but not *imperium*[10]; but it also features some advantages, including neutrality, confidentiality and finality of arbitration. The same advantages also constitute handicaps in establishing solid ground for the application of competition law. The issue of confidentiality renders the arbitral awards not public, hence resulting in little information on the application of competition law in arbitration. In addition, the neutrality of arbitration has the following downside: the arbitral court cannot take invasive actions, whereas the judicial courts and NCAs are able, respectively, to issue injunctions and take appropriate behavioural and structural measures. The finality of arbitration is limited to the private perspective, lacking the general scope of protecting the market in general.

The private enforcement of the EU competition rules focuses on the following objectives: (a) it enables compensation for victims of breaches, (b) it deters the violation of rules and (c) it relieves enforcement pressure in public agencies.

---

[8] Evidently, regulation of follow-on actions leads to a more accurate and specific application, as explained regarding the UK in Alison Jones, Brenda Sufrin, EC Competition Law. Texts, Cases, Materials, 3rd edition, 2008, 1341.

[9] Alison Jones, Brenda Sufrin, EC Competition Law. Texts, Cases, Materials, 3rd edition, 2008, 1344.

[10] Serge Lazareff, Arbitre et concurrence communautaire, in Gazette du Palais, Cahiers de l'Arbitrage no 2003/1, 3.

Although there are some similarities between NCAs and arbitral courts, they follow dissimilar objectives. From the perspective analysed in this chapter, the most relevant common feature of both categories is the possibility to apply European Union rules within their respective procedure, hence the deterrence of illicit behaviour. Considering that arbitration provides remedies, instead of sanctions, to the anticompetitive behaviour, the relief rendered to the workload of NCAs is rather illusory, as the investigation powers and the sanctions rest with the latter. The NCAs or the European Commission would open an inquiry of the most important infringements, regardless of the remedies sought by the victims of illicit deeds in national or arbitral court.

## 8.3 National Arbitration

National arbitration in the EU Member States observes the domestic law, including competition legal provisions, as they indicate which disputes are arbitrable.[11] As Articles 101 and 102 TFEU are applicable in the national law of the Member States, according to the national law requirements, it results that no impediment may be found in the application of EU competition law by the NCAs, the judicial courts, as well as the arbitration tribunals.

One can ask, however, whether the arbitration clause must consider the issue of competition, in order for a matter of competition law to be arbitrable. In civil law systems, where the answer is in the affirmative, the arbitral award taking into account such matter may be considered *ultra petita*,[12] in the absence of an arbitration clause referring thereto. In any case, the arbitrator has to define its status; this is *a minima* argument requiring that any law matter may be discussed within the arbitration frame. In the absence of an arbitral clause pertaining specifically on competition law provisions, the rationale used in order to determine the applicability of specific competition rules comes from the qualification of the legal value of competition rules. This also implies passive enforcement.[13]

Whenever the courts apply Article 101 or 102 TFEU within the legal frame of national or international arbitration of the EU Member States, there is no requirement for a specific provision referring to the applicability of EU law in an arbitration clause, competition rules being *ius cogens.*[14] Further to this rationale, legal systems

[11] Julian D. M. Lew, Loukas A. Misteris, Stefan M. Kroll, Comparative International Commercial Arbitration, Kluwer Law International, 2003, 2003, 194–196.

[12] Yves Derains, L'arbitre, la Commission et la Cour: questions de procedure, in Gazette du Palais, Cahiers de l'Arbitrage no 2003/1, p. 49.

[13] Henry Lesguillons, La solitude ponderee de l'arbitre face au droit de la concurrence, in Gazette du Palais, Cahiers de l'Arbitrage no 2003/1, p. 17.

[14] Assimakis P. Komninos Arbitration and EU Competition Law in International Antitrust Litigation. Conflict of Laws and Coordination (ed. Jurgen Basedow, Stephanie Francq, Laurence Idot), Hart Publishing, 2012, 194.

of states that traditionally exclude from arbitration certain matters[15] are still bound to accept the arbitrability of European Union Competition issues, due to their particular status.

Nonetheless, if the parties desire to include competition law within the aspects to be determined in the arbitration clause,[16] or in case EU law is not intrinsically applicable in the arbitral dispute by means of exclusion,[17] there are no specific requirements for the valid establishment of the incidence of TFEU provisions on competition.

Considering that the rationale sustaining the applicability of EU law stems from that indisputable fact that competition rules are public policy in EU Member States, it results that the ad-hoc arbitration should equally apply these rules. *Ius cogens* is mandatory for national cases; therefore national arbitration is incident in all the cases where the forum is an arbitration tribunal located in an EU Member State. The arbitrators, regardless of whether they are acting within an organized tribunal or ad-hoc, have to answer the question of law in the case of the breach of Article 101 or 102 TFEU, the two articles not being reserved to the administrative authority.

The solution is radically different in the case where one of the parties seeks relief grounded on the legal provisions on competition in front of an arbitral court located in a state which is not a member of the EU. In such a case, the arbitral court may apply Article 101 or 102 TFEU only if the parties provide by means of arbitration clause the incidence of EU competition legal provisions.

The application *ex officio* of competition law in the procedural framework of the arbitral tribunal depends on the distinction made hereinabove. It is understood that the arbitrator may discuss by their own initiative EU competition law only if same law is deemed as *ius cogens* by the domestic law.

Even the sceptics to the applicability of EU competition law in arbitration admit that for hard-core infringements, the tribunal may declare the underlying agreement null and void.[18]

## 8.4 International Arbitration

The general principle applied in determining the arbitration law follows the international conventions of the states of residence of the parties in litigation, or even national law.[19] In international arbitration, the remedies of Article 101 or 102 TFEU are assessed on different bases.

---

[15] For instance Germany, as explained by Julian D. M. Lew, Loukas A. Misteris, Stefan M. Kroll, Comparative International Commercial Arbitration, Kluwer Law International, 2003, 2003, 200.

[16] For instance, deeming arbitrable claims of a tortious nature.

[17] As per the explanation in Sect. 8.1 above.

[18] Assimakis P. Komninos Arbitration and EU Competition Law in International Antitrust Litigation. Conflict of Laws and Coordination (ed. Jurgen Basedow, Stephanie Francq, Laurence Idot), Hart Publishing, 2012, 201, 208–209.

[19] For a review of case-law on arbitrability in general, see Julian D. M. Lew, Loukas A. Misteris, Stefan M. Kroll, Comparative International Commercial Arbitration, Kluwer Law International,

Competition rules may result in arbitration by two ways. The indirect unilateral conflict of rule may be the default option but it is still not favoured by practice, as most of the time arbitration is regulated by the parties by means of an arbitration clause establishing *lex cause*. In the case where none of the parties are seated in an EU Member State, the competition law rules are incident only by introduction in an arbitration clause, whereas, if at least one the parties have their domicile in EU Member States, the solution rests in *lex causae* and the applicability of foreign law, in most of the cases *lex contractus.*[20] Whenever the parties come from both EU and non-EU states, the same parties determine whether EU law is applicable or not.

In the United States, the US Courts can apply the Sherman Act of 1890 in its entirety, whereas part of it is exclusively reserved to the US enforcement authorities. Based on the specific larger ambit of arbitration, some case-law, such as *Mitsubishi v. Soler*[21] included statues to uniformly accepted contracts, as grounds for arbitrability on competition issues. The landmark case where a Puerto Rican distributor used in its defence the competition law provisions in arbitration, validated by the Supreme Court of Justice as serving both remedial and deterrent functions, constituted a powerful example of applicability in EU jurisprudence as well.

Considering the strong similarities between the Sherman Act and the provisions of Articles 101 and 102 TFEU,[22] there should not be actual impediments to the implementation of competition rules in the disputes between EU Member States nationals and the US presented to the arbitrator. Note that there is a caveat: competition rules in general and not EU competition provisions. Nonetheless, there are two different sets of rules, even if apparently similar; the two jurisdictions obstinately promote its legislation in judicial as well as arbitral courts, the US courts (both judicial and arbitral) being reluctant to apply EU law.[23] Symmetrically, the applica-

---

2003, 188–198. The more practical issue of determining the arbitration law according to the conflict of laws, including in arbitration cases, is out of this chapter's scope. Such was the Italian decision of 18 July 1987 XVII YBCA 534/1992 of the Bologna Court of First Instance that was reversed by the Court of Appeal, because it declared the EC competition law matters as not to be arbitrable.

[20] Yves Derains, L'arbitre, la Commission et la Cour: questions de procedure, in Gazette du Palais, Cahiers de l'Arbitrage no 2003/1, p. 45.

[21] *Mitsubishi Motors Corp v. Soler Chrysler Plymouth Inc*, 473 US 614 m, 105 S Ct 3346 (1985). For an extended analysis of this particular case, see Julian D. M. Lew, Loukas A. Misteris, Stefan M. Kroll, Comparative International Commercial Arbitration, Kluwer Law International, 2003, 199.

[22] The literature discusses the globalization of competition law (Alison Jones, Brenda Sufrin, EC Competition Law. Texts, Cases, Materials, 3rd edition, 2008, 1357). The similarities result from the very fact that the Sherman Act served as inspiration for the original Treaty establishing the European Economic Community of 1957.

[23] A good example, however in State aid matters, is the *Micula* case, where the ICSID arbitrators ignored the intervention of the European Commission in arguing that EU law applies. Other examples include *Nippon Paper, Hartford Fire Insurance* (where the Japanese government intervened without success in the case).

tion of US competition law is not embraced by other jurisdictions as well.[24] In Europe, the Commission holds tight control over enforcement,[25] as opposed to the public-private pluralism applied in the United States that has a litigation-oriented system. The Antitrust Division of the US Department of Justice differs from the Commission and there are other important procedural differences as well, in addition to the substance matter discrepancies. The argument on territoriality in competition legal matters is sourced from the limitation in application of sanctions that the European Commission and the US authorities have on undertakings established outside their territory. The distinction made in *ICI*[26] between prescriptive jurisdiction (such as imposition of fines) and enforcement jurisdiction (e.g. annulment of contracts) may further increase the gap between the jurisdictions in international infringements when arbitral disputes are at stake. This approach is however a generalization that may not be valid in all EU Member States jurisdictions.[27]

Regardless, if a matter is not to be solved by a competent court in one of the countries of the two parties, the risk of accessibility to a competition matter, based on the admitted arbitrability according to *lex fori*, is that the award may not be enforceable in the other country. In some more fortunate situations, where agreements are concluded on judicial cooperation between countries,[28] competition law matters are, in principle, addressed. In fact, the cooperation treaties are incapable of rendering adequate solutions. Nonetheless, improving the level of detail in regulating cooperation by means of bilateral agreement may be the way ahead in obtaining a clearer status of both administrative and jurisdictional issues (including arbitration tribunals).

Then, if all the parties in arbitration have their domicile in an EU Member State, the problem is quasi-solved, as the TFEU provisions are EU public policy. The problem whether the parties intervene further to the application of Regulation Brussels 1, is a common issue to arbitral and judicial disputes.[29]

The parties should not abuse the freedom to invoke their rights under Union Law, a limitation to this being the compliance with international public policy and the mandatory public order sovereign laws. This moderation in pursuing the rights results also from the perspective of the arbitrator that is compelled to apply mandatory EU law in case the parties come from EU Member States. However, limitations incurred by the national public policy may prohibit the arbitrability of public poli-

[24] Alison Jones, Brenda Sufrin, EC Competition Law. Texts, Cases, Materials, 3rd edition, 2008, 1358. The authors provide as an example *Timberlane*, where the infringement affected the Honduras market.

[25] For instance, the exemptions to the applicability of Article 101 TFEU are regulated at EU, not national, level.

[26] *ICI v the Commission (Dyestuffs)* Case 48/69.

[27] Alison Jones, Brenda Sufrin, EC Competition Law. Texts, Cases, Materials, 3rd edition, 2008, 1374.

[28] The EC-US Cooperation Agreement, UNCTAD and OECD, WTO and others.

[29] See Chap. 14 in this edited collection.

cies, such as competition, rendering the arbitral award challengeable.[30] For instance, the New York Convention states that recognition may be refused grounded on the fact that the subject matter is not capable of settlement. This may not be the case with competition law (as far as the claims in arbitration do not pertain to infringing of fines or other specific administrative remedies) or the recognition of the enforcement award could be contrary to the public policy.[31]

## 8.5 The Nature of Articles 101 and 102 TFEU

There are two principles governing EU law from which the interpretation and application of the competition rules derive: effectiveness and sovereignty.[32]

The Commission Notice on cooperation between the Commission and the national courts of the Member States in the application of Articles 101 and 102 TFEU clearly explains the relationship between the European competition law and the domestic legislation of the Members States: the provisions of the TFEU prevail even if domestic law offers discretion to apply the national law; therefore the courts must raise the motion issue concerning the breach of the TFEU.

One can ask whether this rule is also applicable for arbitration disputes, given their private nature. Moreover, one can also ask whether an arbitral award is annullable on the grounds that it is inconsistent with Articles 101 and 102 TFEU. The question has now found explicit and non-debatable reasoning further to constant jurisprudence stating that in order to safeguard the effectiveness of EU competition law, the arbitration awards contrary to EU competition law are to be set aside and not recognized at enforcement, due to the inclusion of EU provisions in the *lex fori* of the national court.[33]

The arbitration's private nature does not infer that the substantive law applied by the arbitrator is a stranger to mandatory rules. In fact, once the arbitration law has been elected, the material rules would include the compulsory rules required by the legal system as well.

Certain authors[34] argue that the arbitrator should apply the TFEU on his own initiative and should decline jurisdiction if asked to rule *contra legem*, consequently

[30] Julian D. M. Lew, Loukas A. Misteris, Stefan M. Kroll, Comparative International Commercial Arbitration, Kluwer Law International, 2003, 2003, 197, Alison Jones, Brenda Sufrin, EC Competition Law. Texts, Cases, Materials, 3rd edition, 2008, 1304.

[31] New York Convention, Article V(1)(c).

[32] See Serge Lazareff, Arbitre et concurrence communautaire, in Gazette du Palais, Cahiers de l'Arbitrage no 2003/1, 3, Alison Jones, Brenda Sufrin, EC Competition Law. Texts, Cases, materials, 3rd edition, 2008, 1304 for the extended analysis of the two principles, described by the authors.

[33] ECJ case law includes, more significantly, *Eco Swiss China Time Ltd v Benetton International NV* Case C-295/99; and *Nordsee Deutche Hochseefischere Nordstern AG and Co*, Case 102/81.

[34] Yves Derains, L'arbitre, la Commission et la Cour: questions de procedure, in Gazette du Palais, Cahiers de l'Arbitrage no 2003/1, p. 49.

showing vigilance rather than refrain from applying the TFEU. The extended application of Articles 101 and 102 TFEU would have as a result a uniformity and a certain easement in providing similar solutions.

Even though the arbitrator cannot rule on competition law sanctions, given the imperative nature of European law within the European Union, the nature of the competition law provisions in the TFEU allow an arbitrator to discuss *ex officio* any matter ensued from the application of Articles 101 and 102.

There is a double limitation resulting from the fact that EU competition law is public policy. On the one hand, being public policy, its applicability remains in the exclusive prerogative of the state authorities, this being the very rationale upheld for the initial reluctance in accepting arbitration as a possible resolution modality in competition law matters.[35] On the other hand, the supremacy and effectiveness of EU competition law, in the light of Regulation 1/2003, is the source of applicability in all the dispute resolution alternatives. Actually, the annulment of arbitration originates from the fact that it breaches public policy, not that it tackles public policy issues.

The ECJ states that arbitration agreements are bound to give way in the face of the supremacy and uniform application of Union Law.[36] The principle of Union Law supremacy does not prevent the arbitration to rule in EU competition law matters, but it ordinates the competition rules to prevail when encountering other rules opposed to its principles.

The harmonization also takes place in congruence of the arbitration fundamental techniques with the specific force of the competition rules. The Community public policy serves not only the scope to subordinate EU legislation to national legislation but also allows for the objective of integration. Consequently, the relation between EU law and the rules applicable in arbitration is not one of exclusion, but one of limitation.

## 8.6 Arbitrability Limitations

Most of the arbitration cases resolve contractual disputes (e.g. claims between ex-contractors). Often, the dispute concerns non-compete obligations or exclusivity obligations that entail discussion on the compatibility of the clause with the competition rules. In many cases, arbitration tackles claims pertaining to punitive damages. In order for the award to be issued, the action grounded on domestic law must be admissible.

---

[35] Assimakis P. Komninos Arbitration and EU Competition Law in International Antitrust Litigation. Conflict of Laws and Coordination (ed. Jurgen Basedow, Stephanie Francq, Laurence Idot), Hart Publishing, 2012, 195.

[36] Such was the case of the award in *Eco-Swiss v Benetton* where the ECJ dealt with enforcement of an arbitral award grounded on EC Treaty provisions, Case 126/1997, 1 June 1999.

The principle explained in the previous section states that provisions in an agreement contravening Articles 101 and 102 TFEU are void and unenforceable. Furthermore, the entire agreement will be void if the prohibited provisions cannot be severed from the remainder of the agreement, in application of the interpretation rules.

On the one hand, in contractual arbitrable matters, competition law rules are usable as a shield aimed to protect from claims based on illicit contractual provisions, and, to some extent, as a sword, purported to invalid clauses in conflict with the competition law rules.

On the other hand, antitrust rules do not have a contractual nature, hence the question whether the disputes arising from the application of Articles 101 and 102 TFEU are at all arbitrable. In principle, arbitration is not applicable to tortious claims or unjust enrichment. The disputes resulting from recovery of losses further to an EC or NCA decision are primarily deemed to be solved by judicial courts.

Incidental application in claims grounded on tort remains, in the case of arbitration agreements concluded for the very scope of dispute resolution between the victim and the perpetrator, a situation which is abundantly applicable in systems of law where the arbitration clause covers the damage claim from the null contractual provisions.

There results a distinction between the stand-alone and the follow-on actions, as well. Whereas the European Commission or an NCA issues a decision sanctioning the illicit competitive behaviour, it is very unlikely that an arbitration court may be vested with the solution of damages, due to their tortious nature. In civil law systems the claims of reparation based on the execution of a contract that is decided by the parties as arbitrable may still fall under the arbitration clause in certain situations. Contrary to this situation, the stand-alone actions may be subject to arbitration agreement, especially when the claimant had already entered into a contractual agreement with the defendant governed by arbitration.

The same discussion occurs in the case of remedial procedures concerning merger control or in block exemption compliance assessments. The rationale for limitations stems from the lack of authority of arbitrators concerning the enforcement of EU public policies. Moreover, there is no perfect substitution between a judge and an arbitrator. Contrary to the fact that block exemptions cannot be awarded by the arbitration courts,[37] as their assessment is in the exclusive prerogative of the competition authorities, block exemptions compliance assessment engenders procedural issues that may be covered by arbitration.[38] Merger control procedure con-

[37] Assimakis P. Komninos Arbitration and EU Competition Law in International Antitrust Litigation. Conflict of Laws and Coordination (ed. Jurgen Basedow, Stephanie Francq, Laurence Idot), Hart Publishing, 2012, 196.

[38] Jean-Claude Fourgoux, L'arbitrage et le reglement amiable des differends dans la reglement d'exemption C 1400/2002 relatif aux accords verticaux concernant l'industrie automobile, in Gazette du Palais, Cahiers de l'Arbitrage no 2003/1, 40–44.

cerns the commitments assumed by the entity taking control.[39] This alternative of dispute resolution is introduced by means of an arbitration clause to the European Commission's merger control, as confirmed in jurisprudence.[40] The discussion assumes different approaches, ensued by the commitment typology:

(i) Behaviour commitments entail actions to be taken with the scope to adjust the market behaviour and for this type of commitments third parties (including the arbitrators) are suitable for the commitments' control. This control being a more technical procedure, the undertaking is incentivised to opt for negotiation, for mediation or conciliation, as the negotiation, mediation and conciliation shortcomings in enforceability are to some extent diminished in the case of arbitration of failure in commitment proceedings. Moreover, the enforceability of the arbitration award may be referred to the NCA.
(ii) Substantial commitments represent an exclusively administrative prerogative; hence, the arbitral control is possible to some degree, without excluding the exorbitant prerogative resting with the NCA. The arbitral tribunal is not an administrative control body, but rather verifies the relationship between the parties, and the NCA may refer to an arbitral court the implementation of substantive commitments.

Based on favourable results of the arbitral procedures in this area, results that depend very much on the arbitration clause, the procedure is increasingly popular, proving that some areas believed to be in the exclusive authority of the state may be externalized to private justice.

In order to protect punitive Community rules, injunction measures are the prerogative of ordinary courts. This limitation to arbitration powers is not disputed, due to its exclusive nature in favour of the national courts.

## 8.7 The Arbitral Award

Arbitration is not subject to judicial control in the form of appeal or special reformation procedures. The award remains *res iudicata* and most of the jurisdictions afford review in substance on very limited grounds. The possibility to obtain the

[39] For a synoptic analysis, see Christoph Liebscher, L'arbitrage dans les procedures de contrôle des concentrations: des perspectives, in Gazette du Palais, Cahiers de l'Arbitrage no 2003/1, 24–39.

[40] *Gencor v. Lonrho, Boeing v. McDonnell, MSG v. Media Service*, analysed by Christoph Liebscher, L'arbitrage dans les procedures de contrôle des concentrations: des perspectives, in Gazette du Palais, Cahiers de l'Arbitrage no 2003/1, p. 24–39. The practice shows certain particularities. First, an arbitrator, ad-hoc or institutional, otherwise an expert in the relevant market, may settle the dispute, with various powers and procedural rules. Second, the arbitration clause vary from comprehensive to individual issues. Then, the arbitration award is subject to communication towards third parties or not, or may even contain provisory measures. Moreover, the European Commission may have different roles pertaining to the procedure.

annulment of the arbitral award was subject to reforms in arbitration[41] aimed at reducing the opportunity to appeal against arbitral awards to the courts and maintaining the private nature of arbitration.

There is a dual approach to the review of arbitration jurisprudence.[42] The minimalist approach views only the extreme cases where the arbitrator refuses to discuss hard-core infringements of EU competition law, manifestly sustaining important infringements, such as cartels. Such an approach was visible in *Thales* case,[43] where the court, not dismissing the arguments in merit pertaining to the infringement of EU law, noted that the absence of the arguments on competition during the arbitral procedure did not enable challenge on these grounds. The first perspective is based on the fact that the review of arbitral awards is limited and the judicial review merely verifies if the analysis on competition was comprehensive enough.[44]

The maximalist approach places more emphasis on the effectiveness principle, as illustrated by the *Eco Swiss* case,[45] in the sense that prevents a larger area of competition law violations. The scarcity of grounds for annulment and reformation strengthen the effectiveness of the arbitral award. Moreover, some jurisdictions, such as the United States of America, provide effectiveness grounds by the judicial practice itself. As explained above, the US Supreme Court has held that antitrust law is arbitrable.

The EU Commission has already held in certain cases that the arbitral award is not compliant with State aid rules.[46] The Commission Decision in the *Micula* case stated that by virtue of the arbitration in front of the ICSID tribunal, the Swedish investors were granted illegal aid that should be reimbursed. To the date of publication of this book the ECJ has not ruled in the *Micula* case; nonetheless, from the perspective of the State aid rules, other ECJ jurisprudence has already stated that judicial rulings may infringe Community Law and therefore be reversed.[47] Further to this argument, it results that in the case where the ECJ decision declares an arbitral ruling contrary to the Community Law, then the EU Member States courts are bound to set aside arbitration in order for the parties to refer the case to arbitrators once more, for a compliant solution. Solutions contrary to a decision of the Commission are not enforceable not only from the perspective of State aid rules, but also from the other TFEU provisions, including Articles 101 and 102. As one author

[41] For instance, the United Kingdom, France, Denmark, and the Netherlands.

[42] Assimakis P. Komninos Arbitration and EU Competition Law in International Antitrust Litigation. Conflict of Laws and Coordination (ed. Jurgen Basedow, Stephanie Francq, Laurence Idot), Hart Publishing, 2012, 214.

[43] *Thales v Euromissile* judged by the Paris Court of Appeal in 2004.

[44] Henry Lesguillons, La solitude ponderee de l'arbitre face au droit de la concurrence, in Gazette du Palais, Cahiers de l'Arbitrage no 2003/1, p. 122.

[45] Assimakis P. Komninos Arbitration and EU Competition Law in International Antitrust Litigation. Conflict of Laws and Coordination (ed. Jurgen Basedow, Stephanie Francq, Laurence Idot), Hart Publishing, 2012, 216.

[46] Micula Case, CE Decision 2015/1470.

[47] Asteris Case, Joint Cases 106/87–120/87.

observed, not without irony, should an arbitrator decide against the provisions of TFEU, the same arbitrator may be held liable for a competition infringement.[48]

The arbitration award may decide on the non-infringement of the TFEU, but it cannot decide on the infringement of EU competition law, in the sense that it cannot rule on the merits in deciding on admissibility.

## 8.8 Practical Challenges

The congruence of the issue of arbitrability and EU competition law always engages a disproportion of forces. As explained in the literature, the supremacy of Community Law versus the less important of arbitration leads to an apparent subordination of arbitration to *ius imperium*.

Indeed, to private litigation arbitration may provide private solutions. As private litigation encourages settlement to avoid protracted litigation and as the number of arbitration awards challenged in front of judicial courts is not decreasing, in practice it may result that regardless of the solution given by the arbitrators, the issue of competition law non-compliance is most of the time brought to ordinary courts. The deterring effect to declaring arbitrable competition matters increases especially when the national courts refuse enforcement of arbitral awards.

The comparison between the national or international arbitral awards and the EU Commission decisions that benefit from complementary enforcement and force resources for complex cases is even more asymmetric, rendering almost illusory arbitration in competition substance matters.

Some authors[49] have pointed out several deterring circumstances to arbitration. They include the costs and risks in litigation, the challenges pertaining to administration of evidence (and also the complexity and technicality of economic evidence which is difficult to collect), the length and protraction, the inconsistency risks, the challenges to causation[50] (a condition which is necessary in most of the civil and common law systems), the uncertainty of injunction and enforceability and other limitations.

Another argument constituting a practical challenge to the applicability in front of arbitral courts of Community Law, including competition, rests in the inadmissibility of deterring remedies afforded to arbitration. Whereas the European Commission applies measures aimed to have dissuasive effect on the distortions of competition within the internal market, arbitration is not capable of injunction measures, or any structural or behavioural remedial intervention.

[48] Yves Derains, L'arbitre, la Commission et la Cour: questions de procedure, in Gazette du Palais, Cahiers de l'Arbitrage no 2003/1, p. 48.

[49] Alison Jones, Brenda Sufrin, EC Competition Law. Texts, Cases, Materials, 3rd edition, 2008, 1307.

[50] Alison Jones, Brenda Sufrin, EC Competition Law. Texts, Cases, Materials, 3rd edition, 2008, 1343.

A more sensitive practical problem results from the lack of arbitrators that are specialists in competition law. The complexity of (a very technical) competition law is not accessible enough to arbitrators. It is very unlikely that an arbitrator in EU may notice by their own initiative the occurrence of illicit behaviour pertaining to the execution or performance of an agreement. Even if vested with claims stemming from competition law, the arbitrator, more than the national judge, would require a preliminary ruling of ECJ in order to have a clear interpretation of the Community Law. Despite this, the arbitrator is not enumerated among the beneficiaries of the preliminary referral process.[51]

Moreover, there has been little antitrust litigation brought by private individuals before national courts. The insufficient practice may generate inconsistency at the level of national courts, where uniform practice is still possible by virtue of instruments provided by the national procedure as well as by the Regulation 1/2003. Arbitration tribunals have augmented difficulties in providing consistent solutions to special matters, considering that the awards are not public.

Third parties are not bound by the arbitration clause, nor by the arbitration award and the *erga omnes* effects required by the competition law in order to be effective are impossible to be put into practice when sourced from an arbitration award. Arbitration cannot impose sanctions of any nature, and it cannot award damages against third parties. The duty to inform third parties is not mandatory, and most of the arbitration awards remain undisclosed to other victims of the same infringement. As a result, the other victims cannot benefit from the arbitral award declaring illicit the anticompetitive behaviour, the victims often obtain different solutions from arbitral or judicial courts, and, in the absence of a formal complaint, the NCA cannot be aware of the compensation measures decided by the arbitrator.

The arbitrators also have limited access to evidence. This is a challenge that both arbitration and ordinary courts encounter. Some legal systems that allow inquisitive means of evidence, such as discovery, would have this shortcoming mitigated; still the powers of investigation at the disposition of the NCAs and the European Commission are far superior to any private discovery.

In addition, public-private enforcement coordination still requires some tweaking. The challenges addressable for the actions in court are extended to arbitration, as well. For instance, the application of commitments, leniency or settlements within the administrative procedure affect the administrative liability, but they are out of the scope of the action for damages.

## 8.9 Advantages of Arbitration

Some of the very deficiencies of arbitration may be the source of certain advantages in administrating competition issues. The fact that the parties introduce competition matters chiefly when discussing a contractual relationship entails the possibility to

[51] See Sect. 8.10 below.

compensate damages resulting from a breach which also represents antitrust conduct with contractual objectives.

Moreover, as arbitration represents an expeditious method to resolve the dispute, competition infringement remedies allow the fastest way to seek relief for the victim, in comparison with competition investigations led by an NCA. The competition inquiry led by an NCA or the European Commission does not have a reparatory nature; therefore, claims are brought in front of ordinary courts, which, in most of the EU jurisdictions are not as expeditious as arbitration and entail significant costs.

The justification stands in the urgency of a competition law issue raised by the defendant (in most of the cases) or the claimant (in the odd case where competition rules are used as sword). Costs incentives (and, to some extent, disincentives, accordingly) are another reason for the subtle inclination victims may have for arbitration in obtaining relief. When comparing the duty tax imposed by the ordinary courts and the arbitral fees, the latter comes more advantageous, in most of the jurisdictions. This renders arbitration more financially efficient for the victim. Nonetheless, when comparing from the costs perspective arbitration and investigation procedures led by the NCAs, the balance favours the administrative procedure. Considering these arguments, the victim may prefer to file a complaint first and then get relief in court, than file for a direct claim in court.

This advantage can be added to the other advantages of having the illicit conduct investigated first. These other advantages include: (i) the easement of the burden of proof regarding the facts already established by the decision concluding the inquiry, such as the imputability; (ii) the possibility to settle or waive the claims; and (iii) the benefit of adjacent measures (structural or behavioural) that the NCA may impose on the aggressive competitor.

Another advantage stems from the very auxiliary character of arbitration. The relief sought in arbitration by victims of anticompetitive behaviour is most of the time incidental. Where the arbitrator dismisses the claims, the claimant may file a separate action, grounded on tort, in front of ordinary courts. The victim may also ask simultaneously for the annulment of a contract on more than one ground, such as the infringement of competition rules.

In legal systems, where claims of damages are popular, in practice, settlement and methods of alternative dispute resolution are actually encouraged to resolve antitrust issues.

## 8.10 Cooperation Between the European Commission and the Arbitration Tribunals

One of the sources of debate regarding the applicability of EU law in national or international arbitration is the lack of reference to arbitration tribunals in Regulation 1/2003. Set to unify the national practice in the application of TFEU, the target of

Regulation 1/2003 is the judicial courts, which are vested with the power to directly enforce EU Competition Law.

Further to Article 6 of Regulation 1/2003, the national courts shall have the power to apply Articles 101 and 102 TFEU and order remedies to an agreement infringing competition rules, or to an abusive conduct, so qualified by the court.

Regulation 1/2003 enables the enforcement of remedies for loss in front of the judicial courts, and not arbitration. The interpretation of the legal text cannot however disregard the general recognition of arbitration, especially when organized in institutional form, as an alternative dispute resolution modality having similar effect to the ordinary courts. Consequently, there is no duty to cooperate concerning the arbitral tribunal, as opposed to the case of national courts. Evidently, when applying national law, the arbitral courts may have the possibility to apply Union law which is deemed national law.

To one extreme are the authors denying arbitration access to administrative cooperation.[52] To the other extreme, the more optimistic authors argue, however, that State laws in general do not contain specific provisions on arbitration, rendering it more suitable for assimilation with the judicial courts, except for those situations where it is specifically excluded.[53] The author, using a *per a contrario* argument, explains that in practice it is the very paradoxical application "by the back door" of the same EU provisions which renders useless any restriction in application.

There are some other reasons for which the assimilation of arbitration tribunals to judicial courts renders the arbitration suitable for addressing EU competition law. The judicial court may privately enforce competition rules by awarding damages to the victim of the infringement. The arbitral tribunals may as well solve claims pertaining to damages incurred from the performance of an agreement. Further to the application of Article 16 of Regulation 1/2003, the courts are bound to observe Articles 101 and 102 TFEU; the uniform application of EU legislation prevents the courts to rule against European Commission decisions. Indeed, the courts not only have the power, but also the obligation to apply the TFEU provisions. Moreover, the Commission Notice on the co-operation between the Commission and the Courts of the Member States in the application of Articles 101 and 102 TFEU states that the provisions of the TFEU prevail, even if domestic law offers discretion to apply the national law. Therefore, the Courts must raise the motion issue concerning the breach of the Treaty.

In the absence of a specific provision on cooperation between the arbitration courts and the European Commission, one can ask whether there is a cooperation obligation between the two. According to Article 15 of Regulation 1/2003, the

[52] Henry Lesguillons, La solitude ponderee de l'arbitre face au droit de la concurrence, in Gazette du Palais, Cahiers de l'Arbitrage no 2003/1, p. 18.

[53] Assimakis P. Komninos Arbitration and EU Competition Law in International Antitrust Litigation. Conflict of Laws and Coordination (ed. Jurgen Basedow, Stephanie Francq, Laurence Idot), Hart Publishing, 2012, 197. The author argues that a different solution entails 'serious problems of procedural nature'. Indeed, the ECJ has demonstrated that the problems envisaged are real.

European Commission may provide to the judicial courts not only expert evidence but also opinions on the application of competition rules.

What is the nature of the European Commission's intervention in the judicial procedure? Some literature argues that it holds the position of a witness, but also as *amicus curiae* to national courts.[54] It is my opinion that the procedural status of the European Commission depends on the procedural system the national law applies. Where the judicial system enables *amici curiae*, the European Commission's position may be more flexible. In any case, Regulation 1/2003 requires that the judicial system accommodate the intervention of the European Commission within the procedure. There are legal systems, such as the Romanian one, where procedural rules prevent the intervening of authorities whose decisions are subject to reformation in front of the judicial court. Consequently, the status of *amicus curiae* cannot be extended to the NCA in such situations.

The interventions afforded to the European Commission and the NCAs, analysed from the perspective of arbitration have different solutions, depending on the type of involvement:

(i) Information or evidence on economic or factual matters as well as opinion on legal aspects of the case rendered by the European Commission, on the grounds of Article 15(1) of Regulation 1/2003 might be requested by the arbitration tribunals as well. The European Commission is not bound however to present the same information to the arbitrator, due to the limited circumstances provided by the legal text. In any case, the possibility for the European Commission to intervene ex officio to national courts is quite transposable to arbitration.[55]

(ii) The obligation incurred to Member States to forward any decision on application of Articles 101 and 102 TFEU is not extended to the arbitral awards, even if institutionalized as tribunals. This conclusion is also based on the restrictive interpretation of Article 15 of Regulation 1/2003. Nonetheless, in order to ensure the consistent application of Articles 101 and 102 TFEU, considering that the arbitral courts may apply Community law in their ruling, the Commission should accept copies of the arbitral awards as well. There are some obvious challenges to the application of this instrument of consistent application, the most important one being the lack of procedure in communicating the arbitration activity with the State. Whereas the collection of judicial awards on competition law is an exercise that may be easily implemented by the State, the arbitration tribunals are not integrated in the State institutions and lack institutional communication. The situation where the arbitration is held *ad hoc* is even more arguable to be included in discussion, based on the rationale above.

[54] Yves Derains, L'arbitre, la Commission et la Cour: questions de procedure, in Gazette du Palais, Cahiers de l'Arbitrage no 2003/1, p. 46.

[55] Assimakis P. Komninos Arbitration and EU Competition Law in International Antitrust Litigation. Conflict of Laws and Coordination (ed. Jurgen Basedow, Stephanie Francq, Laurence Idot), Hart Publishing, 2012, 203.

(iii) The possibility for the NCAs to submit written observations to their national courts of their own initiative (or oral submission, with their permission) may be interpreted as a prerogative and not an obligation for the NCA. Nonetheless, the courts may request observations to the case, in which case, in this author's opinion, the NCA cannot refuse submitting a point of view on the matters indicated in the court's reference. The possibility for the NCA to intervene in cases where Articles 101 and 102 TFEU are in debate cannot be extended to arbitration disputes. This solution is not at least contrary to the solution explained hereinabove for the opinion rendered by the European Commission. Whereas, according to Article 15(1) of Regulation 1/2003, the European Commission acts further to the request received from the judicial court, the NCA is afforded by Article 15(3) of Regulation 1/2003 to take its own initiative in intervening in the process. It is difficult to imagine the intervention in private nature case-law of the arbitral courts.

Considering these three instruments are dedicated to the consistent application of Articles 101 and 102 TFEU, the challenges to their effectiveness in arbitration are quite inopportune. Ideally, their application and procedure should be extended so that all types of courts may benefit from these modalities without prejudice to the independence, confidentiality and private nature that render State monitoring quite questionable.[56] As the arbitration practice is confidential, the arguments and the grounding remain outside of the discussion. The same author, quoting national case-law where ad hoc tribunals proceeded to informal cooperation with the Commission, indicates that the same type of assistance required by the national courts is also valid for the arbitrators.[57] In that situation, the European Commission has already intervened in cases deemed appropriate, by means of communicating observations, without having the effect of setting aside the arbitral award.[58] Aside from this latter jurisprudence example, the disregard for the necessity of consulting the European Commission in cases involving arbitration of competition law matters might affect the stability of the award, even though the Commission is not a reform authority for arbitration. Another negative consequence may be, as the literature noted,[59] in the solitude of the arbitrator in facing complex competition matters. The conclusion reached for extending effective cooperation for arbitrators as well may be a notice on cooperation with arbitrators.

[56] Assimakis P. Komninos Arbitration and EU Competition Law in International Antitrust Litigation. Conflict of Laws and Coordination (ed. Jurgen Basedow, Stephanie Francq, Laurence Idot), Hart Publishing, 2012, 203.

[57] Assimakis P. Komninos Arbitration and EU Competition Law in International Antitrust Litigation. Conflict of Laws and Coordination (ed. Jurgen Basedow, Stephanie Francq, Laurence Idot), Hart Publishing, 2012, 205–206.

[58] Prefix v Lipski case (from the Xth report on competition policy, the European Commission).

[59] Henry Lesguillons, La solitude ponderee de l'arbitre face au droit de la concurrence, in Gazette du Palais, Cahiers de l'Arbitrage no 2003/1, p. 18.

## 8.11 Availability of Preliminary Rulings to Arbitration

As explained in the fourth part of this book,[60] the Courts have a right, as well as an obligation to address a preliminary question to the European Court of Justice, when uncertain regarding the interpretation of the Articles 101 and 102 TFEU.

Article 267 TFEU (former Article 234 TEC) provides the Court of Justice of the European Union with the jurisdiction to give preliminary rulings concerning the interpretation of the Treaties and the validity and interpretation of acts of the institutions, bodies, offices or agencies of the Union.

According to the procedure set forth in Article 267 TFEU, the preliminary question may be raised before any court or tribunal of a Member State, if deemed necessary by the court; however it is mandatory for the court in case there is no judicial remedy under national law. No reference is made to the arbitral tribunals. Based on the lack of reference, the case-law, including the *Nordsee* case, concluded that Article 267 TFEU does not apply to arbitration.[61]

It is at least regrettable that arbitration is deprived of access to the consistent application of Articles 101 and 102 TFEU by means of an interpretation ruling rendered by the Court of Justice of the European Union. In the absence of procedural instruments, enabling communication between the arbitration tribunals and the Court of Justice of the European Union, one possible remedy to this problem, stemming from jurisdictional cooperation, may be that the arbitrator addresses the preliminary question to the Court of Justice of the European Union, indirectly, via the ordinary court. Despite the institutional availability of this solution, there are procedural impediments to this in certain procedural systems, as well as some difficulty in harmonizing the celerity of arbitration with this procedural incidental matter, even more delayed by the interposition of the judicial court. A specific procedure provided to arbitration may be the effective solution to the challenge of the harmonization of EU application even in arbitration courts.

The arbitral tribunal is a non-national institution; it has no *lex fori* in the conventional sense,[62] and does not represent a jurisdiction from a member State in the sense of Article 267 TFEU. Consequently, the arbitral court cannot refer to the Court of Justice of the European Union in order to obtain a preliminary ruling, in the case of uncertainty regarding the interpretation of Articles 101 and 102 TFEU, regardless of whether the arbitration takes place in a Member State of the European Union or not.

---

[60] See Chaps. 9 and 10 in this edited collection.

[61] Serge Lazareff, Arbitre et concurrence communautaire, in Gazette du Palais, Cahiers de l'Arbitrage no 2003/1, 3.

[62] Assimakis P. Komninos Arbitration and EU Competition Law in International Antitrust Litigation. Conflict of Laws and Coordination (ed. Jurgen Basedow, Stephanie Francq, Laurence Idot), Hart Publishing, 2012, 200.

## 8.12 Conclusion

Despite the challenges for the enforcement of the EU competition law rules by means of arbitration, the necessity of uniform solutions remains. Arbitration, international or national by case, provides a valuable instrument for the private resolution of claims pertaining to damages resulting from anticompetitive behaviour. Eliminating the full implications of this modality of alternative dispute resolution in competition matters may be against the general and compulsory application of EU competition law, but it may also be harmful for the credibility of arbitration whose status is still far from the one of judicial courts.

In case the arbitration substantive law is the law of an EU Member State, the mandatory provisions of the Treaty are fully applicable, whether a party invokes these provisions or they are invoked *ex officio*, by the arbitrator.[63] In the application of the same provisions, the arbitrator cannot refer a preliminary question to the Court of Justice of the European Union, in the absence of specific provision in the TFEU and a lack of an appropriate procedural instrument. The arbitrators are not to communicate their awards to the European Commission, when applying EU competition law. Neither an NCA nor the European Commission may intervene in the arbitration process, considering that the cooperation instruments provided for in Regulation 1/2003 do not refer to arbitration, but to national courts.

Eventually, a workable solution may be the specialized tribunals. It is the solution that not only solves the lack of adequate competition knowledge of arbitrators but also increases the chances that the European Union legislation takes more seriously arbitration as an forum capable of issuing remedies to competition.

[63] The possibility to raise ex officio a matter of arbitrability in international arbitration where EU competition law is not mandatory for the parties is further analysed in Julian D. M. Lew, Loukas A. Misteris, Stefan M. Kroll, Comparative international commercial arbitration, Kluwer Law International, 2003, 2003, 119–221. See also Assimakis P. Komninos Arbitration and EU Competition Law in International Antitrust Litigation. Conflict of Laws and Coordination (ed. Jurgen Basedow, Stephanie Francq, Laurence Idot), Hart Publishing, 2012, 193.

# Part IV
# Preliminary Rulings – Instruments for the Consistent Application of Articles 101 and 102 TFEU

# Chapter 9
# The National Judge and Preliminary Rulings: Recent CJEU Case Law on Articles 101 and 102 TFEU

**Camelia Toader**

## 9.1 Introduction

The Court of Justice's preliminary rulings form part of the foundation of the European Union's jurisprudence. Preliminary rulings are a unique feature of the Court; not only does the ability to refer a question to the Court for a preliminary ruling encourage active cooperation between the national courts and the Court of Justice, but it also promotes uniform application of European Union law throughout the EU.

This chapter aims to describe the interplay between the national judge – that is the jurisdiction responsible for making a reference to the Court for a preliminary ruling – and the Court's preliminary rulings with respect to cartel and abuse of dominant position practices. It further contains a brief description of the Court of Justice in the larger scheme of European Union law and provides an overview of the preliminary ruling procedure. Finally, it gives examples of certain judgments (recent preliminary rulings from the Court) concerning Articles 101 and 102 in order to demonstrate how preliminary rulings help both the national judge and the development of EU law.

C. Toader (✉)
Court of Justice of the European Union and Faculty of Law, University of Bucharest, Bucharest, Romania
e-mail: camelia.toader@drept.unibuc.ro



A. Almăşan, P. Whelan (eds.), *The Consistent Application of EU Competition Law*, Studies in European Economic Law and Regulation 9,
DOI 10.1007/978-3-319-47382-6_9

## 9.2 Role of the Court of Justice

The Court of Justice has a key role in the life and work of the EU. From the early beginnings of the European integration process, the Court has contributed to establishing the autonomy of the EU legal order. The Court of Justice of the European Union includes two separate institutions: the Court of Justice (which I will refer to as 'the Court') and the General Court.[1]

The Court is composed of 28 Judges and 11 Advocates General (AGs).[2] The Judges and AGs are appointed by common accord of the Member States' governments after consultation of a panel[3] responsible for giving an opinion on prospective candidates' suitability to perform the duties concerned. They are appointed for a term of office of six years, which is renewable. They are chosen among persons whose independence is beyond doubt and who possess the qualifications required for appointment, in their respective countries, to the highest judicial offices, or who are of recognized competence. The AGs assist the Court. They are responsible for presenting, with complete impartiality and independence, an 'opinion' in the cases assigned to them.

The Court itself may sit as a full court, in a Grand Chamber of 15 judges or in Chambers of three or five judges. The Court sits as a full court in the particular cases prescribed by the Statute of the Court (including proceedings to dismiss the European Ombudsman or a Member of the European Commission who has failed to fulfil his or her obligations) and where the Court considers that a case is of exceptional importance.[4] The court sits in a Grand Chamber when a Member State or an institution which is a party to the proceedings so requests, and in particularly complex or important cases.[5]

The Court plays the role of the Union's constitutional court, that is to say the guardian of the objectives and rules laid down in the EU Treaties. The Court rules in cases in which constitutional issues come to the fore, such as the legality of Union secondary legislation, the preservation of institutional balance, the demarcation of Union and national spheres of competence, and the protection of fundamental rights. As summarized by Article 19(3) TEU, the Court rules on actions brought by a Member State, an institution or a natural or legal person; gives preliminary rulings on interpretation and validity of Union law; and adjudicates other cases provided for in the Treaties.

---

[1] Article 3 § 5 TEU. See also Regulation (EU, Euratom) n°2015/2422, in the O.J. 24 december 2015, L 341, P.14.

[2] Pursuant to Council Decision 2013/336/EU of 25 June 2013, the number of AGs was increased to eleven.

[3] The creation of this panel was introduced under the Treaty of Lisbon, Article 253, 1 §, TFEU; Art. 255 TFEU.

[4] Protocol N° 3 on the Statute of the Court of Justice of the European Union, Article 16, ex. *Pringle* case.

[5] Ibid.

## 9.3 The Court of Justice in the Legal Order of the European Union

Although it was inevitable that the Union Treaties would in due course come into conflict with inconsistent provisions in the national laws of the Member States, these treaties did not say anything about how such conflicts were to be resolved. This could have been taken to imply that the Union Treaties were no different from ordinary international treaties, whose effect within the legal order of the contracting parties will depend on a rule of domestic constitutional law. Indeed, the internal effect of a treaty may differ from one contracting party to another. In particular, the question whether a provision of a treaty confers rights on private parties which can be invoked before the national courts, and if so in what circumstances, may receive different answers in different countries. Moreover, legal systems may differ on the question whether treaties take precedence over national law. They may also take different approaches to the interpretation of treaties, so that the effect of a provision in a given set of circumstances might vary.

The principle that the effect of treaties in national courts depends on domestic law is liable to have adverse consequences for the effectiveness of all international treaties. In the case of the Union Treaties, however, those consequences might have threatened the viability of the project its authors had in mind. It was thus apparent that the effect of the Treaties had to be the same throughout the territory of the Member States. Nevertheless, the concepts of direct effect and primacy have not been expressly spelt out in the Treaties, but only implicit in the system that they created. Given the duty imposed on the Court by Article 19 TEU to ensure observance of the law, this jurisdiction, through its case-law, has found solutions to insure a uniform application of the Community and, later, of EU law.

It thus identified an obligation on administrations and national courts to apply EU law in full within their sphere of competence and to protect the rights conferred on citizens by that law (direct application of EU law), and to disapply any conflicting national provision, whether prior or subsequent to the EU provision (primacy of European Union law over national law).

In its case-law (starting with *Van Gend en Loos* in 1963), the Court introduced the principle of the direct effect of Community law in the Member States, which now enables European citizens to rely directly on rules of European Union law before their national courts.

In 1964, the *Costa* judgment established the primacy of Community law over domestic law. In that case, an Italian court had asked the Court whether the Italian law on nationalization of the production and distribution of electrical energy was compatible with certain rules in the EEC Treaty. The Court introduced the doctrine of the primacy of Community law, basing it on the specific nature of the Community legal order, which is to be uniformly applied in all the Member States.

In 1991, in *Francovich and Others*, the Court has also recognized the principle of the liability of Member States to individuals for damage caused to them by a breach of Community law by that State which, first, plays an important part in consolidating the protection of the rights conferred on individuals by EU provisions and, secondly, may contribute to more diligent application of EU provisions by Member States.

## 9.4 Preliminary Rulings in EU Law

### *9.4.1 Overview*

It is self-evident that the constitutional issues of Union law may also arise in cases brought before national courts or the General Court. Therefore, the Court is not the sole guardian of the Union legal order. But national courts may (and, in some cases, must) still bring the constitutional issue before the Court by submitting a question for a preliminary ruling. Likewise, an appeal might be brought or, in exceptional cases, a review procedure initiated against decisions of the General Court, which means that here again the Court can have the last word in determining the legal questions with constitutional implications.

The treaties, as amended by the Treaty of Lisbon, and Article 51 of the Statute of the Court of Justice of the European Union, grant the Court jurisdiction over a number of matters. Article 267 TFEU in particular grants the Court jurisdiction over preliminary references.

The number of references for preliminary rulings has increased over the last years. In 2014 for instance, there were 428 new preliminary references from national courts to the Court.

### *9.4.2 Who Can or Must Refer a Question for a Preliminary Ruling*

According to Article 267 TFEU, any national court seized has the possibility of submitting a question to the Court for a preliminary ruling as far as the question concerns the interpretation of a Union rule of law, and which the national court believes an answer is necessary before it can rule on the issue for which it was seized.[6]

The Court cooperates with all the courts of the Member States, which are the ordinary courts in matters of European Union law. To ensure the effective and uniform application of European Union legislation and to prevent divergent interpretations, the national courts may, and sometimes must, refer to the Court and ask it to clarify a point concerning the interpretation of EU law. National courts may do so

[6] Court of Justice of the European Union Recommendations 2012/C 338/01 to national courts and tribunals to the initiation of preliminary ruling proceedings [2012] OJ C338/2.

in order to ascertain whether their national legislation complies with EU law, or to review the validity of an act of EU law.

However, only the Court can declare that an act of an EU institution or organ is invalid; this power is not reserved to the courts of the Member States. Therefore, when a national court is unsure about the validity of an EU institution's act, it must refer this issue to the Court for a preliminary ruling.

However, according to the Court's *CILFIT* judgment,[7] which was incorporated into the Court's procedural rules, a national court whose decisions will not be subject to appeal under domestic law must refer such questions to the Court unless there is EU precedent on that particular issue, or where the correct interpretation of the rule of law is self-evident.[8] Therefore, a national court can, when it believes it is sufficiently enlightened by the Court's jurisprudence, decide for itself the correct interpretation of Union law and its application to the case at issue.[9] Nevertheless a preliminary ruling can be extremely useful in two situations: first, when it concerns a new interpretation that would be of general interest for the uniform application of Union law, and second when the existing jurisprudence is not applicable to the issue at hand.

### 9.4.3 At What Stage in the National Proceedings Should a Question Be Referred?

The national court can refer its preliminary question to the Court as soon as it realizes that its decision is dependent on the interpretation or validity of a Union law.[10] This national court is clearly in the best position to determine when it should refer the question to the Court.[11] Of course, it is best for the referring court the main proceeding is sufficient developed such that the referring court can define the legal and factual issues of the case.[12] This ensures that the Court has all of the elements necessary to check that Union law is in fact applicable to the main proceedings.[13] The lodging of a request for a preliminary ruling calls for the national proceedings to be stayed until the Court has given its ruling.[14]

---

[7] *CILFIT*, C-283/81, EU:C:1982:335, para. 21.

[8] Court of Justice of the European Union Recommendations 2012/C 338/01 to national courts and tribunals to the initiation of preliminary ruling proceedings [2012] OJ C338/2.

[9] Ibid.

[10] Ibid.

[11] Ibid.

[12] Ibid.

[13] Court of Justice of the European Union Recommendations 2012/C 338/01 to national courts and tribunals to the initiation of preliminary ruling proceedings [2012] OJ C338/3.

[14] Ibid.

### 9.4.4 The Form and Content of the Submission for a Preliminary Ruling

The decision by which the national court refers one or more questions to the Court may be in any form allowed by national law as regards procedural steps.[15] However, given that the referred question must be translated into all the official languages of the Union, the request for a preliminary ruling should be drafted simply, clearly and precisely, avoiding superfluous detail.[16]

Ten pages are sufficient to outline the request and the factual and legal context of the main proceedings.[17] The request must be succinct but also provide all relevant information to give the Court and those entitled to submit observations a clear understanding of the factual and legal context of the main proceedings.[18] In making the preliminary reference request, it is important for the national court to highlight and articulate the relevant EU law provision(s) and the arguments of the parties to the main proceedings.[19] Lastly, if the referring court considers it can do so, it can briefly state its opinion on the answer to the question it refers for a preliminary ruling.[20] In fact, this can be particularly useful when the Court is called upon to give a preliminary ruling in an expedited or urgent procedure.[21]

The parties to the proceedings before the referencing court, the Member States and the EU institutions may take part in the proceedings before the Court.

Several important principles of EU law have been laid down by preliminary rulings. The Court revisited the abilities of national courts to submit a preliminary ruling in its *Križan* judgment in 2013. The Court reiterated that a national law cannot take away the discretion of a national court, at any level, to refer questions of interpretation concerning EU law. The national court must consider itself to have the discretion to refer questions of EU law to the Court if the former believes that a higher national court's legal ruling could lead it to deliver a judgment contrary to EU law.[22] The Court underlined that this procedure had avoided the application of national laws that risk undermining the unity and effectiveness of Union law.[23]

---

[15] Ibid.

[16] Ibid.

[17] Ibid.

[18] Ibid.

[19] Ibid.

[20] Ibid.

[21] Ibid.

[22] *Križan and others*, C-416/10, EU:C:2013:8, para. 68.

[23] Ibid, para. 70.

### 9.4.5 *Effect of the Court's Preliminary Ruling*

The Court's role is only to give an interpretation of the Union law at issue in the main proceedings[24] and it is for the national court to apply this interpretation of the ECJ.[25]

The Court's subsequent preliminary ruling is not merely an opinion; it takes the form of a judgment or reasoned order. Therefore, the national court to which the order is addressed is bound by the interpretation given by the Court. The Court's judgment likewise binds other national courts before which the problem is raised.

Moving to the main subject, I will discuss some of the recent application of the preliminary ruling proceedings to competition issues.

## 9.5 Article 101

Although Articles 101 and 102 TFEU were drafted and became effective recently, these articles promote and protect competition principles that existed prior to this Treaty. They were formerly Articles 81 and 82 of the EC Treaty.

Article 101 TFEU, formerly Article 81 TEC, prohibits cartel arrangements. It specifically prohibits agreements, between entities, that have as their purpose to distort natural competition forces of the market and create artificial conditions that benefit these entities. However, these artificially created conditions can be legal if all the conditions in Article 101(3) are met. This occurs when the agreement in question "contributes to improving the production or distribution of goods or to promoting technical or economic progress, while allowing consumers a fair share of the resulting benefit." Therefore, Article 101 is "intended to protect the interests of competitors or consumers" and "the structure of the market and thus competition as such."[26]

Over the last three years the Court has issued a series of preliminary rulings providing additional shape to the scope of Article 101. In the interests of time, I will discuss those more recent cases. These cases have predominantly dealt with the intent of those entities that are part of the cartel in question.

In *T-Mobile Netherlands and Others,* for example, certain representatives of mobile operators in the Netherlands market met to discuss the reduction of "standard dealer remunerations" for monthly subscriptions.[27] The Netherlands Competition Authority held that the representatives had entered into a concerted

---

[24] Court of Justice of the European Union Recommendations 2012/C 338/01 to national courts and tribunals to the initiation of preliminary ruling proceedings [2012] OJ C338/2.

[25] Ibid.

[26] *Slovenská sporiteľňa*, C-68/12, EU:C:2013:71, para. 18.

[27] *T-Mobile Netherlands and others*, C-8/08, EU:C:2009:343, paras 9, 11–12.

practice in the summer of 2001 which violated Article 81(1) TEC.[28] The mobile representatives brought action before the District Court of Rotterdam after the Competition Authority's decision.[29] That Court annulled the Competition Authority's decision and ordered it to adopt a new decision.[30] The operators and the Competition Authority appealed the District Court's judgment to the college van Beroep voor het bedrijfsleven, which was required to determine "whether the concept of concerted practice was interpreted correctly in light of established case law".[31] The latter court grappled with a few questions, including whether the direct object of the concerted practice was in fact prices of consumer subscriptions or the amount paid by the operators to dealers that were supplying services to assist the consumers.[32] The Netherlands court then referred the following question to the Court: if the concerted practice targeted remuneration to service providers, and not consumer prices, was this concerted practice a restriction or distortion of competition within the meaning of Article 81(1) of the EC[33]?

In its analysis, the Court noted that "close regard must be paid in particular to the objective" which the concerted practice is intended to attain, and its economic and legal context[34]"; it is sufficient that it have the potential to negatively affect competition. The Court went on to emphasize that it is important to determine the purpose of the concerted practice, and if that is not possible then the consequences of the practice on competition should be considered when determining if the practice is anti-competitive.[35]

However, if it is clear that an anti-competitive object is the purpose of the practice, then it is not necessary to consider the effects of the practice; in that case, it is already clear that the practice is anti-competitive.[36] Concerning the referred question mentioned previously, the Court noted that it was not a treaty requirement that there be a direct link between the concerted practice and the impact on the consumer.[37] Here for example, it was evident that the remuneration paid to the service providers would ultimately be reflected in the price the operators charged to the consumer and, therefore, the concerted practice concerning the service provider was linked to the consumer.[38] Therefore, there does not need to be a direct link between the practice and consumer prices.[39] Given all these considerations, the Court ruled that a practice has an anti-competitive purpose when it "is capable in an individual

[28] Ibid, paras 13, 15.

[29] Ibid, para. 16.

[30] Ibid, para. 16.

[31] *T-Mobile Netherlands and others*, EU:C:2009:343, para. 17.

[32] Ibid, para. 19.

[33] Ibid, para. 20.

[34] Ibid, paras 26, 31.

[35] Ibid, para. 28.

[36] Ibid, para. 30.

[37] Ibid, para. 38.

[38] Ibid, para. 37.

[39] *T-Mobile Netherlands and others*, EU:C:2009:343, para. 39.

case of resulting in the prevention, restriction, or distortion of competition within the common market. It is not necessary for there to be actual prevention, restriction or distortion of competition or a direct link between the concerted practice and consumer prices. An exchange of information between competitors is tainted with an anti-competitive object if the exchange is capable of removing uncertainties concerning the intended conduct of the participating undertakings".[40]

Also along the lines of intent, the Court ruled in a judgment issued in 2013 that it is only the intent of those individuals or entities involved in the anticompetitive agreement that is important. In that case, the Competition Authority of the Slovak Republic requested a preliminary ruling concerning the importance of the legal status of the entity impacted by a cartel's anti-competitive practice.[41] Three banks had agreed to terminate their contracts, on the condition that the other two banks did the same, relating to current accounts with the company Akcenta, which itself was found to be operating illegally at the time of the agreement.[42] In its preliminary ruling, the Court held that Article 101 TFEU must be interpreted as meaning that the legal status of an undertaking adversary affected by an agreement that restricts competition is not relevant to whether the agreement itself is an infringement on competition.[43] The Court further ruled, in response to a second referred question, that it is not necessary for an agent to be authorized to enter into an agreement that restricts competition.[44]

The Court revisited the notion of intent and an entity's awareness of its anti-competitive actions in its preliminary ruling in the *Schenker* case. There, the Court ruled that even if the undertaking involved in a cartel believed that its involvement in the cartel was legal, based on information received from a competent authority, it couldn't be exempted from the imposition of a fine if its conduct were found to be anticompetitive.[45] Also in the same case, and as a side note, the Court provided what might be seen as good news for those entities participating in a cartel: those entities that have infringed Article 101 TFEU but that have participated in a national leniency program,[46] may, at the discretion of the national competition authorities, be exempted from the imposition of a fine.[47]

Recently, the Court signalled the scope of those entities that can claim damages under Article 101 in its *Kone* preliminary ruling. There the Court ruled that Article 101 precludes the application of national legislation that excludes civil liability of undertakings, who in making their agreement caused losses to a third party in response to the market distortions resulting from the cartel agreement.[48]

---

[40] Ibid, para. 43.

[41] *Slovenská sporiteľňa*, EU:C:2013:71, para. 12.

[42] Ibid, para. 4.

[43] Ibid, para. 21.

[44] Ibid, para. 28.

[45] *Schenker & Co.* and others, C-681/11, EU:C:2013:404, paras 38;43.

[46] Ibid, para. 31.

[47] Ibid, para. 50.

[48] *Kone and others*, C-557/12, EU:C:2014:1317, para. 37.

Lastly, in its decision of 23 October 2014, *flyLAL-Lithuanian Airlines AS v Starptautiskā lidosta Rīga VAS and Air Baltic Corporation AS*., the Court, interpreting the Regulation N° 44/2001 of 22 December 2000 on jurisdiction and the recognition and enforcement of judgments in civil and commercial matters, ruled that an action seeking legal redress for damage resulting from alleged infringements of European Union competition law, comes within the definition of "civil and commercial matters" within the meaning of Article 1(1) of the Regulation N° 44/2001 and, therefore, falls within the scope of that regulation. By that action, flyLAL seeked compensation for damage resulting, first, from the abuse of a dominant position by Air Baltic on the market for flights from or to Vilnius Airport (Lithuania) and, second, from an anti-competitive agreement between the co-defendants. To that end, the applicant in the main proceedings applied for provisional and protective measures.[49]

## 9.6 Article 102

Jumping to Article 102, this article prohibits entities from abusing their dominant position in the marketplace to their advantage to the extent that this abuse affects trade between Member States. There have been fewer preliminary questions and rulings concerning Article 102, or previous Article 82 when compared to those questions referred under Article 101. Nevertheless, a common theme of questions referred concerning Article 102 is *when* a particular practice by a dominant market player may be considered an abuse of that entity's dominant position, and particularly with respect to prices charged by that entity to consumers. Generally, and perhaps not surprisingly, the CJ's case law signals that these types of matters must be assessed on a case-by-case basis because the type of market, the number of market players involved, and the impact on consumers and competition must be analysed.

Recent preliminary rulings indicate that entities with a dominant market position have some leeway in using this position to their advantage. For example, in *Konkurrensverket v. TeliaSonera Sverige* the question referred concerned whether the practice at issue could constitute an abuse of dominant market condition.

The Court declared in its preliminary ruling that "a pricing practice [whereby] the spread between the prices applied on that market and those applied in the retail market is not sufficient to cover costs which that undertaking must incur in order to gain access to that retail market *may* (emphasis added) constitute an abuse within the meaning of Article 102 TFEU." The Court then somewhat qualified its use of "may" by providing additional guidance to the national court that referred the question. When determining whether the pricing practice is "abusive," the national court must take the following items in particular into consideration:

[49] *flyLAL*, C-302/13, ECLI:EU:C:2014:2319.

- "the prices and costs of the undertaking concerned on the retail services market" and, if these are not available, then the national court can refer to and examine the costs and prices of competitors on the same market,
- "that the practice produces an anti-competitive effect, at least potentially, on the retail market, and that the practice is not in any way economically justified".[50]

The Court provided even further guidance in this particular preliminary ruling by highlighting those factors that are **not** relevant to this particular assessment. These include:

- the absence of any regulatory obligation on the undertaking concerned to supply asymmetric digital subscriber line input services on the wholesale market in which it holds a dominant position;
- the degree of dominance held by that undertaking in that market in the retail market for broadband connection services to end users
- whether the customers to whom such a pricing practice is applied are new or existing customers of the undertaking concerned;
- the fact that the dominant undertaking is unable to recoup any losses which the establishment of such a pricing practice might cause, or
- the extent to which the markets concerned are mature markets and whether they involve new technology, requiring high levels of investment.[51]

Similarly, in *Post Danmark* the Court ruled that exclusionary abuse does not exist simply because the undertaking's charging price "to one of its customers is lower than the average total cost attributed to the activity concerned, but higher than the average incremental costs pertaining to that activity in order to assess the existence of anti-competitive effects in circumstances such as those of that case, it is necessary to consider whether that pricing policy, without objective justification, produces an actual or likely exclusionary effect, to the detriment of competition and, thereby of consumers' interests".[52]

## 9.7 Conclusion

Therefore, as we can see, the preliminary rulings of the Court assist in shaping the competition laws of the Union. In so far as cartels are concerned, the intent of those entities participating in the anticompetitive agreement plays an essential role in determining whether or not there has been a violation of Article 101 TFEU. With respect to abuse of dominant market positions however, it is necessary to make additional investigations as to whether the entity's pricing strategy really is an abuse of its dominant market position. The nature of the market and interactions among market players requires that the Court provides guidelines, and not definitive answers, to national courts concerning competition matters.

---

[50] *TeliaSonera Sverige*, C-52/09, EU:C:2011:83, para. 115.

[51] *TeliaSonera Sverige*, EU:C:2011:83, para. 115.

[52] *Post Danmark*, C-209/10, EU:C:2012:172, para. 45.

# Chapter 10
# The Role of Preliminary References in the Uniform Application of EU Competition Law

**Jules Stuyck**

## 10.1 Introduction

This chapter discusses the role of preliminary references by national courts to the Court of Justice of the EU in the field of competition law. In the first part of this chapter (Sect. 10.2), I will briefly discuss the state of the case-law of the Court on preliminary references in general. In the second part (Sect. 10.3), I will look at the consequences of that general case-law for competition law and to issues, regarding preliminary references that are specific for competition law. As will be seen the existence of comparable competition rules at the EU level and the level of most of the Member States raises interesting questions on the possibility to refer questions to the ECJ where in reality the application of national law alone is at stake.

## 10.2 Preliminary References in General Under Article 276 TFEU

### *10.2.1 Which Courts and on What Points*

Pursuant to Article 267 TFEU national courts can refer questions on interpretation of the treaties and the validity and the interpretation of acts of the institutions and other EU bodies to the European Court of Justice; national courts that decide in last

J. Stuyck (✉)
University of Leuven (KU Leuven), Leuven, Belgium

Radboud University Nijmegen, Nijmegen, The Netherlands
e-mail: jules.stuyck@law.kuleuven.be



A. Almăşan, P. Whelan (eds.), *The Consistent Application of EU Competition Law*, Studies in European Economic Law and Regulation 9,
DOI 10.1007/978-3-319-47382-6_10

resort (such as typically supreme courts) are under an obligation to do so if a question on the interpretation of Union law arises.

The Court of Justice has determined that Article 267 TFEU also applies to international agreements concluded by the EU and to acts of bodies established by such agreements.[1] According to standing case-law of the ECJ the obligation of courts that decide in last resort to refer questions on interpretation does not apply where the answer to the question is obvious ("acte claire") or where the answer has already been given by the Court ("acte éclairé").[2] The obligation also exists where the national court has to follow the opinion of the Constitutional Court.[3]

All courts, including lower courts, are under an obligation to refer questions on the *validity* of secondary Union law, since they cannot decide, without a ruling by the ECJ, that a provision of secondary law is invalid.[4]

'Court or tribunal of a Member State' in Article 267 TFEU embraces any national institution exercising a judicial function, even if it does not constitute a court or tribunal for the purposes of its own domestic law.[5] Article 267 also applies to courts situated in territories which do not form part of a Member States if the Treaties are applicable there as well as to courts common to certain Member States, such as e.g. the Benelux Court.[6]

Pursuant to settled case-law of the Court, in order to determine whether a body making a reference is a 'court or tribunal' within the meaning of Article 267 TFEU, which is a question governed by EU law alone, the Court takes account of a number of factors, such as whether the body is established by law, whether it is permanent, whether its jurisdiction is compulsory, whether its procedure is *inter partes*, whether it applies rules of law and whether it is independent.[7]

In the light of these criteria, a conventional arbitration tribunal is not a 'court or tribunal of a Member State', where the parties are under no obligation, in law or in fact, to refer their disputes to arbitration and the public authorities of the Member State concerned are not involved in the decision to opt for arbitration nor required to intervene of their own accord in the proceedings before the arbitrator.[8] By contrast the Court has held admissible preliminary questions referred to it by an arbitral tribunal, where that tribunal had been established by law, whose decisions were binding on the parties and whose jurisdiction did not depend on their agreement.[9]

---

[1] See further K. Lenaerts – I. Maselis – K. Gutman, *EU Procedural Law*, Oxford University Press 2014.

[2] *CILFIT*, 283/81, EU:1982:335.

[3] *Krizan*, C-416/10, EU:C:2013:8.

[4] *Foto Frost*, C-314/85, EU:C:1987:452,paragraphs 12–20; for a recent example, see *Vodafone*, C-58/08, EU:C:2010:321, re a preliminary reference by the High Court of Justice of England and Wales on the validity of the Roaming Regulation 717/2007 (which the Court held to be valid).

[5] *Broekmeulen*, C-246/80, EU:C:181:218.

[6] *Parfumes Christian Dior*, C-337/95, EU:C:1997:517.

[7] *Belov*, C-394/11, EU:C:2013,paragraph 38.

[8] *Denuit and Cordenier*, in C-125/04, EU:C:2005:69, paragraph 13.

[9] *Danfoss*, Case 109/88, EU:C:1989 :383, paragraphs 7–9.

Recently in *Merck Canada*,[10] the Court held that the jurisdiction of the Tribunal Arbitral necessário (Portugal) does not stem from the will of the parties, but from a national law that law confers upon that tribunal compulsory jurisdiction to determine, at first instance, disputes involving industrial property rights pertaining to reference medicinal products and generic drugs. In addition, if the arbitral decision handed down by such a body is not subject to an appeal before the competent appellate court, it becomes definitive and has the same effects as a judgment handed down by an ordinary court.

### 10.2.2 No Rulings on National Law as Such

It is obvious that Article 267 TFEU does not allow the ECJ to interpret national law. Neither can the Court rule on the compatibility of national rules with Union law.[11] However in *Dzodzi* the ECJ decided to accept questions for interpretation 'in the specific case where the national law of the Member State refers to the content of that provision in order to determine rules applicable to a situation which is purely internal to that State'.[12] By contrast in *Kleinwort Benson*[13] the Court declined competence to interpret a national law provision that was merely mirroring the Brussels Convention. Again *in Leur-Bloem*[14] the Court confirmed *Dzodzi* and said that the Court of Justice has jurisdiction under Article 267 to interpret Union law where the situation in question is not governed directly by Union law but the national legislature, in transposing the provisions of a directive into domestic law, has chosen to apply the same treatment to purely internal situations and to those governed by the directive, so that it has aligned its domestic legislation to Union law. As will be seen hereafter this case-law, which is not confined to national law that transposes an EU directive, is important for competition law.

### 10.2.3 Binding Force of a Preliminary Ruling

A preliminary judgment given by the ECJ is obviously binding on the national court that referred the matter or will deal with the case at a later stage. But its effects go far beyond that. A preliminary judgment on interpretation or validity has *erga omnes* (and *ex tunc)* effect,[15] because it is declaratory, it does not lay down any new

[10] Order in *Merck Canada*, C-555/13, EU:C: 2014:92, paragraph 19.

[11] K. Lenaerts e.a., p. 237 *et seq.*

[12] *Dzodzi*, C-297/88 and C-197/89, EU :C :1990:360.

[13] *Kleinwort Benson*, C-346/93, EU :C :1995:85.

[14] *Leur-Bloem*, C-28/95, EU:C:1997:369.

[15] But the Court sometimes limits the temporal effect of its ruling, e.g. to mitigate the financial consequences for a Member State of the retro-active effect of the judgment (see e.g. *Grelczyk*, C-184/99, EU:C:2001:458 and *Bidar,* C-209/03, EU:C:2005:16).

rule but it is incorporated into the body of provisions and principles of Union law on which it is based and because preliminary rulings secure the uniform application of Union law.[16]

### 10.2.4 Inadmissibility of a Reference for a Preliminary Ruling

The procedure for a preliminary ruling is based on a cooperation between the national court and the ECJ. Each of the two actors has its proper role. Subject to the obligation for each national court to refer in the case where it needs to rule on the validity of a Union act, and for the national court that decides in last resort to refer a question on interpretation, it is up to the discretion of the national court to decide whether or not to refer to the ECJ.

The Court of Justice is normally under an obligation to answer questions for a preliminary ruling. It can however reformulate questions to arrive at a useful interpretation and come to the conclusion that it is not necessary to answer all the questions referred to give the referring judge sufficient guidance.[17]

The Court can even refuse to answers questions in the following cases: either (i) where it is quite obvious that the interpretation of European Union law that is sought bears no relation to the actual facts of the main action or its subject-matter, (ii) where the problem is hypothetical or (iii) where the Court does not have before it the factual or legal material necessary to give a useful answer to the questions submitted to it.[18]

### 10.2.5 Rules of Procedure and Requirements of the Order for Reference

Apart from Article 267 TFEU the following rules are relevant for preliminary references: Article 23 and 23a of the Statute of Court of Justice, Articles 93–114 Rules of Procedure (RP) of the ECJ. The Court has also issued an Information note on references by national courts for preliminary rulings, which can be found on the Court's website.

---

[16] K.Lenaerts e.a., p. 245.

[17] For examples in the case-law, see K. Lenaerts e.a., p. 235.

[18] See recently *Allianz Hungária*, C-32/11, EU:C:2013:162, paragraph 26, with references to already standing case law in, inter alia, *PreussenElektra,* Case C-379/98, EU:C:2011:160, paragraph 39; *Cipolla and Others,* C-94/04 and C-202/04, EU:C:2006:758, paragraph 25; and *Bericap Záródástechnikai,* C-180/11, EU:C:2012:717, paragraph 58.

Article 94 RP relates to the content of a request for a preliminary ruling and provides that, in addition to the text of the questions referred to the Court for a preliminary ruling, the request for a preliminary ruling shall contain:

(a) a summary of the subject-matter of the dispute and the relevant findings of fact as determined by the referring court or tribunal, or, at least, an account of the facts on which the questions are based;
(b) the tenor of any national provisions applicable in the case and, where appropriate, the relevant national case-law;
(c) a statement of the reasons which prompted the referring court or tribunal to inquire about the interpretation or validity of certain provisions of European Union law, and the relationship between those provisions and the national legislation applicable to the main proceedings.

With regard, more particularly, to the information that must be provided to the Court in an order for reference, that information does not serve only to enable the Court to provide answers which will be of use to the national court. It must also enable the governments of the Member States and other interested parties to submit observations in accordance with Article 23 of the Statute of the Court of Justice of the European Union. For those purposes, it is necessary that the national court should define the factual and legislative context of the questions which it is asking or, at the very least, explain the factual circumstances on which those questions are based.[19]

The parties to the main procedure can participate in the procedure before the Court. Member States, the European Commission and the Member States can also intervene (Article 96 RP). Experience shows that the Commission always intervenes. There is just one round of written submissions. There is usually a hearing.

Pursuant to Article 99 where a question referred is identical to a question on which the Court has already ruled, where the reply to such a question may be clearly deduced form existing case-law or where the answer to the question referred admits of no reasonable doubt, the ECJ may, at any time, on a proposal from the Judge-Rapporteur and after hearing the Advocate General, decide to rule by a reasoned order. Recently the Court has done so quite frequently.[20]

### *10.2.6 Duration*

In 2011 a preliminary ruling took an average of 16.4 months between the date of the order of referral and the delivery of the judgment, which is much quicker than e.g. in 2004, where it still took, 23.4 months. There is also an expedited procedure

[19] Case C-25/11 *Varzim Sol* [2012] ECR, paragraph 30; *Allianz Hungaria* C-32/11, EU:C:2013:162.

[20] See e.g. on the Unfair Commercial Practices Directive 2005/29: Orders in *Wamo*, C-288/10, EU:C:2011:443, *Inno*, C-126/11, EU:C:2011:851 and *Euronics Belgium*, C-343/12, EU:C:2013:154.

(Article 105 RP), the average duration of which is 4.5 months. The Court has to grant leave for such a procedure and it has so far only done so in a limited number of cases.[21]

## 10.3 Preliminary References in Competition Matters

### *10.3.1 EU Competition Law: (Also Horizontal) Direct Effect of the Treaty Provisions and of Block Exemption Regulations*

Preliminary references are meant to help national courts in the (uniform) application of EU law. EU rules that are directly effective can be invoked by individuals in national courts.

Articles 101 and 102 TFEU (respectively on restrictive agreements and abuse of a dominant position) are directly effective.[22] Contrary to the situation before 2004 (under the predecessor of Regulation 1/2003: Regulation 17/62) the Commission has no exclusive power to grant individual exemptions. There is therefore no obstacle for a national court to decide e.g. on the validity of an agreement that is restrictive of competition and adversely affects trade between Member States even where it needs to check whether the conditions of a declaration of inapplicability of Article 101(3) are fulfilled.

Article 101(2) contains a private law sanction: agreements that are contrary to Article 101(1) are null and void. The sanction is applied by national courts, mostly where a defendant in a claim concerning the performance of a contract raises the nullity of the contract arguing that it is restrictive of competition. In the early years of EU competition law many questions were referred to the ECJ on the meaning of this provision.[23]

Block exemption regulations are also directly effective. Regulation 330/2010 on Vertical restrictions is often applied in national courts.

References for a preliminary ruling on the interpretation of the EU competition rules can also be made by national courts on the occasion of public enforcement of these rules, i.e. by courts of law that can review decisions of NCAs.

[21] B. Wägenbaur, *Court of Justice of the European Union. Commentary on Statue and Rules of Procedure*, München, Beck, 2013, p. 321 and p. 346.

[22] See Article 1 Regulation 1/2003.

[23] See *Brasserie de Haecht*, 23/67, EU:C:1967:54 and more recently *van Schijndel*, C-43/93 and 431/93, EU:C:1995:441.

### 10.3.2 The Existence of Parallel and Similar Systems of EU and National Competition Laws

EU competition law is unique in that, without harmonisation directive to that effect, but i.a. as a result of Article 3 of Regulation 1/2003, Member States have progressively adopted national competition rules that are very similar to EU competition rules, i.e. Articles 101 and 102 TFEU. The national equivalents of Articles 101 and 102 largely follow the same principles and concepts as these Articles. They do not however require an adverse effect on trade between Member States as Articles 101 and 102 do. They can be simultaneously applicable with the EU rules (and Regulation 1/2003 contains specific rules to cope with that situation.) National merger rules, on the contrary, often differ from the EU merger rules, but the EU merger rules cannot be applied simultaneously with any national merger rules. Pursuant to Article 21(2) of the Merger Regulation (Regulation 139/2004), subject to review by the Court of Justice, the Commission shall have sole jurisdiction to take the decisions provided for in this Regulation and pursuant to Article 21(3). Where the threshold of the Merger Regulation (MR) is exceeded, ("Community dimension") national merger rules cannot be applied and national competition authorities (NCAs) cannot decide. It may happen that below EU threshold mergers have to be notified simultaneously in several Member States. An EU notification (above the MR threshold) is a one stop shop.

National antitrust rules (restrictive practices) can indeed be applicable simultaneously with of Articles 101 and 102 TFEU. Article 3(1) of Regulation 1/2003 contains the basic rule that where the competition authorities of the Member States or national courts apply national competition law to agreements, decisions by associations of undertakings or concerted practices within the meaning of Article 101(1) TFEU which may affect trade between Member States within the meaning of that provision, they shall also apply Article 101 to such agreements, decisions or concerted practices. Where the competition authorities of the Member States or national courts apply national competition law to any abuse prohibited by Article 102, they shall also apply Article 102. The second and the third paragraph of that Article contain exceptions to that basic rule that do not need to be discussed in detail here. To put it simply, the system of Regulation 1/2003 amounts to this: first, where a national authority or court applies domestic antitrust law it is under an obligation to apply simultaneously the corresponding EU article (101 or 102) where the provisions are applicable (because there is a potential adverse effect on trade between Member States) and, second, normally the application of national competition law may not lead to the prohibition of restrictive practices which may affect trade between Member States but which do not restrict competition within the meaning of Article 101(1), or which fulfil the conditions of Article 101(3) or which are covered by a Regulation for the application of Article 101(3) (such as a block exemption regulation).

All this means that the application of EU and national competition rules is very much intertwined. Each time Article 101 or 102 TFEU may be applicable the national court or national competition authority that applies national antitrust law will have to broaden its assessment to the EU competition rules for which it can – and sometimes must(see above) – refer questions on interpretation to the ECJ.

### *10.3.3 Preliminary References by a National Court That Applies National Competition Law Only*

Even where national courts only apply the domestic equivalent of Article 101 TFEU (or 102 TFEU) the Court of Justice has accepted preliminary references on the interpretation of the EU antitrust rules.

Applying its standing case-law mentioned above[24] the Court reiterated in *Allianz Hungária*[25] that it has jurisdiction to give preliminary rulings on questions concerning European Union law in situations where the facts of the cases being considered by the national courts are outside the direct scope of European Union law but where those provisions have been rendered applicable by domestic law, which adopted, for internal situations, the same approach as that provided for under European Union law. In those circumstances, it is clearly in the interest of the European Union that, in order to forestall future differences of interpretation, provisions or concepts taken from European Union law should be interpreted uniformly, irrespective of the circumstances in which they are to apply.[26] More particularly with regard to the specific case the Court observed that the relevant provision of the Hungarian Competition Act faithfully reproduces Article 101(1) TFEU and that it is apparent from the preamble to and the explanatory memorandum for that Act that the Hungarian legislature sought to harmonise domestic competition law with that of the European Union and that, in particular, Paragraph 11(1) of that Act aims to prohibit ‘in application of Article 85 of the EEC Treaty’ (now Article 101 TFEU), ‘everything which distorts competition’. It is therefore not contested that that legislature decided to treat internal situations and situations governed by European Union law in the same way. Moreover the referring national court considers that the concepts referred to in Paragraph 11(1) must in fact be interpreted in the same way as the equivalent concepts in Article 101(1) TFEU and that it is bound in that regard by the interpretation of those concepts provided by the Court. In those circumstances, the ECJ holds that it has jurisdiction to answer the question submitted, concerning Article 101(1) TFEU, even though the latter provision does not directly govern the situation at issue in the main proceedings.

The judgment means that the Court will look at the similarity in text and the harmonization rationale of domestic law before concluding that it can answer a

---

[24] See above Section 7.1.2.

[25] See footnote 18 above.

[26] Paragraph 20 with references to i.a. *Dzozi, Leur-Bloem* and *Confederación Española de Empresarios de Estaciones de Servicio*, C-217/05, EU:C:2006:784.

preliminary question on the EU competition rules that will ultimately only serve for the application of domestic antitrust law.

Finally it can be observed that in several Member States EU block exemption regulations also apply in the domestic legal order, meaning that an interpretation of the provisions of such a regulation can also help the national court to interpret its national law. An example, where the Court was asked to interpret a provision of the former block exemption regulation for exclusive purchasing obligations, Regulation 1984/83, is the judgment in see C-217/05 in case *Confederación Española de Empresarios de Estaciones de Servicio*.[27] A Spanish law provided for a block examption form the Spanish prohibition of restrictive agreements for exclusive purchasing agreements that fulfilled the conditions of Regulation 1984/83. A party in the case before the ECJ submitted that the request for a preliminary ruling was inadmissible in view of the lack of effect on interstate trade. Referring to *Leur- Bloem*[28] the Court disagreed and proceeded to answer the question.

It results from that judgment that national courts can refer questions to the ECJ on the interpretation of EU block exemption regulations where in reality they only have to apply the domestic equivalent of the regulation or a national legal provision that extends the block exemption to purely national situations.[29]

## *10.3.4 What Kind of Preliminary Questions in Competition Law Matters?*

The case-law so far shows a variety of questions referred to the ECJ. I will discuss a few of them which have been quite topical in recent years, namely:

- general notions of competition law, e.g. the notion of concerted practice and restriction by object or effect;
- rules of procedure before NCAs because they are also responsible to apply EU competition law General;
- general principles, e.g. fine for Infringement of Article 101 TFEU on the basis of erroneous legal advice; and
- claims for damages.

Hereafter I will discuss recent case-law in thes four areas, by taking one of example in each area.

---

[27] *Confederación Española de Empresarios de Estaciones de Servicio*, see preceding footnote.

[28] See footnote 14 above.

[29] In *La Retoucherie* (C-217/05, EU:C:2006:784) – this time on the Spanish law extending the then new block exemption Regulation fort Vertical Agreements 2790/1999 and the direct predecessor of Regulation 330/2010 – it was argued that the Court shouldn't answer the preliminary question because (without referring to its purely national character) allegedly the question was not necessary to resolve the dispute. The ECJ reiterated its restraint to declare preliminary questions inadmissible for that reason (see above I.4).

## A General Substantive Notion of Competition Law: Restriction by Object

A question that has been heavily debated recently is that of restriction by object or effect. Article 101 TFEU mentions both categories and questions have arisen on the scope of restrictions by object, because, contray to what is the case with restrictions by effect, its application does not require evidence of effect on the market.

Most recently in *Groupement des Cartes bancaires*[30] the Court of Justice made a clear statement on the necessity to confine "restrictions by object" (for whih the effect does not need to be demonstrated) to certain categories of hard core cartels.

The Court ruled[31]:

> Secondly, in the light of that case-law, the General Court erred in finding, in paragraph 124 of the judgment under appeal, and then in paragraph 146 of that judgment, that the concept of restriction of competition by 'object' must not be interpreted 'restrictively'. The concept of restriction of competition 'by object' can be applied only to certain types of coordination between undertakings which reveal a sufficient degree of harm to competition that it may be found that there is no need to examine their effects, otherwise the Commission would be exempted from the obligation to prove the actual effects on the market of agreements which are in no way established to be, by their very nature, harmful to the proper functioning of normal competition. The fact that the types of agreements covered by Article 81(1) EC do not constitute an exhaustive list of prohibited collusion is, in that regard, irrelevant.

Some type of hard core restrictions would uncontestbaly qualify as restrictions by object: horizontal price fixing, output limitation and market sharing (sharing of geographical or products markets or customers).[32] For more complex or novel kinds of restrictions the qualification is rather contestable. This issue has indeed been hotly debated in recent years[33] and it also emerged in prelilminary references, such as *Allianz Hungária,* already quoted, and *Expedia.*[34] These judgments suggested that the notion of restrictions by object is rather broad.

In *Allianz Hungária* the Court e.g. decided that agreements whereby car insurance companies come to bilateral arrangements, either with car dealers acting as car repair shops or with an association representing those dealers, concerning the hourly charge to be paid by the insurance company for repairs to vehicles insured by it, stipulating that that charge depends, inter alia, on the number and percentage of insurance contracts that the dealer has sold as intermediary for that company, can be considered a restriction of competition 'by object' within the meaning of that provision, where, following a concrete and individual examination of the wording and aim of those agreements and of the economic and legal context of which they form a part, it is apparent that they are, by their very nature, injurious to the proper functioning of normal competition on one of the two markets concerned. This type of

[30] *Groupement des cartes bancaires*, C-67/13 P, EU:C:2014:2204.

[31] See paragraph 59 of the judgment.

[32] See Guidance accompanying the de minimis Notice 2014, website Commission.

[33] See e.g. Grant Murray, "In Search of the Obvious: Groupement des Cartes bancaires and 'By Object' Infringements under EU Competition Law", *European Competition Law Review*, 2015, 47–51.

[34] *Expedia*, C-226/11, EU:C:2012 :795.

agreement does obviously not belong to the limited category of incontestable restrictions by object.

It is not certain that this ruling still holds after *Groupement des Cartes bancaires*. In any event the bold declarations of the Court in *Expedia*, another preliminary ruling, that an agreement that may affect trade between Member States and that has an anti-competitive object constitutes, by its nature and independently of any concrete effect that it may have, an appreciable restriction on competition, now seems to be definitely overruled.

This means that a national court that will have to consider whether there is an "acte éclairé" will also have to check judgments of the ECJ in other cases than preliminary rulings, such as the appeal case in *Groupement des Cartes bancaires*.

### Rules of Procedure Before NCAs Because They Are Also Responsible for Applying EU Competition Law

Preliminary references in the field of competition law can also relate to national procedures. *Vebic*,[35] a judgment of the grand chamber of the ECJ, is a good example. It concerned a rather astonishing situation in Belgium that has been remedied under the new competition rules (the Code of Economic Law, that entered into force in 2014). Belgian bakers and their association (VEBIC) had been condemned by the Competition Council (at that time te body that was responsible at the national level to decide on infringements of the EU and Belgian competition rules) for having entered into price-fixing agreements. When VEBIC lodged an appeal for annulment of the decision before the Court of Appeal of Brussels, that Court noted that Belgian law did not allow the Auditoraat, which was the body responsible for investigations within the Competition Council, to take part in the proceedings before it. Only the Federal Minister responsible for the Economy was entitled to do so. Since the minister did not avail himself of the opportunity to submit written observations, the only party to have taken part in the appeal proceedings is VEBIC, which has acted as the appellant. On a preliminary reference by the Court of appeal the ECJ ruled that Article 35 of Regulation 1/2003[36] precludes national rules which do not allow a national competition authority to participate, as a defendant or respondent, in judicial proceedings brought against a decision that the authority itself has taken. It is for the national competition authorities to gauge the extent to which their intervention is necessary and useful having regard to the effective application of EU competition law. However, if the national competition authority consistently fails to enter

[35] *Vebic*, C-439/08, EU:C:2010:739.

[36] "1. The Member States shall designate the competition authority or authorities responsible for the application of Articles 81 and 82 of the Treaty in such a way that the provisions of this regulation are effectively complied with. The measures necessary to empower those authorities to apply those Articles shall be taken before 1 May 2004. The authorities designated may include courts. 2. When enforcement of Community competition law is entrusted to national administrative and judicial authorities, the Member States may allocate different powers and functions to those different national authorities, whether administrative or judicial."

an appearance in such judicial proceedings, the effectiveness of Articles 101 TFEU and 102 TFEU is jeopardised. In the absence of EU rules, the Member States remain competent, in accordance with the principle of procedural autonomy, to designate the body or bodies of the national competition authority which may participate, as a defendant or respondent, in proceedings brought before a national court against a decision that the authority itself has taken, while at the same time ensuring that fundamental rights are observed and that EU competition law is fully effective.

## Fines for Infringement of Article 101 TFEU on the Basis of Erroneous Legal Advice

In another grand chamber judgment, *Schenker*,[37] the ECJ ruled that Article 101 TFEU must be interpreted as meaning that an undertaking which has infringed that provision may not escape imposition of a fine where the infringement has resulted from that undertaking erring as to the lawfulness of its conduct on account of the terms of legal advice given by a lawyer or of the terms of a decision of a national competition authority.

## Claims for Damages

A domain in which preliminary references are obvious is that of claims for damages for infringements of the EU (and national) antitrust rules, especially claims of victims of cartels. In fact the Court of Justice developed, on the basis of answers to preliminary references from national courts, an important jurisprudence that forms the basis of a hybrid system of compensation of victims of competition infringements: the general principles developed by the Court itself and legislative provisions building on these principles, i.e. a recent Directive discussed hereafter. I shall first look at the case law of the ECJ.

In *Francovich*[38] the Court of Justice set the principle that Member States have to compensate the victims of their infringements of Union law. In *Courage and Crehan*[39] the Court of Justice has extended this principle to private conduct and recognised that where undertakings (businesses) have infringed Article 81 or 82 EC (now Articles 101 and 102 TFEU), any individual who suffers a loss as a result of that infringement can claim compensation from these undertakings. The Court thus recognized that *Union law* gives the victims of such conduct a right to damages. At the same time the Court stressed that in the absence of Union rules governing the matter, it is for the domestic legal system of each Member Sate, to designate the courts and tribunals having jurisdiction and to lay down the *detailed procedural*

[37] *Schenker*, C-681/11, 2013:404.

[38] *Francovich e.a.*, Joined cases C-6/90 and C-9/90 EU:C:1991:428; see also *Brasserie du Pêcheur and Factortame*, joined cases C-46/93 and C-48/93 EU:C:1996:79.

[39] *Courage and Crehan*, C-453/99, EU:C:2001:465.

*rules* governing actions for safeguarding rights which individuals derive directly from Union law, provided that such rules are not less favourable than those governing similar domestic actions (principle of equivalence) and that they do not render practically impossible or excessively difficult the exercise of rights conferred by Union law (principle of effectiveness).[40] The principle of effectiveness opposes *i.a.* the rule of English law barring the victim to claim damages on the sole ground that he is a party to the restrictive agreement. The Court however did not address the more general question as to what extent the substantive conditions of liability for damages in case of infringement of the EU competition rules are governed by Union law or rather by national law.

In *Manfredi*[41] the Court reiterated the principles of *Courage* and, again, without addressing in general Union law's impact on substantive aspects of liability, it ruled that in the absence of Union law on the matter, it is for the domestic legal system of each Member State to prescribe *the detailed rules*[42] *governing the exercise of* that right,[43] including those on the concept of "causal relationship", provided again, that the principles of equivalence and effectiveness are observed.[44] Obviously the causal relationship is not a procedural rule. The detailed substantive rules governing the liability therefore still remained a matter for domestic law, subject to the principles of equivalence and effectiveness. In *Manfredi* the Court however ruled itself that the principle of effectiveness dictates that the injured person must be able to seek compensation not only for actual loss (*damnum emergens*) but also for loss of profit (*lucrum cessans*) plus interests.[45]

Although the victim can rely on the definitive finding (i.e. it has not been overruled by a court) of an infringement by the Commission[46] or, but less certainly under the present state of the law, by a NRA,[47] he might be in need to corroborate the effects of that infringement (including the actual prejudice and the causal link) by elements from the file of the competition authority. Victims however do not have automatic access to the administrative file and some elements may be confidential. Since recently cartels are generally discovered on the basis of whistle blowing by a member of the cartel, which is encouraged by a leniency programme (immunity for the whistle blower who fulfils certain conditions), the question arose whether the victim can also have access to documents relating to a leniency procedure.

---

[40] Paragraph 29 of the judgment.

[41] *Manfredi and Others,* Case C-298/04, EU:C:2006:461.

[42] Note the absence of the adjective 'procedural' in this ruling (which occurred in *Courage and Crehan*).

[43] Such as the statute of limitation (paragraph 80), punitive damages (paragraph 93) or unjust enrichment (paragraph 94).

[44] Paragraph 64 of the judgment.

[45] Paragraph 100 of the judgment.

[46] *Masterfoods*, C-344/98, EU:C:2000:689.

[47] See for the future: Directive 2014/04, Article 9(1): Member States shall ensure that an infringement of competition law found by a final decision of a national competition authority or by a review court is deemed to be irrefutably established for the purposes of an action for damage.

In *Pfeiderer*[48] the Court of Justice answered that question in the affirmative but left it to the national courts, on the basis of their national law, to determine the conditions under which such access must be permitted or refused by weighing the interests protected by European Union law. In *Donau Chemie*[49] the Court added that European Union law, in particular the principle of effectiveness, precludes a provision of national law subjecting such access solely to the consent of all the parties to those proceedings, without leaving any possibility for the national courts of weighing up the interests involved.

In the elevator's cartel case, which was heavily fined by the Commission and which also indirectly led to the *Kone* judgment, the Commission itself brought a claim for damages, on behalf of the European Union, against the members of the cartel, because various institutions and bodies of the EU that awarded public contracts were affected by the cartel. In *Otis*[50] the CJEU ruled that nothing prevents the Commission from doing so. According to the Court of Justice the Commission is not both judge and party in its own cause in breach of the *nemo judex in sua causa* principle.

Finally in *Kone*,[51] the Court reiterates the principles developed in *Courage* and *Manfredi,* including that the concept of "causal relationship" is governed by the domestic law of the Member States, subject to the principle of equivalence and effectiveness. As it did in *Manfredi* with regard to the heads of damage to be covered, in *Kone* the Court rules on the causal relationship by ruling that domestic law cannot categorically exclude civil liability of undertakings belonging to a cartel for loss resulting from "umbrella pricing".

A further judicial debate on causality, and to what extent it is governed by Union law or domestic law, remains necessary since the recent Directive 2014/104 on certain rules governing actions for damages under national law for infringements of the competition law provisions of the Member States and of the European Union (hereafter: antitrust damages Directive) does not directly address the causal relationship.[52] In this respect the Directive only provides that it shall be presumed that the cartel causes harm and that the infringer shall have the right to rebut that presumption (Article 17(2)).

Directive 2014/104 builds on the case-law of the ECJ. The Directive reaffirms the *acquis communautaire* on the right to compensation for harm caused by infringements of Union competition law, particularly regarding standing and the definition of damage, as stated in the case-law of the Court of Justice, and does not pre-empt any further development thereof. Anyone who has suffered harm caused by such an infringement can claim compensation for actual loss (*damnum emergens*), for gain of which that person has been deprived (loss of profit or *lucrum cessans*), plus interest,

---

[48] *Pfeiderer*, C-360/09, EU:C:2011:389.

[49] *Donau Chemie*, C-536/11, EU:C:2013:366.

[50] *Otis*, C-199/11 EU:C:2012:684.

[51] *Kone*, C-557/12, EU:C:2014:1317; see J. Stuyck in *European Review of Private Law,* 2015, p. 460 et seq.

[52] (2014) OJ L349/1. The Directive has to be implemented by 27 December 2016.

irrespective of whether those categories are established separately or in combination in national law. The Directive applies to infringements of both Articles 101 and 102 EU and national competition rules. Its main focus is on problems arising from the overcharge to purchasers as a result of cartels. It is noteworthy that the Directive applies both to damages claims for infringement of Articles 101 and 102 TFEU and their domestic equivalents, implying again that both set of provisions are intertwined. Since the directive is an act of Union law, falling within the ambit of Article 267 TFEU, preliminary references that relate to its application to purely domestic situations will be possible without further conditions (of a sufficient link with Union law because it is Union law). Further preliminary references will undoubtedly follow, perhaps also with follow on questions on the causal relationship, after *Kone*. In this judgment the Court has *de facto* set some common (Union law) principles of causality. In this way the partial harmonisation brought along by Directive 2014/104 is accompanied by a creeping harmonisation through case-law of elements that are not harmonised, such as the causal relationship.

## 10.4 Conclusion

Preliminary references have proven to be a central tool in the development of EU competition law. EU competition rules (those of the Treaty as well as block exemption regulations) are directly effective, i.e. they can be applied by national courts. National courts are even under an obligation to contribute to the application of these rules. There are two other reasons why, in the area of competition law, national courts can (and sometimes must) refer questions to the ECJ in the area of competition law. The first is that they are the natural judges of private enforcement of the EU, both with regard to disputes on the validity of contracts and claims for damages by victims of competition infringements. The second is that the Court of Justice largely accepts references on the interpretation of the EU competition rules where in fact national courts only apply national competition rules, in particular in appeals brought before them against decisions of NCAs, to the extent that these national rules are very similar to the EU competition rules.

Finally, national courts deciding on competition cases should also look at judgments of the ECJ in direct actions, in particular appeal cases against judgments of the General Court in Commission cases, because the judgments may contain important principles that sometimes depart from what the Court had previously held in preliminary references.

# Part V
# Selected National Application of Articles 101 and 102 TFEU

# Chapter 11
# The Uniform Application of Articles 101 and 102 TFEU in German Competition Law

**Bernd Oppermann and Ahmad Chmeis**

## 11.1 The Decentralised Application of Articles 101 and 102 TFEU

The decentralized application of law characterizes competition law enforcement to an extent hardly matched by any other field of law within the European Union. While the European Commission in her function as the European cartel authority necessarily has to realize her decision solely on the grounds of Articles 101 and 102 of the technical part of the Lisbon Treaty (TFEU) and of other provisions of EU competition law, national cartel authorities have to go beyond their national cartel enactments due to the decentralized application of EU law. In competition law proceedings, national competition authorities and national courts shall apply Articles 101 and 102 TFEU in addition to national competition law if the subject matter of the proceedings may affect trade between Member states. Such an approach may lead to contradictions whenever the application of European and German competition law provisions follow different measures or criteria, which may ultimately compromise the effective and efficient application of Articles 101 and 102 TFEU. While the present shape of the European cartel rule and its exemptions (Article 101 (1) and (3) TFEU) and the respective German provisions can be considered largely equivalent, German specificities still remain in the field of anti-abuse rules. National particularities also concern the German merger control provisions despite a certain legislative approximation as a result of the Eighth Amendment to the German Act against Restrictions of Competition (GWB), e.g. the ministerial approval under Section 42 GWB. In the context of the interpretation of Articles 101 and 102 TFEU, substantive requirements may vary as regards the concept of an

B. Oppermann • A. Chmeis (✉)
Leibniz University of Hanover, Hanover, Germany
e-mail: oppermann@jura.uni-hannover.de; ahmad.chmeis@jura.uni-hannover.de



A. Almăşan, P. Whelan (eds.), *The Consistent Application of EU Competition Law*, Studies in European Economic Law and Regulation 9,
DOI 10.1007/978-3-319-47382-6_11

undertaking and the interpretation of the 10 % turnover threshold in determining the amount of a fine pursuant to Article 23 (2) Reg. 1/2003 and Section 81 (5) GWB. From a procedural point of view, a distinction should be drawn between administrative and judicial competition proceedings. In administrative proceedings, the different requirements as regards disclosure obligations shall be considered. However, the largest differences concern judicial proceedings. While proceedings before the Court of Justice are administrative in nature, principles of criminal law and criminal procedural law prevail in German fine proceedings. Moreover, the most crucial aspects of cartel matters in Germany are treated by civil law courts to the result that cartel litigation to a large extend is governed by the law of civil procedure. This persitance of such differences may ultimately complicate the cooperation between competition authorities through the European Competition Network.

The implications of the decentralised application of European competition law not only affect proceedings against private undertakings, but also against public entities. Article 106 (1) TFEU provides that Member States shall neither enact nor maintain in force of any measure contrary to the rules contained in the Treaties regarding public undertakings. However, an exception shall be made in so far as the application of these rules would (in law or in fact) obstruct the performance of specific tasks assigned to them, Article 106 (2) TFEU. This contribution shall therefore also address the application of competition law to public undertakings.

Finally, private competition law enforcement has constantly gained in importance in the European Union as well as in national laws, culminating in the new directive on antitrust damages actions. The relation of private enforcement to public enforcement on the one hand and to constitutional law on the other shall therefore be examined.

## *11.1.1 Basic Concepts*

### The Term "Undertaking" in German Competition Law

Quite some years before the question of a harmonized application of European competition law has aroused, the importance of the concept of an undertaking has been aware in German competition law.[1] Its functional concept of an undertaking differs substantially from other fields of German law,[2] explicitly from commercial law. The concept has been specifically debated facing market behaviour of public or state enterprises.[3]

[1] For early decisions of the German Supreme Court, cf. BGH of 27.2.1962, BGHZ 37, 1, 17 – AKI; BGH 22.3.1976, BGHZ 67, 81, 84 – *Auto-Analyzer*; Urteil v. 18.12.1981, GRUR 1982, 425, 427 – *Brillen-Selbstabgabestelle*; GmS OGB 10.4.1986, BGHZ 97, 312, 314 – *Orthopädische Hilfsmittel*; Urteil v.14.3.1990, BGHZ 110, 371 – *Sportübertragungen*.

[2] *Emmerich*, Kartellrecht, 13th ed. 2014, § 3 Rn. 24 ff.

[3] Cf. fn. 1 for early German Supreme Court decisions. For more recent developments, see: *Oppermann*, Wasserpreise, öffentliche Unternehmen im Kartellrecht und Staatsinterventionismus,

### The Single Economic Entity Doctrine

In the context of liability for competition law infringements, European and German law differ as to the correct addressee of a fine. According to the law, both the European Commission and the German Federal Cartel Office impose fines on "undertakings". However, the respective interpretation of the term "undertaking" in question differs considerably: In European competition law, an "undertaking" is defined as designating an economic entity, even if the law states that the economic entity consists of several legal or natural persons.[4] In the first instance, the single economic entity doctrine may be beneficial to the companies involved as it leads to a so-called "group privilege", which implies that agreements between companies forming the economic unit do not infringe the cartel prohibition under Article 101 TFEU and that merger control rules will not apply to possible restructuring activities within the economic entity. However, this concept may also extend the circle of possible addressees for competition law sanctions. Provided a parent company and its subsidiary form a single economic unit, the parent company may be held jointly and severally liable for infringements of that subsidiary without being personally involved. This will particularly apply to the situation in which the parent company is in a position to exert and in fact exercises decisive influence on its subsidiary's commercial policy.[5] According to the case-law of the European courts, the parent company can exercise such influence and there is a rebuttable presumption that it does in fact exercise decisive influence in the specific case where a parent company holds a 100 % shareholding in its subsidiary.[6] However, the parent company concerned will hardly ever succeed at rebutting the presumption. The concept of a single economic entity therefore merely results in sanctions that are dramatically increasing in practice, as the total turnover of the "undertaking" relevant for the setting of the fine will consequently also include the parent company's total turnover. It is asserted that this decisional practice is justified by the notion of prevention and the aspect of deterrence as provided by competition law.[7]

The situation is different in German. According to the GWB in conjunction with the German Act on Administrative Offences (OWiG), fines for breaching competition law are imposed on natural or legal persons only (Section 81 GWB in conjunction with Section 30 OWiG). Group-based sanction mechanisms as practiced by the European Commission and courts are initially unknown to the German legal system. Therefore, the legitimacy and the implementation of the single economic entity doctrine into German law are highly controversial. In the wake of the legislative approximation regarding the framework for the setting of fines in 2005, the concept

in: Klees/Gent [Ed.], Energie – Wirtschaft – Recht. Festschrift für Peter Salje (2013), 331–355.

[4] See in particular Case C-170/83 *Hydrotherm* [1984] ECR 2999, para. 11.

[5] Case C-286/98 P *Stora Kopparbergs Bergslags* [2000] ECR I-9925, para. 28 f.

[6] Case C-90/09 P *General Química* [2011] ECR I-30, para. 13 f.

[7] See *Ackermann*, ZWeR 2010, 329ff. and ZWeR 2012, 3ff.; see however *Schwarze/Bechtold/Bosch*, Rechtsstaatliche Defizite im Kartellrecht der Europäischen Union, 2008, p. 45f. and *Bechtold/Bosch*, ZWeR 2011, 160ff. for a critical perspective.

of an economic entity was introduced into the GWB in order to determine the turnover relevant for the calculation of fines (see Section 81 (4) 3 GWB). It was subsequently argued that this approximation had also led to the adoption of the European system of imputation of liability, but this position has not been successful.[8] However, the introduction of the single economic entity doctrine is a logical consequence of the decentralized application of Articles 101 and 102 TFEU. A possible approach might be the adoption of the concept in the legal form of a personal company constituted under German civil law ("GbR")[9] in order to respect constitutional premises.[10]

### Competition Law Provisions on Legal Succession

The introduction of the single economic entity doctrine into German sanctions law would also alleviate the key issue of legal succession, which has not been solved by the eighth amendment to the GWB and the introduction of Section 30 (2a) OWIG. Although the latter provision explicitly applies to legal succession, certain forms of restructuring within a group may prevent liability for fines in respect of competition law infringements.[11] Section 30 (2a) OWIG only establishes additional liability of a legal successor in instances of universal succession, especially in the context of a merger pursuant to Sections 2 ff. of the German Transformation Act (UmwG), full transfer pursuant to Section 174 (1) UmwG, or partial transfer pursuant to Section 123 (1) UmwG. The main purpose of Section 30 (2a) OWIG is to eliminate the possibility for undertakings involved in competition law infringements to circumvent liability by dissolving the legal entity and subsequently breaking down the assets concerned by the infringement. Though the German legislature draws the circle of possible addressees of fines closer to the concept of an undertaking in European law in the partial context of universal succession, there are still various possibilities to avoid liability by restructuration. For instance, Section 30 (2a) OWIG does not apply to constellations involving a natural person on the part of the legal predecessor or successor. Furthermore and foremost, the provision does not apply to situations of singular succession, especially by means of an asset deal (disposition of assets and continuation of business operations by the successor on the one side, mere existence of an empty corporate shell on the other side), but also in the way of a share deal (transfer of the company's shares). Therefore, differences to European competition law practice still remain, which hinders the decentralized application of Articles 101 and 102 TFEU.

---

[8] *Bechtold*, GWB, § 81, para. 33f.

[9] *Kersting*, WuW 2014, 1156f. and Der Konzern 2011, 445f.

[10] Serious constitutional law concerns have been raised against the adoption of the single economic entity doctrine into German competition law, see *Schwarze/Bechtold/Bosch*, Rechtsstaatliche Defizite im Kartellrecht der Europäischen Union, 2008, p. 48f.

[11] *Dannecker/Dannecker/Müller*, ZWeR 2013, 417, 430.

Consequently, one may conclude in comparison between German and European law that the application of the functional concept of an undertaking is governed by the same principles while the details differ. The differences increase as the view shifts from the substantial understanding of an entrepreneur towards details of the concept needed for procedure and enforcement.

#### The 10 % Turnover Threshold

Finally, the substantive interpretation of the framework for the setting of fines as set out in Section 81 (4) 2 GWB causes great difficulties. This legal rule provides that the fine to be imposed must not exceed 10 % of the total turnover of an undertaking (or association of undertakings) achieved in the business year preceding the authority's decision. It is assumed that the German legislature understood this turnover threshold as a cap limit in accordance with the European provision in Article 23 (2) 1 Reg. 1/2003. However, in its *Grauzement* judgment, the German Federal Supreme Court (BGH) has ruled that the turnover threshold must be understood as an upper boundary in order to meet constitutional law requirements.[12] The principle of legal certainty provided by Article 103 (2) of the German Constitution ("Grundgesetz") especially demands to establish requirements for criminal and administrative penalties with such a degree of precision that the scope and consequences of provisions regarding criminal and administrative offences can be deduced directly from the law.[13] Nevertheless, the German legislature must provide for effective sanction mechanisms in the case of competition law infringements. Altough the interpretation of the turnover threshold under Section 81 (4) 2 GWB may comply with German constitutional principles, the assumption of an upper limit/maximum to competition fines substantially compromises the uniform application of Articles 101 and 102 TFEU.

### *11.1.2 Competition Procedure*

In addition to the national peculiarities described above as regards substantive competition law, certain administrative and judicial procedural rules may also considerably differ. While differences in the context of administrative procedures mainly concern disclosure obligations imposed on undertakings, the object of criticism regarding judicial procedures consists in concept and structure as well as in respect of their lengthy duration.

[12] BGH NZKart 2013, 195, paras. 50ff.

[13] See *Bosch*, GWB-Kommentar, § 81, para. 29 f.

### Administrative Competition Proceedings

In competition proceedings before the European Commission, undertakings are subject to extensive disclosure obligations in order to simplify competition investigation. In addition to leniency programs and settlement procedures, under which applicants can cooperate with the Commission on a voluntary basis for the purpose of immunity from or mitigation in fines, the success of administrative competition law enforcement is based on the obligation of undertakings to provide comprehensive information during administrative investigations. A partial approximation to European competition law has been implemented by the Eight Amendment of the GWB with the provision of disclosure obligations regarding turnover in Section 81a GWB. However, these obligations are limited to information unrelated to the infringement, that is primarily relevant for the determination of the turnover threshold pursuant to Section 81 (4) 2 GWB as well as for the calculation of market turnover.[14] The German provision thus remains well behind Article 18 of EU Regulation 1/2003 on cartel procedure, which provides the Commission with a powerful investigative tool. The limitation to unrelated information as in the German GWB does not seem appropriate, particularly in view of the fact that the Federal Government has conceded that the protection against self-incrimination emanates from the principle of human dignity and that the latter is not applicable to legal entities or groups of persons as such pursuant to Article 19 (3) of the German Constitution ("Grundgesetz").[15] Therefore, substantial harmonisation is necessary to guarantee a uniform application of Articles 101 and 102 TFEU.

### Judicial Competition Proceedings

For reasons of procedural economy, judicial competition proceedings in Germany must be seen critically, especially with regard to their lengthy duration. The extensive procedural guarantees applicable in proceedings pursuant to the OWIG may lead to substantial delays and thus to a frustration of effective competition law enforcement (e.g. due to a loss of evidence). Furthermore, the distribution of roles in judicial proceedings does not seem practicable. After the German Federal Cartel Office has been engaged in a thorough investigation for several years and has therefore acquired profound knowledge of the case, it loses competence directly after an appeal has been filed against its decision, whereupon the case is referred to public prosecution and the investigation begins anew. Such a formal breakdown of competence may cause a delay of several months. Moreover, it must be critically scrutinised in the view of the fact that competition authorities' position must be strengthened under European law. A reform of the German legal framework is

[14] *Ost*, in: Bien, Das deutsche Kartellrecht nach der 8. GWB-Novelle, p. 305 (325).

[15] Cf. the explanatory memorandum of the Federal Government to the Draft of the eighth amendment to the GWB, BT-Drucks. 17/9852, p. 34f.

imperative in order to meet the requirements resulting from the decentralised application of Articles 101 and 102 TFEU.

## Obtaining Evidence as a Procedural Issue in Competition Law

The existing rules on obtaining evidence in competition law proceedings should especially be reconsidered by such a reform.[16] The embedding of competition law proceedings in the Law of Administrative Offences (OWiG) leads to a predominance of the principles prevailing in criminal proceedings, especially being the principles of orality, immediacy and publicity. These constitutional principles are more pronounced in German than in European competition law proceedings. Thus, the results of administrative proceedings cannot be transferred to forensic proceedings appropriately. The reason lies in Section 261 of the German Code of Criminal Procedures (StPO), according to which the court may only decide on the result of the evidence taken according to its free conviction based on the "epitome of the trial". Section 261 StPO is a manifestation of the principles of orality and immediacy.[17] As a result, judgments can only be based on materials presented and discussed orally before the court.[18] This may raise issues related to leniency programs, because leniency applicants may have to testify in court. The principle of publicity may therefore put pressure on applicants in apprehension of possible damage claims. This may lead to the unfortunate consequence of two different statements, depending on the context. Apart from this potential danger for leniency programs, a strict separation of the administrative investigation of the facts on the one hand and the taking of evidence by the court on the other hand causes a mere repetition of the authority's findings without any additional value. A procedural alternative within constitutional boundaries may be found in administrative procedural law. According to Section 108 (1) of the German Code of Administrative Court Procedure (VwGO), the court shall base its decision on its free conviction gained from the "overall outcome of the proceedings". Though, according to Section 101 (1) VWGO, the principle of oral hearing also applies to administrative proceedings, oral hearings are often limited to the discussion of essential and controversial points in practice. This also results from Section 84 (1) VWGO, according to which the court may rule without oral hearing if the case does not show any particular difficulties. Competition law proceedings in accordance to the principles provided by the German Code of Administrative Court Procedure – VwGO – may guarantee a more efficient enforcement of the law, which would be beneficial for leniency programs and cartel prosecution as a whole.

[16] The German Federal Cartel Office has regularly proposed such a reform, cf. Zwischenbericht des Expertenkreises Kartellsanktionsrecht of 13 January 2015, available at: http://www.bundeskartellamt.de/SharedDocs/Publikation/DE/Berichte/AG_Kartellsanktionenrecht_Zwischenbericht.pdf?__blob=publicationFile&v=2

[17] *Meyer-Goßner/Schmitt*, StPO-Kommentar, § 261, paras. 1, 7.

[18] BGH, Beschluss v. 10.08.1989, 4 StR 393/89, StV 1989, 519.

### 11.1.3 Criminalization of German Competition Law?

Since the implementation of the GWB, a possible criminalization of competition law has been discussed in Germany recurrently.[19] The main argument is that competition law enforcement would supposedly become more effective and efficient. Moreover, the deterrent effect of custodial sanctions has been emphasised.[20] However, a criminalization of competition law would hinder the uniform application of Articles 101 and 102 TFEU in line with the principle of effectiveness. While large, international cartels would only imply administrative sanctions on the EU level, much smaller, national cartels would be exposed to criminal sanctions. Thus, the nature of the penalty would depend on the size, the geographic scope of activities and the turnover of the undertakings involved in the infringement. Such a difference in legal assessment is hardly justifiable. Moreover, the criminalization of German competition law would complicate the cooperation between the German Federal Cartel Office and the Commission (or other competition authorities) within the European Competition Network (ECN). For instance, case allocation among the network may cause difficulties, as national competition law proceedings may pass into proceedings before the Commission in accordance with Article 11 (6) of EU Regulation 1/2003 on competition procedure. While a national authority would assume to conduct criminal proceedings pursuant to national law, the Commission may still take up the case. Therefore criminal proceedings would abruptly turn into administrative proceedings, which would lead to severe legal uncertainty. Criminalization would also considerably impair information exchange between the members of the ECN. According to the second indent of Article 12 (3) Reg. 1/2003, information exchanged within the ECN cannot be used by the receiving authority to impose custodial sanctions. The rationale of the provision is the fulfilment of the undertakings' fundamental rights in the context of criminal proceedings in the respective Member States.[21] The European legislature was perfectly aware of the fact that competition law proceedings featured different structures throughout the ECN when it adopted Reg. 1/2003. Therefore there was a need to protect the procedural rights of defendants in national proceedings when establishing the provisions regarding information exchange among the members of the ECN. However, the protection of procedural rights and (indirectly) the apparent acceptance of existing criminal sanctions regimes in the context of competition law (like in the United Kingdom in accordance with the Enterprise Act 2002) shall not be misunderstood as an encouragement to criminalize national competition law in reverse.[22] Article 12 (3) Reg. 1/2003 shall rather be seen as a compromise by which the existing liability regimes within the EU ought to be balanced. As for the rest, a criminalization of

[19] Cf. *Dannecker*, in Festschrift für Tiedemann, Der strafrechtliche Schutz des Wettbewerbs: Notwendigkeit und Grenzen einer Kriminalisierung von Kartellverstößen, p. 789f.

[20] See *Wagner-von Papp*, WuW 2010, 271ff. for a comprehensive overview of the discussion.

[21] *De Bronett*, Kommentar zur VO 1/2003, Art. 11, para. 7.

[22] See, by contrast, *Wils*, Word Competition 28 (2005), p 177ff.

German competition law would reduce information exchange between the Commission and the German Federal Cartel Office and therefore complicate cooperation between both authorities; a criminalization would compromise the dezentralised application of Articles 101 and 102 TFEU. Accordingly, competition law enforcement should not be criminalized in Germany.

### *11.1.4 Market Dominance and Other Anti-competitive Behaviour*

**Introduction**

The German cartel enactment GWB provides distinct substantive rules as regarding the control of dominant positions (Sections 18–20 GWB) and addresses several individual issues in the context of merger control. Section 19 GWB prohibits the abuse of market dominance pursuant to Section 18 GWB. Section 20 GWB extends the scope of the prohibition on dominance abuse to undertakings with relative market power. Sections 18–20 GWB are the result of the eighth amendment to the GWB, by which the prohibitions of abusive or discriminatory behaviour of market dominant undertakings and undertakings with relative market power were revised and condensed.[23] Unlike the German provisions regarding the prohibition of cartels, Sections 18–20 GWB have only partially been approximated to Article 102 TFEU. It is understood that this difference shall primarily be justified by the third sentence of Article 3 (2) Reg. 1/2003 (the so-called "German clause"), by which Member States shall not be precluded from adopting and applying *stricter* national laws in regard of the prohibition or sanctioning of anti-competitive, unilateral conduct. Sections 18–20 GWB are therefore also applicable in the situation that they go beyond the rules set out in Article 102 TFEU. A supremacy of Union law as in the context of Article 101 TFEU and thus an exclusionary effect towards respective national provisions do not exist.

In contrast to the TFEU, the GWB contains a *ban on discrimination*, which has not been substantially altered to date. According to the initial ban on discrimination, market-dominant undertakings were not allowed to unfairly hinder business activities of undertakings or to treat undertakings differently without objective justification. In 2013, the Eighth Amendment to the GWB has condensed the ban on discrimination (old version of Section 20 (1) GWB) and the ban on unfair hindrance (old version of Section 19 (4) No 1 GWB) into Section 19 (2) No 1 GWB. The general ban on discrimination has no counterpart at the European level, at least in this form. Besides Article 18 TFEU, Article 101 (1) (d) and Article 102 (c) TFEU contain only partial bans on discrimination. Therefore, the scope of application of the German provisions is wider than that of the respective rules on a European level. Though this German specificity was not subjected, there was agreement until the

[23] See *Bechtold*, GWB-Kommentar, Vorbemerkung § 18, para. 1.

Eighth Amendment to the GWB that the scope of application of the rules set out in Sections 19 and 20 (1) GWB could not exactly be distinguished. Especially the implications of the parallel applicability of the bans on unfair hindrance and on discrimination on the one side and the European provision in Article 102 TFEU on the other side remained elusive.[24] These deficiencies could only be corrected partially by the Eighth Amendment to the GWB. Some differences to Article 102 TFEU still remain.

## The Concept of Market Dominance

The concept of market dominance is central in competition law. Market-dominant undertakings are subject to the strict abuse prohibitions in Section 19 (1) and (2) GWB. The (possible) emergence of a dominant position on the market may also lead to measures in the context of merger control according to Section 36 GWB. Thus, the legislature has decided to legally define the concept of market dominance in the Eighth Amendment to the GWB in 2013, which was reinterpreted on this occasion and separated into monopolistic and oligopolistic dominance (respectively Art 18 (1) and (5) GWB). As only an "undertaking" may be dominant pursuant to these provisions, the differences between the traditional German understanding and the European concept of an undertaking might have had an impact in the context of dominance abuse. However, the single economic entity doctrine can only bind the German Federal Cartel Office in the context of Section 1 GWB, though not in the frame of an abuse of dominance pursuant to Sections 19 GWB.[25]

In European competition law, the concept of market dominance also plays a central role regarding the determination of the addressee towards whom the abuse prohibition pursuant to Article 102 TFEU is directed to, as well as for the substantive assessment criteria set out in Article 2 (2) and (3) of EU Regulation 139/2004 in a merger context. In the area of merger control, the creation or strengthening of a dominant position is the principal example case for a significant impediment to effective competition, which ultimately leads to the issuance of a prohibitive decision (so-called SIEC test). The SIEC test has also been implemented into German competition law by the Eighth Amendment to the GWB. For the finding of market dominance, consequently, the relevant product and geographic markets must be defined in both jurisdictions. By contrast, market share thresholds differ in European and German competition law. At European level, they tend to be higher than the thresholds defined under Section 18 (4) and (6) GWB in order to assume market dominance. The Court of Justice has repeatedly confirmed that "very large" market shares may in themselves be evidence of the existence of a dominant position, which would be the case with a market share of 50 %.[26] If the market share of the undertaking keeps considerably below this level, market dominance may only be

[24] Cf. *Bechtold*, Kommentar zum GWB, § 18, para. 2.

[25] *Bechtold*, Kommentar zum GWB, § 18, para. 3.

[26] Case C-62/86 *Akzo* [1991] ECR I-3359, para. 60.

found where additional conditions of some relevance are proved to exist.[27] This may be the case where considerable barriers to entry into the respective market prevail for newcomers.[28] The GWB follows a different approach. It contains several presumptions of market dominance (Section 18 (4) for single dominance and Section 18 (6) and (7) for collective dominance. Though the presumption of single market dominance initially applied to undertakings with a market share of at least one third of the market, the thresholds has been elevated to 40 % in the wake of the Eighth Amendment to the GWB. This increment has been justified with the fact that administrative practice had shown the exceptional nature of market dominance.[29] Until the Sixth Amendment to the GWB in 1998, the legislature had even deliberately desisted from such a presumption, arguing that the provisions previous to Article 102 TFEU did not presume market dominance under any circumstances.[30] After the dominance presumption was incorporated into the GWB during the sixth amendment, it has been maintained until the Eighth Amendment. In consequence, by the latter the old version of Section 19 (3) GWB has been only technically divided into a presumption for single and for collective dominance. Although, Article 102 TFEU is basically applicable to collective market dominance ("by one or more undertakings"), it has been of minor importance in the Commission's decisional practice to date.[31] By contrast, the creation or strengthening of a collective dominant position has often been under examination in European merger control proceedings in order to establish whether a concentration would significantly impede effective competition.[32]

### Market-Dominant Undertakings Pursuant to Section 19 GWB

Whereas Section 18 GWB generally defines the concept of market dominance, Sections 18 and 19 GWB relate to the absolute *or* relative market position of an undertaking and prohibit a respective abuse or certain practices. The new structure of the prohibition provisions described above did not really implicate any substantive changes.[33] Apart from that, the wording and the interpretation of Sections 19 and 20 GWB are quite close to Article 102 TFEU.

---

[27] *Fuchs/Möschel*, in IM, Art. 102 AEUV, para. 87.; auch *Gergmann*, in L/M/R, Art. 82, para. 102.

[28] *Bechtold*, Kommentar EU-Kartellrecht, Art. 102, para. 23.

[29] Explanatory memorandum of the Federal Government to the draft eighth amendment to the GWB, BT-Drucks. 17/9852, p. 23.

[30] Cf. BR-Drucks. 852/97, p. 37.

[31] Cf. Commission decision of 7 December 1988 No. 89/93/EEC (*flat glass*) 1989 O.J. L 33/44, pp. 65f.

[32] Cf EuG EuZW 1998, 299, 308 Kali + Salz; EuG Slg. 2002 II-2585 Airtours/Kommission; Commission decision of 22 July 1992 Nestlé/Perrier, ABl. L 1992, 352/1; see also *Bechtold/Bosch/Brinker* as regards Article 102 TFEU and Article 2 of Regulation 139/2004.

[33] Explanatory memorandum of the Federal Government to the Draft eighth amendment to the GWB, BT-Drucks. 17/9852, p. 23.

Section 19 GWB provides a general prohibition on the abuse of market dominance. While Section 19 (1) GWB contains a general clause providing that the abuse of a market-dominant position by one or more undertakings is prohibited, Section 19 (2) GWB sets out non-exhaustive examples of such an abuse of dominance. The normative structure of the provision therefore resembles of Article 102 TFEU. Furthermore, the concept of abuse tends to correspond with the respective concept under Article 102 TFEU.[34] From a substantive point of view, Section 19 GWB also resembles Article 102 TFEU, which prohibits any abuse by one or more undertakings within the internal market or in a substantial part of it in so far as it may affect trade between Member States. However, it appears conspicuous that the requirements as provided by Section 19 (2) GWB are more differentiated than the examples set out in Article 102 (2) TFEU. While the GWB recognises exclusionary and discriminatory abuses as circumscribed under Section 19 (2) No 1 and 2 GWB being the most important scenarios of dominance abuse.[35] Corresponding cases may at best fall within the general clause of Article 102 (1) TFEU in European competition law. Consequently, the case-law or casuistry became extensive in the frame of the norm. This situation has influenced the European courts in cooperation with the Commission to develop a non-exhaustive practice in order to enhance the application of Article 102 TFEU.

The approximation of the national abuse concept to Article 102 TFEU can clearly be seen in Section 19 (4) No 4 GWB, in which the so-called *essential facilities doctrine* developed under European law plays a predominant role.[36] According to this principle, a company has a right of access to such facilities that are essential for the entry into a downstream market and cannot be duplicated.[37] A facility again is duplicable, if it could be provided at least by particularly effective competitors.[38] The purpose of Section 19 (2) No. 4 GWB is to guarantee competition on downstream markets in which competition is only possible if an existing network or infrastructure installation can be used by several competitors.[39] The German legislature initially bore the telecommunication, energy and rail sectors in mind, though these segments have been regulated separately afterwards. These and similar regulations or even enactments include provisions that ultimately oblige a company to provide

---

[34] Cf. BGH WuW/E DE-R 2268 Soda Club II.

[35] This is the consequence of the systematic list of examples in Section 19 (2) GWB.

[36] See EuGH EuZW 1995, 339 Magill (and comment by *Bechtold* EuZW 1995,345f.); EuGH WUW/E EU-R 127 = WRP 1999, 167 Oscar Bronner/Mediaprint und Entscheidungen der Kommission v. 14.1.1998 Flughafen Frankfurt, ABl. L 72/30; v. 11.3.1998, Van den Bergh Foods Limited, ABl. L 246/1 v. 4.9.1998.

[37] *Eilmannsberger* in MünchKomm, Art. 82 EG, para. 332; *Temple Lang*, Defining legitimate competition: companies' duties to supply competitors, and access to essential facilities in *B. Hawk (Hrsg.)*, International Antitrust Law & Policy, 1994, p. 245ff.

[38] *Bechtold*, Kommentar EU-Kartellrecht, Art. 102, para. 53.

[39] See Bundeskartellamt, WuW/E DE-V 253, 261 – Puttgarden.

access to a network or installation that is essential for competition to actual or potential competitors.[40]

However, the current version of Section 19 GWB, which is mainly inspired by Article 102 TFEU, is based on the several amendments to the German cartel enactment during the past decades. While the initial version of GWB did not distinguish between a general clause and the enumeration of exemplary cases, the first amendment to the GWB created a general clause already in 1965, which has been progressively specified by exemplary cases later on.[41] The development of Section 19 GWB outlined above shall not obscure the fact that the five enumerated example cases only cover some most important forms of abusive behaviour. The wording of Section 19 (2) GWB ("in particular") implicates that only a few out of the imaginable groups of cases are included in the enumeration. The further specification of the general clause in Section 19 (1) GWB (as well as in Article 102 (1) TFEU) shall be in line with the purpose of the provision. Section 19 GWB protects the freedom of entrepreneurial action within the sphere of influence of market-dominant undertakings, in order to enhance the development of competitive processes.[42] Competition namely will only develop on the condition that undertakings can exercise their commercial freedom within the limits of what is legally possible, without being illicitly impaired by market-dominant undertakings. The behaviour of the latter will therefore face the verdict of being abusive if it hinders or damages other entrepreneurs on the basis of the undertaking's market dominance, which would not be possible if effective competition existed.[43] In such context, the Commission's more economic approach does not only apply as regards to the frame of Article 101 TFEU, for which it initially has been developed, but also to Article 102 TFEU. This approach has progressively gained in influence at national level and aims at a stronger orientation of competition rules towards a comprehensive protection of consumer welfare.[44] German authorities and courts must therefore deal with these standards in the context of the application of the general clause in Section 19 (1) GWB, especially if the supposedly abusive behaviour affects third markets.[45] Furthermore, Section 19 (1) GWB may also apply to the behaviour towards consumers, which do not fall

[40] Cf. *Bechtold*, GWB-Kommentar, Vor § 28, paras. 13ff., 19ff. and 28 ff. as regards specific regulations.

[41] See *Bechtold*, GWB-Kommentar, § 19, para. 2.

[42] See *Emmerich*, Kartellrecht, 13th. ed. 2014, § 27, paras. 4 ff.

[43] *Mestmäcker*, in: FS Hallstein, 1966, S. 329; *idem*, AcP 168 (1968), 251; *idem*, DB 1968, 1800; *idem*, Medienkonzentration und Meinungsvielfalt, 1977, pp. 197ff.

[44] See *Kroes*, Tackling Exclusionary Practices to avoid Exploitation of Market Power: Some preliminary Thoughts on the Policy Review of Article 82 in: 29 Fordham International Law Journal (2006) 593, 596; also see *Monti*, EU Competition Policy after May 2004, Speech from 24 October 2003; *idem*, A Reformed Competition Policy: Achievements and Challenges for the Future, Speech from 28 October 2004; (both speeches available at http://ec.europa.eu/comm/competition/speeches/); *Lowe*, DG Competition's Review of the Policy on Abuse of Dominance, 2003 Fordham Corp. L. Inst. 163 (B. Hawk, Ed. 2004).

[45] Cf. BGH WuW/E DE-R 1055, 1057 Ruhrnet; OLG Düsseldorf WuW/E DE-R 880, 883 Strom & Fon; KG WuW/E 3124, 3129 Milchaustauschfuttermittel.

within the scope of the exemplary cases provided by Section 19 (2) GWB. For instance, discriminatory behaviour within the meaning of Section 19 (2) No 1 GWB explicitly applies to discrimination against other undertakings.[46] Discriminatory behaviour towards the consumers might therefore only fall within the scope of Section 19 (1) GWB.[47] This finding suggests that, despite a certain specification by comprehensive exemplary cases, the German general clause as such still has an independent and huge scope of application, which will have to be shaped more precisely by official and judicial practice as well as in the wake of further amendments of German cartel law.

### Undertakings with Relative Market Power Pursuant to Section 20 GWB

Section 20 (1) GWB expands the scope of prohibition of abuse of market dominance on exclusionary and discriminatory behaviour pursuant to Section 19 (2) No. 1 in conjunction with Section 19 (1) GWB by undertakings with relative market power. The prohibition on abusive behaviour pursuant to Section 20 (1) GWB is applicable if and to the extent to which small and medium sized enterprises depend upon the respective undertaking as suppliers or demanders of a certain kind of goods or services (i.e. in a vertical relationship) in a manner that sufficient or reasonable alternatives to the respective undertaking do not exist on the market.[48] While Section 19 GWB relates to the absolute market position of an undertaking, Section 20 GWB focuses on the relative market position (i.e. in relation to the respective small or medium enterprise). By contrast, Article 102 TFEU does not contain any provision comparable to Section 20 GWB as regards discriminatory or exclusionary behaviour by an undertaking with *relative market power* as opposed to undertakings with *absolute market dominance*. The expansion of the abuse prohibition to undertakings with relative market power traces back to the Second Amendment to the German cartel enactment in 1973. The purpose of the amendment in this respect was to close loopholes or protection gaps caused by the abolition of price maintenance for brand products in 1973.[49] To date, the GWB has adhered to this statutory system. Therefore, the level of protection provided by German cartel law appears much higher than under Article 102 TFEU.

### Boycott Prohibition Pursuant to Section 21 GWB

The boycott prohibition pursuant to Section 21 GWB constitutes an additional German specificity. It is applicable regardless of the market position of the undertaking concerned. Competitors might be particularly hindered in the case that

[46] *Bechtold*, GWB-Kommentar, § 19, para. 35.

[47] BGH WuW/E DE-R 3145, 3155 Entega II.

[48] *Emmerich*, Kartellrecht, 13th ed. 2014, § 28, para. 3.

[49] See *Bechtold*, GWB-Kommentar, § 20, para. 6.

suppliers or customers are requested to discontinue business relations with them. The unilateral behaviour of the requesting undertaking is particularly anti-competitive, regardless of a corresponding agreement or concertation. A general boycott prohibition has therefore been developed from Section 4 No. 10 of the Act against Unfair Competition (UWG), Section 21 GWB and Section 823 of the German Civil Code (BGB). Thus, undertakings and associations of undertakings must not demand another company to discontinue supply to or purchase from a third party with intent to unfairly harm the latter. The importance of the boycott prohibition primarily lies with corresponding requests of special business information services to discontinue supply or purchase in order to discipline particularly active competitors.[50] The Eighth Amendment to the GWB has brought only slight changes by recasting Section 21 (2) GWB and including infringements of European law into the circle of illicit conducts within the meaning of the provision. By contrast, an explicit boycott prohibition does not exist in European law, to the result that corresponding behaviour would have to be assessed under the general clause in Article 102 TFEU on a case-by-case basis.[51]

### *11.1.5 Dissolution of Market-Dominant Undertakings?*

Sections 19–21 GWB are exclusively directed against any *abuse* of market dominance, although, the approach does not go against a strong market position resulting from organic growth as such. The *mere existence* of market dominance does not fulfil the requirements of the prohibition on its abuse under German law. In the past, the introduction of (general) dissolution instruments into German competition law has been discussed repeatedly. Newly suggested instruments would have been created in order to terminate competition law infringements as well as to improve market and competition conditions regardless of the sector concerned.[52] However, the debate on the introduction of a dissolution instrument is not exactly new.[53] The peak of the discussion was reached after government plans for a cartel law amendment –

[50] *Emmerich*, Kartellrecht, 13th ed. 2014, § 29, para. 1a.

[51] *Bechtold*, Kommentar zum GWB, § 21, para. 23.

[52] Cf. *Klees/Hauser*, Entflechtungen von Unternehmen als Instrument des allgemeinen Wettbewerbsrechts? RATUBS Nr.4/2010.

[53] Cf. *inter alia Herrmann*, Die Entflechtung als Instrument der Wettbewerbspolitik, 1981; *Scholz*, Entflechtung und Verfassung, 1981; *Selmer*, Unternehmensentflechtung und Grundgesetz, 1981; *Schulte-Braucks*, Die Auflösung marktbeherrschender Stellungen, 1980; *Steffen*, Die Unternehmensentflechtung im Spannungsfeld zwischen Wettbewerb und effizienten Unternehmensgrößen, 1981; MÖSCHEL, Entflechtungen im Recht der Wettbewerbsbeschränkungen, 1979; *Oehler*, Entflechtung und Kontrahierungszwang, 1976; *Möhring*, Entflechtungsmaßnahmen der EWG-Kommission bei Unternehmenskonzentrationen nach deutschem Recht, 1967; *Jens*, WuW 1978, 264 ff. cf. recently *Müller*, Entflechtung und Deregulierung, 2004; *Klees/Hauser*, WuW 2007, 596 ff.; *Haus*, WuW 2001, 659ff.

"Law on the introduction of a power to impose dissolution and a right to comment for the German Federal Cartel Office in legislative procedures" – have been proposed in Germany since January 2010.[54] However, the possibility to establish dissolution measures regardless of an infringement of law raised constitutional and European law concerns.[55] The introduction of a dissolution instrument as initially stipulated in the German government's coalition agreement for the 17th legislative period could therefore not be included in the eighth amendment to the GWB by the year 2013.

Though the German legal system does not provide the possibility to dissolve market-dominant undertakings or undertakings with relative market power irrespective of an infringement of competition law, the GWB allows at least structural measures in accordance with Reg. 1/2003 in case of an infringement. Such structural interventions may include dissolution measures. According to Section 32 (1) GWB, the German Federal Cartel Office may require undertakings or associations of undertakings to terminate an infringement of the competition law provisions in the GWB or Articles 101 and 102 TFEU. To this effect, it may impose all measures that are necessary and proportionate. These measures may be behavioural as well as structural in nature, whereby the subsidiarity of structural measures must be respected (first sentence of Section 32 (2) GWB). Until the Eighth Amendment of the GWB in 2013, Section 32 GWB did not contain the explicit power to impose structural measures. On the contrary, such measures had been explicitly rejected in the Seventh Amendment of the GWB in 2005.[56] It is only in the course of the Eighth Amendment that the wording of the old version of Section 32 (2) GWB has been approximated to Article 7 Reg. 1/2003, by which the Commission may impose behavioural and structural remedies that are proportionate to the infringement of Articles 101 and 102 TFEU and necessary to terminate the infringement effectively on a subsidiary basis. The eighth amendment to the GWB has also added a new subsection 2a to Section 32 GWB, by which the German Federal Cartel Office may require the undertaking to refund the illicit advantages it received by its anti-competitive behaviour. The approximation of Section 32 (2) GWB to Article 7 Reg. 1/2003 is particularly welcome with regard to the effective and efficient application of Articles 101 and 102 TFEU, especially in view of the fact that the harmonisation of powers facilitates cooperation among the competition authorities in the European Competition Network (ECN).

[54] Cf. *Klees/Hauser* (Fn. 49), RATUBS Nr.4/2010; Bundeskartellamt, Diskussionspapier, http://www.bundeskartellamt.de/SharedDocs/Publikation/DE/Diskussions_Hintergrundpapier/Bundeskartellamt%20-%20Entflechtung%20als%20Instrument%20des%20Kartellrechts.pdf?__blob=publicationFile&v=6.

[55] Cf. *Bechtold* BB 2010, 451, *Lange* EWS 2010, 3rd issue, 1, *Säcker* WuW 2010, 370 and *Nettesheim/Thomas*, Entflechtung im deutschen Kartellrecht, Tübingen 2011.

[56] *Bechtold*, GWB-Kommentar, § 32, para. 3.

## 11.2 Merger Control

### *11.2.1 The Introduction of the "SIEC Test" into Section 36 GWB and Its Effects on Ministerial Approvals Pursuant to Section 42 GWB*

Unlike acting or judging within the scope of Articles 101 and 102 TFEU, national authorities and courts are not obliged to apply European merger control rules *in addition* to national law. On the contrary, both control regimes are exclusive within their respective scope of application. In the case that the turnover thresholds of Articles 1 (2) and (3) of EU Regulation 139/2004 (Merger Regulation – EUMR) are met, the Commission shall have exclusive jurisdiction to examine the concentration based on European merger control rules, with reservation of the possibilities of referral pursuant to Articles 4 (4) and 9 EUMR. Conversely, if the conditions of application of the European merger control regime are not met, but the German provisions are applicable in accordance with Sections 35 (1) and (2) GWB, the European Merger Regulation (EUMR) shall not apply. The European merger control regime is therefore not taken directly into consideration in the course of national proceedings.

However, the respective German provisions have been (in part almost literally) approximated towards the EUMR by the Eighth Amendment to the GWB. This is especially the case regarding prohibition criteria. According to Article 2 (3) EUMR, a concentration which would significantly impede effective competition in the common market or in a substantial part of it, shall be declared incompatible with the common market, especially if the impediment to competition results from the creation or strengthening of a dominant position. The introduction of this so-called SIEC criterion (or "SIEC test") was mainly motivated by two considerations[57]: On the one hand, the legislature wanted to fill existing gaps in the context of uncoordinated effects in oligopolies. On the other hand, the SIEC test provided the possibility to take efficiency gains into consideration. These advantages may include non-competitive aspects, such as the realisation of a primary objective in line with public interests (e.g. resulting from industrial, technological, social, or regional policy).[58] The SIEC test has been fully implemented into the German provisions on merger control by the Eighth Amendment to the GWB. Consequently, the new version of Section 36 GWB will not primarily assess concentrations according to the initial market dominance test anymore, but rather following the European approach as expressed in the SIEC test. However, the market dominance criterion is still relevant as it functions as a presumptive main example for an impediment to effective competition.

The introduction of the SIEC test, which allows the consideration of non-competitive aspects into German competition law raises the question about the

[57] Cf. *Simon*, in: *Loewenheim/Meessen/Riesenkampff*, Einf. FKVO, para. 37.

[58] Cf. 3. Bericht über die Wettbewerbspolitik, Brüssel-Luxemburg 1974, 38–56.

legitimacy of the ministerial approval pursuant to Section 42 GWB. However, German legislature decided to adhere to the ministerial approval concept despite the approximation of substantive assessment criteria to the EUMR. The main argument was that this solution allows a transparent separation of the German Federal Cartel Office's competitive assessment and the consideration of non-competitive aspects of public welfare by the Federal Minister of Economics in order to keep away political pressure from the Cartel Office and therefore re-establish its enforcement activity.[59] However, this evaluation may prove to be wrong. Besides concerns in regard of regulatory policy (e.g. dirigisme and public interventionism),[60] the desired effects of a ministerial approval have only been achieved in a few cases.[61] This has been particularly evident in respect of the protection of employment,[62] which has regularly proved to fail afterwards.[63] Non-competitive effects that fall within the scope of the ministerial approval may be addressed by the SIEC test in the context of the balancing clause pursuant to Section 36 (1) sentence 2 No. 1 GWB, which has been designed precisely in order to take efficiency gains into account. This may be the case for macroeconomic benefits such as the long-term protection of energy supply in Germany[64] as well as the protection of employment (subject to the foregoing).[65] According to the provision, a concentration shall not be prohibited if the parties to the transaction demonstrate that the concentration improves the conditions of competition and that these improvements overweigh the impediment to competition established under the first sentence of Section 36 (1) GWB. Certain public interests within the meaning of Section 42 GWB, such as restructurings, rationalisation benefits or military aspects,[66] cannot be taken into consideration under the substantive assessment criteria pursuant to Section 36 GWB. However, these aspects have played a minor role in the context of ministerial approvals anyway. In particular, they have never justified such approval by themselves. The legitimacy of a "foreign body" in the GWB such as the ministerial approval will therefore have to be assessed critically in future. This is particularly true considering that a review of concentrations by another authority matching the German ministerial approval system does not exist in European law. Once the Commission has declared a concentration incompatible with the common market pursuant to Article 2 (3) EUMR, an

---

[59] Explanatory memorandum of the Federal Government to the Draft eighth amendment to the GWB, BT-Drucks. 17/9852, p. 20.

[60] Cf.. *Mestmäcker*, in: Festschrift v.d. Groeben, pp. 9, 28.

[61] See for a comprehensive representation *Roth/Voigtländer*, ZfW 2002, 231, 248 f.

[62] See the special report of the German Monopoly Commission 36, WuW/E BWM 225, 228, para. 138.

[63] This conclusions is also reached by the Federal Ministry of Economics and Technology in its progress report in 1992, p. 4.

[64] Federal Minister of Economy, WuW/E DE V 573, 584 f., 589 E.ON/Ruhrgas.

[65] Cf. Federal Minister of Economy, WuW/E 225, 228 Kali + Salz/PCS; WuW/E 177, 181 IBH/WiBau; WuW/E DE-V 573, 592 f. E.ON/Ruhrgas; most recently Federal Minister of Economy, WuW/E DE-V 1691 Universitätsklinikum Greifswald.

[66] See *Bechtold*, GWB-Kommentar, § 42, para. 9 for benefits in line with public interest.

administrative revision (by a second authority) is not possible. The German Monopoly Commission (*Monopolkommission*) therefore considers that a ministerial approval can possibly be incompatible with European law.[67] As this question must be assessed on a case-by-case basis, the ministerial approval system as such does not compromise the effective and efficient application of Articles 101 and 102 TFEU by German competition authorities or courts.

### 11.2.2 The Concept of a Concentration within the Meaning of Section 37 GWB, Especially the Acquisition of Non-controlling Minority Shareholdings

Section 3 (2) and (3) EUMR and Section 36 GWB both address "concentrations" between undertakings. The review of a proposed transaction therefore starts with the preliminary question whether a project as filed to the Commission or the German Federal Cartel Office constitutes a "concentration" within the meaning of the respective merger control provisions. In this respect also, the EUMR has served as a model for the GWB (i.e. for the current Section 37 GWB). In particular, the introduction of the "acquisition of control" concept pursuant to Article 3 (1) (b) and (2) EUMR enables to capture a wide range of possible transaction structures. By contrast, the acquisition of shares in another undertaking constitutes a transaction within the meaning of Section 37 (1) No. 3 GWB regardless of a possible acquisition of control, if the shares amount to at least 25 % of the capital or the voting rights of the other undertaking. The German legislature assumed that such shares typically suffice to provide a special influence within the respective company.[68] However, the German provision is discussed critically, since a minority shareholding does not provide the existence of an economic entity as required by substantive merger control rules as such.[69] The concept as regards the acquisition of minority stakes under German cartel law therefore goes well beyond the approach of the European merger regulation that will not review the acquisition of a minority shareholding as long as it does not simultaneously result in an acquisition of control pursuant to Article 3 (1) (b) EUMR. However, the Commission is currently examining whether the acquisition of a minority shareholding shall fall within the scope of the European merger regulation. The Commission has therefore launched a public consultation on a possible reform of EU merger control and published the white paper "*Towards More Effective EU Merger Control*".[70] The Commission's proposals ultimately aim at a more effective and efficient EU merger control. The German merger control provisions may therefore serve as a model for the EUMR.[71]

[67] Monopoly Commission, WuW/E DE-V 543 E.ON/Ruhrgas.

[68] See the reasons for the draft bill, BT-Drucks. 13/9720, p. 43.

[69] *Emmerich*, Kartellrecht 13th ed. 2014, § 33, para. 25.

[70] http://ec.europa.eu/competition/consultations/2013_merger_control/merger_control_en.pdf.

[71] Which would historically be in line with the creation of European competition law, cf.

### 11.2.3 Merger Control in the Context of Joint Ventures

European and German merger control rules also differ in respect of the assessment of joint ventures. Joint ventures are defined as undertakings jointly controlled by at least two other undertakings (the parents) by Article 3 (1) (b) and (4) EUMR. As a means of cooperation between undertakings, a joint venture is on the edge between the concepts of cartel and of concentration.[72] Thus, the creation of a joint venture may give rise to competitive issues, especially with regard of the fact that the parent companies, though (formally) competing with each other, may show consideration towards their cooperation. Such a group effect would cause decreased competition. European and German merger control regimes therefore both try to control this group effect. However, they take different approaches: The EUMR deals with the described group effects since 1997. According to Article 3 (1) (b) EUMR, the acquisition by one or more persons already controlling at least one undertaking, or by one or more undertakings of direct or indirect control of the whole or parts of one or more other, shall also fall within the scope of EUMR. Article 3 (4) EUMR clarifies that the creation of a joint venture performing on a lasting basis all the functions of an autonomous economic entity shall constitute a concentration within the meaning of Article 3 (1) (b) EUMR. If the turnover thresholds in Articles 1 (2) and (3) EUMR are met, the European merger regulation is exclusively applicable to the creation of the joint venture concerned. Finally, Article 2 (4) EUMR provides that to the extent that the creation of a joint venture constituting a concentration as described above has as its object or effect the coordination of the competitive behaviour of undertakings that remain independent (regularly the parents), such a coordination will additionally be reviewed under Articles 101 (1) and (3) TFEU (i.e. according to the procedure as set out in Reg. 1/2003). However, this only applies to so-called cooperative full-function joint ventures, which perform all the characteristic features of an autonomous economic entity in the long term.[73] In summary therefore, the Commission tries to coordinate possible group effects in the context of joint ventures by examining the matter both under the EUMR on the one hand and additionally under Articles 101 (1) and (3) TFEU and Reg. 1/2003 on the other.

German competition law follows a different approach. According to Section 37 (1) No. 3 sentence 3 GWB, if several undertakings simultaneously or successively acquire shares in another undertaking, this shall also be deemed to constitute a concentration among the acquiring undertakings themselves in regard to the market on which the target undertaking operates. Such a fiction of a partial merger between the parent companies conceptually differs from the European merger regulation as regards legal doctrine to the extent that joint ventures are subject to a double review under both the EUMR and Articles 101 (1) and (3) TFEU, whereas German law fictitiously assumes an additional concentration between the parents. However, joint ventures may impede competition between the parents *inter alia* because of the

---

[72] Cf. *Emmerich*, Kartellrecht, 13th ed. 2014, § 17, paras. 1ff.

[73] *Bechtold/Bosch/Brinker*, Kommentar EU-Kartellrecht, Art. 3 FKVO, para. 28.

above-mentioned group effect, which would correspond with a cartel under German law. There is a debate whether, in this case, Section 1 GWB is applicable in addition to the merger control rules, and, if so, how cartel prohibition and merger control relate to each other.[74] A comparable provision as seen in the EUMR does neither exist in the GWB nor in Art. 3 (4) EUMR. However, the so-called double-barrier theory has prevailed, according to which the provisions on cartel prohibition and merger control are applicable to joint ventures in parallel.[75] Thus, it is decisive whether the requirements of the ban on cartels (applicability of Section 1 GWB) or those of the merger control regime (applicability of Sections 36, 37 GWB) are fulfilled in the individual case. A legislative measure comparable to the relevant provisions in the EUMR would nevertheless be preferable in order to avoid legal uncertainty. In consequence, as far as Section 1 GWB is applicable, it now basically has priority over merger control rules.[76]

## 11.3 Public Business Activities

The uniform application of Articles 101 and 102 TFEU in Germany is also important in the context of public business activities, especially as regards the application of European competition law to public undertakings. Article 106 (1) TFEU provides that Member States shall neither enact nor maintain in force any measure contrary to the rules of the Treaties, especially to the competition rules as set out in the TFEU, in the case of public undertakings and undertakings to which Member States have granted special or exclusive rights. Article 106 (2) TFEU adds the restriction that undertakings entrusted with the operation of services of general economic interest or having the character of a revenue-producing monopoly shall be subject to the same rules in so far as the application of these rules does not legally or factually obstruct the performance of the particular tasks assigned to them. These two subsections of Article 106 TFEU differ from each other in so far as the first subsection is directed to the Member States, whereas the second subsection directly addresses the undertakings concerned. However, the provision must be understood as a unity in view of its genealogy.[77] Therefore, as far as Article 106 (2) TFEU provides exemptions, they shall apply to public undertakings and to enterprises with special or exclusive rights within the meaning of Article 106 (1) TFEU as well.

[74] Cf. *Emmerich*, Kartellrecht, 13th ed. 2014, § 33, para. 40f.

[75] BGHZ 96, 69 (77 ff.) = NJW 1986, 1874; BGHZ 147, 325 (331, 333, 335 ff.) = NJW 2001, 3782; BGH WuW/E DE-R 2361 (2362 Tz. 14) NordKS/Xella; NJW-RR 2010, 615 = NZG 2010, 76, Tz. 14 = JuS 2010, 547 – Gratiszeitung Hallo; OLG Düsseldorf AG 2006, 506 (509 f.) = WUW/E DE-R 1625 (1630 f.) – Rethmann/GfA Köthen; NZKart 2013, 377 (380) = WuW/E DE-R 3993 – Chemikalienhandel; Bien, NZKart 2014, 247.

[76] *Emmerich*, Kartellrecht, 13th ed. 2014, § 33, para. 44.

[77] Cf. Case C-320/01 *Paul Corbeau* [1993] ECR 1–2563.

Article 106 TFEU is not without controversy in respect of the constitutional fabric of the European Union. The provision's rationale is to exclude the possibility that Member States release themselves from the obligation to protect and enforce European competition law by performing business activities under the umbrella of a public undertaking.[78] However, a full extension of the competition rules set out in the TFEU to public undertakings (as proposed by some Member States) could not prevail, whereupon the Member States did agree only on some exemptions. The exclusions provided from European competition law should in their relevance to the market not been underestimated, especially as regards services of general interest (such as the supply of electricity, Gas and water, health care and other social law matters),[79] which are addressed by Article 106 TFEU. Within the scope of these exemptions, competition law is not applicable. Only a few exclusions are provided by the GWB under Sections 28 ff., and were restructured by the latest amendment of the enactment. At the same time, the economic activity of public authorities has been exempted from the control of price abuse, as long as they charge fees or dues subject to public law (second sentence of Section 130 (1) GWB). As a consequence, there is some concern that public authorities may "escape into public procurement and fees" in order to avoid competition law requirements.[80] The issue is accentuated in view of the control of abusive behaviour, e.g. regarding the question whether such a control shall be of competitive or supervisory nature. The advantages of a competitive assessment are obvious, especially with regard to the wide harmonisation of competition law within the European Union.[81] The application of competition law would guarantee more dynamics in the respective markets and could contribute to decrease prices. In Germany, the opposite may be observed as a consequence of the exemption mentioned above, especially by observing the local supply of water.[82] A possible cause might be the current uncertainty as regards the legal concept of an undertaking in respect of public entities.[83] However, the creation of further exemptions should not be encouraged. Exceptions within a competition framework cannot be justified in objective terms, as only free competition can regulate free pricing. Though modern-day Germany is far away from being the "land of cartels" it once was, there are still numerous monopolies in diverse markets. This may be harmful to the decentralised application of Articles 101 and 102 TFEU.

---

[78] See in detail *Emmerich*, Festschrift Steiner, 2009, pp. 173ff.

[79] See in detail *Oppermann*, in: Festschrift Salje 2013, p. 331 passim.

[80] Cf. Stellungnahme des Bundeskartellamts zum Referentenentwurf zur 8. GWB-Novelle, WuW 2012, S. 257, 266.

[81] Cf. *Oppermann*, in: Festschrift Salje 2013, p. 331, 352 f.

[82] Cf. Hannoversche Allgemeine Zeitung of August 14, 2012, p. 7.

[83] Cf. most recently: *Suchsland/Rossmann*, Verpflichtet die Kartellschadensersatzrichtlinie zur Übernahme des europäischen Unternehmensbegriffs in das deutsche Recht?, WuW 2015 (vol. 10), p. 973. For a more general analysis of "undertaking" in competition law: *Oppermann*, in: FS für Salje 2013, p. 331, passim.

## 11.4 Private Enforcement

### *11.4.1 Introduction*

Public enforcement of competition law as described so far may be accompanied by private enforcement. Private action has increasingly gained importance over the last years. Its significance has been evidenced recently by the Directive 2014/104/EU on certain rules governing actions for damages under national law for infringements of the competition law provisions of the Member States and of the European Union issued on November 26th, 2014 (hereinafter "the Directive").[84] The Member States shall bring corresponding national law into force by December 27th, 2016 in order to improve the application of Articles 101 and 102 TFEU that is in line with the principle of effectiveness as regards actions for damages.[85] In the past, the development of private enforcement has often been inhibited by its uncertain relationship to public enforcement, as there might be cases where private enforcement appears not suitable for supplementing public measures. On the contrary, public and private enforcement may affect each other in some situations, e.g. in the case that a leniency applicant must fear damage claims by injured parties. The issue becomes very clear with regard to the fact that private damage claims are protected by constitutional law, rather than being merely at public disposal in the general interest of effective and efficient enforcement of competition law. The Regulation can be seen as an attempt of the Commission to enforce the Articles 101 and 102 TFEU in a manner that balances public and private enforcement adequately. The success of this endeavour as well as the effects of the implementation of corresponding provisions into national law on public enforcement (especially as regards leniency programs) remain to be seen. Furthermore, the Regulation requires some additional minor amendments to German competition law that will promote the effective and efficient application of Articles 101 and 102 TFEU.[86]

### *11.4.2 Constitutional Requirements Regarding Private Enforcement*

In its rulings in the cases *Courage*[87] and *Manfredi*,[88] the ECJ acknowledged the necessity for private claims in order to guarantee an overall effective and efficient enforcement of competition law, which would be put at risk if it was not possible to claim damages suffered by anticompetitive behaviour of others. The German

---

[84] 2014 O.J. L 349, 1.

[85] Cf. *Bosch*, NJW 2015, p 1734f.

[86] See in detail *Makatsch/Mir*, EuZW 2015, p. 7ff.

[87] Case C-170/83 *Courage* [2001] ECR I-6297.

[88] Case C-298/04 *Manfredi* [2006] ECR I-6619.

Federal Court of Justice has approved this line of decision in its *ORWI* judgment[89] and explicitly stressed that the right to claim damages was not merely an instrument of competition law enforcement, but rather, and foremost, guaranteed as an individual right. Individual rights do not only have relative effects of claims between the parties, moreover, they are protected against public interventions by constitutional law. It is worthwhile emphasising the injured party's fundamental right to property in this context.[90] The material area protected by the right to property is not confined to tangible property, but rather includes non-tangible property rights[91] such as contractual claims.[92] Consequently, the injured party's damage claims are protected by European law as property rights (Article 17 CFREU). The correct standard of review as regards fundamental rights, however, depends on the applicable law. If applying German law, only the fundamental rights provided by the Constitution ("Grundgesetz") are relevant. By contrast, in the context of European competition law enforcement by German authorities and courts, European fundamental rights are addressed, as the decentralised application of Articles 101 and 102 TFEU by the Member States constitutes an implementation of Union law within the meaning of Article 51 (1) CFREU.

### 11.4.3 Relationship to Public Enforcement

The process of implementing the CFREU covers of course some more aspects, which are discussed presently.[93] We do not follow up, turning towards a more general approach on private claims in structural competition law.

The standard of fundamental rights may be counteracted if public enforcement is given preference to private enforcement. Despite the Commission's efforts to intensify private competition law action, the primacy of public law enforcement still prevails. This approach will not be a matter of disposal by a new Directive after, e.g., years of successful leniency policy.

If public and private enforcement collide, it is argued that compensating damages should take precedence over public enforcement, which should be ensured procedurally.[94] Thus, the risk that claims under civil law might not be enforced because of the prior payment of a fine would be banned. This opinion should not be

---

[89] BGH 28.06.2011 - KZR 75/10, NJW 2012, 928, 931, Rn. 36 f. = WRP 2012, 209 – *ORWI*.

[90] Cf. *Glöckner*, WRP 2015, 410 f.

[91] *Dolzer*, in: *Merten/Papier*, Handbuch der Grundrechte, 2010, § 140, para. 7; cf. ECHR, 26.06.1986 – A101, para. 40 f. – Van Marle et al. ./. The Netherlands.

[92] *Jarass*, in: *Jarass*, Charta der Grundrechte der Europäischen Union, Art. 17, para. 8.

[93] Cf. *Weitbrecht*, Die Umsetzung der EU-Schadensersatzrichtlinie, WuW 2015 (vol. 10), p. 959; *Schnitzler*, Vorwirkungen der Kartellschadensersatzrichtlinie, WuW 2015 (vol. 10), p. 992; *Suchsland/Rossmann*, Verpflichtet die Kartellschadensersatzrichtlinie zur Übernahme des europäischen Unternehmensbegriffs in das deutsche Recht?, WuW 2015 (vol. 10), p. 973.

[94] Cf. *Glöckner*, WRP 2015, 410 f.

followed because such a provision might deter possible leniency applicants from cooperating with competition authorities. Strengthening private enforcement in this manner would therefore compromise the decentralized application of competition law. It might therefore be discussed to dispense leniency applicants from damage claims in proportion to the degree of cooperation and the benefits to investigations provided. In a case of conflict of public and private measures, such a dispense would constitute a justified intervention into the injured party's fundamental rights, as the strengthening and maintenance of the primacy of public enforcement serves the effectiveness and efficiency of competition law, which is a legitimate aim of public interest.

Besides the problem of colliding measures, the strengthening of private enforcement would be desirable for the future even in acknowledgement of leniency programs which stand for a good collection of evidence and intelligence.[95] Added value is achieved by hindering upcoming and maintaining cartels to develop an organizational structure. Leniency also increases uncertainty on the side of the cartel members and makes it more difficult for cartel participants to reach an agreement. Last but not least, the costs of adjudicating may decrease due to the legal goal-oriented activity of whistle blowers.

In contrary, there are a few adverse effects. In a theoretical approach, the notion of leniency is contradictory since blowing the whistle is the second best choice only. Making the exemption to become the rule gives wrong incentives to the market members to opt for the first best choice, in order to build a cartel either not punished or not discovered and keep silent. For some principle reasoning such an option would create an obstacle. Moreover practically, some adverse effects could be identified.[96] Leniency programs are thought to help to find out well hidden cartels, in other words to encourage discovery in hard cases. Instead, leniency is not eligible to be the main tool of cartel enforcement. Besides the public measures mentioned, the encouragement of private claims should be welcomed.

## 11.5 Summary

Although there has not been a fundamental change of paradigm, however, some approximation of German provisions to European competition law has taken place, not least in the wake of the amendment to the GWB in 2013. This process of harmonization or, moreover, adherence, simplifies the decentralized application of Articles 101 and 102 TFEU and enhances the cooperation between competition authorities within the European Competition Network (ECN). The debated criminalization of German competition law would clearly jeopardized positive effects of such

[95] Cf. Oppermann, Leniency Policy in European Cartel Enforcement, in: Duc In Altum - Caderno de Direito, Vol. 6, No 10 (2014), 27 ff.

[96] See in detail: *Oppermann*, in: Oppermann, Leniency Policy in European Cartel Enforcement, in: Duc In Altum - Caderno de Direito, Vol. 6, No 10 (2014), 27, 49 f.

advantageous development, which is why this approach must be clearly rejected. On the contrary, special focus should be laid on enhancing efficiency and effectivity of competition law. This applies to the substantive as well as to the procedural aspects of the GWB. Some specificities of German competition law do not compromise the decentralised application of Articles 101 and 102 TFEU, as demonstrated by discussing the provisions regarding abuse control or the so-called ministerial approval. Nevertheless, the latter should be subject to revision, as there is no equivalent at EU level. Furthermore, the transposition of the Directive on antitrust damages actions into national law will be subject to thorough observation. In the process of implementation, the German legislature should consider the effectiveness and efficiency of leniency programs at the same time be aware of their hidden problematics. The transposition of the Directive 2014/104/EU should be regarded as a first step towards better private enforcement of cartel and competition claims. In any subject envisaged, however, the uniform application of Articles 101 and 102 TFEU is a primary goal which has been enhanced by the measures reported. Further developments remain to be seen.

# Chapter 12
# Recent Developments in the Application of Articles 101 and 102 TFEU by French Courts

**Rafael Amaro**

## 12.1 Introduction

There is no ideal model of private enforcement, two sharp-eyed observers of the evolution of competition law once stated.[1] This thoughtful assertion perfectly applies to the French model of private enforcement of EU competition rules. It is a common view among French lawyers, especially those of the plaintiffs', that private competition law enforcement is far from ideal. Nonetheless, if it is true that the success rate of private actions in French courts is low, it seems to be slightly increasing in the past few years. Moreover, we can take for granted that the "total underdevelopment" of damages actions depicted by the *Ashurst study* a decade ago is out of date. This leads us to a first assumption: if it remains far from being perfect, the French model of private enforcement is a little bit less imperfect than what it used to be. Two explanations might be advanced here. First, the French government acknowledges the need to promote the development of an efficient enforcement system and inserted some innovative rules into French statutes. Although these efforts are to be welcomed, they are slow to bear fruit and do not appear to really explain the rise of private litigation in French courts. As a matter of fact, the French government was guided, as the European institutions where when preparing Directive 2014/104/EU, by one overriding objective: the need to protect the efficiency of public enforcement from being jeopardized by the development of private enforcement. Based on the (debatable) supposition that public enforcers should lead the struggle against infringements of competition law, the major changes in French law

[1] A. A. Foer and J. W. Cuneo, "Toward an Effective System of Private Enforcement", in A. A. Foer, J. W. Cuneo (ed.), *The International Handbook on Private Enforcement of Competition Law*, Edward Elgar, 2010, p. 590 *sqq.*, at pp. 592 and 593.

R. Amaro (✉)
Université Paris Descartes – Sorbonne Paris Cité (CEDAG), Paris, France
e-mail: rafael.p.amaro@gmail.com

 
A. Almăşan, P. Whelan (eds.), *The Consistent Application of EU Competition Law*, Studies in European Economic Law and Regulation 9,
DOI 10.1007/978-3-319-47382-6_12

aim to protect the confidentiality of the information collected by the competition authority, and to make sure that private lawsuits follow public enforcement proceedings rather than taking their place.

Hence, to explain the recent progress of private enforcement in France, another factor seems much more decisive – although less detectable: the human factor. More precisely, from the observation of the recent French courts' activity, it could be supported that the mindset of French judges regarding private litigation has changed. A few years ago, many lower courts felt uncomfortable with complex economic evidence. It was not unusual then to see them dismissing claims for the sole reason that they were not convinced by the quantification of harm. The truth was that, due to their lack of experience, they preferred to deem the harm uncertain – which is sufficient under French tort law to exempt a defendant from civil liability – rather than taking a clear stand on its plausible amount. Now, some French courts (not all of them...) handle with more ease complex disputes and are less reluctant to award damages even where a doubt remains concerning the exact amount of the claimant's loss. This victim-friendly case law has been thriving on the basis of the *Code civil* and the *Code de procédure civile*'s general rules and did not require any modifications of French statutes. It is not to say that legal reforms are without merit but, as often, we must face the fact that human factors prevail. This is perhaps the key to an efficient application of EU competition law in French courts.

To support this hypothesis, I will describe in Sect. 12.3 the promising rise of individual actions. In Sect. 12.4, some of the major modifications regarding the interactions between private and public enforcement – illustrating the French legislator's bias to only pursue this objective – will be discussed and in Sect. 12.5 I will get onto the lingering difficulties claimants have to deal with. But first, Sect. 12.2 will provide the reader with a quick introduction to the French competition law enforcement model.

## 12.2 Introduction to Competition Law Enforcement in the French Legal System

As in all Member States of the European Union, the application of Articles 101 and 102 TFEU in France is governed by the principles of EU primary and secondary law. This is true for both public and the private enforcement. Note also that there are very few differences in the application of EU and French competition law (which is governed by Article L. 420-1 *seq.* of the *Code de commerce*). After a quick overview of the French legal system (Sect. 12.2.1), this section will then describe the rules applicable to the main private actions brought in French courts: actions for damages and for nullity (Sect. 12.2.2) and actions for interim relief (Sect. 12.2.3).

### *12.2.1 Overview of the French Legal System*

**Public Enforcement** The French national competition authority, the *Autorité de la concurrence*, is responsible for the application of French and European competition law in public enforcement procedures. Appeals can be lodged against its decision in Chamber 5-7 of the *Cour d'appel de Paris* (Paris Court of Appeal), which has an exclusive jurisdiction in public enforcement matters.

**Private and "Administrative" Litigation** French courts, competent for civil and criminal matters, decide private and criminal cases: the *juridictions judiciaires*. The *juridictions administratives* are competent for litigation between the State and private parties. At the first instance level, claimants can seize two kinds of *juridictions judiciaires*: the *tribunaux de grande instance* (civil courts) and the *tribunaux de commerce* (commercial courts). As they frequently involve business disputes, most of first instance private enforcement cases are actually dealt by the *tribunaux de commerce*. It follows from Article L. 420-7 and R. 420-3 to R. 420-5 that 16 first instance courts are specialized in the application of French and European competition law.[2] As for public enforcement, the *Cour d'appel de Paris* has an exclusive jurisdiction to decide on appeals. The *juridictions judiciaires*, which are competent for civil and commercial litigation, may award the claimants domestic remedies for breaches of Article 101 and 102 TFEU, such as damages, nullity or interim relief.[3]

**Criminal Enforcement** Usually, criminal enforcement cases are handled by the *tribunaux de grande instance's* criminal formations. They apply the only criminal provision that remains in French competition law: Article L. 420-6 of the *Code de commerce*.[4] This Article applies to French competition law infringements, but in general, breaches of EU competition law accompany breaches of national competition law. It can be argued then that in cases where EU law is applied, criminal proceedings should be possible on the basis of a breach of national law.

---

[2] Eight *tribunaux de commerce* and eight *tribunaux de grande instance* from the following cities: Marseille, Bordeaux, Lille, Fort-de-France, Lyon, Nancy, Paris and Rennes.

[3] For an overview on the topic, see: R. Amaro, *Le contentieux privé des pratiques anticoncurrentielles. Étude des contentieux privés autonome et complémentaire devant les juridictions judiciaires*, avant-propos G. Canivet, préf. M. Béhar-Touchais, Bruylant, 2014; M. Béhar-Touchais, C. Prieto, D. Bosco (eds), *L'intensification du private enforcement*, Travaux du Réseau Trans-Europe-Experts, SLC, 2016; M. Chagny, *Droit de la concurrence et droit commun des obligations*, préf. J. Ghestin, Dalloz, "Nouv. bibl. de theses", 2004; E. Claudel, *Ententes anticoncurrentielles et droit des contrats*, th. Paris X, 1994, dir. M.-C. Boutard-Labarde; M. Dumarçay, *La situation de l'entreprise victime dans les procédures de sanction des pratiques anticoncurrentielles*, préf. B. Lasserre, Litec, "Bibl. Dr. entreprise", 2010; S. Pietrini, *L'action collective en droit des pratiques anticoncurrentielles*, Université Paris-Ouest Nanterre La Défense, 2010.

[4] The first paragraph of this Article provides that: "If any natural person fraudulently takes a personal and decisive part in the design, organisation or implementation of the practices referred to in Articles L. 420-1 and L. 420-2, such person shall be punished by a prison sentence of 4 years and a fine of 75,000 Euros."

**A Mix of *Règles de Droit Commun* and *Règles de Droit Special*** If we set aside the few principles designed by the ECJ landmark cases, like *Courage*,[5] *Manfredi*[6] or *Otis*,[7] the private litigation is governed by French procedural and substantive rules, in compliance with the autonomy principle. To the foreign observer new to private enforcement in France, the French legal framework could appear somehow intricate. Indeed, it mixes general rules from the *Code civil* and the *Code de procédure civile* (*"règles de droit commun"*) and specific rules from the *Code de commerce* and the *Code de la consommation* (*"règles de droit special"*). This complexity is an inevitable pitfall of the French lawyers' "codification obsession". That said, one of the underlying principles that should be kept in mind to have a clearer picture of the exact solution French law lays down is the *Specialia generalibus derogant:* if no specific rule from the *Code de commerce* and the *Code de la consommation* provides for a solution, then general rules from the *Code civil* and the *Code de procédure civile* apply.

**Procedural Rules** Procedural matters are ruled by the common principles of the French civil procedure of the *Code de procédure civile*[8] complemented by the specific provisions of the *Code de commerce* and *the Code de la consommation.*[9] Under the general rules of the *Code de procédure civile*, especially Articles 30 and 31, there is no doubt that a breach of EU competition law gives rise to a cause of action in French courts for remedies. Individual actions adhere to the *Code de procédure civile*, while collective actions, only available for consumers, are framed by the *Code de la consommation*. The new 5 year limitation period of Article 2224 of the *Code civil*, introduced by the major reform of the Act of 17 June 2008,[10] applies to private actions. Most of the legal issues related to evidence are governed by the *Code de procédure civile*, especially 11,[11] 138 *seq.*[12] and 142 *seq.*,[13] except when it

[5] Case C-453/99, EU:C:2001:465.

[6] Case C-295-04,EU:C:2006:461.

[7] Case C-199/11, EU:C:2012:684.

[8] S. Amrani-Mekki, "Inciter les actions en dommages et intérêts en droit de la concurrence: le point de vue d'un processualiste", in L. Idot (ed.), *Livre blanc sur les actions en dommages et intérêts pour infraction aux règles communautaires sur les ententes et les abus de position dominante*, co l'Institut de droit comparé de Paris II, 13 June 2008, *Concurrences*, n° 2-2009, p. 11 *seq*.

[9] These specific rules will be dealt with below.

[10] Loi n° 2008-561 *portant réforme de la prescription en matière civile*.

[11] Article 11 provides for the obligation of the parties and third parties to contribute to ascertaining the truth and empowers French courts to order the disclosure of evidence on the parties' request.

[12] Article 138 applies when the evidence is in the possession of a third party. It states that "If, during the proceeding, a party wishes to rely on a notarial deed or a deed under private signature to which he was not a party or a document held by a third party, he may request the judge, to whom the matter is referred to, to order the delivery of a certified copy or the lodging in court of the deed or the document." Article 139 adds the following: "The request may be made without any formality. The judge, if he considers that the request is well-founded, will order the delivery or the production of the original, copy or extract of the deed, as the case may be, under the conditions and guarantees that he determines, if necessary, under a periodic penalty payment."

[13] Article 142 applies when the evidence is in the possession of another party (claimants or defendants). Article 142 extends the principles laid down by Articles 138 and 139 for the *inter partes* disclosure.

comes to the disclosure of the *Autorité de la concurrence*'s file, which is governed by the *Code de commerce*.

**Substantive Rules** For substantive matters, the general rules of the *Code civil*, and the extensive case law that clarifies its provisions for the last 200 years, establish a consistent framework that will be marginally affected by the transposition of the Directive 2014/104/EU. The main changes will concern the various rebuttable and irrebuttable presumptions created by the directive and the civil leniency awarded to SME and immunity recipients.

### 12.2.2 Rules Applicable to Actions for Damages and for Nullity

**General Principles of French Tort Law** As pointed out above, common principles of French tort law apply to damages actions: former Article 1382 *seq.* (now Article 1240 *seq.*) of the *Code civil* complemented by the prolific case law of the *Cour de cassation* govern the three threshold requirements: fault, causation and harm.[14] Damages actions may be brought against companies, as legal persons, who violate French or EU competition law[15] on the basis of Article 1382 of the *Code civil* but individuals may be held liable too. Corporate executives, as natural persons, may be sued on the basis of Articles L. 225-251 or L. 223-22 of the *Code de*

[14] For an overview: A. Bénabent, "La mise en jeu de la responsabilité civile", *in Les sanctions judiciaires des pratiques anticoncurrentielles*, 29 April 2004, *LPA*, 20 January 2005, n° 14, p. 31 seq.; S. Carval, "L'estimation du montant des préjudices concurrentiels. Un possible apport de la directive n° 2014/104 au droit commun de la responsabilité civile", *D.*, 2015, p. 1290 *seq.*; M. Chagny, "Quelle(s) réforme(s) et adaptation(s) du droit français? Approche critique et prospective ?" in M. Chagny (ed.), *La réparation des dommages concurrentiels en France et en Europe: État des lieux et changements à venir*, Paris, 13 May 2014, *Concurrences*, n°3-2014, p. 59 *seq.*; M. Chagny, "La place des dommages-intérêts dans le contentieux des pratiques anticoncurrentielles", *RLC*, 2005/4, p. 186 seq.; G. Decocq, "Leçon sur la responsabilité civile du fait d'une pratique anticoncurrentielle", in *Leçons du Droit Civil. Mélanges en l'honneur de François Chabas*, Bruylant, 2011, p. 197 seq.; F. Dreifuss-Netter, "Droit de la concurrence et droit commun des obligations", *RTD civ.*, 1990, p. 369 seq.; F. Dupuis-Toubol, "Action civile en matière de pratiques anti-concurrentielles: éléments de problématique", in *La réparation du préjudice causé par une pratique anti-concurrentielle en France et à l'étranger: bilan et perspectives*, Cour de cassation, Paris, 17 October 2005; D. Fasquelle, "La réparation des dommages causés par les pratiques anticoncurrentielles", *RTD com.*, 1998, p. 763 seq.; J.-L. Lesquins, "L'établissement de pratiques anticoncurrentielles lors du procès civil", in *Les sanctions judiciaires des pratiques anticoncurrentielles*, l'Université Paris I, 29 April 2004, *LPA*, 20 January 2005, n° 14, p. 17 seq.; C. Momège, L. Idot, "Application of Articles 81 & 82 EC by the French Ordinary Courts. A Procedural Perspective", in C.-D. Ehlermann, I. Atanasiu (eds), *European Competition Law Annual 2001: Effective Private Enforcement of EC Antitrust Law*, Oxford, Hart Publishing, 2003, p. 230 seq.; R. Saint-Esteben, "La réparation du préjudice économique résultant d'infractions au droit de la concurrence (point de vue d'un 'juriste français')", in *Risques, assurances, responsabilités*, 26 April 2007.

[15] Cass. com., 1 March 1982, No. 80-15834, *Bull. Civ.* IV No. 76.

*commerce.*[16] Article L. 225-251 for the *"sociétés anonymes"*[17] and Article L. 223-22 for the *"sociétés à responsabilité limitée"*[18] rule that corporate executives committing misconducts can be held personally liable.[19] employees who participated in the commission of the anti-competitive practice may be sued as well on the basis of Article 1382 of the *Code civil.* It has to be borne in mind that employees' personal liability is narrowed by a rather protective case law[20] but they can still be held liable when they commit a criminal offense or an intentional civil fault.[21]

**General Principles of French Contract Law** As for damages actions, the substantive rules applicable to actions for nullity are the general principles of the *Code civil* that deal with all types of contracts, *ie* Article 1101 *seq.* (*droit commun des contrats*). These rules must comply with the principles outlined by ECJ case law, especially the *Courage* case that limits the scope of the *Nemo Auditur* principle.[22] French courts apply Article 101 paragraph 2 TFEU and its French counterparts, Article L. 420–3 of the *Code de commerce.*[23] Under French contract law, claimants can apply for total or partial nullity. This nullity is qualified as "absolute" (*absolue*) which means that any interested party may ask the court to declare the contract void and unenforceable, including third parties and public prosecutors (*ministère public*). In compliance with the *Van Schijndel* ruling,[24] the common rules of civil procedure only require, since a landmark case of 21 December 2007, that

---

[16] E. g. CA Aix-en-Provence, ch, 2, 4 December 2008, *SA Eurelec Midi Pyrénées v Max D.*, No. 07/09250.

[17] The French legal form of limited liability corporation for major companies.

[18] The most wide-spread French legal form of limited liability corporation for SME's.

[19] Article L. 225-251 paragraph 1 states that: "The directors and managing director shall have individual or solidary responsibility to the company or third parties either for infringements of the laws or regulations applicable to limited companies, or for breaches of the constitution, or for tortious or negligent acts of management." Translation from: http://www.legifrance.gouv.fr/Traductions/en-English/Legifrance-translations.

[20] The *Cour de cassation* based this protective case law on the ground of Article 1384 paragraph 5. In two famous cases (*Costedoat* and *Cousin*), the French Supreme Court granted employees a civil immunity in most situations where harm has been caused by their faults. In such situations, the employer's strict liability is engaged (*"responsabilité sans faute du commettant du fait du préposé"*). See the *Costedoat case*: Cass. ass. plén., 25 February 2000; *Grands arrêts*, No. 217; *Dalloz*, 2000, p. 673, note P. Brun; *Rev. trim. dr. civ*, 2000, p. 582, obs. P. Jourdain; and the *Cousin* case: Cass. ass. plén., 14 December 2001, No. 00-82.066; *Dalloz*, 2002, p. 1230, note J. Julien; *JCP G*, 2002, II, 10026, note M. Billiau; *Rev. trim. dr. civ.*, 2002, p. 109, obs. P. Jourdain.

[21] Cass. civ. 2, 21 February 2008, No. 06–21.182; *Dalloz* 2008, p. 2125, note Laydu; *JCP G*, 2008, I, 186, No. 5, obs. Stoffel-Munck. See M.-P. et C. Lucas de Leyssac, "L'inquiétant Article L. 420-6 du Code de commerce et comment se rassurer", in *Les droit et le Droit. Mélanges à Bernard Bouloc*, Dalloz, 2007, p. 651 *seq.*

[22] Case C-453/99, EU:C:2001:465, at 22 and 24.

[23] That states: "Any undertaking, agreement or contractual clause referring to a practice prohibited by Articles L. 420-1, L. 420-2 and L. 420-2-1 shall be invalid."

[24] Case C-430/93 and C-431/93, EU:C:1995:441, at 13 and 22; the ECJ laid down that national courts have the obligation to declare a contract void on their own motion, only if their national rules oblige them to do so.

courts may decide on their own motion whether it is appropriate or not to declare the contract void. In other words, French courts have an option and not the obligation to hold that a contract violates EU or French competition law.[25] Actions for nullity based on a breach of Articles 101 and 102 TFEU are common in French courts and many cases can be recorded.[26]

### *12.2.3 Rules Applicable to Actions for Interim Relief*

**The *Référé* and *Requête* Proceedings** French procedural rules allow any claimant to seek interim relief in national courts. Such relief is usually awarded after fast track proceedings, as the *référé* and the *procédure sur requête*. These two proceedings, governed by the *Code de procédure civile*, are not specific to competition law litigation and may be initiated in any commercial or civil courts. The *référé* proceedings governed by Article 484 *seq.* of the *Code de procédure civile* allow courts to grant interim relief after a contradictory debate, whereas the *requête* proceedings, governed by Article 493 *seq.* of the same code, precludes the need for such debate when specific conditions are met. By their orders (*ordonnances*), courts do not rule on the merits of the case; but they are empowered to order a wide range of measures, immediately enforceable.

**The Three Purposes of Interim Relief** Depending on the type of measures ordered, applicants might pursue three purposes: prepare for a forthcoming trial; preserve their situation during the trial's lapse of time; and anticipate the final judgment on the merit.[27] Interlocutory proceedings differ from main proceedings on the merits to get a final judgment (*procédure au principal*) in that the measures courts may order are temporary and their rulings do not bind courts seized on the merits of the case in a following procedure. However, it is noteworthy that, in most cases, interlocutory judgments are not subject to challenge on the merits by a subsequent

[25] Cass. ass. plén., 21 December 2007 (2 judgments) No. 04-10672 and 06-11343, *Bull. ass. plén.*, No. 8 et 10; *JCP G*, 2008, I, 138, No. 9, obs. S. Amrani-Mekki; *Rev. dr. contr.*, 2008/2, p. 327, obs. A. Bénabent; *Resp. civ. et ass.*, 2008/3, comm. 112, note S. Hocquet-Berg; *Defrénois*, 2008, p. 1457, note E. Savaux; *JCP G*, 2008, II, 10006, note L. Weiller.

[26] See for an overview, see R. Amaro, *Le contentieux privé des pratiques anticoncurrentielles*, Bruylant, 2014; C. Lucas de Leyssac, G. Parléani, "L'atteinte à la concurrence, cause de nullité du contrat", in *Le contrat au début du XXIe siècle: études offertes à Jacques Ghestin*, LGDJ, 2001, p. 601 seq.; M. Malaurie-Vignal, "Droit de la concurrence et droit des contrats", *D.*, 1995, p. 51 seq.; J. Mestre, B. Fages, "L'emprise du droit de la concurrence sur le contrat", in Y. Picod (ed.), *Droit du marché et droit commun des obligations, Rev. trim. dr. com.*, 1998, p. 71 *seq.*; B. Oppetit, "La liberté contractuelle à l'épreuve du droit de la concurrence", *Rev. sc. mor. pol*, 1995/3, p. 241 *seq.*; D. Houtcieff, "La nullité des pratiques anticoncurrentielles à la croisée du droit de la concurrence et du droit des contrats", *in Regards croisés sur les pratiques commerciales*, l'Université du Maine, 16 May 2003, *Revue juridique de l'Ouest*, 2005/1, p. 14 *seq.*

[27] J. Normand, "Préface", *in* A. Lacabarats, B. Mathieu, *Les procédures d'urgence en droit des affaires*, Joly éd., "Pratique des affaires", 2010, p. IX.

action. Therefore, if the measures ordered by the courts are "temporary", legally speaking, in fact, they often are definitive.

## 12.3 The Promising Rise of Individual Actions

The last several years have seen an increased number of damages actions against companies. The most visible actions followed public enforcement procedures, but stand-alone actions can also be reported. This demonstrates that claimants may succeed in stand-alone litigation, especially when they invoke the harm caused by an abuse of a dominant position or anticompetitive vertical agreements. Generally, consumers take very few damages actions and virtually all cases involve undertakings. This growing litigation gave French courts the opportunity to refine the case law and provide useful clarifications on certain issues. It also highlights some lingering difficulties in the quantification of harm. Aside from the fact that new patterns of follow-on actions have developed (Sect. 12.3.2), there is also a very significant stand-alone litigation (Sect. 12.3.3), albeit "under the radar", that demonstrates the strategic interest of private actions in competition litigation. That being said, litigants may also seek for interim relief. It is even one of the most valuable asset of French procedural rules that explains the increasing number of private actions in French courts (Sect. 12.3.1).

### *12.3.1 The Success of Actions for Interim Relief*

**The *Mesures d'instruction in Futurum*** First and foremost, Article 145 of the *Code de procédure civile* offers a sort of discovery "à la française" which is very useful for collecting evidence before a trial. Accordingly, French courts may order preparatory inquiries necessary "to preserve or to establish, before any legal process, the evidence of the facts upon which the resolution of the dispute depends".[28] These inquiries, called *"mesures d'instruction in futurum"*, could relate to, for instance, expertise or a disclosure of documents.[29] This procedural mechanism is all

[28] Its provisions are written as follows: "If there is a legitimate reason to preserve or to establish, before any legal process, the evidence of the facts upon which the resolution of the dispute depends, legally permissible preparatory inquiries may be ordered at the request of any interested party, by way of a petition or by way of a summary procedure." The "legally" measures are those available on the ground of Articles 232–284-1 CPC.

[29] R. Amaro, "Le référé de droit commun en droit des pratiques anticoncurrentielles: brève analyse du contentieux porté devant le juge français", *Concurrences*, n° 4-2013, p. 216 *seq.*; E. Claudel, "Les injonctions", *in Les sanctions judiciaires des pratiques anticoncurrentielles*, l'Université Paris I, 29 April 2004, *LPA*, 2005, n° 14, p. 23 *seq.*

the more interesting given that Article 145's requirements are not very onerous: applicants only have to establish that they have a legitimate interest to ask for the measures; whether the claim is well founded or not is not relevant at this stage of the litigation.

**The *Référé-Sauvegarde*** To preserve their situation, claimants may also apply for interim measures on the basis of Articles 809 paragraph 1[30] and 873 paragraph 1.[31] These provisions empower French courts to order all permissible measures necessary "to avoid an imminent damage *(dommage imminent)* or to abate a manifestly illegal nuisance *(trouble manifestement illicite)*".[32] Insofar as this proceeding adheres to the *référé* procedural rules, it is called *"référé-sauvegarde"*. As for Article 145, the requirements to be fulfilled under Articles 809 and 873 are flexible. Their wordings specify that interim measures may be ordered even where the applicant's argument is "confronted with a serious challenge" from the defendant. In competition law litigation, it means that applicants do not need to establish undoubtedly the existence of the alleged anticompetitive practice.[33]

**The *Référé-Provision*** The *référé* or *requête* proceedings may also serve to anticipate the final judgment. Even if courts are not entitled to declare a party liable in their summary orders, Article 809 paragraph 2 or 873 paragraph 2 of the *Code de procédure civile* allow them to award an "interim payment" (*une provision*) "in cases where the existence of the obligation is not seriously challenged".[34] The *Cour de cassation*'s case law specified that the quantum of the sum paid to the creditor on the basis of this provision could amount to 100 % of the alleged sum due by the debtor. As a result, the so-called *"référé-provision"* is often considered as a way to definitively resolve a dispute. In practice, applicants favour the Articles 809 or 873 paragraph 1 pathway for at least two reasons. First, it is often faster than the *Autorité de la concurrence's* similar procedure for interim measures of Article L. 464-1 of the *Code de commerce*. Second, it allows applicants to maintain a broader control over the process.

---

[30] Before the *tribunaux de grande instance.*

[31] Before the *tribunaux de commerce.*

[32] Their provisions are written as follows: "The president may always, even where confronted with a serious challenge, order in a summary procedure such protective measures or measures to restore (the parties) to (their) previous state as required, either to avoid an imminent damage or to abate a manifestly illegal nuisance.

[33] Cass. com., 10 July 1989, Bull. n° 216, for a case where an abuse of dominant position was invoked.

[34] Their provisions are written as follows: "In cases where the existence of the obligation is not seriously challenged, he may award an interim payment to the creditor or order the mandatory performance of the obligation even where it is an obligation to do a particular thing."

### 12.3.2 The Diversification of Follow-On Damages Actions

**The *DKT* Case** Follow-on damages actions are usually brought to French courts after final decisions have been issued by competition authorities finding infringements of competition law. However, new patterns of follow-on actions, can be observed. For instance, the *DKT*[35] case illustrates the existence of a follow-on litigation consecutive to commitment proceedings. The claimant (DKT) complained of predation on the recycling of plastics market from two other undertakings. It requested 2.3 million euros for its loss and submitted the *Autorité de la concurrence*'s commitment decisions.[36] After several developments on the question of the access to the *Autorité de la concurrence's* file,[37] the claimant continued its damages action before the *Tribunal de commerce de Paris* (Paris Commercial Court). In its judgment, the court significantly relied on the *Autorité*'s decision to find that the two defendants were guilty. It thus raised the dominant position of each of these two defendants and deducted from the "competition concerns" identified by the *Autorité*, the existence of abuses of dominant position constituting civil wrongs. The court concluded that the claimant's harm is "necessarily implied by these practices." It then awarded it 50,000 euros for the actual loss, 200,000 euros for the loss of profit and 100 000 euros for the moral prejudice resulting from the loss of reputation, a total of 350,000 euros.

### 12.3.3 The Increasing Efficiency of Stand-Alone Damages Actions

**The Main Features of Stand-Alone Litigation in French Courts** One of the main findings of recent empirical studies on the application of EU and French competition law is the steady development, over the last decade, of stand-alone litigation. A ratio of 80 % stand-alone actions for 20 % follow-on actions is sometimes assumed.[38] Stand-alone litigation is manifold but some recurring features may be

[35] T. com. Paris, 15e ch., 30 March 2015, RG no J2012000109, *SARL DKT International c/ SA Eco-Emballages et Valorplast, Lettre Creda-concurrence*, 13 April 2015, note A. Ronzano, *Contrats, conc., consom.* 2015, comm. 155, obs. G. Decocq.

[36] Aut. conc., dec. No. 10-D-29, 27 September 2010, *relative à des pratiques mises en œuvre par les sociétés Eco-Emballages et Valorplast dans le secteur de la reprise et de la valorisation des déchets d'emballages ménagers plastiques.*

[37] CA Paris, ch. 5-4, 24 September 2014, RG no 12/06864, *SARL DKT International c/ SA Eco-Emballages et Valorplast, Lettre Creda-concurrence*, October 8th, 2014, obs. A. Ronzano, overruling T. com. Paris, 15e ch., 16 March 2012, RG no 2011023307, *SARL DKT International c/ SA Eco-Emballages et Valorplast, Lettre Creda-concurrence*, 10 March 2012, obs. A. Ronzano.

[38] R. Amaro, *Le contentieux privé des pratiques anticoncurrentielles*, Bruylant, 2014, annexe 2.

outlined: it involves business disputes; most litigants are contractual partners; an imbalance in their respective negotiating power may also be observed; and the illegal conducts are predominantly abuses of dominant position and vertical restraints. The success rate of stand-alone actions is similar to that of follow-on actions, notwithstanding the lack of previous decisions of the competition authorities. Two possible explanations may be advanced to elucidate this startling conclusion. First, insofar as the offenses punished in stand-alone litigation are infrequently hardcore cartels agreements but rather assumed business practices whose illegality is closely related to the dominant position of the defendants, it is therefore quite easy for claimants to prove the existence of such offenses. This differs from secret pricing and market-sharing agreements that require more coercive means of investigation to be established, means which are only available to public authorities. Second and as noted above, since abuses of a dominant position or vertical restraints occur in contractual relationships, it is possible to quantify at least approximately the harm through the milestone that constitutes the contract. Therefore, courts tend to estimate the damage by using simple quantification on the basis of the missed transactions due to the unlawful practice, multiplied by the gross margin, actually realised by the claimant on the market.

Two cases decided by the *Cour d'appel de Paris* illustrate the increasing efficiency of stand-alone actions.

**The *SPPS* Case** In the *SPPS* case, a newsstand operator (Mr Merhi) wanted to open a new store to sell various publications. The Paris Company Press Services (SPPS), enjoying a monopoly on the Paris market supply of newspapers, agreed to supply the new store on one condition: Mr Merhi had to sign a standard contract stipulating that the approval to be supplied by SPPS was personal and revocable without cause within 48 h. Mr Merhi refused to sign this contract and filed a stand-alone claim for abuse of a dominant position. The *Cour d'appel de Paris* ruled in his favour and stated that the contracts submit the Parisian newsstand operators to a total dependence on SPPS. The Court condemned SPPS for an abuse of a dominant position and awarded up to 25 000 euros for the loss of a chance to get gains from the second store the claimant could not open.[39]

**The *Aviscom* Case** In the *Aviscom v La Montagne* case, the claimant was a company editing an online condolence books service (Aviscom). It filed a claim against a local newspaper (La Montagne) who refused to insert the link in its website (avis-dedécès.fr) in the newspaper's obituaries. The *Cour d'appel de Paris* found that the newspaper was in a dominant position in "the market of obituaries" of the Puy-de-

[39] CA Paris, ch. 5-4, 27 April 2011, *M. B. Merhi v SNC Société Presse Paris Services*, Juris-Data no 2011-007393.

Dome (a French territorial division) since it was the only daily publishing obituaries in this territory. It also established that the link to Aviscom's website was absolutely necessary for this company to develop its service. It then concluded that, by refusing for no legitimate reason to insert the links to the website avisdedécès.fr, La Montagne committed an abuse of dominant position and forced Aviscom out of the market. The loss of revenue was quantified through a basic method: for each link that La Montagne refused to insert, an average damage of 10 euros was awarded due to the fact that without the link, Aviscom charged its customers 5 euros instead of 15 euros. Aviscom proved 4 839 refusals by La Montagne and received 48 390 euros.[40]

## 12.4 The Search for Better Interactions Between Private and Public Enforcement

Once a private lawsuit is filed, disclosure measures are ordered by French courts on the basis of Article 138 (disclosure ordered to third parties) and Article 142 (*inter partes* disclosure) of the *Code de procédure civile*.[41] When assessing the merits of the disclosure demands, French lower courts enjoy a wide margin of appreciation, but they have to respect the limits set out by the general rules of the *Code de procédure civile* laid down by Article 141[42] and by the special provisions of Articles L. 463-6 and L. 462-3, paragraph 2 of the *Code de commerce*, which are designed to protect the effectiveness of the public enforcement.[43] In the past five years, the application of these two rules (described below) has been adapted to cope with the new challenges thrown up by the development of private litigation. The French government clearly endorsed the European Commission's view to restrict the claimants' access to the *Autorité*'s documents (Sect. 12.4.1). Yet, the new rules concerning limitation in follow-on litigation set forth recently seems more favourable to the claimants (Sect. 12.4.2), as do those concerning the fault requirement (Sect. 12.4.3).

---

[40] CA Paris, ch. 5-4, 17 September 2014, *SA La Montagne v SAS Aviscom*, R. G. no 12/10322; *Lettre Creda-Concurrence*, 13 October 2014, note A. Ronzano; *AJCA*, 2015, p. 70, note M. Chagny.

[41] Note that Article 145 of the Code de procédure civile only applies before the trial (see No. 16).

[42] This Article establishes that: "In case of difficulty, or if (an argument of) a legitimate impediment is raised, the judge who ordered the delivery or the production in court may, on informal request made to him, retract or modify his decision. The third party may appeal against the new decision within 15 day as from its pronouncement." The legitimate impediment could be the protection of business secrets.

[43] For an overview: L. Idot, F. Zivy, "L'accès au dossier des autorités de concurrence dans le cadre des actions privées: État des lieux deux ans après l'arrêt Pfleiderer", *Concurrences*, No. 3-2013, p. 34 *seq*.

### *12.4.1 The Restricted Disclosure of the* Autorité de la concurrence*'s Documents*

**The "Investigative Privilege" Set Out by Article L. 463–6** In order to protect the confidentiality of the *Autorité de la concurrence*'s investigations, Article L. 463-6 of the *Code de commerce* prohibits any disclosure from a party that had access to the competition authority's files during a public enforcement procedure.[44] Any violation of this "investigative privilege" exposes the offenders to criminal charges. This deterrent obstacle to the spontaneous disclosure used to be enforced strictly by French courts until the *Cour de cassation* decided to relax Article L. 463-6's prohibition. In its *Semavem* judgment, issued on 19 January 2010, a defendant was allowed to disclose documents covered by the investigative privilege on the ground of Article 6 paragraph 1 of the European Convention of Human Rights, the provision that protects the right to due process.[45] The *Cour* was convinced that this disclosure was "necessary" for the litigant's defence and agreed to establish an exception to the principle of Article L. 463-6. Two further decisions extended the *Semavem* exception to claimants.[46]

**The Grey and Black Lists of Documents Created by Article L. 462–3 § 2** The *Loi Lurel* of 20 November 2012[47] completed the limitation to the disclosure of the *Autorité de la concurrence's* documents by creating a grey and a black lists of documents that the Autorité shall not communicate. It inserted into Article L. 462-3 of the *Code de commerce*, a new paragraph designed to anticipate the transposition of Article 6 of the Directive 2014/104/EU.[48] Article L. 462-3 does not cover the production by the parties themselves (as Article L. 463-6 does), but the disclosure ordered by the courts to the *Autorité de la concurrence*. It follows from its provision that:

[44] It states: "The disclosure by one of the parties of information regarding another party or a third party, which it could only have known as a result of the notifications or consultations which have occurred, shall be punished by the penalties specified by Article 226-13 of the Penal Code. Any failure to comply with this prohibition expose the claimants (and sometimes the defendants) to a 15 000 euros fine or a 1 year jail sentence."

[45] Cass. com., 19 January 2010, No. 08-19761, *Bull. civ.* IV, No. 8; *Contrats conc. consom.*, 2010, comm. 105, note G. Decocq; *Rev. jurid. écon. publique*, 2010, No. 677, comm. 36, note A. Friboulet; *Concurrences*, No. 2-2010, p. 136, obs. C. Lemaire, S. Naudin.

[46] CA Paris, ch. 5-4, 20 November 2013, *Président de l'Autorité de la concurrence c/ SAS Ma Liste de courses* et al., R. G. No. 12/05813; *Lettre Creda-concurrence*, November 18-22, 2013, note A. Ronzano; CA Paris, ch. 5-4, 24 September 2014, *SA Eco-Emballages et Valorplast c/ Autorité de la concurrence et SARL DKT International*; R. G. No. 12/06864; *Lettre Creda-concurrence*, 29 September – 3 October 2014, note A. Ronzano.

[47] No. 2012-1270.

[48] Its probable content was already known in 2012.

> The *Autorité de la concurrence* may send all information that it has concerning the anti-competition practices concerned, except for documents prepared or gathered under IV of Article L. 464-2, to any court that consults it or asks it to submit documents that are not already at the disposal of a party to the proceedings. It may do this within the same limits when it makes observations on its own initiative before a court.

This Article makes a distinction between two types of documents, depending on the nature of the public enforcement proceeding in which the *Autorité de la concurrence* obtained them. The principle set out by this Article concerns a first category of documents: those obtained during an ordinary proceeding – *i.e.* not opened after a leniency application. For such documents the *Autorité* is entitled to accept or to decline to accept their disclosure, as suggested by the word "may" (the grey list principle). The exception laid down by this Article concerns a second category of documents: those obtained during a leniency procedure (the one mentioned at point "IV of Article L. 464-2"). Anticipating the provisions of Article 6 § 6 of Directive 2014/104/EU, the *loi Lurel* totally prohibits the disclosure of these documents by the *Autorités* (black list principle). So far, no case law, such as the *Semavem* judgment, has relaxed this exception. As a result, claimants who did not take part in the public enforcement procedure might have a very restricted access to the *Autorité*'s files; this may jeopardise their chances of a positive outcome.

### *12.4.2 The New Limitation Periods Rules Designed to Encourage Actions by Claimants*

**The Easier Interruption of the Limitation Period** The *loi Hamon* of 17 March 2014 added a specific rule to the general provisions of the *Code civil* that apply to private litigation. This new rule, inserted in a new paragraph 4 of Article L. 462-7 of the *Code de commerce*, provides that the opening of proceedings before the *Autorité de la concurrence*, the national competition authority of another Member State or the European Commission interrupts the private action's limitation period. It also specifies that the interruption takes effect until the date on which the decision on the public enforcement procedure is final. This new rule applies to individual actions and collective redresses, *i.e.* the *action en représentation conjointe* and *the action de groupe* (see below No. 30). It aims to prevent the victims' actions from being time-barred before the end of the public enforcement procedure, as occurred under the former case law.[49] It's worth noting that the *Cour d'appel de Paris* reversed this case law, still applicable to past situations arising prior the entry into force of Article L. 462-7 paragraph 4 of the *Code de commerce*,[50] and aligned it with the new provisions of this Article.

---

[49] E. g. TGI Paris, ord., 15 January 2009, *Conseil régional d'Île-de-France et Région Île-de-France*, No. 08/55030, 08/59948, 08/59949; *RLC*, 2009/19, p. 97, note M. Chagny.

[50] CA Paris, ch. 5-5, 2 July 2015, *SA EDF et SA ERDF c/ SAS Nexans et SAS Prysmian*, R. G. No. 13/22609; *Lettre Creda-Concurrence*, 29 June-3 July. 2015, note A. Ronzano.

The new rules on limitation are clearly more favourable to claimants than the former case law. They also anticipate the solution adopted in Article 10 paragraph 4 of Directive 2014/104.[51]

### *12.4.3 The Relaxation of the Fault Requirement in Follow-On Litigation*

**The Lightening of the Burden of Proof** Another step toward the effectiveness of follow-on action has been taken by French courts. French case law admits that a breach to competition law is a ground for civil liability.[52] Whether this breach is to be considered as an irrebuttable presumption of a civil fault, a rebuttable presumption, or nothing more than an indication of a civil fault is not well-defined yet. However the most recent case law tends to ignore this conceptual debate, by simply declaring the infringer, liable. For instance, the *Cour d'appel de Paris* considered that:

> "The violation of the (competition) law necessarily constitutes a civil fault; however, it falls to the claimant who seeks to obtain compensation, to prove its loss, as well as the causal link between that fault and this loss."[53]

This solution could give credence to the irrebuttable presumption thesis, but it is not certain. What is sure, though, is that this ruling of the *Cour d'appel de Paris* is claimant-friendly to the extent that it lightens the burden of proof required to establish the defendants' liability.

**Civil Liability of Subsidiaries (*JCB Service* Case)** Recently French courts went even further to ease the difficulty with claimants' actions. By a first judgment of 15 November 2011, issued in the *JCB Service* case, the *Cour de cassation* ruled that the "group" of companies - which is referred to in the "motifs" (the reasons of the judgment / decision) of the European Commission's decision - *including subsidiaries*, was insufficient to automatically result in the subsidiaries' liability as only the

---

[51] It states that: "Member States shall ensure that a limitation period is suspended or, depending on national law, interrupted, if a competition authority takes action for the purpose of the investigation or its proceedings in respect of an infringement of competition law to which the action for damages relates. The suspension shall end at the earliest one year after the infringement decision has become final or after the proceedings are otherwise terminated."

[52] Cass. com., 1 March 1982, No. 80-15834, *Bull. civ.*, No. 76; Cass. com., 15 June 2010, No. 09-1581; *Dalloz*, 2010, p. 2781, note Y. Utzschneider, H. Parmentier; *Contrats conc. consom.*, 2010, No. 232, obs. Malaurie-Vignal; *Gaz. Pal.*, 12 February 2011, No. 43, p. 43, obs. J. Philippe, M. Trabucci; *Concurrences*, No. 4-2010, p. 205, obs. C. Lemaire.

[53] CA Paris, ch. 5-4, 27 May 2015, n° RG 14/14758, Sté Lectiel (en liquidation) c/ SA Orange (anciennement SA France Telecom); in the same litigation and already supporting this point of view: Cass. com., 23 March 2010, No. 08-20427; CCE, 2010/12, comm. 122 note M. Chagny; Contrats conc. consom., 2010/5, comm. 131, G. Decocq; RTD. com., 2010, p. 317, note F. Pollaud-Dulian.

parent company was identified in the "*dispositif*" (the formal court / authority order) as the infringer.[54] Nonetheless, a further judgment in the same case, issued on 6 October 2015,[55] specified that such subsidiaries might be held liable if the claimants were able to establish that they participated in the infringement. Yet, this participation seems easy to prove considering that the simple fact of taking part in the commercial policy of the parent is enough for a subsidiary to be considered at fault. The *Cour de cassation* approved the *Cour d'appel de Paris*'s position set forth in these terms:

> "These two companies [the subsidiaries] notify distributors [the victims] the anti-competitive distribution agreements on the order of JCB SERVICE [the parent] [...] apply the instructions of the commercial policy of JCB SERVICE and contribute to the achievement of violations reported; (...) they have thus committed a fault under French law; the claim to be dismissed from the lawsuit is not justified and in this regard, the fact that they [the subsidiaries] are not condemned in the European Commission's decision does not prevent the national court from deciding in the light of those elements, including the European Commission's decision, the part of their behaviour that constituted a fault".[56]

It is not possible yet to assess the progress these changes will bring for the victims but what appears clearly is that lingering obstacles keep hampering the surge of an efficient private enforcement model in France.

## 12.5 Lingering Obstacles to Private Actions

Recently, it seems that the main drawbacks to overcome under French law concern damages actions. The ineffectiveness of collective redresses is spectacular considering the number infringements found by the *Autorité de la concurrence* (Sect. 12.5.1). Another explanation of the poor outcome of private litigation lies in the fact the two other threshold requirements to establish a defendant's liability – causation (Sect. 12.5.2) and harm (Sect. 12.5.3) – are not so easy to prove.

---

[54] Cass. com., 15 November 2011, No. 10-21701; *Contrats conc. consom.*, 2012/3, comm. 66, obs. M. Malaurie-Vignal; *Bull. Joly Sociétés*, 2012, p. 395, note C. Prieto; *Rev. Sociétés*, 2012, p. 37, note S. Prévost.

[55] Cass. com., 6 October 2015, No.13-24.854, ECLI:FR:CCASS:2015:CO00871; *AJCA*, 2015, p. 526 note R. Saint-Esteben; *Concurrences*, No. 1-2016, note R. Amaro.

[56] CA Paris, ch. 5-4, 26 June 2013, *Sté JCB Sales Ltd, Sté JC Bamford Excavators Ltd et Sté JCB Service v SA Central Parts*, R. G. No. 12/04441; *Lettre Creda-Concurrence*, 15-19 July 2013, obs. A. Ronzano. See also the *Arkopharma* case, one of the "*Vitamins cartel*

" follow-on litigation, where the Nanterre Commercial Court of 1st instance ruled that a subsidiary, is liable as it had: "(...) obviously carried out the instructions of the authors of the cartel and participated in the commission of the offense."; T. com. Nanterre, ch. 6, 11 May 2006, *SA Les Laboratoires pharmaceutiques Arkopharma v sté Roche et sté F. Hoffmann La Roche AG*, R. G. No. 2004\F02643, *Rev. Lamy Concurrence*, 2007/10, p. 62, note M. Chagny.

### 12.5.1 The Ineffectiveness of Collective Redresses

**Opt-in Actions Limited to Harms Suffered by Consumers** The French procedural rules provide two kinds of collective redresses that may fit with competition law litigation: the *action en representation conjointe* and the *action de groupe*. Both are opt-in schemes and are governed by the *Code de la consommation.* As such, their scopes are limited to harm suffered by consumers. In other words, in the current state of French procedural rules, business companies are not eligible for collective redresses.

**The *Action en Représenation Conjointe*** The first collective redress created in French law is the *action en representation conjointe*, which is governed by Article L. 622-1 to L. 622-3 of the *Code de la consommation.* Articles L. 622-1 paragraph 1 enables consumers associations to represent consumers in private litigation by this *action*, provided that they obtain a mandate (*mandat*) of at least two consumers. Paragraph 2 of this article prohibits the association from using publicity measures.[57] These two legal requirements explain the dramatic failure of this collective redress.

**The "Mobile Phones" Cartel Case** The example of the "mobile phones" cartel brings clear evidence of this failure. After mobile phones operators were convicted of price and market sharing conspiracy and fined 534 million euros by the former *Conseil de la concurrence*, the leading consumer association, *UFC-Que Choisir?*, tried to obtain compensation for the 1.2–1.6 billion euros[58] of overcharges paid by the 20 million subscribers of Orange, SFR and Bouygues. It then brought an *action* in French courts. Following a costly and time-consuming lawsuit, the association only gathered 12 500 mandates, representing not more than 0.06 % of the victims.[59] And above all, after a short-lived success, the *action* was ultimately deemed illegal by the *Cour de cassation* because *UFC-Que Choisir?* used prohibited means of public appeal to inform consumers.[60]

**The *Action de Groupe*** Many stakeholders have viewed this disappointing result with consternation. It was partly to address the weaknesses of the *action en representation conjointe* that the *Loi Hamon*, signed into law in March 2014, created the *action de groupe.* This opt-in class action was inserted in a new chapter of the *Code*

[57] It states that: "The mandate may not be solicited by means of a public appeal on radio or television, nor by means of posting of information, by tract or personalised letter. Authorisation must be given in writing by each consumer."

[58] According to the association's quantification.

[59] Que choisir, "Action de groupe : 99,94 % des victimes de l'entente entre les opérateurs mobiles ne seront pas indemnisées!", Press release of 13 October 2006 : http://www.quechoisir.org/communiques/99-94-des-victimes-de-n-entente-entre-les-operateurs-mobiles-ne-seront-pas-indemnisees/F0AA7CFAB02CD7AFC1257206002A862B.htm)

[60] Cass. civ. 1, 26 May 2011, No. 10-15676; *D.*, 2008, p. 1884, note N. Dupont; *RTD com.*, 2011, p. 627, obs. B. Bouloc.

*de la consommation*, at Articles L. 623-1 *et seq*. Article L. 623-1 narrows its scope to harms suffered by consumers, including harms caused by breaches to competition law, and only allows consumers associations to act as representative entities. Neither consumers acting as individuals nor businesses may initiate an *action de groupe*. Article L. 623-17 of the *Code de la consommation* also limits the *action de groupe* to a follow-on litigation pattern. Consumers associations cannot bring an action prior to the issuing of a definitive decision from the competition authority or the court empowered to review the competition authorities' decisions.

**Scepticism** These choices may be questioned given the current reality of private litigation, which involves mostly business disputes without any prior action from competition authorities. It is also very likely that the few consumers associations entitled to bring *actions de groupe* (sixteen in 2015) will face practical difficulties to cope with the scale of this mass litigation. Many observers showed scepticism with regard to these limits and it is likely that the French government will sooner or later extend the possibility to individuals and business to act as representative entities. The opt-in scheme has also been criticized for its structural inadequacy to mass litigation, as the "mobile phones cartel" demonstrated under the rules of the *action en représentation conjointe*. Last, among the various others accusations against the *action de groupe*, it is sometimes put forward that the prohibition to bring the action before a final decision of the competition authority would, in practice, condemns follow-on actions to fail. As the infringements sanctioned by competition authorities will be old (sometimes more than 15 years old) no consumer will still have material evidence, such as bills, of their relationships with the defendants.

So far, no *actions de groupe* have been brought to French courts in competition law litigation.[61]

### 12.5.2 *The Heavy Burden of Proof of Causation*

**The *Actori Incumbit Probatio* Principle** It follows from the former Article 1315 (now Article 1353) of the *Code civil* and Article 9 of the *Code de procédure civile* that it is for the victim to establish causation, according to the *Actor incumbit probatio* principle. This rule applies widely to most types of civil and commercial

[61] See among many contributions on the topic: S. Pietrini, *L'action collective en droit des pratiques anticoncurrentielles*, Bruylant, 2012; M. Bacache, "Action de groupe et responsabilité civile. Loi n° 2014-344 du 17 mars 2014 relative à la consummation", *RTD civ.*, 2014, p. 450 *seq.*; M. Béhar-Touchais, "L'action de groupe à la française, voie prometteuse ou (trop) Limitée ?", in M. Chagny (ed.), *La réparation des dommages concurrentiels en France et en Europe : État des lieux et changements à venir*, *Concurrences*, n°3-2014, p. 51 *seq.*; E. Claudel, "Action de groupe et autres dispositions concurrence de la loi consommation : un dispositif singulier", *RTD com.*, 2014, p. 339 *seq.*; C. Marechal, "Le volet 'concurrence' de la loi n° 2014-344 du 17 mars 2014 relative à la consommation", *Contrats conc. consom.*, 2014/ 5, dossier 4; N. Molfessis, "L'exorbitance de l'action de groupe à la française", *D.*, 2014, p. 947 *seq.*

litigation, including the private litigation of competition law. But it is noteworthy that in complex matters, such as medical malpractices litigation, French courts sometimes make exceptions to this principle and shift the burden of proof to the defendant in order to ease the success of claimants.[62] However, neither the *Code civil* nor the case law provides an exception to this principle for competition law litigation. It means that direct purchasers and indirect purchasers will support the burden of proof of causation. For instance, in situations where overcharges may have been passed onto indirect purchasers by direct purchasers, the *Cour de cassation* in its *"Le Gouessant"* judgment ruled that no exception was to be made to the principle of Article 1315 of the *Code civil.*[63] It confirmed the previous case law of the *Cour d'appel de Paris* that refused to shift the burden of proof to the defendant[64] by this wording:

> "That passing on is the usual and normal business practice, (the plaintiffs) do not demonstrate that they had not been able to pass the effects of rising prices of lysine on their clients; that the condition of these findings and assessments which it concludes that (the plaintiffs) do not establish to have suffered damage resulting from lysine additional costs caused by the cartel, the court of appeal that has not reversed the burden of proof, was able to rule as it did".

In other words, direct purchasers need to prove that they have been harmed by the overcharge and that they have not passed it onto indirect purchasers.

This case law is at odds with Article 13 of the Directive 2014/104/EU[65] and it could be seen as a major obstacle to the success of claimants. The transposition act will probably have to reverse the *"Le Gouessant"* ruling to introduce into French law a more victims-friendly rule.

### *12.5.3 The Unpredictable Decision-Making of the French Courts in Quantifying Damages*

**A Lack of Legal Certainty** Quantifying antitrust harm is a lingering difficulty in French courts, as elsewhere. French tort law does not give a clear methodology and the courts have no other choice than relying on assumptions more or less substantiated by economic studies. The observation of the recent case law gives the unpleasant feeling that the quantification of harm and even the decision to award remedies will depend upon the courts' abilities to handle economics. This may seem

[62] Since the *Distilbène* case law: Civ. 1ère, 24 September 2009 (2 decisions), No. 08-16305, *Bull. civ.* I, No. 187; No. 08-10081, *Bull. civ.* I, No. 186; *Dalloz*, 2009, p. 2342, note I. Gallmeister; *Rev. trim. dr. civ.*, 2010, p. 111, note P. Jourdain.

[63] Cass. com., 15 May 2012, No. 11-18495.

[64] CA Paris, ch. 5-4, 16 February 2011, *SCA Le Gouessant v SA Ceva Santé et SAS Ajinomoto Eurolysine*, R. G. No. 08/08727.

[65] It states that "The burden of proving that the overcharge was passed on shall be on the defendant, who may reasonably require disclosure from the claimant or from third parties."

questionable as it weakens legal certainty for litigants. Recent cases illustrate the fact that some courts are more comfortable than others in quantifying antitrust harm.

**The *Outremer Telecom* Case** The first interesting case in this respect is the *Outremer Telecom* case, judged by the *Tribunal de commerce de Paris* (Paris commercial court) in March 2015.[66] This follow-on litigation was initiated after France Telecom (now Orange) and its subsidiary Orange Caraïbes were found guilty by the *Autorité de la concurrence* of anticompetitive agreements and abuses of a dominant position on the market of mobile telephony in the Antilles and Guyana. The claimant, *Outremer Telecom*, then sought remedies. It claimed approximately 75 million euros as compensation for various alleged harms. The gist of the commercial court's judgment focuses on the analysis of the harm alleged by the claimant. The commercial court refused to compensate three of the five heads of damage alleged by the claimant and ruled in its favour for the other two. The first of these two harms resulted in the loss of profit related to loyalty deals offered by Orange to its customers. These offers locked Orange's market share, preventing the claimant from entering the market. The court then quantified this damage by reference to one of the studies submitted by the claimant. The study based its quantification on the number of subscribers that have renewed their contract with Orange because of the loyalty offers but that would not have done so in the absence of these offers (30 %). Then it multiplied this number by the gross margin the claimant would have achieved for each of these subscribers. The court found that the loss amounted to 3.39 million euros. It also compensated a second loss resulting from a practice of tariff advantage for professional subscribers to France Telecom. The court ruled that such a tariff advantage had hindered the development of Outremer Telecom in both the fixed and mobile telephony markets. To quantify the damage, it dismissed the comparative analysis submitted by the claimant based on a comparison with other geographical markets. Without really explaining it, it quantified the loss to 2 million euros for the mobile phone market and 0.28 million for the fixed telephony market.

**The "Cable-Layers" Case** In the second case, the so-called "cable-layers" case,[67] a follow-on action was brought by EDF (the incumbent electric utility operator) in Chamber 5-5 of the Court of Appeal of Paris after the former French competition authority (the *Conseil de la concurrence*) sanctioned two anticompetitive agreements committed by cable manufacturers during a call for tender.[68] As the contracting company, EDF was seeking the annulment of contracts concluded as a result of

[66] T. com. Paris, 15ᵉ ch., 16 March 2015, n° 2010073867, SAS Outremer Telecom c/ SA Orange Caraïbe et SA Orange (anciennement SA France Telecom).

[67] CA Paris, ch. 5-5, 2 July 2015, *SA EDF et SA ERDF c/ SAS Nexans et SAS Prysmian*, R. G. No. 13/22609; *Lettre Creda-Concurrence*, 29 June – 3 July 2015 note A. Ronzano.

[68] Cons. conc., dec. No. 07-D, 26 July 2007 *relative à des pratiques mises en œuvre dans le cadre de marchés de fourniture de câbles à haute tension.*

this tender with the two cable-layers on the basis of Article 1116 of the *Code civil* and L. 420-3 of the *Code de commerce*. EDF also claimed damages for the loss suffered. This claim was rejected on the ground that EDF did not establish with certainty its damage for three reasons. First, the counterfactual submitted by EDF to quantify its harm was based on competitive pricing assumptions and not on prices provided by a bidder who had not taken part in the cartel. Second, a lingering uncertainty affected EDF's quantification. Third, EDF agreed to contract at the conditions offered by the defendants convicted despite agreements. Each of these three reasons could be discussed but to focus only on the second one, the Court of Appeal of Paris' refusal to compensate EDF's loss exemplifies a recurring hesitation[69]: some French courts tend to disregard quantifications based on economic counterfactuals due to their speculative dimension's being seen as incompatible with the certainty of harm requirement.

If we compare this ruling with *Outremer Telecom*, it appears that the Commercial Court of Paris demonstrated more ease with counterfactual analysis. It even decided to retain one of the two studies produced by the applicant, while correcting certain valuations.

**Three Conclusions** From this comparison, three conclusions may be drawn. First, this difference is unsatisfactory and one can hope that a uniform decision-making will grow out in the next years. Second, if the victims are not able to establish beyond reasonable doubts the quantum of their losses, French courts could still rule on the existence of the loss and ask for a complementary expertise on its quantification. In the *Lectiel* case, that is what another formation of *Cour d'appel de Paris* (Chamber 5-4) did.[70] Third, in the absence of any economic study submitted by the parties, the harm can still be evaluated through simple methods, as was so in the *DKT* case. A quantification based on a summary formula and a limited number of data does not prevent it from being very close to reality. This method can be satisfactorily while being inexpensive and easy to control. Moreover, when the existence of the harm is ascertained, it seems preferable to retain a rough and even simplistic quantification of the harm, rather than dismissing the victim, a practice that could seriously undermine the principle of full compensation. More generally, these differences illustrate the main conclusion defended in this article: the human factor definitely prevails. The upcoming transposition of Directive will undoubtedly change the state of French law but it will take several years to see results. Meanwhile, the ball is in the judges' court... *March 2016*

[69] See CA Paris, ch.5-4, February 16th, 2011, RG No. 08/08727, *SCA Le Gouessant c/ SA Ceva Santé et SAS Ajinomoto Eurolysine* confirmed by Cass. com., 15 May 2012, n° 11-18.495.

[70] CA Paris, ch. 5-4, 27 May 2015, R. G. 14/14758, Sté Lectiel (en liquidation) c/ SA Orange (anciennement SA France Telecom).

## Glossary and Abbreviations

| Name in French | Translation into English | Abbreviation used in the footnotes or in the text |
|---|---|---|
| *Action de groupe* | Group action introduced by the Loi Hamon in the Consumer Code at Articles L. 423-1 | - |
| *Autorité de la concurrence* | French competition authority | "Aut. conc." |
| *Code civil* | Civil Code | "C. civ." |
| *Code de commerce* | Commercial Code | "C. com." |
| *Code de la consommation* | Consumer Code | "C. consom." |
| *Code de procédure civile* | Code of Civil Procedure | "C. pr. civ." |
| *Conseil constitutionnel* | French Constitutional court | "Cons. const." |
| *Conseil de la concurrence* | Former French competition authority, replaced in 2009 by the *Autorité de la concurrence* | "Cons. conc." |
| *Cour d'appel* | Court of Appeal | "CA" followed by the indication of the city, e. g. CA Paris and of its division when known e. g. "ch. 5-4" for section 4 of the pole 5 or "ch. civ." for the "civil division") |
| *Cour de cassation* | French Supreme Court for civil, commercial and criminal matters | "Cass.", followed by the abbreviation of the Court's division, e. g. "com." for "commercial division", "civ. 1" for "1st civil division" |
| *Loi* | Act | "Loi" followed by the name of the minister who presented the act |
| *Référé* | French fast track proceedings | réf. |
| *Tribunal de commerce* | Commercial court of first instance | "T. com." followed by the indication of the city |
| *Tribunal de grande instance* | Civil court of first instance | "TGI" followed by the indication of the city |

# Chapter 13
# Recent Developments in Romanian Jurisprudence Regarding the Application of Articles 101 and 102 TFEU

**Sorin David**

## 13.1 Introduction

Modern Romanian anti-trust legislation has a relatively new history. In 1996, Romania enacted Law no. 21 on Competition (RCL), modelled after Articles 81 and 82 of the Rome Treaty of 1957 (Articles 101 and 102, respectively in the current Treaty on the Functioning of the European Union or TFEU) and the European Commission' anti-trust legislation, although at that time Romania was not an EU member. The RCL created the Romanian Competition Council (RCC), an autonomous public authority (not subordinated to the Parliament, Government or the Presidency) having the powers to enact the anti-trust secondary legislation and enforce the RCL and its implementing regulations.

The RCL was amended a number of times with the most significant amendments taking place in 2003 and 2010. The 2010 amendments are particularly important because they were adopted after Romania's accession to the EU. Their purpose was to harmonize the RCL with the latest EU anti-trust regulations.

In the first years of the RCL's application, the RCC's activity was mostly focused on merger clearance. Gradually, the RCC became more confident and started to develop its cartel and vertical agreements practice. Since 2009, the RCC's activity in these areas has grown significantly. For instance, in 2014 the RCC finalised 21 investigation procedures (mostly on horizontal and vertical agreements) and started 12 new such procedures.[1] More importantly, its investigations and other administrative procedures tackled increasingly complex cases. Since Romania's accession to the EU on 1 January 2007, the RCC has applied both the competition provisions of

[1] Consiliul Concurentei, Raport Anual 2014, http://www.consiliulconcurentei.ro/ro/publicatii/rapoarte-anuale.html. Accessed 29 Oct 2015.

S. David (✉)
University of Bucharest, Faculty of Law, Bucharest, Romania
e-mail: sorin.david@david-baias.ro



A. Almăşan, P. Whelan (eds.), *The Consistent Application of EU Competition Law*, Studies in European Economic Law and Regulation 9,
DOI 10.1007/978-3-319-47382-6_13

the TFEU and the RCL to the anti-trust cases under its investigation (in case the facts started or continued after the accession), based on Regulation (CE) no. 1/2003 and the relevant provisions of the RCL.

From a procedure standpoint, once the RCC decides that an anti-trust infringement took place, it applies the sanctions prescribed by the RCL. Such sanctions are almost entirely in the form of fines. Together with the fact analysis and the interpretation of the law, they are included in RCC decisions and are subject to further judiciary scrutiny.

The Romanian judicial system is a two-tier system (first instance and appeal) with the possibility, in certain cases, to have in addition an extraordinary recourse (recourse in cassation) regarding the correct application of the law. Accordingly, the courts comprise local courts (*judecatorii*) or tribunals (*tribunale*), courts of appeal (*curti de apel*) and the High Court of Justice and Cassation (ICCJ).

The judicial review of RCC decisions has the peculiarity of consisting in only two courts, the Court of Appeal of Bucharest (CAB) and the ICCJ (in both cases, through their respective administrative sections), similarly to the system of the Court of Justice of the European Union. The main difference is that ICCJ acts in a double capacity: as court of appeal and court of cassation and thus it can hear appeals on both the points of law and the facts.

In this chapter, I shall analyse the most relevant anti-trust issues decided by the Romanian courts after 1 January 2007.

## 13.2 Jurisdiction of Articles 101 and 102 TFEU in Romanian Courts

In a number of cases, the courts had to decide on the challenges mounted by the sanctioned enterprises in connection with the right to apply Article 101 TFEU by the RCC. In these situations, the respective enterprises argued that there was no distortion of trade between Member States. Responding to such challenges, in one case the ICCJ decided that Article 101 was applicable since the relevant geographical market was Romania, itself considered to be a substantial part of the Common Market, and the participants to the respective horizontal agreement represented 90 % of the product and geographical market. Moreover, an EU undertaking located in another country was allowed to sell the respective service in Romania and that service could be attractive cross-border for EU undertakings established in other countries (dec. 7240/2013[2]).

Similarly, the CAB decided that when the geographical market is Romania and the anti-trust action takes the form of a cartel, the respective action has the potential to affect trade between the Member States and therefore it is not necessary to prove such an effect on EU trade and EU consumers, especially since the participants'

[2] http://www.scj.ro/1093/Detalii-jurisprudenta?customQuery%5B0%5D.Key=id&customQuery%5B0%5D.Value=105415. Accessed 28 Oct 2015.

turnovers significantly exceeded 40 million euro and some of the raw materials used to produce the affected product where procured from other EU countries (dec. 2046/ 2013,[3] upheld by the ICCJ).

On the other hand, the ICCJ decided that the geographical market represented by a Romanian county does not have the size to qualify as a significant part of the Common Market and thus the anti-trust infringement - limited geographically to the respective county – could not affect trade between the Member States (dec. 5027/2011,[4] dec. 3384/ 2012[5]). However, these pronouncements should not be considered the prevailing jurisprudence with respect to the limitation of the geographical market to one Romanian county. Depending on the facts of future cases, the ICCJ may rule to the contrary.

With respect to the anti-trust infringements that took place and ended prior to Romania's accession to EU, the ICCJ decided that Article 101 TFEU cannot be applicable (dec. 3384/ 2012,[6] dec. 5027/ 2011[7]).

## 13.3 Right of Defence of the Accused Undertaking

Since anti-trust law is considered similar to criminal law from the perspective of the protection of the defence rights of the accused enterprise,[8] there is a particular concern of the RCC and the investigated enterprises regarding the protection of the defence rights. It is not therefore surprising that in many instances the enterprises sanctioned invoke before the courts the infringement of such rights as a cause for the nullity of RCC decisions.

The Romanian courts admit, as a matter of principle, that undertakings accused of breaching anti-trust law enjoy the presumption of innocence as regulated under Article 6 (2) of European Convention of Human Rights; consequently, any doubt must be interpreted in favour of the accused undertaking (CAB dec. 2046/ 2013,[9] upheld by ICCJ).

---

[3] Not published (the decisions that are not published are the ones that for specific reasons are not included on the website of the deciding court or in the judicial reporters published later).

[4] http://www.scj.ro/1093/Detalii-jurisprudenta?customQuery%5B0%5D.Key=id&customQuery%5B0%5D.Value=89693. Accessed 28 Oct 2015.

[5] http://www.scj.ro/1093/Detalii-jurisprudenta?customQuery%5B0%5D.Key=id&customQuery%5B0%5D.Value=93097. Accessed 28 Oct 2015.

[6] http://www.scj.ro/1093/Detalii-jurisprudenta?customQuery%5B0%5D.Key=id&customQuery%5B0%5D.Value=93097. Accessed 28 Oct 2015.

[7] http://www.scj.ro/1093/Detalii-jurisprudenta?customQuery%5B0%5D.Key=id&customQuery%5B0%5D.Value=89693. Accessed 28 Oct 2015.

[8] A.Menarini Diagnostics S.r.l. v. Italy, ECHR, appl. No.43509/08, decision of 27.09.2011, paras.38–44.

[9] Not yet published.

In 1999, the ICCJ ruled for the first time that the RCC has the obligation to employ "solid evidence" when establishes a breach of anti-trust law, in order for the courts to be able to verify how it reached its respective conclusion (dec. 2719/1999[10]).

In furtherance of this principle, the ICCJ decided in its landmark cartel decision (*Carpatcement Holding v. RCC*) that the key piece of evidence invoked by the RCC, together with other circumstantial evidences must prove "without doubt" the anti-trust behaviour of the accused enterprises. The ICCJ held, with regard to one of the alleged participants (Carpatcement), that the RCC did not prove beyond reasonable doubt the lack of validity of the alternative explanations for the similar price increases in the oligopolistic market where the participants operated or the involvement of Carpatcement in the drafting, by one of the cartel participants, of the written note used by the RCC as the main evidence (dec. 1358/ 2007[11]).

Also in case of horizontal agreements, the Romanian courts – in accordance with ECJ jurisprudence – apply consistently the rule that by participating to the conclusion of the agreement without publicly distancing itself from the anti-trust elements of that agreement, the participant is presumed to have contributed to the conclusion of the agreement. Therefore, it is the burden of the participant to rebut the presumption, a burden that in practice proves to be very onerous (ICCJ decisions 3434/ 2012[12]; 4562/ 2011[13]).

In one case, which is exceptional from the perspective of how it developed, the ICCJ suspended its proceedings because a local Prosecutor Office commenced a criminal investigation and lodged an annulment action against one of the written documents considered an essential piece of evidence in that case. Subsequently, a lower court admitted the prosecutor's request and decided irrevocably that the respective document was forged and therefore null and void. Following the pronouncement of the lower court, the ICCJ resumed its proceedings and ruled in favour of the respective undertaking by cancelling the RCC decision because the infringement was not properly demonstrated since it relied on a forged document (dec. 5185/ 2013[14]). This case proves once more that the Romanian courts tread carefully when assessing whether the defence rights of the undertakings are observed.

In many instances, RCC investigations may extend over a long period without coming to a conclusion. In one such case, the ICCJ ruled that the excessive duration of RCC proceedings might affect the rights of the undertaking who lodged the complaint that triggered the RCC investigation, in particular its right to the proper

[10] Curtea Suprema de Justitie. Buletinul Jurisprudentei. 1999.

[11] http://www.scj.ro/1093/Detalii-jurisprudenta?customQuery%5B0%5D.Key=id&customQuery%5B0%5D.Value=85008. Accessed 28 Oct 2015.

[12] http://www.scj.ro/1093/Detalii-jurisprudenta?customQuery%5B0%5D.Key=id&customQuery%5B0%5D.Value=98697. Accessed 28 Oct 2015.

[13] http://www.scj.ro/1093/Detalii-jurisprudenta?customQuery%5B0%5D.Key=id&customQuery%5B0%5D.Value=73123. Accessed 28 Oct 2015.

[14] http://www.scj.ro/1093/Detalii-jurisprudenta?customQuery%5B0%5D.Key=id&customQuery%5B0%5D.Value=101320. Accessed 28 Oct 2015.

administration of justice enshrined in Article 41 of the European Charter of Fundamental Rights. The ICCJ found that, considering the circumstances of the case and the object of the infringement (abuse of market power), the elapse of 5 years without the RCC finalising its investigation breached the claimant's right to a reasonable deadline; it therefore ordered the RCC to finalise its investigation within 6 months (dec.3221/2010[15]). This pronouncement is unique in Romanian anti-trust jurisprudence. Generally, the Romanian courts are reluctant to dictate to the administrative authorities how to exercise their executive powers. We can expect that in the future, if the particular situation will warrant it, the Romanian courts may extend the application of this ruling to the cases when the long duration of RCC proceedings will infringe the rights of the investigated undertakings.

I cannot conclude this section without mentioning a judgment running against the jurisprudential current mentioned above. In one isolated instance, the ICCJ stated that a court reasoning does not need to respond to all arguments invoked by one party as long as such arguments are not relevant for the solution of the case (dec. 5218/ 2011[16]). This decision – if followed – would open the gate for abuse of the courts because it would allow them, in their discretion, to select and further assess the arguments of the undertakings or the RCC that they consider relevant for solving the case. The arguments ignored could not be subject to judicial review and the predictability of the law's application would be severely affected.

## 13.4 Restriction of Competition by Object

Since 2009 one can notice in RCC practice a tendency of investigating with priority those agreements that restrict competition "by object". The RCC prefers these cases because the burden of proof in order to demonstrate the infringement is less onerous: they do not require complex economic analysis as to their effects on the market as opposed to the agreements having an anti-competitive effect. The downside of such an approach is the risk of the RCC's expanding the area of the agreements having the object of restricting competition, beyond the agreements which by their very nature are indeed harmful to competition.[17] Therefore, it is a useful reminder for any competition authority to avoid the error of not exercising restraint in determining whether an agreement has the object of restricting the competition.[18]

---

[15] http://www.scj.ro/1093/Detalii-jurisprudenta?customQuery%5B0%5D.Key=id&customQuery%5B0%5D.Value=60976. Accessed 28 Oct 2015.

[16] http://www/scj.ro/1093/Detalii-jurisprudenta?customQuery%5B0%5D.Key=id&customQuerry%5B0%5D.Value=80643. Accessed 30 Oct 2015.

[17] The same issue is apparent at the level of the Court of Justice of the European Union. This can explain why ECJ felt compelled in the case of *Groupement des Cartes Bancaires v. Commission* (C-67/13 P) to re-affirm the basic difference between agreements restricting the competition by "object" and those that only have the effect of restricting it, by emphasizing the former do not represent the rule.

[18] C-67/13 P, para.58.

On their side, the Romanian courts take the traditional stance that in the case of a "per se" restriction (price fixing, market partitioning, etc.), the RCC does not need to prove the effects on the market and on the consumers in order to demonstrate the anti-trust infringement (ICCJ, dec.6791/2013[19]). If the courts support the RCC's finding of the agreement having an anti-competitive object (which they do in the overwhelming majority of the cases), this does not necessarily mean they automatically embrace the RCC's view on the gravity of the infringement. Thus, whether the RCC qualifies "per se" infringements, rather mechanically, as breaches of a very serious or medium gravity (for horizontal agreements) and medium to low gravity (in case of the vertical ones), the courts do not feel bound by the RCC's fine determination. As shown in Section 13.6 below, there has been numerous instances when the Romanian courts lowered the fine amount by ascribing a lower gravity to the respective breach.

The Romanian courts started to recognize that even in the case of infringements "by object", the RCC and subsequently the courts must still perform some assessment of the effects in order to properly determine the base level of the fine. In one case the ICCJ stated that as long the RCC did not prove that the infringement was complex and on the other hand the evidence in the file indicated the impact on the market was reduced, the infringement was of low gravity even if the agreement concerned vertical price fixing (ICCJ, dec. 6390/ 2013[20]).

The courts face an increased complexity in case of multi-party agreements having an anti-trust object. The additional difficulty results from the fact that Romanian civil procedure does not allow in such instances the cases to be joined, although someone may argue this could be permitted if all the parties would agree. Therefore, each undertaking challenging the RCC decision will have its own file and quite likely a panel of judges different from the ones siting in the other cases opened in connection with the same the RCC decision. Each court panel will assess the participation of the plaintiff-undertaking to the respective agreement on its own merits, sometimes without knowing the legal arguments used by the other plaintiffs before their respective panels and as a result it may reach different conclusions and determine different levels of the fine. The following example is illustrative.

In 2007 the Romanian Supervision Commission for Private Pensions (CSSPP) issued secondary legislation regulating the initial subscription and allocation of clients for Pillar II pension funds. The allocation system provided for two phases: in the first phase the pension administrators (limited by law to Romanian-authorised companies irrespective of the nationality of their shareholders) would compete without restriction for the pension subscribers and in the second phase those who subscribed for two or more administrators and the individuals who did not subscribe would be allocated, pro rata to the market share acquired by each administrator at the end of phase I. Due to some unforeseen practical situations that appeared in

---

[19] http://www.scj.ro/1093/Detalii-jurisprudenta?customQuery%5B0%5D.Key=id&customQuery%5B0%5D.Value=105357. Accessed 28 Oct 2015.

[20] http://www.scj.ro/1093/Detalii-jurisprudenta?customQuery%5B0%5D.Key=id&customQuery%5B0%5D.Value=105330. Accessed 28 Oct 2015.

phase I, the pension administrators agreed, with the apparent blessing of CSSPP, to change the allocation rule for phase II and replace it with bilateral agreements between the administrators. Subsequent to the conclusion of the final client allocation, the RCC opened an investigation into this practice and eventually sanctioned the participants, under Article 101 TFEU and RAL, for concluding a horizontal agreement on market partitioning. The pension administrators challenged each RCC decision at CAB level before different panels of judges. Not surprisingly, some CAB court panels ruled for maintaining in full the RCC decision, others supported the RCC's legal analysis on the agreement but reduced the fine applied to the respective undertakings, and one even cancelled the RCC decision with respect to that plaintiff-undertaking. The divergence of the solutions continued before the ICCJ. Thus, one panel of ICCJ judges decided that the fine for a certain undertaking should be reduced to a level specific for low gravity infringements, even though it ruled that the agreement was of medium gravity (dec. 7240/ 2013[21]). However, a different ICCJ panel decided – with respect to another participant to the respective allocation agreement – to cancel its fine entirely by reasoning that the RCC did not take into account the legal and economic circumstances of the case and thus failed to observe that, due to such circumstances, the respective participant did not act with the intention of harming competition, but it was forced to adopt a practical solution in order to deal with a complex and novel issue under the pressure of time (dec. 1203/2013[22]). It is worth mentioning that in reaching different solutions, the two court panels assessed differently the impact of the same circumstance (i.e., the enactment of a subsequent CSSPP regulation that validated the incriminated behaviour). The third ICCJ panel then decided to obtain some clarity on the interpretation of the European law applicable in this case (i.e., Article 101 (1) (c) TFEU) and lodged a request for preliminary ruling with ECJ. The other ICCJ panels stayed their respective proceedings in anticipation of the ECJ preliminary ruling.

The ECJ had to answer the question whether agreements to share clients constitute agreements having an anti-competitive object and whether the number of clients affected by such agreements is relevant in the light of the condition relating to the existence of a restriction of competition on the internal market. The European Court issued its judgment in the preliminary ruling on July 2015 (case C-172/ 14 *ING Pensii – Societate de Administrare a unui Fond de Pensii Administrat Privat v. Consiliul Concurentei*). The ECJ restated its position on the criteria that should be used by the authorities and the courts in assessing whether an agreement has an anti-competitive object. It further confirmed that agreements to share customers are clearly among ones most restrictive of competition (referring to its previous judgment in *Commission v. Stichting Administratiekantoor Portielje* – case C-440/ 11 P) and from this perspective the number of shared customers is irrelevant for the

[21] http://www.scj.ro/1093/Detalii-jurisprudenta?customQuery%5B0%5D.Key=id&customQuery%5B0%5D.Value=105415. Accessed 28 Oct 2015.

[22] http://www.scj.ro/1093/Detalii-jurisprudenta?customQuery%5B0%5D.Key=id&customQuery%5B0%5D.Value=101040. Accessed 28 Oct 2015.

purpose of determining if there is a restriction on competition.[23] With respect to the impact of particular factual circumstances in determining whether the agreement affected trade between the Member States, the ECJ ruled that irrespective of the limitation (under Romanian law) of the access to the new obligatory private pension fund market to Romanian authorised companies, the agreement made more difficult the penetration of the Romanian market by companies established outside Romania.[24] This latter pronouncement can raise some eyebrows since pension administration companies located outside Romania and not authorised to participate in the allocation of the clients under the initial formula for phase II, could not in any event sell Pillar II pension services to such allocated customers, even if no agreement would have been in place.

Not all the cases of multi participant agreements having an anti-competitive object follow the saga of the private pension case. In another case with multiple parties (this time, a vertical agreement for market partitioning), again CAB panels ruled differently (the majority of them upheld the RCC decision but reduced the fines applied to the distributors; one of them cancelled the fine applied to a participant based on the specific circumstances of the respective case). However, this time the different panels of ICCJ judges took a more consistent approach among themselves. Thus, they upheld the CAB decisions on the reduction of the RCC fines and reversed the cancelation of the fine in the lower court in that one case, by ruling that with respect to that participant the conditions of *Bayer Adalat*[25] were not met, since the respective distributor (together with the others) did not oppose but followed the plan of the producer, therefore it did not distance itself from the other distributors (dec. 345/ 2013[26]). Interestingly, the fine of the latter distributor was reduced by a lesser amount than in the case of the other two, even if the court found the same circumstances were applicable.

Concluding this section, I would like to note the tendency of the panels of ICCJ judges to rule uniformly on matters of law in the cases resulting from the same infringement sanctioned under the same RCC decision, occasionally even invoking the need for unitary jurisprudence (see for instance ICCJ dec. 5185/ 2013[27]). Nevertheless, this does not imply the solution given earlier by an ICCJ or CAB panel with respect to one of the undertakings represents *res judicata* for another participant in the same "lot" or a reason to suspend the proceedings in the latter case (ICCJ, dec. 241/ 2011[28]).

---

[23] Case C-172/14, para. 54.

[24] Case C-172/ 14, para. 51.

[25] http://curia.europa.eu/juris/liste.jsf?num=C-2/01&language=en.

[26] http://www.scj.ro/1093/Detalii-jurisprudenta?customQuery%5B0%5D.Key=id&customQuery%5B0%5D.Value=93102. Accessed 28 Oct 2015.

[27] http://www.scj.ro/1093/Detalii-jurisprudenta?customQuery%5B0%5D.Key=id&customQuery%5B0%5D.Value=101320. Accessed 28 Oct 2015.

[28] http://www.scj.ro/1093/Detalii-jurisprudenta?customQuery%5B0%5D.Key=id&customQuery%5B0%5D.Value=65278. Accessed 28 Oct 2015.

## 13.5 Abuse of Dominant Position in Romanian Courts

Compared to the number of RCC decisions and court cases on anti-trust agreements, there are very few cases on abuse of dominance. This situation can be partly explained by the difficulties of the process for the determination of the abuse and the need for complex economic analysis in order to prove the infringement. In accordance with RCC regulations, abuse of dominance is considered an infringement of medium to very serious gravity.

The majority of the abuse of dominance cases required the application of the RCL only because they occurred prior to Romania's accession to EU. Thus, Article 102 TFEU has not had a chance of being applied in court practice so far. As to the application of its Romanian version, by analysing the Romanian judgments one cannot escape the feeling that the Romanian courts struggled either with the proper determination of the relevant market, or with the economics of the infringement. Consequently, the courts were forced to order the input of economic, technical or even competition experts; such expertise played an important role in their decisions.

In one earlier case (on predatory pricing), the courts cancelled the RCC decision because the economic analysis performed by the court-appointed expert did not reveal that the dominant undertaking practiced sale prices below its costs (ICCJ, dec. 710/ 2010[29]).

In another case, the ICCJ took a stance different from the lower court (CAB) and accepted the findings of the economic expertise provided by the RCC earlier in the administrative file. As a result, it disregarded the expertise provided by the expert appointed by the CAB and found that the dominant undertaking charged excessive prices to its customers without objective reasons (dec. 3055/ 2010[30]). Under Romanian law judges have discretion in accepting the findings of the experts appointed by them, as well as those of the experts appointed by the parties.

Recently, the ICCJ ordered the retrial of two cases and returned the files back to CAB because of insufficient evidence. For the retrial, the ICCJ instructed the CAB to provide expertise (technical and in competition) in order to determine the relevant market, whether the undertaking had a dominant position and if its incriminated behaviour (that is, refusal to supply) affected competition (dec. 1841/ 2014[31]; dec. 2605/ 2014[32]).

[29] http://www.scj.ro/1093/Detalii-jurisprudenta?customQuery%5B0%5D.Key=id&customQuery%5B0%5D.Value=69968. Accessed 28 Oct 2015.

[30] http://www.scj.ro/1093/Detalii-jurisprudenta?customQuery%5B0%5D.Key=id&customQuery%5B0%5D.Value=60836. Accessed 28 Oct 2015.

[31] Not yet published.

[32] Not yet published.

## 13.6 Determination of the Fines

The Romanian courts often exercise their review on whether the fines applied by the RCC respect the proportionality principle. The RCC determines the fine under its own secondary legislation. The Romanian anti-trust fining system has a peculiarity compared to the correspondent mechanism employed by the Commission. In Romania, the base level of the fine is established as a percentage of the total annual turnover of the undertaking in the year prior to the application of the fine, and not by reference to the annual sales of the incriminated product or service (i.e., product turnover). Therefore, there are numerous instances when the RCC fines burdened excessively the sanctioned enterprises.

As a result, the courts are increasingly under pressure to review fines from the perspective of their proportionality with the gravity of the infringement. Such reviews have led them on numerous occasions to reduce the RCC fines either by deciding that the infringement had a lower gravity, or by maintaining the gravity found by RCC but lowering the fine amount. In acting so, the courts have made it clear they could use different reasoning from the RCC in determining the fine amount. More importantly, they did not feel bound to use the fine computation formula prescribed under the RCC instructions. Although the courts observed the mitigating and aggravating circumstances included in RCC regulations, when they felt compelled by the facts of the case they gave such circumstances a different weight than the RCC and even applied circumstances that were not specifically described in RCC regulations.

Nevertheless, the circumstances invoked by the undertaking for the reduction of the fine must be real and not hypothetical (ICCJ, dec. 7042/ 2013[33]).

In one case dealing with a vertical agreement having an anticompetitive objective, the RCC took into account the effect of the infringement on competition and consumers, the subjective mind set of the parties, the lack of secrecy of the agreement, the specific economic circumstances (in that case, the economic crisis was invoked) and decided to significantly lower the fine amount (dec. 6390/ 2013[34]).

In other cases, the courts observed the existence of confusing administrative regulations or that the actions of a governmental agency induced parties to adopt inappropriate behaviours and as a result qualified such situations as mitigating circumstances (ICCJ decisions 7240/ 2013[35] and 352/ 2012[36]).

Recently, in a case concerning a vertical agreement that infringed Article 101 TFEU and the RCL, the CAB ruled that the RCC is bound to apply the criteria used

[33] http://www.scj.ro/1093/Detalii-jurisprudenta?customQuery%5B0%5D.Key=id&customQuery%5B0%5D.Value=106650. Accessed 28 Oct 2015.

[34] http://www.scj.ro/1093/Detalii-jurisprudenta?customQuery%5B0%5D.Key=id&customQuery%5B0%5D.Value=105330. Accessed 28 Oct 2015.

[35] http://www.scj.ro/1093/Detalii-jurisprudenta?customQuery%5B0%5D.Key=id&customQuery%5B0%5D.Value=106650. Accessed 28 Oct 2015.

[36] http://www.scj.ro/1093/Detalii-jurisprudenta?customQuery%5B0%5D.Key=id&customQuery%5B0%5D.Value=67800. Accessed 28 Oct 2015.

by European jurisprudence and the European Commission in order to respect the proportionality principle (CAB, dec. 1032/ 2013,[37] maintained in appeal by ICCJ, dec. 2802/ 2014[38]). The respective CAB judgment even mentioned that the proportionality principle would require the taking into account of the product turnover as an indication of the economic significance of the infringement; however, the judgment of the ICCJ in appeal does not retain this reasoning.

## 13.7 Conclusions

Traditionally, the Romanian courts have followed closely the jurisprudence of the Court of Justice of the European Union, including its latest developments. As this chapter shows, they are increasingly sophisticated in applying Article 101 TFEU. As to Article 102 TFEU, it is expected that once the RCC starts to enforce it and once RCC decisions become subject to judicial review, they will look for guidance from EU jurisprudence and the European Commission's practice. This way, they will continue to contribute to the uniform application of EU anti-trust law.

[37] Not yet published.

[38] Not yet published.

# Chapter 14
# Application of EU Competition Law by the Hungarian Judiciary: Cooperation with the ECJ and Relying on the Case Law of the ECtHR

Mónika Papp

## 14.1 Introduction

This chapter will address some aspects of the application of EU antitrust rules by the Hungarian judiciary. The main focus of the first part of the chapter will be on the procedural framework these rules are applied within and the cooperation with the European Court of Justice (ECJ) via preliminary rulings. In this first part I will first sketch the contours of requesting a preliminary ruling from the ECJ as an ordinary practice of Hungarian courts. Hungarian courts are quite active in applying EU law and posing preliminary rulings to the ECJ. If we have a quick look on the statistics, we can detect different areas of EU law where this phenomenon is visible. The most numerous group of cases deals with tax law generally and VAT tax law specifically. The second biggest area with significant number of requests for a preliminary ruling is the EU consumer law acquis, where the unfair contract terms Directive is applied in most of the cases.[1] As the Hungarian courts are very active in posing preliminary questions, it comes as a surprise that in competition law matters the judiciary seems to be more inclined to autonomously interpret EU competition law without the help of the ECJ. From accession until 2015 only two ECJ judgments were adopted

[1] Somssich Réka: Előzetes döntéshozatali eljárások a számok tükrében- a 2004-ben csatlakozott országok bíróságai által kezdeményezett eljárások 10 évvel a csatlakozás után. Európai Jog, 2015/2. pp. 1–13.

M. Papp (✉)
Law School, University of Eötvös Loránd, Budapest, Hungary

Center for Social Sciences, HPOPs- Lendület Research Group, Hungarian Academy of Sciences, Budapest, Hungary
e-mail: mpapp@ajk.elte.hu



A. Almăşan, P. Whelan (eds.), *The Consistent Application of EU Competition Law*, Studies in European Economic Law and Regulation 9,
DOI 10.1007/978-3-319-47382-6_14

under the request of Hungarian courts on antitrust matters, in the cases *Allianz*[2] and *Generali*.[3]

In the second part of the paper, the context is changed and I will turn the attention of the reader to another challenge posed by the European Convention on Human Rights.[4] As Hungary is a signatory to the Convention, in addition to Union law, the law of the Convention is binding on Hungarian courts. The standard of judicial review in competition cases is put to the test by the European Court of Human Rights (EctHR) under the right to a fair trial. The penal nature of antitrust procedures and its implication on the standard of proof was at the center of discussion at the highest level of the court system in Hungary. Before I provide a deeper examination of a recent Supreme Court judgment and a Constitutional Court judgement, I briefly explain the position of the European Court of Justice on the standard of judicial review and the right to a fair trial.

## 14.2 The National Context

The pre-accession period goes back to 1991 when the Europe Agreement was signed, by which Hungary was obliged to approximate its national law, particularly, among other areas, competition law, with European Community law as far as possible.[5] One year before, in 1990, the first Competition Act was adopted by the Parliament after the transformation to a market economy and an independent agency, the Hungarian Competition Office (Gazdasági Versenyhivatal or GVH), was established to enforce competition law. Later, Act LVII of 1996 on the prohibition of unfair and restrictive market practices (hereinafter: Hungarian Competition Act or HCA) came into force; it regulates competition law in Hungary and has been subject to several amendments. Article 11 of the Act contains a prohibition modelled on the text of Article 101 TFEU.[6] Article 21 of the HCA entails a prohibition on abuse of a dominant position.[7] The Preamble of the HCA refers to EU competition

[2] C- 32/11. *Hungária Biztosító Zrt v Gazdasági Versenyhivatal*, ECLI:EU:C:2013:160.

[3] C-470/13. *Generali-Providencia Biztosító Zrt v Közbeszerzési Hatóság Közbeszerzési Döntőbizottság*, ECLI:EU:C:2014:2469.

[4] Convention for the Protection of Human Rights and Fundamental Freedoms, Act XXXI of 1993.

[5] Europe Agreement establishing an association between the European Communities and their Member States, of the one part, and the Republic of Hungary, of the other part, OJ L 347, 31/12/1993, p. 2–266. According to Article 67, Hungary shall act to ensure that future legislation is compatible with Community legislation as far as possible.

[6] Article 11(1): Agreements or concerted practices between undertakings and decisions by social organisations of undertakings, public corporations, associations or other similar organisations (hereinafter together: agreements), which have as their object or potential or actual effect the prevention, restriction or distortion of competition, shall be prohibited. Agreements concluded between undertakings, which are not independent of each other do not qualify as such kind of agreements.

[7] Article 21: It shall be prohibited to abuse a dominant position.

law as a model for formulating domestic legislation.[8] Voluntary law approximation has taken place after Hungary's accession to the EU, the most important modifications were introduced in procedural law under Council Regulation 1/2003/EC.[9] The former notification system was abolished and the GVH received powers similar to the European Commission's.[10]

Administrative decisions of the GVH are frequently based on Articles 101 and 102 TFEU, alongside national competition law. According to practice, the reasoning of a GVH decision follows a compound pattern, meaning that the reasoning based on EU law and Hungarian law is not divided in separate sections. The GVH relies on the similar wording of the two legal bases to justify its positions such that there is no need to apply these provisions separately. The GVH consistently uses EU hard and soft law to substantiate its decisions, even in cases decided exclusively upon Hungarian competition law. National courts reviewing GVH decisions have agreed with this approach. In 2010 in the *Allianz* case[11] the Supreme Court argued that in decisions based solely on Article 11 of the HCA, the GVH can base its prohibition decision completely on the interpretation of Article 101, because the wordings of the two provisions are almost identical. Consequently, the interpretation given by the ECJ on the meaning of Article 101 will have a binding effect on the interpretation of the national cartel prohibition. In its request for a preliminary ruling, the Supreme Court pointed out that there is a clear interest in having a uniform interpretation of the provisions and concepts of EU law. The ECJ declared its jurisdiction and argued that EU law has been rendered applicable by domestic law, which adopted for internal situations the same approach as that provided under EU law. The wording of the preamble and the explanatory memorandum of the HCA on the approximation of Hungarian law to EU law was a significant argument of the Supreme Court and the ECJ alike.

In Hungary, judicial review of GVH decisions takes place at three levels. During the two instances of ordinary review, courts examine the legality of the administrative decision based on points of law and facts. Afterwards, on points of law only, the Supreme Court reviews these judgments.[12]

The Hungarian Code on Civil Procedure[13] sets the following limit on the competence of the two instance review courts: 'An administrative decision rendered on a discretionary basis shall be considered lawful if the administrative body has

---

[8] "In order to attain these objectives – also taking into consideration the requirements of the approximation to the law of the European Community and the conventions of domestic competition law – Parliament passed the following Act."

[9] Council Regulation (EC) No 1/2003 of 16 December 2002 on the implementation of the rules on competition laid down in Articles 81 and 82 of the Treaty, OJ L 1, 4.1.2003, p. 1–25.

[10] On the history of the reception of EU competition law, see Tihamér Tóth: The reception and application of EU competition rules in Hungary: An organic evolution In: The law of the European Union in Hungary: Institutions, processes and the law, edited by Márton Varju and Ernő Várnay, HVG-Orac, Budapest, 2014.

[11] C-32/11, *Allianz Hungária Biztosító Zrt et al v. Gazdasági Versenyhivatal* ECLI:EU:C:2013:160.

[12] The Supreme Court cannot order the taking of evidence; its judgment is based on the file.

[13] Act III of 1952 on the Code of Civil Procedure.

appropriately ascertained the relevant facts of the case, complied with the relevant rules of procedure, the points of discretion can be identified, and the reasoning of the decision demonstrates a causal relation as to the weighing of evidence'.[14]

The Supreme Court sets aside the judgment of the review courts if it is incompatible with the law, or if any breach of procedural rules has occurred which had an impact on the merits of the case.[15]

Since the new Fundamental Law in Hungary came into force (2012) the Constitutional Court has the competence to review, on the basis of a constitutional complaint, court decisions for conformity with the Fundamental Law and to annul any court decision that is contrary to the Fundamental Law.[16]

### *14.2.1 Practice of the Hungarian Competition Authority*[17]

Ten years after accession, 99 procedures were initiated by the GVH under a double legal basis (i.e. under both EU and Hungarian law). Out of the 99 proceedings, 87 were closed by 1 May 2014. Proceedings commenced under a double legal basis make almost 40 % of the total number of cases. Out of the 87 proceedings closed: 14 were closed with a finding of violation with fines; 2 without fines; 8 commitment decisions were issued; in 16 proceedings, the proceeding was closed on the basis of lack of inter-state effect; in 2 proceedings, Articles 101 and 102 were found inapplicable; and in the majority of cases (45) the alleged breach was not proven and the file was closed. The problem usually faced by the GVH is that at the beginning of its procedure, information gathered is not enough for the verification of a potential or actual effect on inter-state trade. Faced with the dilemma whether to commence a proceeding under EU competition law as well, the GVH tends to start the investigation under a double legal basis. The reason for that is that cooperation with the European Competition Network is open only in proceedings based on EU Competition Law.[18] This results in the high number of proceedings (16) closed with the reasoning that the conduct is not capable of affecting trade between Member States.

---

[14] Article 339/B.

[15] Article 275(3).

[16] Article 24(2) d, Basic Law. The so-called constitutional complaint procedure may be submitted when a right guaranteed by the Fundamental Law of the petitioner is violated by a judicial action and the possibilities for legal remedy have already been exhausted by the petitioner. Consequently, it is not a claim for judicial review.

[17] The data is taken from the following article written in Hungarian by Decsák Péter- Sárai József-Szilágyi Gabriella: The experience of the GVH in the application of EU competition law ten years after accession; A 10 éves uniós tagság tapasztalatai a GVH jogalkalmazásának tükrében. Versenytükör 2014. 1. szám, pp. 19–30.

[18] Ibid., p. 24–25.

Under Act CXL of 2004 on the General Rules of Administrative Proceedings and Services, the GVH shall assess each piece of evidence separately and as a whole and shall establish the facts according to its conviction based on this assessment.[19]

## 14.3 The Standard of Proof and Judicial Review in EU Competition Law

The ECJ has emphasised, relying on ECtHR case-law, that competition law does not belong to the hard core of criminal law and therefore the guarantees in matters of criminal law laid down in Article 6 of the ECHR will not necessarily apply with their full stringency.[20] Therefore, it is quite difficult to draw the exact level of protection Member States and the European Union have to provide to companies accused of a violation of national or EU antitrust law.

### *14.3.1 The Standard of Proof*

The standard of proof shows us the conditions which must be satisfied for facts to be regarded as proven. Under settled case law of the ECJ, it is incumbent on the Commission to prove the infringements found by it and to adduce evidence capable of demonstrating to the requisite legal standard the existence of the circumstances constituting an infringement.[21]

According to established ECJ practice, the Commission must establish 'sufficiently precise and coherent proof' of an infringement,[22] and the Commission must provide a "firm, precise and consistent body of evidence" to justify its view.[23]

Alison Jones and Brenda Sufrin note that[24] 'a breach of the competition rules appears, therefore, to have to be established only on the balance of probabilities and the Commission does not have to adduce proof beyond reasonable doubt of the

---

[19] Article 50(6).

[20] See for example T-541/08, *Sasol and others*, ECLI:EU:T:2014:628, para 206.

[21] C-185/95 P, *Baustahlgewebe GmbH v Commission*, ECLI:EU:C:1998:608, para 58, Claus-Dieter Ehlermann and Mel Marquis (eds): European Competition Law Annual 2009: *The Evaluation of Evidence and its Judicial Review in Competition Cases*, Hart Publishing, Oxford and Portland, Oregon, 2011.

[22] Case 29 and 30/83, *Compagnie Royale Asturienne des Mines SA and Rheinzink GmbH v Commission* [1984] ECR 1679.

[23] C-89/85, C-104/85, C-114/85, C-116/85, C-117/85 and C-125/85 to C-129/85, *Ahlström Osakeyhtiö and Others v Commission* [1993] ECR I-1307, para 127. See also Jacques Buhart, Romain Maulin: Proof in Cartels: State of Play and Perspectives. Concurrences No 4-2011, pp.51–64.

[24] Alison Jones and Brenda Sufrin: *EU Competition Law*, Oxford University Press, Oxford, 2014., p.126

existence of the infringement'. However, any doubt of the Court must benefit the undertaking to which an infringement decision is addressed.[25]

The principle of unfettered evaluation of evidence applies, meaning that the only relevant criterion for the purpose of assessing the probative value of evidence lawfully adduced relates to its reliability.[26] The intimate conviction of the judge refers to the continental law systems in which the level of proof is the one which is convincing for the court.[27] According to Gippini-Fournier the law usually does not frame how strong this 'personal conviction' of the judge should be and that is the case with the EU Courts as well, which is not inclined to frame in general terms the standard of proof in competition cases.[28]

Under Court practice, it is not necessary for every item of evidence produced by the Commission to satisfy those criteria in relation to every aspect of the infringement. It is sufficient if the body of evidence relied on by the institution, viewed as a whole, meets that requirement.[29] The ECJ takes a holistic view of the evidence by

---

[25] Joined cases T-44/02 OP et al, *Dresdner Bank AG and others*, ECLI:EU:T:2004:302, para 60, Case T-441/08, *International Confederation of Societies of Authors and Composers (CISAC) v Commission*, ECLI:EU:T:2013:188. para 91. and T-348/08; *Aragonesas Industrias y Energía SAU v Commission*, ECLI:EU:T:2011:621, paras 92–93; C-199/92 P, *Hüls AG v Commission*, ECLI:EU:C:1999:358, para 149–150.

[26] C-411/04 *Salzgitter Mannesmann GmbH v Commission*, ECLI:EU:C:2007:54, para 45.,Opinion of Judge Vesterdorf acting as Advocate General of 10 July 1991 in Case T-1/89, *Rhône-Poulenc v Commission*, ECLI:EU:T:1991:38, at page II-954., Joined Cases T-67/00, T-68/00, T-71/00 and T-78/00, *JFE Engineering Corp*, ECLI:EU:T:2004:221, para 273. Heike Sweitzer claims that 'with a view to Article 101 and Article 102 decisions imposing fines, a significantly higher standard of proof applies, analogous to what in the common law system would be qualified as 'beyond reasonable doubt'. (Ioannis Kokkoris: The Reform of EC Competition Law: New Challenges In Mel Marquis and Roberto Cisotta (eds): *Litigation and Arbitration in EU Competition Law*, Edward Elgar Publishing, 2015, p. 113.) She refers to *the Siemens* judgment, according to which the Court must come to a "firm conviction" that the alleged infringement took place. In the *Toshiba* judgment in 2014 the General Court allegedly raised the standard of proof to beyond reasonable doubt, as it has declared that 'the evidence submitted by the Commission must permit the conclusion beyond all reasonable doubt that there was an infringement.' As that judgement has not yet been confirmed by the ECJ, the prevailing view applies according to which the balance of probabilities standard is enough to be satisfied by the Commission. See T-519/19, *Toshiba Corp v Commission*, ECLI:EU:T:2014:263 and the appeal pending:C-373/14. P.

[27] Eric Gippini-Fournier: The Elusive Standard of Proof in EU Competition Cases http://papers.ssrn.com/sol3/papers.cfm?abstract_id=1433744, p. 5., Per Hellström: A Uniform Standard of Proof in EU Competition Proceedings in: Claus-Dieter Ehlermann and Mel Marquis (eds): *European Competition Law Annual 2009: The Evaluation of Evidence and its Judicial Review in Competition Cases*, Hart Publishing, Oxford and Portland, Oregon, 2011.
http://papers.ssrn.com/sol3/papers.cfm?abstract_id=2147705, p. 2.

[28] Eric Gippini-Fournier: The Elusive Standard of Proof in EU Competition Cases http://papers.ssrn.com/sol3/papers.cfm?abstract_id=1433744, p. 5 and p. 9.

[29] Joined Cases C-238/99 P, C-244/99 P, C-245/99 P, C-247/99 P, C-250/99 P to C-252/99 P and C-254/99 P *Limburgse Vinyl Maatschaapij and Others v Commission*, ECLI:EU:C:2002:582, paragraphs 513–523.

focusing on the body of evidence on which the Commission relies when viewed as a whole.[30]

### 14.3.2 Standard of Judicial Review

Jones and Sufrin note that 'the question of the intensity of the review in which the General Court engages when reviewing Commission competition decisions is a burning issue. ... As the Commission is not a tribunal for the purposes of Article 6(1) of the ECHR or Article 47 of the Charter the supervision by the GC must satisfy the requirement of a fair and public hearing before an independent and impartial tribunal if the competition proceedings are to comply with the Convention and the Charter.'[31]

Recently in the *Microsoft* judgment the Court observed that it follows from consistent case law that, although as a general rule the Community Courts undertake a comprehensive review of the question as to whether or not the conditions for the application of the competition rules are met, their review of complex economic appraisals made by the Commission is necessarily limited to checking whether the relevant rules on procedure have been complied with, whether the reasons for the decision have been stated, whether the facts have been accurately stated and whether there has been any manifest error of assessment or a misuse of powers.[32]

Likewise, in so far as the Commission's decision is the result of complex technical appraisals, those appraisals are in principle subject to only limited review by the Court, which means that the Community Courts cannot substitute their own assessment of matters of fact for the Commission's.[33]

However, while the Community Courts recognise that the Commission has a margin of appreciation in economic or technical matters, that does not mean that they must decline to review the Commission's interpretation of economic or technical data. The Community Courts must not only establish whether the evidence put forward is factually accurate, reliable and consistent but must also determine whether that evidence contains all the relevant data that must be taken into consideration in appraising a complex situation and whether it is capable of substantiating the conclusions drawn from it.[34]

[30] Ioannis Kokkoris: The Reform of EC Competition Law: New challenges. In Mel Marquis and Roberto Cisotta (eds): *Litigation and Arbitration in EU Competition Law*, Edward Elgar Publishing, 2015, p.114. See Joined cases T-305/94 to T-307/94 *Linburgse Vinyl Maatschappij and others v Commission (PVC II.)* ECLI:EU:T:1999:80, para 768–778 and recent cases *Toshiba*, para 38 and *Intel v Commission*, para 64.

[31] Alison Jones and Brenda Sufrin: *EU Competition Law*, Oxford University Press, Oxford, 2014., p.1029.

[32] T-201/04, *Microsoft Corp. v Commission*, ECLI:EU:T:2007:289, para 87–89.

[33] Para 88.

[34] Para 89.

In the *KME Germany v Commission and Chalkor v Commission* judgment[35] the issue of the Commission's margin of discretion with regard to complex economic and technical matters was challenged again by pleading a violation of Article 6(1) of the ECHR. By that time the ECtHR has issued its well-known *Menarini* judgment. Although the ECJ did not refer explicitly to *Menarini* in *KME*, it has repeated its interpretation discussed above, the effect of which is that in its view its own interpretation is in conformity with the Charter and supposedly with ECHR jurisprudence. The Commission's margin of appreciation does not mean that the Court of the European Union must refrain from reviewing the Commission's interpretation of information of an economic nature.[36] According to Igor Nikolic 'the courts limit themselves to verifying whether the Commission has applied the Fining Guidelines correctly, and in doing so, it will only look for manifest errors of appraisal. The General Court often did not engage in significant proportionality review of fines'[37]

On the other hand, the ECJ in *Otis*[38] held that the review provided by the Treaty meets the requirements of the principle of effective judicial protection in Article 47 of the EU Charter of Fundamental Rights.[39]

Recently Pieter Van Cleynenbreugel pointed out the difference between comprehensive and limited review and the tendency of the ECJ to submit more cases to a comprehensive review.[40] The comprehensive review consists in an exhaustive review of both the findings of facts and the legal appraisal of those facts.[41] A limited review takes place if the Union Courts confine their review to whether the Commission has committed a manifest error of assessment.

Under the limited review the Commission is capable not only of developing the competitive harm theory, but also of deciding occasionally on policy issues. José Carlos Laguna de Paz also reflected on the 'need to strike the right balance between

[35] C-272/19 P, ECLI:EU:C:2011:810.

[36] C-272/19 P, *KME Germany v Commission*, ECLI:EU:C:2011:810, paras 94, 102; C-386/10 P, *Chalkor AE Epexergasias Metallon v Commission*, ECLI:EU:C:2011:815, para 54. See also Igor Nikolic: Full judicial review of antitrust cases after KME: a new formula of review? E.C.L.R. 2012, 33(12), 583–588.

[37] Igor Nikolic: Full judicial review of antitrust cases after KME: a new formula of review? E.C.L.R. 2012, 33(12), 583–588., at page 587. Wils has also admitted that with regard to the amount of the fine, Regulation 1/2003, the case law of the EU Courts and the Guidelines and Leniency Notice still leave the European Commission a significant margin of discretion. Wouter P.J. Wils: The compatibility with fundamental rights of the EU antitrust enforcement system in which the European Commission acts both as investigator and as first-instance decision maker, http://papers.ssrn.com/sol3/papers.cfm?abstract_id=2363440, at page 13. Nonetheless, his final conclusion is that the combination of the review of legality and this unlimited jurisdiction meets the "full jurisdiction" standard laid down in the case law of the European Court of Human Rights; at p. 14.

[38] C-199/11 *Europese Gemeenschap v Otis and others*, ECLI:EU:C:2012:684.

[39] paras 56–63.

[40] Pieter Van Cleynenbreugel: Efficient justice in the service of justiciable efficiency? Varieties of comprehensive judicial review in a modernised EU competition law enforcement context. The Competition Law Review, Volume 10, Issue 1, pp. 35–6, at p.37.

[41] P.37.

the conflicting forces of improving courts' scrutiny as a means to protect the citizens' rights, on the one hand, and leaving the competition authority the necessary room to shape and implement competition policy, on the other.'[42]

Pieter Van Cleynenbreugel on the other hand, claims that 'rhetoric does not match results in this area of the law'.[43] In his view recent case law demonstrates that the application of the comprehensively tailored review amounts to *de facto* deference to the Commission's interpretation of facts and classifications in law and that the Court of Justice appears unwilling to determine – as a matter of EU law – clear-cut standards in accordance with which the General Court has to take account of tailored pleas and the margin of appreciation entrusted to the Commission.[44]

As the President of the General Court has noted, the Court is marginalising the marginal review test, and therefore the tendency is to put each case under the full review test.[45]

This view is confirmed by other academics citing among others the *Telefonica*[46] and *Deutsche Telekom*[47] judgments to reason that the Commission's leeway has been considerably reduced by several decades of case law, which set out standards of proof and very detailed interpretation criteria.[48] The marginal review test probably has also reflected the institutional division between the Commission and the Court under which the Court has refrained to engage in its own appraisal based on a different methodology than the Commission.[49]

The ECJ's interpretation of the required standard of proof to be met by the Commission does not necessarily have a determinative effect on the standard of proof applied by the national competition authorities and national courts, because,

---

[42] José Carlos Laguna de Paz: Understanding the limits of judicial review in European competition law, Journal of Antitrust Enforcement, Vol. 2, No. 1 (2014), pp. 203–224, at p. 204.

[43] P. 41.

[44] P.44. He is relying on the judgments of *Schindler* and *Kone*: C-501/11P,, ECLI:EU:C:2013:522 and C-510/11P, *Kone Oyj et al v Commission*, ECLI:EU:C:2013:696.

[45] Marc Jaeger: The Standard of Review in Competition Cases Involving Complex Economic Assessments: Towards the Marginalisation of the Marginal Review? (2011) 2:4 Journal of European Competition Law & Practice: 295–314. See also the editorial comments in the October 2011 issue of The Common Market Law Review: '... generally, the 'margin of appreciation' doctrine has not prevented the General Court from looking into any economic or technical detail of a case that appeared remotely promising as a basis for a successful ground of appeal. Therefore, much would be won if the Court stopped paying lip-service to the old 'complex appraisals' formula'.

[46] T-336/07 *Telefónica SA and Telefónica España SA v Commission*, ECLI:EU:T:2012:172, paras 110–144.

[47] T-271/03, *Deutsche Telekom AG v Commission*, ECLI:EU:T:2008:101, para 185; and on appeal C-280/08. P, ECLIEU:C:2010:603.

[48] José Carlos Laguna de Paz: Understanding the limits of judicial review in European competition law, Journal of Antitrust Enforcement, Vol.2, No. 1 (2014), pp.203–224, p.216. Heike Schweitzer also explains that "the intensity of judicial control exercised by the GC does not decrease, but rather increase with the complexity of the fact patters and the economic assessment at issue." p. 511.

[49] Heike Schweitzer, p. 512.

according to Recital 5 of Regulation 1/2003/EC,[50] the Regulation affects neither national rules on the standard of proof nor obligations of competition authorities or courts of the Member States to ascertain the relevant facts of a case, provided that such rules and obligations are compatible with general principles of Community law.

Thus, decentralisation of the application of Articles 101 and 102 TFEU does not result in the obligation on national enforcers to apply the same standard of proof as that applied by the ECJ.

## 14.4 The Standard of Proof and Judicial Review Debate in Hungary[51]

Recently the most important question raised by the parties at national court level was whether review of a GVH decision by the competent administrative courts is penal or administrative by nature. Given that different arguments and answers surfaced, the debate was finally decided by the Supreme Court and the Constitutional Court.[52] To allow one to follow the judgments in chronological order, one first summarises the judgment of the Supreme Court from May 2014.

### *14.4.1 Judgment of the Supreme Court*[53]

Several years ago the GVH found that a bid-rigging cartel had been created back in 2004 and adopted a negative decision under Article 101 TFEU and Article 11 of the HCA, fining the participant undertakings quite heavily. The leniency applicant received immunity from the fine. The legality of the decision and judgments issued by the review courts was challenged before the Supreme Court.

The central question of this case was the standard of proof in competition law procedures. The parties challenged the decision on the ground that the GVH cannot rely on evidence coming only from one source, namely the leniency applicant. In their submission it would not fulfil the standard of proof, that is 'beyond reasonable

[50] Council Regulation (EC) No 1/2003 of 16 December 2002 on the implementation of rules on competition laid down in Article 81 and 82 of the Treaty, OJ L 1, 04/01/2003, pp. 1–25.

[51] See the study of Nagy Csongor István in Hungarian: Tisztességes eljárás és bírósági felülvizsgálat a versenyfelügyeleti eljárásban. In Verseny és szabályozás 2014 (szek.: Valentiny Pál, Kiss Ferenc László, Nagy Csongor István) MTA KRTK Közgazdaság-tudományi Intézet, pp. 55–72., http://econ.core.hu/file/download/vesz2014/felugyelet.pdf.

[52] For earlier literature see in Hungarian: Ruszthiné Juhász Dorina- Zavodnyik József: A bizonyítási mérce, a bizonyítási teher és a bizonyítékok értékelése versenyügyekben, Jogtudományi Közlöny, 2014/6, pp. 286–299.

[53] Kfv. III.37.690/2013/29. Case annotation by Dorkó Dalma in Hungarian in Versenytükör. Dorkó Dalma: Vasútépítő kartell a Kúria ítéletének tükrében. Versenytükör 2014/1, pp. 69–77.

doubt' as established by the jurisprudence of the European Court of Human Rights.[54] Hence, the plaintiff claimed a violation of its right to a fair trial[55] under the European Convention on Human Rights.[56]

The GVH argued that the standard of proof is not the 'beyond reasonable doubt' test, but that applied by the ECJ. According to this reasoning, the ECJ accepted evidence originating from one single source, if the evidence was consistent and sufficiently precise.

The Supreme Court noted at the outset that the penal nature of the fine has the consequence that the procedural guarantees flowing from the jurisprudence of the European Court of Human Rights have to be respected. The Supreme Court relied especially on the *Menarini* judgment.

The Supreme Court found that the fine applied by the GVH is of a criminal nature, but that does not mean that the court should review the decision in a penal procedure or that the standard of proof is 'beyond reasonable doubt.' According to the Supreme Court the ECHR, as interpreted in the *Menarini* judgment, does not oblige national courts to apply a specific standard of proof, because standards of proof applied in civil procedures are different in the Member States. Legal doctrine in some countries, like in Hungary, has not developed a uniform standard of proof applicable in each civil law proceedings.

In the Supreme Court's view, the ordinary courts should view the GVH's decision as an indictment in penal law and during judicial review the plaintiffs can prove that a more reasonable assessment of the evidence exists.

With regard to the standard of judicial review in the Supreme Court's judgment the plaintiffs do not have to prove that the competition authority has exercised its discretion in a gravely unreasonable manner.

Ordinary courts cannot rely on the limits of review set by the Hungarian Code on the Civil Procedure in Article 339/B; full review of the discretionary powers of the competition authority should be exercised by the Hungarian courts.

It is in line with the *Menarini* judgment that Hungarian procedural law limits the competence of the Supreme Court to review judicial decisions on points of law only, because the two level ordinary court review fulfils the requirements of full judicial review as flowing from the *Menarini* judgment.

Concerning the evidence of the GVH in the given case, the Supreme Court recalled that the ECJ had accepted evidence coming only from one source if the evidence was consistent and sufficiently precise. Hence, the Supreme Court was willing to approve the findings of the GVH in that respect.

---

[54] The judges relied on the following judgments: *Engel and others v The Netherlands*, Application no. 5100/71, 5107/71, 5102/71, 5354/72, 5370/72, 08/06/1976, *Öztürk v Germany*, Application no. 8544/79, 21/02/1984, *Jussila v. Finland*, Application no. 73053/01, 23/11/2006, *Menarini Diagnostics S.R.L. v Italy*, Application no. 43509/08, 27/09/2011.

[55] Article 6.

[56] Convention for the Protection of Human Rights and Fundamental Freedoms, Article 6(1): "In the determination of his civil rights and obligations or of any criminal charge against him, everyone is entitled to a fair and public hearing within a reasonable time by an independent and impartial tribunal established by law".

In consequence, the leniency application of a cartelist and the document obtained during the dawn raid was found sufficient to prove the existence of the cartel.

Furthermore, the parties made a motion to the Supreme Court to initiate a preliminary ruling procedure at the ECJ on the interpretation of the applicable standard of proof.

The Supreme Court has refused to ask for a preliminary ruling by stating that according to the *CILFIT* judgment[57] it is not obliged to do that, because the ECJ has extensive case-law on that point.

The Supreme Court also noted that Article 52(3) of the EU Charter of Fundamental Rights incorporates the ECtHR jurisprudence in those cases where the Member State's implement Union law.[58] By applying Article 101, Hungary implements Union law, resulting in the obligation for national court to set aside national law not in conformity with the ECHR. The Supreme Court explicitly ruled that Article 339/B of the Procedural Code has to be set aside as it is incompatible with the ECHR.

Another considerable statement of the Supreme Court was the implication flowing from Article 3(2) of Regulation 1/2003. That article contains the so-called convergence rule according to which the application of national competition law may not lead to the prohibition of agreements, decisions by associations of undertakings or concerted practices which may affect trade between Member States but which do not restrict competition within the meaning of Article 101(1) of the Treaty, or which fulfil the conditions of Article 101(3) of the Treaty or which are covered by a Regulation for the application of Article 101(3) of the Treaty. In the Supreme Court's view, this provision is also applicable to the determination of standard of proof in Article 101 cases; nonetheless the wording of it is confined to the legal assessment. The contrary view would lead to the prohibition of cartels by national competition authorities or courts that are to be considered as compatible with Article 101 by the European Commission or by the ECJ. This, in turn, would not only violate the principle of uniform application of Union law, but also hamper the achievement of the objectives of Article 101.

### 14.4.2 Judgment of the Constitutional Court

In parallel with the review of the cartel decision forming the subject matter of the judgment of the Supreme Court, another cartel decision was reviewed by the ordinary courts and later by the Constitutional Court.[59] The competition authority had

[57] C-283/81, *Srl CILFIT and others v Ministry of Health*, ECLI:EU:C:1982:335.

[58] 'In so far as this Charter contains rights which correspond to rights guaranteed by the Convention for the Protection of Human Rights and Fundamental Freedoms, the meaning and scope of those rights shall be the same as those laid down by the said Convention. This provision shall not prevent Union law providing more extensive protection.'

[59] Decision of the Constitutional Court of 30 September, 2014 (No.30/2014. (IX.30.) Case annotation by László Bak in Hungarian in Versenytükör. Bak László: Alkotmányos versenyjog-a versenyfelügyeleti eljárás az Alkotmánybíróság fókuszában. Versenytükör pp. 52–60.

found a single and continuous infringement of Article 11 of the Hungarian Competition Act in the so-called road construction bid-rigging cartel case. The petitioner claimed that the judgment of the Supreme Court violated its fundamental rights.

In September 2014, the Constitutional Court rendered its judgment on the same questions of law as those answered by the Supreme Court in the railway cartel case discussed above. The petitioner practically challenged the entire system of competition law enforcement in Hungary. This summary is focusing only on the most important allegations.

The first head of claim of the petitioner was about the violation of its right to a fair trial, as the Competition Authority itself had charged it with the cartel and imposed fines on it. In its second claim the undertaking alleged the breach of its right to presumption of innocence, because the Supreme Court has based its decision on a single piece of evidence. The third head of claim concerned the violation of the right to a fair trial again, on the basis of the fact that Supreme Court had weighed the evidence without having a competence under Hungarian procedural rules to do so.

In sum, the arguments centred on the administrative or penal nature of the review proceeding and the standard of proof and the weighing of evidence.

The Constitutional Court first recalled Article 6(1) of the European Convention on Human Rights[60] and Article 47 of the EU Charter of Fundamental Rights[61] on the right to a fair hearing and interpreted Article XXVIII of the Hungarian Basic Law[62] in this international context. Another right relied on by the applicant was the right to the presumption of innocence[63] and *nullum crimen sine lege, nulla poena sine lege*.[64] The petitioner claimed that as the decision of the competition authority was based on the single and continuous infringement, a concept unknown in

[60] Convention for the Protection of Human Rights and Fundamental Freedoms, Act XXXI of 1993. On the relationship of the Convention, EU Charter of Fundamental Rights and Hungarian Constitutional Law see Juhász Miklós: Kriminális versenyjog? – gondolatok az emberi jogok és a versenyjog kapcsolatáról, Magyar Jog 2013.9. szám, pp 515–524. See also a Hungarian ECHR case: *DEBÚT Zrt and others v Hungary*, application o 24851/10, 20/11/2012.

[61] Charter of Fundamental Rights of the European Union, OJ C 326, 26.10.2012, p. 391–407.

[62] Basic Law of Hungary, 25 April 2011, Article XXVIII (1) ‘Everyone shall be entitled to have any charge against him or her, or his or her rights and obligations in any litigation, adjudicated within a reasonable time in a fair and public trial conducted by an independent and impartial court established by an Act.’

[63] Convention for the Protection of Human Rights and Fundamental Freedoms, Article 6(2), Charter of Fundamental Rights of the European Union, Article 48, Fundamental Law, Article XXVIII (2) ‘No one shall be considered guilty until his or her liability under criminal law has been established by the final decision of a court.’

[64] Article 48 of the Charter for the Protection of Human Rights and Fundamental Freedoms, Hungarian Fundamental Law, Article XXVIII (4): ‘No one shall be found guilty and subjected to punishment for an act that, at the time it was committed, was not a criminal offence under the law of Hungary or – within the sphere specified by an international treaty or a legal act of the European Union – under the law of another State.’

Hungarian competition law, its right to *nullum crime sine lege* was violated during the procedure.

At the outset, the Constitutional Court held that the procedure in front of the Competition Authority has to be considered as having a criminal nature under ECHR and ECJ jurisprudence.[65] The Court proceeded by arguing that entrusting the prosecution and punishment of breaches of competition rules to administrative authorities is not inconsistent with the ECHR or the EU Charter of Fundamental Rights in so far as the person concerned has an opportunity to challenge any decision made against him before a tribunal that offers guarantees.

The Court argued that any violation of fundamental rights can be avoided by having a full review provided by a judicial body. The characteristics of such a body include the power to quash in all respects, on questions of fact and law, the decision. The judicial body must in particular have jurisdiction to examine all questions of fact and law relevant to the dispute before it.[66]

The Court has contended that the principles claimed by the petitioner and enshrined in the international documents and in the Hungarian Fundamental Law should be applied also in competition proceedings outside the ambit of Hungarian penal law, but the level of protection is lower than in penal proceedings as competition proceeding does not belong to the hard core of criminal law.[67]

The above statement has considerable consequences also on the standard of proof. The Court, without saying anything specific about the applicable standard of proof in Hungarian law, has underlined that the standard of proof is not that of beyond reasonable doubt. It was further suggested by the Court that the Competition Authority has to base its decision on consistent, direct or indirect, evidence.

The review court has the obligation to assess the evidence produced by the Authority. The judge has to weigh freely the evidence produced by the Authority.

By turning back to the question of full judicial review, the Court observed that under Articles 339(1) and 339(2) of the Procedural Code, Hungarian courts have the competence to annul the decision, to order reopening and to alter the decision itself. Furthermore, the courts have the competence to order the taking of evidence as well. Nonetheless the text of Article 339/B of the Procedural Code sets a limit on the competence of the courts to review the administrative decisions based on discretion; in practice, in reviewing the fines, the courts have the competence to overrule de facto the discretion exercised by the HCA with the reasoning that the facts established by the court are in contradiction with the records.

In the second part of its the decision, the Constitutional Court interpreted the petitioner's right to the presumption of innocence and whether this right was violated as there was a single piece of evidence relied on by the Competition Authority. Part of that right is the principle of *in dubio pro reo* under which, if reasonable doubt

---

[65] The *Engel, Jussila v. Finland, Janosevic v Sweden*, and *Menarini* cases were referred to by the Constitutional Court from the ECHR jurisprudence; C-501/11.P. *Schindler v Commission*, ECLI:EU:C:2013:522 was referred to from the case-law of the ECJ.

[66] Para 65 of the decision.

[67] My emphasis; para 62 of the decision.

remains, the accused is to be acquitted. After citing ECJ judgments in the cases *E.ON Energie v Commission*,[68] *Baustahlgewebe v Commission*[69] and *United Brands*,[70] the Constitutional Court came to the conclusion that the *in dubio pro reo* principle has to be respected by the Competition Authority and by the review courts. That means in practice that the GVH has to rely on consistent and convergent evidence, not on speculations or hypothesis.[71] The body of evidence cannot contain conflicting evidence; it should be consistent by nature. On the other hand, the probative force of the evidence has to be decided by the judge relying on his or her own conviction. Hence, the Constitutional Court has no competence to overrule the probative force of evidence determined by judges. With this, the Constitutional Court established that Hungarian courts have to rely on their intimate conviction in competition procedures.

The petitioner claimed the breach of the principle of *nullum crimen sine lege* as well, arguing that the concept of single and continuous infringement is unknown in Hungarian law and therefore the violation of competition rules was not foreseeable. In this context the Constitutional Court has pointed out that the concept developed by the ECJ is not a new form of conduct, but a series of several individual conducts already declared incompatible with law. Criminal charges can be determined legally not only by the legislator and also by the jurisprudence if the illegality of the conduct is foreseeable. The Constitutional Court hinted that the latter was the case.

## 14.5 Conclusion

We can see that the eagerly awaited judgments of the Supreme and Constitutional Court have considerable implication in practice. The standard of proof and judicial review debate is to be closed in Hungary. Lower courts charged with the everyday application of EU and national antitrust rules should follow the decisions of the Supreme and the Constitutional Court. From the analysis above it can be seen that the Constitutional Court has remained faithful to the jurisprudence of the ECHR; nonetheless the EU Charter provides room for stricter protection for fundamental rights. The Constitutional Court established that Hungarian courts have to rely on their intimate conviction in competition procedures.

On the other hand, the Supreme Court has set aside a procedural rule in the Hungarian Procedural Code by arguing that the full review requirement of the ECHR is not fulfilled otherwise. De jure full review provides more protection for undertakings than de facto practice of courts.

It is interesting to note that the Supreme Court decided not to ask for a preliminary ruling, instead it interpreted the convergence rules of Regulation 1/2003/EC,

[68] C-89/11.P, ECLI:EU:C:2012:738.

[69] C-185/95.P,ECLI:EU:C:1998:738.

[70] 27/76, ECLI:EU:C:1978:22.

[71] Para 71.

the requirement of uniform application of competition law and ECtHR case law alone. After the Supreme Court's ruling, the standard of judicial review is based in Hungary on de jure full review which seems higher than the standard provided currently by Union law.[72]

**Acknowledgments** Research was also financed by OTKA (No K-109414 project). The author would like to thank Márton Varju, Zoltán Marosi and András Kovács for their helpful comments on this topic. Any error or omission remains the author's.

[72] Nagy Csongor István in Hungarian: Tisztességes eljárás és bírósági felülvizsgálat a versenyfelügyeleti eljárásban. In Verseny és szabályozás 2014 (szek.: Valentiny Pál, Kiss Ferenc László, Nagy Csongor István) MTA KRTK Közgazdaság-tudományi Intézet, pp. 55–72, http://econ.core.hu/file/download/vesz2014/felugyelet.pdf, p. 62.

# Chapter 15
# The Application of EU Competition Law in Poland

**Krystyna Kowalik-Bańczyk**

## 15.1 Introduction

The Republic of Poland joined the European Union on 1 May 2004. Since that date EU competition law has been applied directly in the Polish legal system, in parallel to the provisions of Polish competition law. Polish competition law itself is deeply influenced by the EU competition system and its provisions are very often interpreted in line with the EU *acquis*.[1] The direct application of Articles 101 and 102 of the Treaty on the Functioning of the European Union (TFEU[2]) by the President of the Office of Consumers and Competition Protection ("Polish National Competition Authority" or "OPCC")[3] depends on the identification of the effect on trade between the Member States in the possible anticompetitive practice. Therefore the main concern of this chapter is to identify how this criterion conditioning the direct application of EU competition law has been used during the last 12 years (Sect. 15.2). If the

[1] On this issue, see: Miąsik D, (2010) Solvents to the Rescue – A Historical Outline of the Impact of EU Law on the Application of Polish Competition Law by Polish Courts. Yearbook Antitrust and Regulatory Studies 3(3): 11; Kolasiński M, (2010) Influence of the General Principles of Community Law on Polish Antitrust Procedure. Yearbook Antitrust and Regulatory Studies 3(3): 29; Kuik K, Mościbroda A, (2012) 2010 and 2011 EU Competition Law and Sector-Specific Regulatory Jurisprudence and Case Law Developments with a Nexus to Poland. Yearbook Antitrust and Regulatory Studies 6(7): 157. Broader on the issue of convergence in competition law in EU: Albors-Llorens A, (2014) Competition and Consumer Law in the European Union: Evolution and Convergence. Yearbook of European Law 33: 163–193.

[2] Treaty on the Functioning of the European Union (OJ C 202, 7.06.2016, p. 47–200).

[3] If there is a reference to National Competition Authorities within the European Competition Network, the abbreviation 'NCA' is applied.

K. Kowalik-Bańczyk (✉)
Institute of Law Studies of the Polish Academy of Sciences, Warsaw, Poland

General Court of the European Union, Luxembourg City, Luxembourg
e-mail: kowalikkrystyna@wp.pl



A. Almăşan, P. Whelan (eds.), *The Consistent Application of EU Competition Law*, Studies in European Economic Law and Regulation 9,
DOI 10.1007/978-3-319-47382-6_15

criterion is fulfilled, the Polish NCA and the Polish courts rely on Regulation 1/2003 as well as the Polish rules on substantive and procedural competition law. Regulation 1/2003 refers, inter alia, to the division of tasks between the European Commission and the National Competition Authorities within the EU. One of the few Polish preliminary references linked with the EU competition law[4] referred to the scope of the decisive powers of the President of the OCCP the Regulation 1/2003 and remains an illustration of a rather distrustful attitude of the European Commission towards the NCAs. The limitation of autonomy of the NCA in the direct application of the EU competition rules is thus a significant concern and might influence the low level of direct application of EU competition law (Sect. 15.3).

## 15.2 Defining the Effect on Trade Criterion

The President of the OCCP issues about hundred decisions yearly in matters related to the practices infringing the competition protection rules.[5] Only a few of them per year (if any) implies the application of Article 101 or 102 TFEU. To the knowledge of this author, in the years 2004–2014 the President of the OPPC issued altogether about thirty decisions where Article 101 or 102 TFEU was applied.[6] On the other hand, the statistics of the European Commission indicate that in the analysed period there were only 13 such decisions issued by the Polish NCA, with 29 new investigations pending.[7] Thus the official statistics are even less optimistic.[8] Only about one third of identified decisions found an infringement of either Article 101 or 102 TFEU.

Considering the scope of the Polish market, the presence of foreign investment on this market and the general activity of the OCCP, this number of decisions referring to Article 101 or 102 TFEU is surprisingly low. In order to contrast it with other

[4] Case C-375/09 *Prezes UOKiK v Tele2, now Netia*, ECLI:EU:C:2011:270.

[5] Cf Report on the Activity of the OCCP of 2013 (which is the latest available report), p. 2, available at: <https://uokik.gov.pl/sprawozdania_z_dzialalnosci_urzedu.php>. Accessed 30 September 2015. In 2013 OCCP issued 98 such decisions.

[6] Based on the reports on the activity of OCCP published each year at the webpage of the OCCP: and on the author' analysis of decisions published on the OCCP' webpage.

[7] <http://ec.europa.eu/competition/ecn/statistics.html#1>. Accessed 7 October 2015.

[8] For instance decisions in which the application of Articles 101 and 102 TFEU was considered but did not occur, mainly due to the fact that the infringement ceased before the decision was adopted, include i.a.: decision of the President of OPCC of 16 April 2007 in case RWA 10/2007 *Związek Polskich Artystów Fotografików w Warszawie*; decision of the President of OPCC of 10 June 2009 in case RWA 6/2009 *Stowarzyszenie Artystów Wykonawców Utworów Muzycznych i Słowno Muzycznych SAWP*; decision of the President of OPCC of 21 July 2009 in case RWA 10/2009 *Stowarzyszenie Autorów ZAiKS*; decision of the President of OPCC of 21 December 2009 in case DOK 8/2009 *Telekomunikacja Polska S.A.*; and decision of the President of OPCC of 15 July 2015 in case DOK 1/2015 *Grabikowski-Grabikowska PPHU "INEX"*.

Member States, one can cite the statistics of the European Commission; they reveals that in other 'new' Member States, there have been since their accession to the European Union: 7 decisions in Bulgaria; 6 decisions in Cyprus; 9 decisions in the Czech Republic; 3 decisions in Estonia; 33 decisions in Hungary; 6 decisions in Latvia; 20 in Lithuania; 30 in Romania; 17 in Slovakia; 28 in Slovenia; and 3 in Malta.[9] This very low number of "Polish" decisions where EU competition law had been applied can be explained in different ways. The European Commission presumes that it might be a result of relatively low number of employees and means involved in antitrust investigations.[10] However it seems that it might also quite viably be explained by the hypothesis that the President of the OCCP had applied a very narrow definition of the criterion conditioning this application, namely that of an effect on trade between Member States of the EU, as required by Article 3 of the Regulation 1/2003, or that this criterion is not taken into account while applying the national law.

Article 3(1) of Regulation 1/2003 on the implementation of Articles 101 and 102 TFEU[11] sets the relationship between the EU and national competition law provisions. According to this provision, the National Competition Authorities and national courts are bound to apply, next to the national competition law provisions, the EU ones towards the anticompetitive practices which "may affect trade between Member States".[12] The President of the OCCP is thus bound to identify if a given practice infringes Article 101 or 102 TFEU, in parallel to the considerations on possible infringements of the Polish antitrust rules. It seems, however, that there is no such practice to raise the application of Articles 101 and 102 TFUE *ex officio*.[13]

[9] <http://ec.europa.eu/competition/ecn/statistics.html#1>. Accessed 3 September 2015. Broader statistics given in: Botta M, Svetlicinii A, Bernatt M, (2015) The Assessment of the Effect on Trade by the National Competition Autorities of the "New" Member States: Another Legal Partition of the Internal Market?. Common Market Law Review 52: 1247–1276, 1275.

[10] European Commission, Staff Working Document – Enhancing Competition Enforcement by the Member States' Competition Authorities: Institutional and Procedural Issues. Published in Brussels on 9.7.2014, COM (2014)453. <http://ec.europa.eu/competition/antitrust/legislation/swd_2014_231_en.pdf>, para 21.

[11] Council Regulation (EC) No 1/2003 of 16 December 2002 on the implementation of the rules on competition laid down in Articles 81 and 82 of the Treaty (OJ L 1, 4.1.2003, p. 1–25).

[12] Banasiński C, Bychowska M (2009) Kompetencje decyzyjne Komisji Europejskiej i Prezesa UOKiK wynikające z rozporządzenia Rady UE nr 1/2003 w świetle zasady równoległego stosowania wspólnotowego i krajowego prawa antymonopolowego. Przegląd Prawa Handlowego 3:6; Kohutek K (2006) Stosunek między art. 81 i 82 Traktatu a krajowym prawem konkurencji (reguły konwergencji). Przegląd Ustawodawstwa Gospodarczego 4.

[13] On this obligation: Kowalik-Bańczyk K (2007) Uwzględnianie przez sąd z urzędu zarzutów opartych na prawie wspólnotowym. Europejski Przegląd Sądowy 12: 10–20.

### 15.2.1 The Notion of Effect on Trade in EU Practice

The notion of effect on trade lays at the core of the initial construction of the European Community's competition rules. The Spaak report prepared by the Intergovernmental Committee on European Integration in 1956[14] referred to rules applicable to undertakings if their actions affect "interstate trade", similarly to solutions adopted in the US constitution and in the GATT.[15]

The notion of "effect on trade" (as it is used instead of affectation on trade)[16] is interpreted in the same way for both Article 101 TFEU and Article 102 TFEU. There is no clear definition of this notion in EU law; therefore the interpretation stems both from the Court of Justice of the European Union's ("CJEU") jurisprudence and the guidelines issued by the European Commission in 2004[17] ("the Guidelines"). Those Guidelines sum up the CJEU jurisprudence and might be considered as a one-sided obligation of the Commission to follow the rules expressed in them.[18] However, there is no legal basis for any binding effect of those Guidelines for the National Competition Authorities of EU Member States.

The notion of effect on trade was for the first time considered by the CJEU in the case 56/65 *Société Technique Minière (STM) v Maschinenbau Ulm.*[19] The CJEU was answering the preliminary question of a French court that was considering a dispute between the parties of an agreement on exclusive right of sell of diggers, where one of the parties was claiming that the agreement was null and void. The CJEU stated that the agreement must be one which "may affect trade between Member States" if it is possible:

[14] Brussels Report on the General Common Market prepared by the Intergovernmental Committee on European Integration, June 1956, available at: http://aei.pitt.edu/995/01/Spaak_report.pdf. Accessed 8 September 2015.

[15] On those similarities, see Roda J-C in : Bosco D, Luc I., Rincazaux P., Cardonnel P., Roda J-C (2011) Affectation du commerce entre États membres et pratiques anticoncurrentielles: Une question d'actualité. Concurrences 2: 17–32, 30.

[16] Cf in the Commission Notice—Guidelines on the effect on trade concept contained in Articles 81 and 82 of the Treaty (OJ C 101, 27.4.2004, p. 81–96).

[17] Commission Notice—Guidelines on the effect on trade concept contained in Articles 81 and 82 of the Treaty (OJ C 101, 27.4.2004, p. 81–96).

[18] Senden L, Soft Law in European Community Law, Oxford and Portland Oregon 2004, p. 45. Cf case C-322/88 *Grimaldi* [1989] ECR 440, para. 18: "national courts are bound to take recommendations into consideration in order to decide disputes submitted to them, in particular where they cast light on the interpretation of national measures adopted in order to implement them or where they are designed to supplement binding Community provisions". The EU courts have repeatedly stressed that the Commission is bound by its own guidelines: C-3/06 P *Groupe Danone v Commission* [2007] ECR I-1331, para. 23; T-119/02 *Royal Philips Electronics v Commission* [2003] ECR II-1433, para. 242; T-71/03, T-74/03, T-87/03 and T-91/03 *Tokai Carbon v Commission* [2005] ECR II-10, para. 157; Case T-16/99 *Lögstör Rör* [2002] ECR II-1633, para 344.

[19] Case 56–65 *Société Technique Minière (L.T.M.) v Maschinenbau Ulm GmbH (M.B.U.)*, ECLI:EU:C:1966:38.

> to foresee with a sufficient degree of probability on the basis of a set of objective factors of law or of fact that the agreement in question may have an influence, direct or indirect, actual or potential, on the pattern of trade between Member States" [and that this agreement is] "capable of bringing about a partitioning of the market in certain products between Member States and thus rendering more difficult the interpenetration of trade which the treaty is intended to create.[20]

In that very early case, the assessment of the relevant clause contained in an exclusive sale agreement can lead to a division of product markets between Member States, hindering in this way any mutual influence of those markets, in violation of the provisions of the Treaty. It is not necessary that each individual part of such an agreement, including clauses that restrict competition, should affect the trade.[21] If an agreement as a whole can affect trade between Member States, it should be covered by the EU competition law rules, including those parts of any agreement that on their own do not exercise this influence. If the agreement in question covers various forms of activity, those spheres of activity should be directly linked and constitute parts of the same agreement.[22] Otherwise, each of the activities should be considered separately as a separate agreement. In case T-2/89 *Petrofina*,[23] the General Court found that even if an effect on trade caused by one of the parties of the agreement is irrelevant, it does not mean that that party would be liberated from the liability for infringement of Article 101 TFEU. As far as Article 102 TFEU is concerned, the abuse of a dominant position should affect trade between Member States, but it does not mean that one has to consider each 'behaviour' of the abusing undertaking separately. All activities forming part of a general strategy adopted by the entity dominating the market should be assessed in light of the effects brought by the strategy as a whole. If a dominant entity adopts different practices, all bound to achieve the same aim (for instance, the elimination of competitors), in order to apply Article 102 TFEU it is sufficient that at least one of the practices can affect trade between Member States.[24]

[20] This definition is still in use, cf case 42/84 *Remia BV and others v Commission of the European Communities*, ECLI:EU:C:1985:327, para 22; case C-475/99 *Firma Ambulanz Glöckner v Landkreis Südwestpfalz*, ECLI:EU:C:2001:577, para 48; joint cases C-295/04 to C-298/04 *Vincenzo Manfredi v Lloyd Adriatico Assicurazioni SpA* (C-295/04), *Antonio Cannito v Fondiaria Sai SpA* (C-296/04) and *Nicolò Tricarico* (C-297/04) and *Pasqualina Murgolo* (C-298/04) *v Assitalia SpA*, ECLI:EU:C:2006:461, para 48.

[21] Para 14 of the Guidelines on the effect on trade; case 193/83 *Windsurfing International Inc. v Commission of the European Communities*, ECLI:EU:C:1986:75, para 96; case T-77/94 *Vereniging van Groothandelaren in Bloemkwekerijprodukten, Florimex BV, Inkoop Service Aalsmeer BV and M. Verhaar BV v Commission of the European Communities*, ECLI:EU:T:1997:70, para 126.

[22] Para 14 of the Guidelines on the effect on trade, case T-77/94 *Vereniging van Groothandelaren in Bloemkwekerijprodukten, Florimex BV, Inkoop Service Aalsmeer BV and M. Verhaar BV v Commission of the European Communities*, ECLI:EU:T:1997:70, paras 142–144.

[23] Para 15 of the Guidelines on the effect on trade, case T-2/89 *Petrofina* [1991] ECR II-1087, para 226.

[24] Para 17 of the Guidelines on the effect on trade; case 85/76 *Hoffman-La Roche* [1979] ECR 461, para 126.

In the case C-226/11 *Expedia*[25] the CJEU was in fact intermingling the effect on trade criterion with a different criterion present in Articles 101 and 102 TFEU (the object of the questioned practice).[26] And thus in para 20 it stated: "It follows that the competition authorities of the Member States can apply the provisions of national law prohibiting cartels to an agreement of undertakings which is capable of affecting trade between Member States within the meaning of Article 101 TFEU only where that agreement perceptibly restricts competition within the common market".

In addition to the judicial definitions (that, as it will be shown, correspond to the interpretation adopted by the President of the OPCC), there are also clear hints how to identify an effect on trade in the Guidelines of the European Commission of 2004.[27] There are three conditions that need to be fulfilled: (1) the practice has to affect trade between Member States, (2) the effect must be possible and (3) the effect must be appreciable.[28]

According to the Guidelines, for horizontal agreements, there is a presumption that an effect on trade is not appreciable if: (1) the joint market share of the parties in any relevant market inside the EU is not bigger than 5 %; and (2) the joint turnover, acquired by the undertakings in question on the territory of EU, for the products covered by the agreement, does not exceed 40 million dollars (the so-called "NAAT criteria").

The Commission' Guidelines are not binding on the national authorities; however they can certainly be used as an ancillary tool to identify an effect on trade. The practice of the last 12 years confirms that those guidelines are actually being invoked by the President of the OPCC. Usually, however, in the decisions where only the Polish antitrust rules are applied, there is no explanation if the test for effect on trade had been applied. This omission to even consider an effect on trade might in fact be a main reason for the low number of decisions in which EU Competition rules are applied.

[25] King S, (2015) How Appreciable Is Object? The De Minimis Doctrine and Case C-226/11 *Expedia Inc v Autorité de la concurrence*. European Competition Journal 11 (1) available at: <http://dx.doi.org/10.1080/17441056.2015.1039799> accessed 7 October 2015.

[26] This is not uncommon also in practice of some NCAs: Bailey D, (2009) Appreciable Effect on Trade within the United Kingdom. European Competition Law Review 30(8):353–361, 359.

[27] Kowalik-Bańczyk K, (2008) Pojęcie "wpływu na handel" jako kryterium stosowania przez sądy krajowe wspólnotowego prawa konkurencji. Przegląd Ustawodawstwa Gospodarczego. 2: 24–30.

[28] Cf case 22/71 *Béquelin* [1971] ECR 949, para 16.

### 15.2.2 The Definition of Effect on Trade in the President of the OPCC's Decisions

The following analysis of decisions of the President of the OCCP is based on a selection of those decisions[29] from the very beginning of the Polish membership in the European Union, thus from 2004 until 2015. Most of those decisions were either mentioned in the annual reports of the OCCP or published directly on the webpage of the Authority. Not all of the decisions will be presented, just the most representative ones. In each of the presented decisions, the President of the OPCC applied Article 101 or 102 in parallel to Articles 6 and 9 of the Act on the Protection of Competition and Consumers.[30]

The first decisions where the EU competition rules were applied date from 2006. Those first decisions are worth a broader analysis as they have "set up the scene" for the further continuing practice, introducing the criteria that keep "reappearing" in most of the further decisions. In the decision *Visa International*[31] the President of the OPCC found an infringement of Article 81 TEC (now Article 101 TFEU), whereas in the decision *Telekomunikacja Polska*[32] the President found an infringement of Article 82 TEC (now Article 102 TFEU).

In the decision of 29 December 2006 in the case *Visa International*[33] the President of the OPCC found that the way in which the interchange fee had been agreed constituted an anticompetitive agreement, infringing both Polish and Community competition rules. The interchange fee was acquired at each transaction made by the payment cards belonging to systems of Visa and MasterCard in Poland. The fee had been paid by the acceptant of the payment – the seller. Each transaction involving the payment of such a fee implied four parties: a consumer paying with a card, a seller (acceptant of the payment), the bank of the seller (the so called *acquirer)* and the bank that emitted the card by which the transaction was executed. The President of the OCCP in its decision DAR 15/2006 held that the practice infringing competition consisting of acquiring this fee was followed by twelve banks during 13 years. The fee was set by the banks with no relation to the real costs of payment by card and it substantially increased the transaction costs for the sellers. The relevant product market was set as a market of acquiring services. The relevant geographic market was identified as covering the territory of Poland. While verifying whether there was an effect on trade between Member States, the President of OPCC stated that the practice in question covered the whole territory of Poland; therefore it might

[29] All of the decisions issued by the President of the OCCP are available online at the following website: <https://uokik.gov.pl/decyzje_prezesa_uokik3.php> accessed 7 October 2015.

[30] Consolidated version published in Journal of Laws 2015, item 184; hereinafter the Competition Act.

[31] Decision of the President of OPCC of 29 December 2006 in case DAR 15/2006 *Visa International.*

[32] Decision of the President of OPCC of 29 December 2006 in case DOK 166/2006 *Telekomunikacja Polska.*

[33] Decision DAR 15/2006.

have had an effect on trade between Member States, because it caused "a division of the common market into national markets". The President of the OPCC stated that the increase in the prices of goods and services, connected with the application of the interchange fee, exists, regardless whether a transaction is done in cash or by card. It might have caused a decrease in the import of goods to Poland from other Member States. The effect on trade could be considered as "appreciable", because it concerned "an important part of goods and services sold in the territory of Poland". Most of the participants of the antitrust agreements belonged to international corporations that are active in various Member States of EU. Thus the change in "their competitive position in one Member State might influence the position of the whole group". The President of the OPCC also argued that the NAAT criteria, stemming from the 2004 Guidelines, were not fulfilled; therefore there had been an appreciable effect on trade between Member States. In effect, both the Polish competition rules and Article 101 TFEU were applied.

The other of the "first" decisions concerned abuse of dominant position by the then Polish telecom incumbent Telekomunikacja Polska (TP).[34] In a decision[35] of 29 December 2006 the President of the OPCC found an infringement by TP of Article 82 TEC (Article 102 TFEU) together with the Polish antitrust provisions, consisting of requiring the clients that wanted to buy access to service of broadband internet connection (Neostrada TP) to enter also into an agreement for a phone abonnement. The President of the OPCC ordered TP to stop the aforementioned practice. The identified relevant market was set to cover the country's telecommunication services in the stationery telecommunication network. As it concerned the telecom activity of a regulatory character,[36] the President of the OPCC stated that the geographic scope of the relevant market covered the whole country. According to Article 10 of the Act on Telecommunication Law,[37] the taking up of telecom activity in the territory of Poland is conditioned by an inscription in the register of telecom undertakings, led by the Regulator (President of the Office of Electronic Communication). Upon the inscription, the telecom undertaking can lead its activity on the territory of the Republic of Poland, and thus its clients are only the entities and persons localized in the network of Poland. Thus for the end users of such services there is no substitution for such services outside of Poland, as they belong to different geographic markets. Therefore the market does not stem beyond the frontiers of Poland but covers its whole territory. The President stated that on this market TP had a dominant position and it was abusing it by forcing the consumers/clients that wanted to acquire the service of an internet broadband connection to accept also services of a traditional stable phone connection. The abusive practice led as well to the exclusion of services of other operators (competitors of TP). Thus the President of the OPCC held that the effect on trade consisted of the introduction of barriers to

[34] It was later on acquired by Orange.

[35] Decision DOK 166/06.

[36] According to Article 10 of the Act of Telecommunication Law.

[37] Law of 16 July 2004 – Telecommunication Law, (Journal of Laws no 171 item 1800 with amendments).

entry to the Polish market for potential consumers, regardless of whether the competitors were Polish or foreign entities. The users of Neostrada services were bound by the phone services of TP, including the fact that disloyal customers were punished by an automatic cancellation of the Neostrada contract in cases where the customers had chosen different providers of phone services. It breached the customers' freedom to choose the best offer on the market. The pressure exercised by TP ensured that the users bound by contracts with TP were not eager to change phone services providers. This might have constituted a discouraging factor for potential competitors of TS to invest in the competitive (for TP) telecom activity in the territory of Poland. The behaviour of TP could have influenced the foreign entities decisive process to enter the Polish market with products that would be in competition with TP products. The President of the OPCC stated that the activity of TP led to distinguishing (Pl. *wyodrębnienie*) of the Polish market from the internal market and thus there was an effect on trade.[38]

In the decisions following those first decisions on, respectively, Articles 101 and 102 TFEU, the President of the OPCC often reached out for the same arguments to prove the existence of an effect on trade. Most often it identified this effect when the practice in question covered the whole territory of the Republic of Poland. For instance, in 2007 the President of the OPCC issued another decision directed against TP,[39] this time concerning its practice of degrading in a discriminatory manner the IP connection of competitors, by lowering the quality of or making impossible the transfer of data. This practice constituted an infringement of both Article 102 TFEU and Article 9 of Polish Competition Act. The effect on trade criterion was fulfilled because the practices of TP led to the "cutting out of the national market from the internal market by setting barriers to access the services offered by foreign entities".[40]

Similarly, in the decision concerning a cement cartel – *Lafarge et al.*[41] – the President of the OPCC found that the producers of cement entered an anticompetitive agreement within the scope of Article 101(1) TFEU by setting prices and other conditions of sale of grey cement, setting the division of production and sale of grey cement and allowing for the exchange of confidential commercial information among competitors. Considering the criterion of effect on trade, the President of the OPCC held that the agreement in question was horizontal, including almost all cement producers in Poland, which covered almost 100 % of the territory of the country. All participants to the agreement belonged to the international capital groups, active in many Member States of the EU. The aim of their agreement was to stabilize the cement market as to the participation in market shares and the level of prices, so that no war occurred between the cartel members, whereas without this agreement the cement could have been imported and exported from the neighbouring countries. All cartel members were also trying to control the selling practices of

---

[38] Decision DAR 15/2006, p. 61.

[39] Decision of the President of OPCC of 20 December 2007 in case DOK 98/2007 *Telekomunikacja Polska*.

[40] Decision DOK 98/2007, para 476.

[41] Decision of the President of OPCC of 8 December 2009 in case DOK 7/2009 *Lafarge et al.*

cement produced by a competitor who entered the market during the cartel's existence. The OPCC's President identified that the agreement might have trans-frontal consequences, because the activities of the cartel members introduced barriers to entry to the market. The main consequence of the cartel was the division of the common market.

In decisions of the President of the OPCC following those described above, there is a repetitive set of conditions that are invoked in order to show that there is an effect on trade, implying the application of EU competition law. There is, as a first and foremost argument, in cases concerning either Article 101 or 102 TFEU, an argument that the practice in question had taken place on the territory of entire Poland.[42] Very often the undertakings concerned in a natural way limited their activity to the territory of Poland (like in the case of telecom activity or the cases of collective management of author's rights). Sometimes the cases concerned international corporations (like in cases *Visa International* and *Lafarge*). The criteria that keep reappearing are:

- the criterion that the practice concerned occurred on the whole territory of Poland[43];
- the criterion of distinguishing the Polish market from the internal market[44];
- the criterion of introductions of barriers to entry into the national market[45];
- the criterion of hindering entrance to the national market of competitors from outside[46]; and

[42] TP case of 2006 and interchange fee case of 2006; cement cartel decision of 2009, dominance on the gas market case (decision of the President of OPCC of 13 April 2012 in case DOK-1/2012 *Polskie Górnictwo Naftowe i Gazownictwo*), mobile tv case of 2012 (decision of the President of OPCC of 23 November 2011 in case DOK-8/2011 *Polkomtel SA, PTC, Centertel, C4*), insurance for workers (decision of the President of OPCC of 25 October 2007 DOK *Polski Zakład Ubezpieczeń, PZU*).

[43] Decision of the President of OPCC of the President of OPCC of 5 June 2006 DOK-53/2006 *Telekomunikacja Polska S.A.*; decision of the President of OPCC of 29 December 2006 in case DOK 15/2006 *Visa International*; decision of the President of OPCC of 25 October 2007 in case DOK-96/07 *Polski Zakład Ubezpieczeń*; decision of the President of OPCC of 8 December 2009 in case DOK-7/2009 *Lafarge Cement S.A. et al*; decision of the President of OPCC of 23 November 2011 in case DOK-8/2011 *Polkomtel*; decision of the President of OPCC of 13 April 2012 in case DOK-1/2012 *Polskie Górnictwo Naftowe i Gazownictwo*.

[44] Decision of the President of OPCC of 29 December 2006 in case DAR 15/2006 *Visa International*.

[45] Decision of the President of OPCC of 20 December 2007 in case DOK-98/07 *Telekomunikacja Polska*; decision of the President of OPCC of 29 August 2008 in case DOK-6/2008 *ZAIKS*.

[46] Decision of the President of OPCC of 29 December 2006 in case DOK 166/2006 *Telekomunikacja Polska*; decision of the President of OPCC of 24 August 2010 in case DOK-7/2010 *ZAIKS*; decision of the President of OPCC of 13 April 2012 in case DOK-1/2012 *Polskie Górnictwo Naftowe i Gazownictwo*; decision of the President of OPCC of 8 December 2009 in case DOK-7/2009 *Lafarge Cement S.A. et al*; decision of the President of OPCC of 23 November 2011 in case DOK-8/2011 *Polkomtel*.

- the criterion that the practice was committed by the representatives of international capital groups present at the Polish market.[47]

Therefore at least in situations where one of those criteria occurs, the President of the OPCC should presume the existence of an effect on trade. However in a number of cases, the President of the OPCC closed the proceedings in which Article 101 or 102 TFEU could have been applied, after having stated that the practice in question had been stopped.[48] It was due to the adopted interpretation of Article 5 of Regulation 1/2003 that the decision based on this provision can be issued only if the practice is still in place. Article 5 of Regulation 1/2003 covers only decisions "requiring that an infringement be brought to an end" (fr. *les décisions ordonner la cessation d'une infraction*, niem. *die Entscheideungen mit denen die Abstellung von Zuwiderhandlungen angeordnet wird*), so there is no scope for decisions stating that the infringement occurred but had been finished. It is a different issue than the problem analysed in case C-375/ *Tele 2*, where the statement on non-infringement of Article 101 or 102 TFEU was excluded from the President's competences.

## 15.3 The Application of Regulation 1/2003 by National Authorities

The existence of an effect on trade does not only imply the application of Article 101 or 102 TFEU. It also obliges the authorities that take decisions to do so in close cooperation within the European Commission. In order to guarantee the unified application of EU Competition Rules, Article 11 of Regulation 1/2003 obliges the Commission and the national authorities to apply those rules "in close cooperation". It refers both to the NCAs (Article 11 of Regulation 1/2003) and to the courts (Article 15 of Regulation 1/2003).

### *15.3.1 Cooperation Between the European Commission and the Polish NCA and Courts*

When the NCA acts under Article 101 or 102 TFEU, it should inform the Commission in writing before or without delay after commencing the first formal investigative measure (Article 11(3) of Regulation 1/2003). Before the adoption of a decision where EU competition law is applied is such a way that it leads to:

---

[47] Decision of the President of OPCC of 29 December 2006 in case DAR 15/2006 *Visa International*, decision of the President of OPCC of 8 December 2009 in case DOK-7/2009 *Lafarge Cement S.A. et al.*

[48] Decision of the President of OPCC of 16 April 2007 in case RWA – 10/2007 *Związek Polskich Arystów Fotografików*; decision of the President of OPCC of 10 June 2009 in case RWA 6/2009 *Stowarzyszenie Artystów Wykonawców Utworów Muzycznych i Słowno-Muzycznych SAWP.*

- a request to bring an infringement to an end
- acceptance of commitments or
- the withdrawal of the benefit of block exemption

the NCA should inform the Commission. This explains the difference between the number of decisions visible in the statistics of the European Commission (13) and the actual number of decisions (26). In the decisions where the President of the OPCC brings the proceeding to an end without adjudicating on the infringement, it does not apply Article 11(4) of the Regulation.

Article 15 of Regulation 1/2003 provides for several forms of cooperation between the national courts applying the EU competition rules and the European Commission. Up until now, those possibilities are hardly in use in Poland. The possibility of receiving information from the Commission on questions concerning the application of EU competition rules, provided in Article 15(1) of the Regulation has not been reported by the Commission.[49]

The Polish courts are not very active in forwarding to the Commission copies of judgments of national courts deciding on the application of Article 101 or 102 TFEU, despite the fact that the Regulation imposes such an obligation on them: Article 15(2). The only case reported on the basis of Article 15(2) remains the case XVII AmA 213/10 (*PZU Życie*).[50] The judgment concerns the case in which the preliminary question had been asked by the Supreme Court: the *Tele 2* case.

On the other hand, the European Commission had not yet used the possibility to intervene in a Polish court as an *amicus curiae* (Article 15(3) of Regulation 1/2003).[51]

### *15.3.2 Limited Autonomy of the NCA in the Application of EU Competition Law – Case* **Tele 2**

According to Article 5 of Regulation 1/2003 the National Competition Authority cannot find that there is no breach of Article 101 or 102 TFEU. In the only (to date) Polish preliminary question linked directly with the interpretation of EU competition rules, the CJEU stated that only the European Commission can issue a negative decision on the merits. It might lead to some insecurity for undertakings under investigation, because the closure of a procedure under Polish rules does not exclude the possibility of a parallel proceeding led by the European Commission, creating an important risk of double proceedings.

The case C-375/09 *Prezes UOKiK v Tele 2* explains in fact two novel questions linked with the principle of procedural autonomy. First, it covers the situation when there are EU secondary law provisions on procedural issues. In this case Article 5

[49] <http://ec.europa.eu/competition/court/antitrust_requests.html> accessed 7 October 2015.

[50] <http://ec.europa.eu/competition/elojade/antitrust/nationalcourts/> accessed 7 October 2015.

[51] <http://ec.europa.eu/competition/court/antitrust_amicus_curiae.html> accessed 7 October 2015.

of Regulation 1/2003 provides an enumerative list of decisions that might be issued by the national competition authority in cases where Article 101 or 102 TFEU is applied. One could have reasonably wondered if this provision is exhaustive, and if not, whether it was possible to issue decisions falling outside of this catalogue of decisions (particularly if the national law allowed for such an option). Second, due to the fact that the Regulation 1/2003 covers the procedural issues only in a limited way (a catalogue of decisions), for all other issues the national procedural rules are applied. However in this second case, the CJEU in *Tele 2* indicated an important limitation for national procedural autonomy. Namely, the President of the OPCC cannot apply the provisions of the Polish procedure if it might hinder the uniform application of EU law (in this case Article 102 TFEU). This clearly shows that despite the decentralisation of application of EU competition law, the central competition authority remains the European Commission. The declared decentralisation started on 1 May 2004, so that the EU competition rules were applied mainly by the national competition authorities.

The direct application of Article 101(1), Article 101(2) and Article102 TFEU by the national competition authorities had been possible since the beginning of the functioning of the European Community,[52] but it was since 2004 that the application of EU Competition law should have occurred mainly at the national level.[53] Article 101(3) TFEU became a "legal exception" from the prohibition contained in Article 101(1), and it can now be directly applied by the national authorities. Beforehand the European Commission had an exclusivity for application of this rule and in this sense it was a case of complete centralization.[54] The decentralization that occurred in 2004 was said to be purely pragmatic, as it was introduced to let the European Commission deal with the most evident and grave infringements of EU competition law, whereas all the rest was to be handled by the National Competition Authorities under Article 3 of Regulation 1/2003. Thus, the European Commission was to act only subsidiary to the activities of the National Competition Authorities, leaving the main burden of enforcement on the NCAs.[55]

This logic has not been confirmed by the case *Tele* 2, in which the Polish Supreme Court asked, *inter alia*, about the interpretation of Article 5 of Regulation 1/2003 and its implications for the competences of the NCAs to fully apply the EU compe-

[52] Case 127/73 *BRT v SABAM* [1974] ECR 51.

[53] It was both approved: Jones A, Sufrin B (2011) EU Competition Law. Text, Cases and Materials. Oxford University Press, Oxford, p. 1027; Hiljemark L (2003) Enforcement of EC Competition Law in National Courts – The Perspectives of Judicial Protection in: Dabbah M (ed). The Internationalisation of antitrust policy. Cambridge, p. 87; as criticized: Voet van Vormizeele P (2010) Die Bewärung der Kartellrechtsreform durch die VO 1/2003 aus Unternehmenssicht in: Schwarze J (ed), Rechtsschutz und Wettbewerb in der neueren europäischen Rechtsentwicklung. Nomos, Baden Baden, p. 12.

[54] Goyder J, Albors-Llorens A (2009) Goyder's EC Competition Law. Oxford University Press, Oxford p. 517.

[55] The position of the Czech Government in the *Tele 2* case is very revealing: it argued that Regulation 1/2003 does not introduce any hierarchy between the European Commission and the NCAs, creating the basis for horizontal cooperation between those organs.

tition rules. The competences of the NCAs were in fact set to be only subsidiary to those of the European Commission. They are subsidiary not only to the mechanism introduced by Regulation 1/2003, that once the European Commission "takes over" a case/matter at hand, the NCA should desist further proceedings. They are as it turned out from *Tele 2* also subsidiary on the merits. The NCA can only adjudicate on the possible infringement of Article 101 or 102 TFEU but it cannot issue a decision stating the lack of such an infringement. This is a serious limitation to the procedural autonomy of the NCAs, as it limits their decisional competences.[56] The *Tele 2* case brings an important explanation as to the scope of application of the procedural autonomy principle. Namely, the national authorities are allowed to use this principle as long as it does not bring a risk to the uniform application of EU law. This uniform application can be assured only, if the risk of differing decisions issued on different decisional levels (national and EU levels) are eliminated. But in fact, uniform application seems to be just a good argument to maintain the dominant "decisional" position of the European Commission, as an organ that imposes such a unity. Thus the decentralization announced in 2004 is only apparent, as the European Commission remains the central organ for the application of EU competition law. Laura Parett calls it clearly a "top-down system" in which a decisive role for defining the EU competition policy is still played by the Commission.[57] It seems that the NCAs can only follow the policy set by the Commission, as they are not allowed to act independently when they want to establish non-infringement situations and issue so-called negative decisions on merits.

## 15.4 Conclusions

In the decisions of the President of the OCCP, the appreciable effect is identified in a way required by the *acquis* set by the EU courts and the European Commission. In particular, such an effect would be found where one of these three hypotheses occurred: (i) there was a separation of the Polish market from the EU internal market; (ii) there was a threat that barriers would be introduced for entry into the Polish market; or (iii) there existed a risk of hindering competition for entities coming from outside Poland. Thus a definition of effect on trade is mainly limited to situations where the practices infringing competition occurred in a way concerning the whole territory of the Republic of Poland, in a way "separating" it from the rest of

[56] On the notion of procedural autonomy, see: Claes M (2006) The National Courts' Mandate in the European Constitution. Hart Publishing, Oxford and Portland, Oregon, p. 119; Rideau J (2005) Commentaire à l'article II-107 de la Constitution pour l'Europe. In Burgorgue-Larsen L, Levade A, Picod F (eds) Traité établisant une Constitution pour l'Europe. Commentaire article par article. Partie II la Charte des droits fondamentaux de l'Union, Bruylant Bruxelles, p. 595 ; Prechal S (1998) Community Law in National Courts: The Lessons from Van Schijndel. Common Market Law Review 35: 681; Biondi A (1999) The European Court of Justice and Certain National Procedural Limitations: Not Such a Tough Relationship. Common Market Law Review 36: 1271.

[57] Case C-344/98 *Masterfoods* [2000] ECR I-11369.

the territory of the European Union. Such a restrictive definition of the effect on trade can lead to the extremely low number of decision of the Polish President of the OCCP in which it applies the EU competition rules. However, considering the number of decisions issued yearly by the President of the OPCC, one can as well presume that in all the decisions the criterion of effect on trade was raised *ex officio*, substantially reducing the number of decisions where the EU competition rules are actually applied.

The narrow definition of effect on trade or the situation of not raising this criteria *ex officio* can have broader implications for the effective enforcement of EU competition law in Poland. There is not only a low number of decisions where the infringements of Articles 101 and 102 are considered. There are as well at least three other consequences. First, the judicial *acquis* on material and procedural EU competition law are not applied if there is no effect on trade. The Polish authorities are not bound by this *acquis* if there is no "European Union element" involved – therefore if no effect on trade is identified, Polish undertakings might be deprived of some procedural guarantees that should be applied in EU competition proceedings – like LLP or privilege against self-incrimination, that do not have the same scope in Polish law and in EU law.[58]

Second, as mentioned in the second part of this paper, there is no cooperation between the European Commission and national authorities that deal with infringements of competition law. In the case of a lack of an EU link (effect on trade), the Polish authorities are not obliged to search for cooperation with the European Commission. This, even if there is a general factual tendency of convergence of Polish and EU law solutions and practice, is not a very stable situation for the undertakings. It adds also to the risk of having two parallel proceedings, one led before the Polish NCA on the basis of Polish rules and second, led before the European Commission on the basis of EU competition law provisions. The tendency then not to treat certain cases as cases having an EU element leads to a situation where the undertakings concerned are facing an actual risk of double enforcement.

Third, the lack of identification of effect on trade might influence the possibilities of winning a private enforcement case before the Polish courts. If the party can introduce its claim as a claim with EU elements, there is already a jurisprudence that should enhance the possibility of success of such a claiming party. If one sticks only to the national provisions on private enforcement, the possibilities of winning the case are much reduced.[59]

---

[58] On this: Kowalik-Bańczyk K (2012) Prawo do obrony w unijnych postępowaniach antymonopolowych. W kierunku unifikacji standardów proceduralnych. Wolters Kluwer, Warszawa, Chapter 9; Bernatt M (2012) Convergence of Procedural Standards in the European Commission Proceedings. Competition Law Review 3: 255–282.

[59] Jurkowska-Gomułka A (2013) Private Enforcement of Competition Law in Polish Courts: The Story of an (Almost) Lost Hope for Development. Yearbook of Antitrust and Regulatory Studies 6(8): 107–128.

FSC
www.fsc.org
MIX
Papier | Fördert
gute Waldnutzung
FSC® C083411

Kolibri 360 GmbH
Ferdinand-Jühlke-Straße 7
99095 Erfurt, Deutschland
produktsicherheit@kolibri360.de